MEDIEVALIA ET HUMANISTICA

MEDIEVALIA ET HUMANISTICA
New Series
Edited by Paul Maurice Clogan

Number 1: In Honor of S. Harrison Thomson

Katherine Zell *Roland H. Bainton* • Wyclif and the Augustinian Tradition with Special Reference to His *De Trinitate* *Gordon Leff* • A Collection of Decretal Letters of Innocent III in Bamberg *Stephan Kuttner* • The Tale of the Captive Bird and the Traveler: Nequam, Berechiah, and Chaucer's *Squire's Tale* *Albert C. Friend* • Rhythmic Architecture in the Music of the High Middle Ages *Theodore Karp* • The Tuscan Town in the Quattrocento: A Demographic Profile *David Herlihy* • The University and the Church: Patterns of Reform in Jean Gerson *Steven E. Ozment* • *Epistola Cuthberti De Obitu Bedae*: A Caveat *W. F. Bolton* • The Hussite Revolution and the German Peasants' War: An Historical Comparison *Frederick G. Heymann* • Number Symbolism and Medieval Literature *Edmund Reiss* • Some Common Features of Italian Urban Experience (c. 1200–1500) *Marvin B. Becker* • Flavio Biondo's *Roma Instaurata* *Dorothy M. Robathan* • *The Kambriae Descriptio* of Gerald the Welshman *Urban T. Holmes* • The *Planctus* of Oedipus: Text and Comment *Paul Maurice Clogan* • Verses on the Life of Robert Grosseteste *Richard W. Hunt*.

Number 2: Medieval and Renaissance Studies in Review

Byzantine Studies and Western Literatures: A Foreword *Paul J. Alexander and Mary E. Giffin* • Incunabula in the Gennadius Library *Francis R. Walton* • A Fifteenth-Century Burgundian Version of the *Roman de Florimont* *Charity C. Willard* • Byzantium and the Migration of Literary Works and Motifs: The Legend of the Last Roman Emperor *Paul J. Alexander* • The Addressee and Interpretation of Walahfrid's "Metricum Saphicum" *David A. Traill* • Representations of Charles V of France (1338–1380) as a Wise Ruler *Claire Richter Sherman* • *The Praise of Folly* and its *Parerga* *Genevieve Stenger* • Lord Berners: A Survey *N. F. Blake* • Kingship, Government, and Politics in the Middle Ages: Some Recent Studies *Michael Altschul* • Latin Palaeography in the Later Middle Ages: Some Recent Contributions *Braxton Ross* • The Cataloguing of Mediaeval Manuscripts: A Review Article *M. L. Colker* • *Corpus der italienischen Zeichnungen 1300–1450*: A Review Article *Bernhard Bischoff* • The Future of Medieval History *Joseph R. Strayer* • Table of Contents for Fasciculi I–XVII • Cumulative Index for Fasciculi I–XVII.

MEDIEVALIA ET HUMANISTICA

STUDIES IN MEDIEVAL & RENAISSANCE CULTURE

Founded in 1943 by S. Harrison Thomson

NEW SERIES

NUMBER 3

SOCIAL DIMENSIONS IN MEDIEVAL AND
RENAISSANCE STUDIES

Edited by Paul Maurice Clogan
NORTH TEXAS STATE UNIVERSITY

The Press of
Case Western Reserve University
Cleveland & London
1972

To the memory of
MICHAEL JOSEPH CLOGAN
who lovingly taught his children
how to see and feel the touch of life.

Editorial Note

FOUNDED IN 1943 by S. Harrison Thomson and now under new editorship and management, *Medievalia et Humanistica* continues to publish, in a series of annual volumes, significant scholarship, criticism, and reviews in all areas of medieval and Renaissance culture: literature, art, archaeology, history, law, music, philosophy, science, and social and economic institutions. *Medievalia et Humanistica* encourages the individual scholar to examine the relationship of his discipline to other disciplines and to relate his study in a theoretical or practical way to its cultural and historical context. Review articles examine significant recent publications, and contributing editors report on the progress of medieval and Renaissance studies in the United States and Canada.

Medievalia et Humanistica is sponsored by the Medieval Interdepartmental Section of the Modern Language Association of America, and publication in the series is open to contributions from all sources. The editorial board welcomes interdisciplinary critical and historical studies by young or established scholars and urges contributors to communicate in an attractive, clear, and concise style the larger implications in addition to the precise material of their research, with documentation held to a minimum. Texts, maps, illustrations, and diagrams will be published when they are essential to the argument of the article.

Books for review, inquiries regarding Fasciculi I–XVII in the original series, and manuscripts (which should be prepared in conformity with the second edition of *The MLA Style Sheet* and accompanied by a stamped, self-addressed envelope) should be addressed to the editor, *Medievalia et Humanistica*, P.O. Box 13348, N.T. Station, Denton, Texas 76203 .Numbers 1, 2, and 3 of *Medievalia et Humanistica*, New Series, may be ordered from their publisher, The Press of Case Western Reserve University, Quail Building, Cleveland, Ohio 44106.

Preface

One of the major tendencies of contemporary humanistic scholarship is its move away from traditional interests — archives, biographies, documents, sources — to a concern with social structure, social mobility, and the history of society. In recent decades, there has been a very considerable growth of interest in social history. In the hands of the traditional humanists, social history was a kind of residual category; it was what was left over after the really important topics — constitutional, diplomatic, and political — had been studied. The term "social history" in the past was used in combination with economic history and generally referred to either the history of social movements or manners, customs, and everyday life. G. M. Trevelyan's *English Social History* (London, 1944), which has been called "history with the politics left out," is a good example of the old approach. Today social history is at the center of serious humanistic study. The rapid growth and development of social history in the past twenty years can be explained by the deliberate specialization of economic history and by the general historization of the social sciences, as well as the technical and institutional changes within the academic discipline of the social sciences. Unlike that of intellectual history, which separates written ideas from their human context, the subject matter of social history cannot be isolated and can never become a specialization. The social and societal dimensions of man's nature cannot be isolated from the economic, political, literary, and religious dimensions of his nature. The intellectual historian may ignore economics, or the economic historian Shakespeare, but the social historian who ignores either will not succeed. The new social history is truly interdisciplinary, and requires concepts and methods derived from the social sciences and the convergence of scholars from different disciplines to revise many of the historical interpretations that we have inherited. It is in this context and against this background that this third volume in the new series of *Medievalia et Humanistica* attempts to explore the general topic of "Social Dimensions in Medieval and Renaissance Studies." There is no easy way to represent completely this major new tendency in contemporary humanistic scholarship. One can only point to trends and indicate directions which some humanists seem to consider congenial.

In compiling and editing the articles in this third volume, the editor is most grateful to the members of the editorial board for their expert criticism and to the following consultants who helped in the planning: Joan Gadol (City College of New York), J. Aquin Gimeno (Case Western Reserve University), Erving Goffman (University of Pennsylvania), Talcott Parsons (Harvard University), Lawrence V. Ryan (Stanford University), Meyer Shapiro (Columbia University), Denis Sinor (Indiana University), Margaret Switten (Mount Holyoke College), Kurt Weitzman (Princeton University), and Harry F. Williams (Florida State University). The next volume in the series will explore from different perspectives the subject of spirituality in the Middle Ages and Renaissance. Review articles will examine significant recent publications, and contributing editors will report on the progress of medieval and Renaissance studies in the United States and Canada.

P.M.C.

MEDIEVALIA ET HUMANISTICA

Paul Maurice Clogan, Editor
NORTH TEXAS STATE UNIVERSITY
Julie Sydney Davis, Managing Editor

EDITORIAL BOARD

Contents

THE SOCIAL SIGNIFICANCE OF TWELFTH-CENTURY
CHIVALRIC ROMANCE
ROBERT W. HANNING
Columbia University 3

NATURE AND THE AESTHETIC SOCIAL THEORY OF
LEON BATTISTA ALBERTI
ANDREA DI TOMMASO
Wayne State University 31

PIERRE DE LANGTOFT'S CHRONICLE:
An Essay in Medieval Historiography
ROBERT STEPSIS
Lake Forest College 51

CLERICAL JUDGES IN ENGLISH SECULAR COURTS:
The Ideal Versus the Reality
RALPH V. TURNER
Florida State University 75

MEDIEVAL POEMS AND MEDIEVAL SOCIETY
DONALD R. HOWARD
The Johns Hopkins University 99

"BACHELOR" AND RETAINER
J. M. W. BEAN
Columbia University 117

THE MEDIEVAL LYRIC AND ITS PUBLIC
STEPHEN G. NICHOLS, JR.
Dartmouth College 133

SIMON OF SAINT-QUENTIN AS HISTORIAN OF THE
MONGOLS AND SELJUK TURKS
GREGORY G. GUZMAN
Bradley University 155

QUEST AND QUERY IN THE *CHASTELAINE DE VERGI*
EMILIE P. KOSTOROSKI
Case Western Reserve University 179

THE ILLUSTRATIONS OF THE *CÆDMONIAN GENESIS*:
Literary Criticism Through Art
THOMAS H. OHLGREN
Purdue University 199

THE FIGURAL STYLE AND MEANING OF
THE SECOND NUN'S PROLOGUE AND *TALE*
PAUL M. CLOGAN
North Texas State University 213

CAXTON'S TWO CHOICES:
"Modern" and "Medieval" Rhetoric in Traversagni's
Nova Rhetorica and the Anonymous *Court of Sapience*
JAMES J. MURPHY
University of California at Davis 241

CYNEWULF'S MULTIPLE REVELATIONS
JACKSON J. CAMPBELL
University of Illinois at Urbana 257

THE FAIR FIELD OF ANGLO-NORMAN:
RECENT CULTIVATION
RUTH J. DEAN
University of Pennsylvania 279

MUST WE ABANDON THE CONCEPT OF
COURTLY LOVE?
FRANCIS L. UTLEY
Ohio State University 299

BOOKS RECEIVED   325

MEDIEVALIA ET HUMANISTICA

The Social Significance of Twelfth-Century Chivalric Romance

Robert W. Hanning

It IS NOW generally accepted that the chivalric romances of the twelfth century are documents worthy of scrutiny by anyone interested in the dynamics of European culture during the "Renaissance of the Twelfth Century."[1] In this essay, I would like to examine the conventions of twelfth-century literary chivalry — i.e., the portrayal of love and martial prowess as mutually generating activities — and the generic peculiarities of the romance plot, and thereby to suggest how these two basic elements of the chivalric romance can be interpreted to explain the significance of this literary form for twelfth-century courtly society, its first audience. Specifically, I will resurvey the place of the *topos* of chivalry (love inspires prowess, prowess inspires love) in courtly literature antedating the rise of chivalric romance, indicating the limits of its use by poets in courtly narratives; then I will offer a working definition of the romance genre, stressing its aptness as a literary vehicle for exploring the dynamic consequences of self-awareness and placing chivalric romance within the wide spectrum of romance types; finally, I will offer partial analyses of Chrétien de Troyes' *Yvain* and of the anonymous *Partonopeu de Blois* in terms of their manipulations of the chivalry *topos* and their organizing of a plot around the hero's crisis of self-awareness. My conclusion will be that chivalric romance embodies the conviction of its audience that self-consciousness is the key to successful activity

I should like to acknowledge the debt I have incurred in preparing this paper to the students in my doctoral seminar in Medieval Literature in the Columbia University English Department during the Autumn 1970 semester. Their intelligence and enthusiasm have been a great aid to me and their friendship a great comfort.

3

in the cause of self-fulfillment, and the awareness of its audience of a tension between experienced private needs and imposed public or external values and obligations.

I

Courtly narrative came into being early in the twelfth century as a vernacular literature created under the patronage of great lords and ladies for the entertainment and instruction of the nobility.[2] Even from its beginnings, courtly literature can be distinguished from the Latin literature of twelfth-century clerical culture and from the archaic vernacular literature of the *chansons de geste*.[3] Courtly literature alone combined audacious borrowings from both of the other traditions with simultaneously and self-consciously exploited impulses toward refined idealism and descriptive, often comic, realism in its representation of reality.[4] Among the conventional situations developed in courtly narrative during the twelfth century, one of the most interesting is that in which love and martial valor interact to form a single thematic *topos*. First codified during the 1130's, the chivalry *topos* was destined to become a dominant force in courtly literature with the rise of chivalric romance; its progress to this position of eminence was gradual, however, as the following recapitulation will demonstrate.

The first extant instance of the chivalry *topos* comes in the ninth book of Geoffrey of Monmouth's *Historia Regum Britanniae* (1138?), a Latin work which drew eclectically upon clerical historiography, classical epic, and nascent courtly sensibilities for its matter and outlook.[5] Describing the festivities which accompany Arthur's solemn celebration of Pentecost, Geoffrey says that Arthur's court attracted all the elite of European knighthood, who came seeking the honor of serving the king, conforming to refined standards of dress and conduct, and proving themselves, through deeds of prowess, worthy of the favors of the ladies at court. The relationship of knights and ladies makes the former bolder, the latter more chaste and virtuous; each strives to be worthy of the other.[6] Geoffrey then describes a tournament during which knights joust while ladies watch them from atop the walls of Caerleon and spur them on by flirtatious behavior.[7] The world of chivalry here evoked betrays Geoffrey's awareness of how basic human impulses, sexual and aggressive, can be harmonized within the frame of a precise yet stylized iconography to create a moment at once symbolic and self-consciously elegant. However em-

4

blematic, the passage is also a diversion, ultimately irrelevant to the real concerns of the *Historia* at this point, national self-preservation and imperial conquest. Shortly after the chivalric display, an embassy comes from Rome to challenge Arthur's power; a war council is called, and there Cador, Duke of Cornwall, denounces the years of peace (during which, we recall, chivalry and refinement have flourished) as a period of laziness and decline.[8] No one contradicts this opinion, and in the climactic campaign of Britain versus Rome which soon ensues there is no hint that chivalric considerations inspire any of the warriors. So the *topos* of knights and ladies functions only as an isolated, attractive excrescence on a plot whose main themes have nothing to do with chivalry.

Subsequent appearances of the chivalry *topos* in vernacular, courtly literature attest to its attraction for court poets and their audiences, without its being transformed into a plot. Wace's *Roman de Brut* (1155) and the *Roman de Thèbes* (1150–55?) offer the next examples.[9]

Wace's translation of Geoffrey's *Historia* does not substantially alter Geoffrey's plot, but places it within a rich context of courtly comment and material, by turns refined and down-to-earth, serious and comic.[10] Wace's repeated use of the term *cortoise* in the passage (10493–10516) translating Geoffrey's references to chivalric activity and motivation among Arthur's knights and ladies confirms that to Wace and his audience this is an emblematically courtly moment, encapsulating the *maniera* of a refined, self-conscious aristocracy in an effective tableau.[11] And when Cador later charges, as in Geoffrey, that peace has made the Britons soft, Wace invents a reply by Gawain (often a spokesman in later romances for conventional courtly values) defending peace and concluding with a couplet defining chivalry (the first such statement by a character in a courtly work): "Par amistiez et par amies/ Font chevalier chevaleries" (10771–72). In the Roman war which follows, however, Wace refrains from having Gawain or anyone else act on chivalric principles; the dichotomy between peace-time *topos* and martial plot remains unresolved.

In the *Roman de Thèbes*, chivalry begins to find a place in actual warfare, as part of the anonymous poet's adaptation of epic material from classical antiquity to the tastes of a courtly audience. The structure of *Thèbes* is quasi-episodic within the limits of its inherited plot, which recounts a single, grand, and fatal action — a legendary history deeply significant to an earlier (Roman) audience. The episodes added

5

or modified by the poet draw attention away from the main action without actually supplanting it, and within this looser, ultimately unsatisfactory, structure the chivalry *topos* is given fairly free rein. Besides being stated as a factor motivating heroic activity in war on several occasions, the *topos* is shown becoming a subplot.[12] In Statius' *Thebaid*, the source for the plot of *Thèbes*, Ismene, princess of Thebes, loves Atys, a young Theban warrior, though we do not hear of their love until Atys has died in battle and Statius puts a pathetic lament in the mouth of the bereaved Ismene. Starting here, the French poet expands the love of Ysmaine and Athes, and creates a new, complementary, one between Antigone, Ysmaine's sister, and Parthonopeus, a noble young warrior of the army besieging Thebes. Developing these relationships permits the introduction of new kinds of scenes into courtly narrative, e.g., the first meeting of Antigone and Parthonopeus, while the princess is on a mission of peace from the besieged city to the surrounding army.[13] As the love relationships flower amidst the battle for Thebes, Geoffrey's stylized iconography of knights jousting while women watch them from above becomes a human situation in which Ysmaine, watching from the city walls, can exclaim, "Ce est Athes que je la voi,/ veez com broche a cel tornoi [i.e., the battle for the city]!/ Sor toute rien amer le doi,/ car tout ice fet il por moi."[14] Later, we see the two sisters at their observation post engaging in friendly yet intense debate about the respective merits of their lovers' *prouesce*, during which Antigone complains that she cannot physically enjoy the pleasures of love as easily as can Ysmaine, since Parthonopeus is on the opposing side in the war (5867–97).

At precisely this point, the humanized chivalry *topos* collides with the demands of the inherited plot. The news of Athes' death in battle reaches Ysmaine as she tells her sister of a foreboding dream she has had. A bit later in the story, Parthonopeus is killed during a foray, as the plot moves relentlessly toward general catastrophe, and the final, fratricidal duel of the story's "real" protagonists, Polynices and Eteocles. Chivalry, no longer an ornament irrelevant to the larger narrative in which it appears, has become symbolic of aspirations for happiness which are frustrated by the larger imperatives of fate in history. The juxtaposition of Antigone's complaint about postponed sexual gratification and Athes' death marks chivalry as an ironic *topos* within the imagined world of the *Roman de Thèbes*.[15]

At about the time that the *Thèbes* poet was creating chivalric relationships that moved dynamically in time and space within a courtly narrative, the Ovidian *conte* developed the theme underlying the chivalry *topos*—the power of love, an inner experience, to affect outer behavior—and thereby created a new type of courtly literature whose innovations were crucial for the ultimate flowering and significance of the chivalric romance. The *conte* borrowed from Ovid its plots and its portrayal—at times highly charged with pathos, at times aglow with sophisticated irony—of the impact of love on the feelings and actions of the lover.[16] By means of these inherited resources it explored a completely new topic: the joys and sorrows of self-discovery through love.[17] The *conte* exploited rhetorical, dialectical, and allegorical techniques popular in the Latin intellectual culture of the day[18] to recreate stories like those of Narcissus and of Pyramus and Thisbe as parables of how desire for another stimulates, in a lover, a heightened awareness of identity and reality. The tension between the protagonist's inner state of yearning to complete him or herself through union with the beloved and the recognition of how external forces (conventions of modesty, familial prohibitions) function as obstacles to fulfillment of desire generates soliloquies of self-analysis, and a plot in which hero or heroine acts in the outer world to close the gap that mars the inner world of consciousness: the gap between the self's present situation and envisioned fulfillment.[19] Love links the inner and outer worlds of the *conte*, but the action it stimulates is pathetic and insufficient; the lover is destroyed, through the malevolence of fortune and society (*Piramus et Tisbé*), or the failure of human understanding and compassion (*Narcisus*).

In the *Roman d'Enéas*, however, the inner dynamic of the Ovidian *conte* began to be integrated with the outer dynamic of chivalry developed in the *Roman de Thèbes*.[20] The long additions to Virgil in which the *Enéas* poet creates the love affair of Enéas and Lavine (7857–9274, 9313–42, 9839–10090) reveal a consuming interest—at once clinical and sentimental, ironic and sympathetic—in the agonies of falling in love. Both protagonists must come to grips with their desire, recognize its nature and object, and confront the obstacles to its fulfillment. This Ovidian *tour de force* is grafted onto the epic plot by means both of Lavine's mother, Amata (who in Virgil hates Aeneas and prefers Turnus as a husband for Lavinia), and of the single combat between Aeneas and Turnus to decide the fate of the Trojans in Latium with which the *Aeneid* concludes. In the *Enéas* the queen's hostility to Enéas neatly becomes an external obstacle which sharpens Lavine's awareness of what she desires (Enéas, whom she has seen

7

from her window in a tower — a combination of Ovidian sources and chivalric iconography) and how she must behave (rebelliously and dishonorably) to get him.[21] Her desperate decision to reveal her love to Enéas (via a note wrapped around an arrow, shot from her tower) initiates love in him as well and inspires him to defeat Turnus in order to win her (see 8982–96, 9046–66; the latter passage is a litany of love's effect on prowess, while Lavine states the chivalry *topos* succinctly, 9340–42).

The *Roman d'Enéas* converts its epic hero's victory into an exemplum of chivalry heightened in significance by being linked to the idea of self-discovery through love. But the conversion is far from complete; the actual impression on the reader of the Lavine episode is that love conversations — internal and external dialogues of varying degrees of earnestness — have been massively intruded into an epic action to divert the audience's attention from the plot, or at most to modernize the plot without resolving the contradictions between Virgil's concern with the harsh demands of destiny on the *pius* hero and the more optimistic assumptions of the chivalry *topos*.[22]

Unresolved contradictions, in fact, mark every instance of the chivalry *topos* mentioned thus far. The inhospitality of large plots to the intrusion of a *topos* imaginatively expressing courtly desires for an ethic reconciling private and public needs (love and honor) restricted a full exploration of the possibilities for such an ethic; only with the rise of chilvalric romance did this occur. Historical plots — such as those of Geoffrey and Wace — which traced the ebb and flow of national fortunes demonstrated in the process that, if heroes made history, history could also unmake heroes. Claims for the autonomy of chivalric heroism inspired by love could hardly be made in such a context of large and impersonal forces.[23]

Similarly, the stories of Thebes, Troy, and Rome that provided the plots of *romans antiques* inhibited the dramatic possibilities inherent in the chivalry *topos*. Chivalry suggests that a personal relationship can trigger public action, but also that the ultimate purpose or effect of the relationship remains personal; as Geoffrey puts it, knights become braver, ladies more chaste and honorable. In a chivalric plot, our final concern should be how well the knights and ladies live up to the supposed norms which bind them together; an epic or historical narrative, however, focuses on a portion of the body of legend or tradition shared by its audience and gains thereby a controlling context within which to define or judge personal deeds or interpersonal relationships. The manifest movement of history toward the fall of Troy or the founding of Rome suggests how we should evaluate the deeds of Hector or Achilles, the affair of Dido and Aeneas. In such a context, the more successfully a poet articulates the chivalric *topos* in action, the more ironic (as in *Thèbes*) or disruptive (as in *Enéas*) its relationship with the inherited "overplot" becomes.

The rise of chivalric romance after the middle of the twelfth century created a narrative form within which the chivalry *topos* could thrive, and within which, therefore, the ideals of courtly society could be fully and self-consciously explored at the level of metaphor. The romance plot lacks any context larger than the lives of its protagonists; it permits the simultaneous presentation of external, heroic adventures and of an inner world in which the self-awareness born of love permits the control of martial impulses. The hero's discovery of his identity and his destiny (they are two aspects of the same phenomenon) is an act of realization; his shaping of his powers to attain the perceived goals is self-realization of a longer and more arduous kind. In chivalric romance the chivalry *topos* expands to become the setting for the interaction of these two types of realization. We can understand more clearly how this happens by considering the nature and potentialities of the romance plot.

II

Twelfth-century court poets did not invent the kind of plot critics nowadays call romance. (They did invent the term, but used it simply to distinguish works in the French vernacular from those in Latin.) Chivalric romance reflects the literary conventions of twelfth-century courtly society — the chivalry *topos* with its heroic ideals modified by love, the use of marvellous elements in incidents and descriptions, confinement of interest to protagonists of one social class [24] — within a narrative form which has appeared and reappeared throughout the history of western literature. As I have suggested in the preceding paragraph, the defining attribute of the romance form is its plot, which organizes incidents ranging widely in time and space around the life of the hero without any larger controlling narrative context (as would be the case in the epic or the Victorian novel). The lack of any overt logical sequence connecting one incident to another makes the plot episodic as well as biographical. The easiest distinction among romance plots is that between active romance (usually heroic), in which the hero's adventures — his experience of life in all its variety — are willed and obstacles are overcome by force, and passive romance, in which adventures are initiated by Fortune (shipwrecks which separate families, gypsies who steal children from their cradles, etc.) and must simply be borne by weak or outnumbered protagonists. (Greek romances such as *Daphnis and Chloe* or Xenophon's *Ephesian Tale* are primarily passive romances.)

In the basic structure of episodic romance, a hero moves away from and then back toward a situation of stasis, through an intervening period of often arbitrary adventures involving loss, exile, hazard, or search. Romance is thus a fictional form which incorporates a cyclic perception of life rooted, I suspect, in our recognition (and ritual commemoration) of the endless seasonal cycle of death and rebirth, or loss and recovery of fertility, in nature.[25] Just as the myth of the Golden Age, its loss, and its wished-for recovery is a social version of cyclic rhythms stretched out into history so as to happen only once, so romance is an individual, biographical version of those rhythms, stretched out into personal history. In each case, the uniqueness of the cycle, rather than its periodic recurrence, introduces an element of linearity into experience which exists in tension with the plot's inherent circularity.[26] (Besides its biographical basis, romance also differs from the Golden Age myth in placing the bulk of its plot in the period of loss, i.e., that of adventures between the happy beginning and happy ending.)

The potentiality for complexity and sophistication in a romance plot lies in the fact that human life is a phenomenon extending into time, is biologically irreversible, and is cumulative in terms of learning experiences. That is, man grows in various ways, and the line of his growth is an extra force of linearity in the romance plot, which can increasingly dominate, though never entirely efface, the circularity of the loss-recovery or exile-return plot, depending on the author's presentation of the hero. If the hero is ageless and changeless (as in comic books or other fantasies), there is little linearity in a romance; this is also true if the author simply ignores the fact of growth or aging in recounting the adventures, for example, of a shipwrecked merchant who finally returns to his own city, or of a husband and wife separated by war and later reunited by chance. To introduce the idea of growth (in time) into the world of the romance protagonist's adventures (in space) is to ensure that he never returns to "where he started" as quite the same person he was when he set out. If the romance is about a king's son deprived of his inheritance while still a child and exiled by the villain, then physical growth in time allows him to win back his land once he has grown into a mighty warrior (as in the romances of *Horn* and *Havelock the Dane*). Similarly mental growth makes "the brave man slowly wise," and capable of performing a task he earlier failed through folly. Moral growth is also possible.

Any of these changes may render the hero unrecognizable, on his return, as the person who left long ago; that is, identity is often a major theme of romance. In a truly cyclical world, where all people experience the same endless round of death and rebirth, no identity would be possible. When a plot contains both a large circular movement back to where one started from and constant human growth, paradoxes of identity occur. The hero remains the same person throughout the story, yet may also change his identity during his adventures through a change of personality (amnesia, moral reformation), disguise, or a stroke of fortune (the king's son stolen and raised by gypsies). Making our various identities fall together in and through time is one of the goals of romance, involving various factors — natal, qualitative (the sum of our virtues and vices), circumstantial (who the world judges us to be), and desire or destiny (who we want to be, or become again). Identity in romance is at once a *given*, a *process*, and a *goal* — a past, a present, and a future.

The most sophisticated view of human growth in time subordinates the circularities of experience to the point where they become milestones on the road of progress toward the perfection of personality through the fruitful interaction of our qualities and our experiences. This is moral growth, and its catalyst is self-awareness, that mysterious knowledge of inner identity by which an individual locates himself within the continuum of his life and the context of his character, and thus arrives for the first time at a comprehension of where the concatenation of his virtues (or vices) and his circumstances is leading him. Accordingly, the most sophisticated form of romance is that in which the hero's arrival at self-awareness, and not some external catastrophe or willed quest undertaken simply for profit or honor, initiates the phase of adventures, culminating in a "return" which, even if it completes a spatial circle, in fact marks the new attainment of a fulfilled, perfected self. Love plays a special role in the attainment of self-awareness in romance, for it fills the hero with yearning for the beloved and simultaneously prompts him to act to bridge the gap

11

across which desire reaches out toward its object. Since the end of love is to make a new "person" out of two previously separated selves, the outer adventures of the love quest function concurrently as a metaphor for the self's great inner adventure: its quest to become the image it has generated of its own triumphant perfection.[27]

The two forms of romance which most clearly concern themselves with the growth of the hero in the terms just outlined are religious romance and twelfth-century chivalric romance. In both cases the outer adventures of the protagonists are potentially metaphoric and have their ultimate reference in the inner life, i.e., in the struggle for the perfection and harmony of the self's desires. The two types are best distinguished in terms of their external goals.

Religious romance seeks the full relationship with God which is salvation; its "return" is to heaven at death, to the Maker from whom the soul came into earthly life. The progress toward God is initiated by the hero's recognition of his sinfulness and God's desirability; this is his rebirth in grace (sometimes symbolized by his baptism), at which point he leaves behind worldly pleasure and, physically or mentally, sets off "on adventure" to find the full union with God he has now perceived as the goal of his fulfilled self.

In chivalric romance, the goal of the hero's quest is an earthly beloved (or a reconciliation or reunion with her), and the progress toward that goal — which is also the fulfilled and perfected self of the lover-hero — is instigated by a crisis of self-awareness to which I will shortly return in discussing specific examples. It is worth noting that in the heyday of chivalric literature, the twelfth and thirteenth centuries, courtly poets were also producing religious romances written in the same verse form and style as chivalric ones, and some narratives (the Anglo-Norman *St. Brendan* and *Guillaume d'Angleterre*, apparently by Chrétien de Troyes) which could as easily be called secular as religious romances.[28] Even if we did not have the extraordinarily rich devotional and didactic literature of this period to testify to European culture's rediscovery of the inner life and renewed quest for its perfection, courtly narratives in romance form would reveal this important aspect of a society's evolution.

III

We are now in a better position to assess the marriage of the chivalry *topos* and the romance plot in twelfth-century courtly narratives.

By rooting the plot of romance in the relationship between love and prowess, the court poet invited his audience to identify its aspirations and self-awareness with those of the hero whose activities embodied established *courtoise* ideals. In this way the crises of the hero became those of the audience, metaphorically expressed. The crises of chivalric romance are two: the relationship between chivalry and self-awareness, and the relationship between the chivalric hero and the society which alone can honor him for his deeds.

Self-awareness in chivalric romance results when the smooth interaction between love and prowess (as in Geoffrey of Monmouth's original paradigm) breaks down because of tensions between love's demands on a knight and demands either of honor, of valor, or of obligations related to the knight's social status. Tension leads to crisis, crisis to self-awareness, and self-awareness to a new stage, self-hatred or self-alienation. The consequences of this sequence are explored through heroic adventures which we can also interpret, thanks to symbolic cues, as a metaphor for heroic self-control in the service of self-perfection. In the process, the poet raises questions about the relationship between the hero and his society. The court in the romances is either the home of the hero, or the ostensible golden world to which he turns for honor and approbation. Refined and luxurious, the court is also fallen or flawed, and nowhere more so than in its imposition of values on the hero, or in its opposition to his private quest for happiness. The tensions in the knight's relationship with the court express the concern of the courtly class that personal cultivation and social achievement are not easily compatible, though they are usually resolved at some level in the chivalric romances of the twelfth century.[29]

The romances of Chrétien de Troyes are justly considered the greatest achievement of twelfth-century courtly literature; among them *Yvain* is most esteemed today.[30] *Yvain* is Chrétien's second "classic" statement of the chivalric *topos* as a full plot, the first being *Erec*. The first movement of the plot in both works is through a preliminary adventure toward a deceptive stasis, and then to a personal crisis, the equivalent of external catastrophe in less sophisticated romances, which, one might say, is equal and opposite in the two works. In *Erec*, the hero chooses a life of love at the expense of prowess, and it costs him honor — his "public identity." In *Yvain*, the hero chooses honor earned by prowess, and loses his love and his sanity. The crisis at the center of *Yvain* is a watershed across which the hero moves from one behavioral system inspired by honor to another inspired by love.

Yvain not only attains a new qualitative identity as the Knight of the Lion; he also grounds his new identity in a reinterpretation of the goal of prowess (service instead of honor), and by his own deeds and the reactions of others to them brings about a new hierarchy of chivalric values in Arthurian society, so that a reconciliation of personal desires and social norms becomes at least possible. The key to the metamorphosis of the chivalric hero and his chivalric world in *Yvain* is self-awareness, on which directly depends the control of heroic (or more precisely aggressive) impulses through moral judgment in the service of interpersonal relationships embodying one or another form of love. Ultimately, heroic impulses are transcended altogether by impulses toward love or service; the Arthurian world, no longer ironically golden,[31] seems to become really so and to function as an external metaphor for the attained inner harmony of the chivalric hero.

The structure of *Yvain*, like the façade of a Gothic cathedral, creates unity out of variety through sophisticated organization. There are two prefatory sections. The first offers negative exemplars of chivalric society — Arthur's disordered and disharmonious court (42–149) — and of an individual life of adventure through prowess — Calogrenant's disastrous trip to the storm-causing fountain seven years previously (173–580). The second sees Yvain on the same quest as Calogrenant, though with less random motivation: his cousin's honor, and therefore his own, is (belatedly) at stake. Ironically, he must seek honor secretly lest the King, hearing of his quest, deny him the chance to gain glory through prowess by awarding the adventure to Gawain or Kay (677–90).

At this point, the plot proper of the romance begins; Yvain kills the knight who defends the fountain, falls in love with Laudine, the dead man's wife, and wins her through the aid of Lunete, her witty damsel, who is beholden to Yvain for the hospitality he has formerly shown her at Arthur's court.[32] This first stage of the action already raises questions about the elements of chivalry, and about the importance of self-awareness, which the latter sections of the romance must answer. Falling in love with Laudine provides Yvain with a new, unsuspected goal for the adventure he has so blithely undertaken: he must win her. The change in priorities also reveals to hero and audience, however, that his previous values and desires are inadequate to resolve the paradoxes and meet the conflicting needs of his new situation. He loves the woman who hates him because of his success-

14

ful prowess, and is therefore at once her friend and her enemy. He wishes to return to Arthur's court with some token of his triumph in order to gain honor there, but he also wants to remain imprisoned (as he is) in Laudine's castle so that he can see, and perhaps win, her. Against all logic, love and hate, joy and despair coexist within his situation, as a brilliant, serio-comic, Ovidian monologue makes clear (1343–1544). Chrétien's complication of the chivalric *topos* is reflected in his clever manipulation of its traditional iconography: instead of a lady in a tower feeling love's pangs as she watches a knight jousting below, a knight imprisoned in the upper chamber of a castle feels love's pangs as he watches a lady below who is experiencing the agonies of nearly insane grief as a result of his prowess.

Arthur and his court, arriving at the fountain, bring with them the opportunity for Yvain to gain honor and revenge himself on Kay without leaving Laudine. But Laudine's resultant need for a knight of great prowess to defend the fountain against the intruders and Lunete's skill in pleading Yvain's cause to her grief-stricken but pragmatic mistress also allow Yvain's personal crisis to be resolved with deceptive facility. This questionable dénouement settles none of the larger questions Chrétien has raised about the relationship between love and prowess or between Yvain's private and public desires. The fountain and its accompanying ritual of undiscriminating, amoral prowess are the suspect center of this imagined world, the agent of its disruption and discords but also the occasion for its reconciliation — the objective symbol of prowess without awareness. What awareness of conflicting values and goals Yvain gains when he falls in love lies in abeyance because of the neat handling of this first crisis in *Yvain*.

After his marriage, Yvain is convinced by Gawain, his closest friend, to leave Laudine in order to seek honor in the world through participation in tournaments — a form of prowess even less directed at private needs or desires than the defense of the fountain. Yvain promises to return to Laudine after a year, but is so successful at tourneying that he forgets his deadline. Eventually he remembers his obligation to his wife, but by this time she has sent a damsel to denounce him as a traitor. Shocked, Yvain flees from society in a state of madness. Separated from love and society, he begins a series of episodic adventures which culminate in a return first to Arthur's court, then to Laudine, through reconciliation with whom he regains — or, more accurately, first attains — true personal felicity.

Space prohibits exploring in detail the significance of Yvain's adventures, through which Chrétien chronicles the conversion of prowess from an instrument of amoral disruption, in personal life and in society, into a means of serving those in distress and an element in a new, moral society based on the reciprocal relationship of unselfish aid between individuals. Nor can I more than allude to the poet's skill in presenting the case for heroic self-control, that central theme of internalized romances, through an almost Aristotelian juxtaposition of situations emblematic of too little control (behavior disruptive of one's intentions and goals) or too great constraint (the curbing of one's powers by internal or external restraints which induce impotence).[33] I shall confine myself to indicating how Chrétien presents Yvain's self-awareness becoming the controlling element of his career and therefore of the romance plot, and then how by the end of the work the hero's attainment of self-mastery is reflected in the transformation of the entire chivalric world.

The shock of awareness comes to Yvain at the height of his glory, when his triumphant prowess has made him the center of a world preoccupied by honor (2681–95).[34] He suddenly remembers his broken promise to Laudine, and almost immediately thereafter her damsel appears to reveal publicly his disloyalty and to demand that he return her mistress' ring, symbolizing the end of their love (2696–2782). Yvain had been prevented by shame from reacting to his own discovery of his delinquency (2704–5); now that it is public, grief becomes self-hatred (2792), accompanied by an overwhelming desire to escape from society (2786–91). Thoughts of self-destruction (2793–97) finally give way to the inner storm of madness (2806–7), and Yvain strips himself and flees to the forest where he lives the life of an irrational wildman, hunting game with a bow and arrow, and eating his prey raw.

Yvain's madness follows from his sudden awareness that he has chosen prowess over love, public honor over private happiness. (Chrétien carefully indicates that his hero realizes privately, while in the presence of Arthur and his court, that he has broken his word to Laudine before the arrival and public accusation of the damsel.) His deranged behavior is both an outer mimesis of the implications of his previous behavior — he has been mad and subhuman to leave and forget Laudine [35] — and a response of alienation and despair to his realization of who he has been (a brave and honored knight, but a traitor to his wife) and what it has cost him. By becoming aware of the tremendous gap between what he has accomplished and what he really wants (i.e., Laudine's love), Yvain is redefining himself in terms of desired happiness rather than possessed honor, that is, in terms of an identity perceived but not attained, whose ultimate referent is personal and private. The "inner distance" between his new state of realization and its desired goal is so insurmountable to Yvain as to call forth a negative response of madness and escape to the woods, i.e., an inner and outer escape from the hated self whose hideous distortion stands revealed in the glow of awareness cast by remembered love. Yvain's inner crisis is a negative version of religious conversion, a horrified turning-away from the old self illuminated by grace; it is the lack of grace (or of its secular equivalent) which drives the hero mad. (At the end of the romance, l. 6771, Yvain will describe himself as a *pecheor* on whom Laudine should have mercy.) All of Yvain's responses in madness have inner significance: in running away, stripping himself, and taking bow and arrows, he abandons his social identity and the hateful meaning or form it has given to his martial impulses. He will now hunt for survival with unchivalric weapons instead of jousting in armor to gain honor. His repudiation of his old self involves the repudiation of society and civilization, which have shaped that self through their values; hence he eats his meat raw, an act symbolic of a precivilized state, and lives alone in a presocial one. In sum, for Yvain guilt (negative self-awareness) leads to madness (self-alienation) which is also the repudiation of chivalry, or at least of its social basis.

It follows from this analysis that Yvain's adventures must reflect his progress in facing himself, and controlling his martial powers, but also his ability to find a new mode of relationship with society that will allow him to pursue his happiness and fulfillment in other than complete isolation. The adventure phase of *Yvain* shows Chrétien not only guiding his hero through stages of self-control,[36] but also remaking his fictional world on the basis of a new ethos of service grounded in different types of love, to each of which prowess can beneficially be subordinated. (Thus, Yvain brings animals he has hunted to the cell of the charitable hermit, saves Lunete's life because of her kindnesses to him, and is moved by his affection for Gawain to save the latter's niece from the lust of Harpin of the Mountain [3766ff].) The climax of *Yvain* is accordingly double: the first part shows Yvain returning to Arthur's court, the values of which reflect the purified vision of the hero; the second, final part brings

Yvain back to Laudine, to reconciliation, and to the synthesis of his old and new identities.

Yvain returns to Arthur's court to fight his climactic battle as the Knight of the Lion, loyal friend and defender of wronged ladies — exemplar, that is, of a new, moral chivalry of service. Unrecognized, he enters judicial combat on behalf of a wronged younger sister, while the claim of her unjust older sister is upheld by Gawain, Yvain's old friend. The symbolic import of this battle between two kinds of prowess is obvious, and it is most skillfully treated by Chrétien: Gawain's exhortations to honor through prowess had led Yvain to leave Laudine, and now the two friends, disguised for different reasons, cannot recognize each other, just as the chivalry painfully evolved by one has no recognizable relationship to the honor-loving, amoral prowess espoused by the other. The fight is bitter but inconclusive, and when at last the combatants recognize each other, the hatred of martial encounter gives way to the love of old friends,[37] who because of their mutual affection are each willing to forfeit the honor of victory to the other (6269–6302). Arthur himself now settles the feud of the sisters by realizing who is in the wrong and tricking the older sister into admitting her guilt (6376–92). His awareness and wit succeed where prowess has failed, bringing honor to the knights and to himself (6432–37).[38] This episode unveils a new hierarchy of values. Prowess is at the bottom of this hierarchy, and justice, love and reconciliation at the top. In the brave new Arthurian world, Gawain, former apostle of honor, is ready to sacrifice honor for love (and therefore does not have to), while Arthur, no longer the mindless, irresponsible monarch of earlier episodes, becomes instead a just, perceptive, and therefore powerful king.

The repairing at Arthur's court of a kin relationship in which selfishness and injustice have disrupted love and service prefigures the second part of the romance's resolution. Yvain leaves Arthur's court, and goes to the fountain, determined to make it storm until Laudine is forced to have mercy on him. This desperate act of love brings Lunete to the fountain to tell him that she has convinced Laudine to help the Knight of the Lion regain his lady's favor in return for his agreeing to defend her fountain against the unknown knight who threatens her land![39] Lunete's constant loyalty to Yvain and her unfailing wit thus bring about a final reconciliation of the knight and her lady in a state which represents the summit of the chivalric hero's moral ascent: peace.[40] Yvain's last, symbolic, gesture of prowess at the fountain is again subordinated to loyal friendship, while perception and wit effect the desired healing of a disrupted relationship of love and service. Lunete's efforts at peacemaking surpass Arthur's, since they result in the achievement by the hero of his desired self and the integration of his identities. Yvain thus overcomes his alienation from himself and his world, and constructs a new self as the basis for a new world of purified chivalric values. Through him, the chivalric romance celebrates the birth and triumph of the conscious self, which it declares to be cause and symbol of universal harmony.

IV

One of the most interesting chivalric romances of the twelfth century outside Chrétien's corpus is *Partonopeu de Blois*, written by an anonymous poet in the 1180's.[41] Its plot is full of reminiscences of Chrétien,[42] yet it speaks with its own voice and exploits dramatic possibilities inherent in the chivalric *topos* in new ways.

At the beginning of the romance the hero, Partonopeus, Count of Blois and nephew of the King of France, is a brave and handsome boy of thirteen. Transported in an unmanned boat to a mysterious city of beautiful but empty palaces, Partonopeus goes to bed in the most beautiful one, and in the dark is visited by a woman he cannot see. He rapes her, and she identifies herself as the young Empress of Byzantium, Melior, who, pressed by her vassals to choose a husband, has selected the young count and magically transported him to her. The apparent emptiness of the city is also the result of her magic, and she now tells him that if he wishes to marry her he must stay in the city alone for two and one-half years (until he is old enough to be dubbed knight by her), during which time he can enjoy her at night but must not try to see her face. These conditions are necessary in order to prevent her vassals discovering that she has, out of love, chosen a mere boy as her husband and has granted him her favors before she has either knighted or married him. Discovery would bring disgrace and death to both of them.

Partonopeus, smitten with love, agrees to Melior's scheme, but after a year he asks her permission to return to his home in France. She agrees, saying that he will there be able to save the Franks from invasion by their enemies, and win great glory. Her prediction is borne out, but in France Partonopeus is also subjected to a new danger: his mother and his royal uncle become convinced that his beloved is an

19

evil spirit and insist that he not return to her. With the aid of a love potion they almost force him to marry the King's beautiful, rich niece, but his love for Melior saves him at the last moment, and he returns, shaken and repentant, to Chef d'Oire, Melior's city. When, some months later, he requests leave to return to France again, Melior warns him that this time he will succumb to the wiles of his kin and betray her. Disregarding this prophecy, the young man goes home, and is soon convinced by his mother and by the Bishop of Paris that Melior is an ugly demon who seeks his damnation. They give him a marvellous inextinguishable lantern with which to see her when next he goes to bed with her, and Partonopeus, once back at Chef d'Oire, uses it — only to discover that Melior is young and beautiful, and to realize that he has broken his promise and betrayed her. His self-hatred is matched by Melior's rage and despair; her magic has been impaired by the betrayal, and the lovers suddenly find themselves surrounded by the courtiers of Chef d'Oire. While Melior expects her vassals to arrive momentarily and put an end to them both, her beautiful and witty sister, Urraque, appears instead and urges that she curtail her grief, forgive Partonopeus for his folly, and make hasty plans to deceive her vassals into accepting Partonopeus as her husband.

Neither Partonopeus nor Melior will be comforted by Urraque's Lunete-like advice; the empress rejects her lover, and he leaves Chef d'Oire for France in a state of extreme self-torment and depression. His decline continues in his own country, and in a state of melancholy madness which has changed his appearance to that of a wildman he finally sets out for the wilderness where he hopes to be devoured by the beasts. Instead, he accidentally meets Urraque, who, recognizing him despite his sad metamorphosis, saves him from despair by convincing him (untruthfully) that Melior has forgiven him but dares not recall him because of her vassals. Partonopeus, his will to live regained, goes with Urraque to her island dwelling place, and the shrewd princess now convinces her sister that Partonopeus is dead and that she must ask her vassals to hold a tournament the winner of which will be her husband. The announcement of the tournament sets the stage for the chivalric resolution of the romance's crisis: Partonopeus, dubbed knight by Melior while in disguise, can now fight in the tournament, and after various adventures he does indeed enter the lists, where his love for Melior inspires him to triumph. He reveals himself to his beloved, is reconciled with her, and marries amid great festivities.

Partonopeu is a romance of a young man's coming of age. At the beginning of the story, the hero is an adolescent, full of promise but untested in love or war. The first episode is a superb evocation of his introduction to the mysteries of love, an initiation or rebirth into passion which creates a private world entirely divorced from the life of relationships and activities he has thus far experienced. Melior has structured the world of love as one which must remain a secret from the world of honor (her vassals) until it can present itself to this public world on the latter's terms and receive its blessing. The antagonism and disjunction between a world of love, full of pleasure but hedged round with prohibitions and permitting only limited perception of reality, and a threatening world of honor and public responsibility provides the audience with an anti-chivalric paradigm which must obviously be modified as the hero grows toward physical maturity.

The sensually pleasing but impercipient world of young love in which Partonopeus finds himself reflects both his and Melior's immaturity in its taboos and its fearful avoidance of antagonistic external reality. His noble nature, which has led Melior to choose him as lover and husband, and which has cooperated with her magic in bringing him to a relationship with her,[43] now initiates the crucial phase of interaction between his private world of love and the public world of responsibilities in which a courtly young hero is led by his will to participate. When Partonopeus returns to France after a year with his beloved, he wins honor through prowess prompted by love.[44] But he also discovers that the people whose values controlled him before his discovery, in love, of a private destiny challenge his love vision and thereby test his ability to perceive the true nature and goal of his desire, i.e., to understand himself. His mother and his feudal "father" the King set themselves against his private identity, and propose a pseudo-love identity instead, in the form of a socially sanctioned and apparently desirable marriage. The attractions, symbolized by the love potion,[45] through which society in fact seeks to control the destiny of the young courtier are seductive and perilous. Love, however, has given Partonopeus sufficient self-awareness to perceive that this is not the end he desires, and by thinking of Melior he resists the workings of the potion.[46]

Partonopeus' love cannot counter his fear of damnation, however, and where his blood and feudal relations have failed to trap him, his spiritual father, the Bishop of Paris, succeeds. Respecting the Bishop's insight into his love more than his own, Partonopeus surrenders his autonomous judgment and accepts as a guide to perception the lantern which will ironically allow him only to perceive that the impulse of his love was correct and that his willingness to be swayed by another code of values toward another goal was an act of hideous self-betrayal.[47]

The moment of crisis in *Partonopeu*, like that in *Yvain*, creates negative self-awareness; the hero's conversion to self-hatred and despair[48] results in both romances from a broken promise to the beloved. Partonopeus, like Yvain, flees his own *folie*; his flight from Chef d'Oire to France, and from France to the wilderness, functions again as an external metaphor of the flight from the self, perceived as the hopelessly imperfect subverter of its own real desires. (Yvain's active, wild madness as a hunter of beasts grotesquely parodies the prowess he had earlier set above love, while Partonopeus' passive, melancholy madness and desire to be eaten by beasts recalls his passiveness before, and manipulation by, the figures who embody the restraints and values of his public world.)

This is not to say that the moment of crisis in *Partonopeu* lacks originality. The poet links Partonopeus' betrayal to the sudden, full visibility of Melior's own public world and to the appearance on the scene of Urraque, whose virtues will be so important in bringing the romance to a happy and chivalric conclusion. In other words, he suggests that this is a *felix culpa*, a fortunate fall through which the lovers face the full complexity of their relationship to the external world and its values; from this perception, however painful, they can ultimately move to accepting their own imperfections and the hostility of society to their private love[49] — a hostility neither as terrible nor as insurmountable as ignorance and innocence have led them to believe. The magic of love has been irrevocably destroyed by the fall, but so have its illusions, and the way is clear to discover how to outwit and manipulate society for the sake of love while apparently observing its behests in order to gain honor.[50]

All the positive possibilities of Partonopeus' crisis of self-awareness are summed up in Urraque, who now enters the narrative with counsels of moderation (4963–78), an understanding of Partonopeus' human weakness (4943–50), and schemes which will compensate for his *folie* and counteract the opposition of Melior's vassals to her quest for private fulfillment (5001–38). Through Urraque's eyes we see Melior not as a fairy-mistress but as a petulant young girl who has not learned the necessity for tolerance in love; we also realize that heroic rage or self-laceration can not be final responses to love gone

22

wrong any more than secrecy and isolation can be to its birth. The two protagonists are equally culpable in the dislocation of their love. Both have been guilty of too great respect for the norms and pressures of society: Melior has been led by her fear of her vassals to create the spell of isolation for her love affair, and to impose on her lover the promise that he will not try to perceive who she is, while he has been led by his respect for the advice of his sponsors to break the promise. The lovers' crisis of awareness makes the audience aware, as well, of how limited and immature their earlier felicity had been, and the presence of Urraque assures us that good can come of the end of innocence.

The remainder of *Partonopeu de Blois* records the triumph of Urraque's wit and *mesure* over the self-destructive alienation of both Melior and Partonopeus, and then the triumph of chivalry over the obstacles placed in its path. In the last great crisis of the poem (5947ff.) Urraque accidentally encounters Partonopeus in the wilderness, and begins to move him toward recovery with shrewdness and great humanity. The young count is now a wildman whom she cannot recognize; he, paradoxically, has been driven by negative self-awareness to such a diminished state of consciousness that he does not recognize her. Such has been his flight from himself that he will not tell his name, except as "trahitres provés" (6024); his identity is entirely that of past mistakes. This is the obsession Urraque must break to save his life, and when he faints on hearing her name and she recognizes him, she revives him by saying (untruthfully) that Melior has sent her to find him and bring him back to her. At this news, Partonopeus regains the desire to live and a positive sense of perfectible and desirable identity. Thanks to Urraque, he admits, "sui ge tos revenus en moi" (6116). He swears eternal allegiance to Urraque, thereby suggesting that he has passed definitively under the sway of her particular virtues of resourcefulness and optimistic determination (6099–6103), and leaves the wilderness to go to her castle on a marvellously fertile and abundant island which echoes the new force and vitality of the life-wish within him (6197–6214).

Only after this turning point does the chivalric *topos* begin to function systematically in the plot of *Partonopeu de Blois*. To this court poet, chivalry could only work when those who espouse it do so with full awareness of their own limitations, and those of their "daylight" world, and can still meet the challenge of this world as social beings with deeply personal desires.

23

V

Rather than describe in detail the adventures and final tournament of *Partonopeu*, which constitute a straightforward interaction of love, prowess, and wit (what we might call the chivalry of ingenuity) made possible by the awareness and skills of the three protagonists, I will close this discussion by noting how evanescent was the happy marriage of chivalry and self-awareness which defined chivalric romance in the twelfth century and reflected its audience's desire to make personal fulfillment accord with the demands of an honor-centered social existence. A rupture in the metaphoric unity of the courtly poet's vision already appears in *Partonopeu*; the role of the narrator disturbs the delicate balance of public and private significances created by the plot. The narrator tells his audience that he is in love with a cruel lady who shows no willingness to pity him; at several places in the poem (e.g., 1861–86; 3423–48; 4039–52; 4537–48; 7519–52) he intrudes on the story to compare and contrast the situation of Partonopeus with his own. The effect of his new dichotomy between the optimism of fiction and the pessimism of "experience" is to suggest, however artificially, to the audience that art, no longer a metaphor but a fantasy, contradicts inner reality instead of representing it.

In Renaut de Beaujeu's *Le Bel Inconnu* (ca. 1190?),[51] the gap between narrator and his story widens. Having brought his hero (whose adventure-quest has also been a quest for his own identity and for awareness of his destiny) to the point of secretly loving a fairy mistress but marrying, with the approval of Arthur's court, another lady won through adventure, the narrator ends his romance, saying that he will continue the story, and bring Guinglain back to his *amie*, in return for *un biau sanblant* from his own mistress, whose heartlessness he has frequently bemoaned (6247–66; cf. 1–10, 1237–71; 4189–4210). Renaut's playing off of one literary convention (the narrator's plea to the cruel beloved — originally a lyric *topos*) against another (the chivalry *topos*) reveals an art, and relies on an audience, which have become detached enough to enjoy the manipulation and exploitation of literary themes as self-justifying artistic activities quite apart from any metaphoric content the themes may convey. The result is a type of mannerism in chivalric romance which marks the end of the genre's "classic" phase.

The end of the twelfth century also saw a completely different kind of development in chivalric narratives in the hands of courtly and non-courtly writers, viz., the reintegration of chivalry into historical frame-plots concerned with the rise and fall of Arthur's Round Table and the pseudo-salvation history of the Grail society. The great prose cycles of the early thirteenth century interpreted the ideals inherited from Chrétien and his contemporaries in the context of society's development and decline. The Cistercian *Quest del Saint Graal* and the *Mort Artu* passed very different yet equally adverse judgments on secular chivalry; no society, it seemed, could support adultery between the King's wife and his best *chevalier* — not even that founded by Arthur and guided by Merlin. Nor could a chivalric hero, however valorous, maintain such a liaison and still experience the higher personal fulfillment of the Grail vision. We see here a repudiation of the assumptions that underlay the chivalric romance in its first glories.

Chivalric romances continued to be written for some centuries, but never again did they combine literary sophistication and metaphorical intensity to express the ideals of an audience as they did for courtly society in the second half of the twelfth century in France and England.

NOTES

1. For examples of recent appreciations, see R. W. Southern, *The Making of the Middle Ages* (London, 1953, repr. 1959), Chap. 5, "From Epic to Romance"; F. Heer, *The Medieval World*, trans. J. Sondheimer (Cleveland, 1962), pp. 123–57 (a more idiosyncratic assessment). As will be noted below, I distinguish throughout this paper between chivalric romances and other twelfth-century courtly narratives not using the episodic romance plot form.

2. On patronage, see J. Benton, "The Court of Champagne as a Literary Center," *Speculum*, XXXVI (1961), 551–91; W. F. Schirmer, "Die kulterelle Rolle des englischen Hofes im 12. Jahrhundert," *Studien zum literarischen Patronat im England des 12. Jahrhunderts* (Köln u. Opladen, 1962), pp. 9–23; and M. D. Legge, *Anglo-Norman Literature and its Background* (Oxford, 1963), pp. 1–8. Legge's book offers the best introduction to the rise of courtly literature in northern Europe.

3. See Legge, pp. 8–18.

4. On the impulses of the courtly vernacular style see C. Muscatine, *Chaucer and the French Tradition* (Berkeley and Los Angeles, 1957), pp. 11–57.

5. All references are to the edition of A. Griscom (New York, 1929); see Book IX, Chap. 13.

6. Griscom, p. 457 (IX.13): "Quicumque vero famosus probitate miles in eadem erat unius coloris vestibus atque armis utebatur. . . . Efficiebantur ergo [mulieres] caste et meliores, et milites pro amore illarum probiores."

7. Griscom, p. 458 (IX.14): "Mox milites simulacrum prelii sciendo equestrem ludum componunt; mulieres in edituo murorum aspicientes in furiales amores flammas ioci irritant."

8. Griscom, p. 461 (IX.16): Cador says, "ubi usus armorum videtur abesse alee autem et mulierum inflammationes ceteraque oblectamenta adesse dubitandum non est etiam id quod erat virtutis . . . ignavia commaculari."

9. For Wace, see the edition of I. Arnold (2 vols. [Paris, 1938–40]); for *Thèbes*, that of G. Raynaud De Lage (2 vols. [Paris, 1966–68]). The dating of *Thèbes* is approximate; see De Lage, I, xxvi–xxx. Wace's *Brut* is usually dated by a reference to it in the prefatory remarks of Lazamon's *Brut*.

10. In the crown-wearing episode, for instance, Wace both multiplies rich and refined details and inserts a realistic, rueful description of men gambling amidst the festivities (10557–96).

11. Wace is more explicit than Geoffrey about the precise activities of Arthur's *chevaliers* during the joust (*behorder* 10521–38), and also about the correspondingly appropriate behavior of the ladies: "Qui avoit ami an la place/ Tost li tornoit l'uel et la face" (10541–42).

12. Verbal references occur at 1153ff., 1765–66, and 4379–84. For a perceptive discussion of how the *topos* begins to become a vessel for real human emotions and actions, see R. R. Bezzola, *Les origines et la formation de la littérature courtoise en occident (500–1200), troisième partie* (Paris, 1963), I, 275–78.

13. Bezzola, p. 276, aptly calls this encounter a "pastourelle courtoise." It has about it none of the element of self-recognition which appears in the Ovidian *contes* and chivalric romances discussed below.

14. Ll. 4685–88. She goes on to say that she will sleep with her lover, "ou face bien ou ge foloi" (4691–92), thereby underlining the sensual reality of the passion which Geoffrey presents more formally in his description of the ladies on the walls of Caerleon (cf. note 7). Athes is wearing Ysmaine's "manche de syglaton" (4679–82), which looks back to, and vivifies, Geoffrey's remark that knights and ladies wore clothes of matching colors (IX.13).

15. The French poet describes Athes' death first, and then the sisters' conversation in the tower. The audience's knowledge of the first scene forces it to regard the second from an ironic perspective.

16. The standard treatment of Ovidian sources for courtly narratives, including the *contes*, is E. Faral, *Sources latines des contes et romans du moyen age* (Paris, 1913), pp. 3–157. For more recent studies, see note 18, below.

17. New, that is, in courtly narrative. On similar explorations in Provençal lyrics, see F. Goldin, *The Mirror of Narcissus in the Courtly Love Lyric* (Ithaca, 1967), pp. 69–106.

18. On these borrowings from learned culture, see H. C. R. Laurie, "Narcissus," *Medium Aevum*, XXXV (1966), 111–16; *idem*, "Piramus et Tisbé," *Modern Language Review*, LV (1960), 24–32; C. Muscatine, "The Emergence of Psychological Allegory in Old French Romance," *PMLA*, LXVIII (1953), 1160–82; and F. Branciforti, ed., *Piramus et Tisbé* (Florence, 1959), pp. 13–65.

19. See, e.g., *Piramus et Tisbé*, ll. 269–301, where Tisbé, torn between demands of love and filial obedience, moves toward action that will win Piramus "ou bel me soit ou m'en repente" (299).

20. *Enéas*, ed. J. J. Salverda de Grave (2 vols. [Paris, 1925, 1929]). The in-

fluence of the *Enéas* was thoroughly studied by A. Dressler, *Der Einfluss des altfranz. Eneas-Romans auf die altfranz. Literatur* (Leipzig, 1907); more recently, see H. C. R. Laurie, "*Enéas* and the *Lancelot* of Chrétien de Troyes," *Medium Aevum*, XXXVII (1968), 142–56.

21. See 8445–8662, where Lavine haltingly reveals the name of her lover, syllable by syllable, to her mother, and the latter insists that Enéas is a sodomite and will not return her love. Finally, the beleaguered girl faints and the queen leaves; when Lavine awakes, she quickly comes to the decision that, throwing her honor to the wind, she must reveal her love to the Trojan hero (8708–19). On the Ovidian source of the girl in the tower, see Faral, p. 130.

22. Note especially that, during the battle which leads up to Enéas' final encounter with Turnus and during the duel itself, no mention is made of Lavine at all. The twelfth-century poet retains Virgil's reason why Enéas killed Turnus (vengeance for the slaughter of Pallas by Turnus), despite the fact that it conflicts, at least implicitly, with Enéas' ostensibly chivalric motivation (see 9343–9838; esp. 9792–9814).

23. I have discussed Geoffrey's historiography in *The Vision of History in Early Britain* (New York, 1966), pp. 121–72.

24. On the marvellous, see Faral, pp. 307–88; E. Auerbach discusses the class limitations and interests of chivalric romance in the chapter on "The Knight Sets Forth" in *Mimesis*, trans. W. Trask (Princeton, 1953; repr. New York, 1957), pp. 107–24.

25. The cyclical nature of romance plots has frequently been noted. Chrétien de Troyes' *Yvain*, discussed below, organizes its hero's adventures around returns to a marvellous storm-causing fountain, while simultaneously portraying the hero's inner growth in self-awareness and morality.

26. On the myth of the Golden Age, see H. Levin, *The Myth of the Golden Age in the Renaissance* (Bloomington, Ind., 1969). The Christian history of salvation shares many features with the Golden Age myth, including a tension between linear and cyclic history. See J. Danielou, *Sacramentum Futuri* (Paris, 1950), pp. 3–52.

27. For a provocative discussion of the relationship between love, self-knowledge, and self-perfection, as presented from the ironic perspective of the Narcissus myth, see Goldin, pp. 20–68.

28. The best religious romances of the period are *St. Alexis* (written in the archaic style) and *St. Eustache*; for a secular version of the latter, cf. the Middle English romance *Sir Ysumbras*.

29. The reputation bestowed upon a knight by the court, or by the entire external world, may be equated with what I earlier called the romance hero's circumstantial identity. Chrétien explores this dimension of identity thoroughly in his *Lancelot* by means of the device of the *charette* which Lancelot mounts, thereby shaming himself before the entire chivalric world and earning a new identity as *chevalier de la charette*.

30. I use the edition of M. Roques (Paris, 1960).

31. See the opening of *Yvain*, where Chrétien lavishly praises the honor and love service of the Arthurian court, and proceeds to describe it in action as a place of disorder and skewed priorities: Arthur dishonorably leaves his

knights on the feast of Pentecost (the occasion of Arthur's crownwearing in Geoffrey's *Historia*) and goes to sleep with his wife, while outside his bedchamber Kay sows discord among the knights and Calogrenant is obliged to tell of an adventure which brought him dishonor.

32. See 1001–15. This is the first announcement of the theme of interlocking hospitality and service which will prove central to the romance. Its ultimate and most moving statement, also by Lunete, is at 6685–99.

33. As the Knight of the Lion, Yvain devotes himself to the service of ladies trapped in a variety of destructive or degrading situations. His relationships with the hermit in the woods, with his lion, and, of course, with Lunete are models of mutually beneficial service — that of hospitality offered, and of prowess offered in return. All these features of the adventures offer comments on and inversions of his disloyal, selfish relationship with Laudine. Disruptive images, besides the fountain, include Laudine's grief and above all the self-disruption of Yvain's madness. Images of constraint include all the many instances of imprisonment in the poem: Yvain in Laudine's castle, the lion locked up so that he cannot aid his master, the damsels in the basement of the *chastel de pesme avanture*, etc.

34. Arthur seeks out Yvain, who has set up camp outside the castle where the King is staying; thus the place of honor comes to the hero rather than vice versa.

35. Notice the marvellous irony of 2861–63, explaining the wild, mad Yvain's return to the hut of the hermit who has given him water: "mes n'est nus, tant po de san ait,/qui el leu ou l'en bien li fait,/ ne revaigne molt volentiers." Cf. 6774, when the repentant Yvain tells Laudine, "folie me fist demorer."

36. The lion, whose loyalty to Yvain makes him control even his most basic hunting instincts (3412ff.), is a symbol of self-control; Yvain also rejects suicide (self-destructive prowess) in order to save the wrongly accused Lunete (3486ff.), thereby marking another step forward on the road to control of martial impulses for positive ends.

37. See 5992ff., in which Chrétien deftly exploits the paradox of the situation in which Hate reigns between two who love each other — or would, if they could recognize each other. The import of the paradox is clear: aggressive, destructive prowess is a function of ignorance (including self-ignorance), while with awareness of identity comes the primacy of love.

38. When the King tells the older sister he will declare Gawain the loser of the battle unless she agrees to accept his verdict (6408–22), he reveals a new awareness that only justice should be rewarded with honor. His instructions to the older sister show him to be aware that reconciliation in turn crowns justice: "si l'amez come vostre fame, / et ele vos come sa dame/ et come sa seror germainne" (6435–37).

39. At an earlier meeting with Laudine (4582–98), during which he did not reveal himself, the Knight of the Lion confessed that he had lost his lady's favor and would not cease his adventures until he regained it.

40. The word *pes* appears in the text at 6769, 6783, 6789, 6801, referring specifically to the peace between Yvain and Laudine.

41. Ed. J. Gildea (2 vols. in 3 [Villanova, Pa., 1967–70]). See A. Fourrier,

Le Courant réaliste dans le roman courtois en France au moyen-age (Paris, 1960), pp. 315–446.

42. The figure and function of Urraque is based on Lunete; in *Partonopeu* as in *Yvain* the hero breaks a promise to his beloved, thereby precipitating a crisis; in the latter part of the romance Partonopeus, like Lancelot, is imprisoned in a tower from which he escapes with the aid of his jailer's wife in order to take part in a tournament, etc.

43. See 1363–84, on how she fell in love with him, and her praise of his lineage and *noblesce*, 1501–14; also 921ff., which describe how a *pensers de noblece* leads him to seek out the most beautiful palace in Chef d'Oire in which to eat and sleep — Melior's palace.

44. See 3401–30, where love motivates Partonopeus to win a climactic battle, thereby illustrating for the first time in the poem the chivalry *topos*. Cf. the fuller statement of the *topos*, 7560–76.

45. Fourrier, p. 390, attempts to rationalize the potion as probably the intoxicating effect of wine on a fifteen-year old boy. He misses the point that in this scene Partonopeus is being tempted by all that society can offer him to follow its plans for him and forsake his private destiny. The potion stands for the lure of self-forgetfulness, implicit in accepting the good life lived at court.

46. See 4061–64: "Quant cil ot s'amie [Melior] nomer,/Tantost se prent a porpenser,/Et en la guise del porpens/Li est tos revenus li sens."

47. The lantern has been given to Partonopeus as a stimulus to, and symbol of, spiritual perception to ward off the snares of the devil. When Partonopeus realizes "Qu'il a ovré moult folement" (4532), he throws the lantern against the wall and it goes out (4536), a fact which indicates graphically that his treason has in fact brought a new moral darkness to his love vision. See 4531–42.

48. The long speech by Partonopeus (4783–4820), not only admits his awareness of his *traison* (4790), and *felonie* (4793), and *folie* (4798), but repeatedly expresses his wish to die and his conviction that awareness will make life a living death for him (4805–16). Cf. 5203–58, another soliloquy expressing the same self-condemnation.

49. As Partonopeus denounces his *folie* to Melior and pleads for mercy, the poet says: "A ces paroles vint li jors,/Qui lor devise lor amors" (4821–22). The suggestion of enlightenment is unmistakable, and the double meaning of *devise*, viz., *separate* and *arrange* likewise proposes that the lovers have arrived at a beginning as well as an end.

50. See 4667–70, where Melior tells Partonopeus that his treason has caused the loss of that part of her formidable education in arts which enabled her to perform illusions such as those she has used to hide Partonopeus from her vassals. Her *engiens*, *ars*, and *livres* are still hers (4664–65); it is, in fact, such aids that Urraque will use to make love triumph in the latter part of the poem.

51. Ed. G. Perrie Williams (Paris, 1929). I will discuss this romance and *Partonopeu de Blois* in much greater detail in a forthcoming study of twelfth-century chivalric romance.

Nature and the Aesthetic Social Theory of Leon Battista Alberti

Andrea di Tommaso

Per dare savie leggi a un popolo bisogna essere anche un poco artisti.

Mussolini

What we demand is the unity of politics and art.

Mao Tse-tung

VARIOUS SCHOLARS have already underlined the importance of the position of nature in the thought of Leon Battista Alberti. Anthony Blunt mentions his "complete faith in nature";[1] Saitta points out that nature is Alberti's one true God;[2] Nicola Badaloni says that Alberti uses nature as the basis of his notion of *virtù*;[3] and P.-H. Michel analyses Alberti's admiration for this divinity "ouvrière" and "ordonatrice."[4] It remains to be shown to what extent the example of nature offers a unifying principle which pervades not only Alberti's view of art and architecture, but also his view of man and society.[5]

That Alberti saw nature as active and organized are important observations; such a vision is, however, only a projection of his own *haut bourgeois* mentality onto nature. Like the early Greeks, he sees in nature what is really a reflection of his own intellect. The important point is not so much that nature has a divine force or that man in imitation of nature can, as Alberti says, *essercitarsi*. What is important, rather, is that man and nature are both productive, and that the product is magnificent, a well-made work of art. Neither nature nor man derives "divinity" in Alberti's system from the inherent goodness of the agent. It is derived from the goodness (i.e., the magnificence) of the object made. It is not enough to say that nature is an artificer (*costitutrice*). The important point is that nature is an excellent artificer (*ottima costitutrice*). Not all observers of nature in the Renaissance

31

see her as a creator whose creation is a perfect model for man to admire. Bernardo Daniello in the Cinquecento, for example, observes in his *Poetica* that, along with what is good, that is to say useful to man, nature produces thorns and trees with sour fruit. He concludes that human art (such as grafting trees to produce better fruit) *must* improve upon nature's work. Alberti does say that man through art can in some ways surpass nature, but he does not hold the belief that nature can be improved by man in the same way that man can be improved by nature. What momentary doubts of nature's ability he has are dispelled upon his return to Florence, where reside such geniuses as Brunelleschi, Donatello, Luca della Robbia, and Masaccio. There was a time, however, he tells us in the Prologue to his treatise on painting, when he believed that "Nature, the mistress of things, had grown old and tired," with the result that "she no longer produced so marvellously and abundantly." [6] Save for this doubt, nature remains for Leon Battista the perfect artificer, a *Natura artifex* whose chief virtue is magnificence as Thomas Aquinas explained it.

Aquinas tells us that "it pertains to magnificence to do something great [*magna facere*, as its name implies]," and, quoting Cicero, that " 'magnificence is the considering and administering of great and lofty undertakings, with noble and splendid purpose of mind,' *consideration* (*cogitatio*) referring to the inward intention, and administration (*administratio*) referring to the outward execution. Wherefore just as magnanimity intends something great in every matter, it follows that magnificence does likewise in every act of creation in external matter." "The intention of magnificence," he goes on to say, "is to produce a great work." [7]

For Alberti, nature is just the agent to produce a great work, for, as he says, nature seeks "in all things to produce what is fitting and perfect." [8] She so seeks perfection that, indeed, she will even deprive corrupt children of the "true love" and "entire charity" of their fathers. [9] The importance of this statement increases with our awareness of the importance of the family in Alberti's social theory.

Just as magnificence requires both intention and accomplishment for Thomas Aquinas, so in the *Libri della famiglia* we learn that for Alberti, too, intentions alone are insufficient. In fact, intention without good results is worse than no intention at all. This is clear from the hypothetical illustration he gives of a boat race at Venice:

> You would strive mightily to reach the goal, where garlands
> and trophies of victory were stored and where the prizes and

32

> honors were given out to the winning contestants. You would
> want your ship to share with no more than two others in the
> first three prizes. Perhaps a fourth place might also give you
> if not a supreme prize at least some reputation and remem-
> brance. . . .
>
> The other participants in the race, however, would remain
> unknown. No one would speak of them. These contestants
> might perhaps have been better off if they had remained on
> land, taking no active part.[10]

Alberti would expect no one to wish to be mocked or consigned to
the oblivion of the shores of life, which, we remember from *Fatum
et Fortuna*, are the abode of *le ombre*,[11] the shores of Death. On one
shore there is physical death, on the other spiritual death. Thus everyone, he says later, should "strive hard for first place." [12]

A boat race, however, is not the best example of *essercizio*, since
it does not reflect the greatness Alberti expects an activity to produce.
The first quality of greatness he usually has in mind is usefulness.
Utile is a word as frequent in the *Libri della famiglia* as the word *essercizio*, and in his analysis of productive activities he implicitly agrees
with Palmieri that outside of the *limitata sottigliezza de l'absoluta
verità* [13] what is *utile* is not always *onesto*, and vice versa. If an individual has a choice of activities, Alberti counsels him to choose one
that is most useful to himself and his family.[14] First consideration is
given to final results; in the end one should do the thing he can do
best. Thus Alberti concludes that if a man's only talent is to earn
money his best choice is to do that rather than doing something else
less well.[15] Alberti's systematic imitation of nature not only insists
that each citizen have an *essercizio*, but also defines him by his function, from the architect to the pursuer of seemingly unworthy pecu-
niary activities, as long as the function is well executed.[16] Even to
acquire riches one must have *virtù*, especially since the most important product of one's activities is the self. Saitta has said that Alberti's
position is that being is defined by doing ("noi siamo in quanto
agiamo"),[17] but this falls short of a precise evaluation, since it does
not allow for the utility of *essercizio*. It would be better to say that
"noi siamo in quanto *facciamo*," since by doing man *makes* himself
and becomes a work of art. Alberti says that man "is not born to
stagnate at rest, but to be up and doing [*stare faccendo*]." [18] The Albertian hero, a *homo faber-Deus artifex*, seeing the world around him
from what has been called the perspective of art, also sees himself as
an objectified part of that world, as external matter upon which a form

33

must be impressed.[19] This is simply a reflection of the division of the model into *natura naturans* and *natura naturata*, the creator and the created.[20] The hero imitates nature in order to liberate himself from her through his art, not only by building shelter (although this too is an important function), but also by stepping outside the corruptive process of time into "the a-temporal privileged world of art."[21] It is an inevitable step from praising nature as "maestra delle cose"[22] to asking "Who can doubt that painting is the master art or at least not a small ornament of things?"[23] It is through his art that the painter glorifies himself and "will feel himself considered another god."[24] The same holds for any artificer, for these are various gradations of divinity, as pointed out in *Fatum et Fortuna*: some are *dii* and others are *semidii*.

Alberti's comparison of the human artificer to the divine, so common in Italian Renaissance letters, is more than idle rhetoric, for he sees every individual who forms himself and the world around him as, if not a creator *ex nihilo*, a demiurge. "More and more," he says, "do I find myself appreciating the teaching of Aristotle, who found that whenever man thinks with reason and with virtue, he, in his felicity, is like a mortal god."[25] The "stylized idealization," to use Weise's terminology, of society offered by Alberti requires heroic acceptance of the formative power of *virtù*, but at the same time it rewards the individual with *maestà e dignità sovrumane*.[26]

To understand the desire of modern western man to control nature one must accept the proclamation of the deification of man in the Renaissance as something more than arbitrary praise. It was a total panegyric for the new *Deus artifex*, the man of *virtù*. The cycle of Alberti's thought on the subject runs as follows: nature is a divine artificer; nature gives reason to man; reason gives *virtù* to man; and *virtù* makes man a divine artificer.

Nature is divine; she is a *maestra delle cose* and possesses a *forza divina*,[27] a creative force which Alberti understood as an operative deity.[28] Furthermore, nature always seeks perfection; she is an *ottima costitutrice*.[29] Man as a divinity can only be compared to divine nature the *ottima costitutrice*, the producer of magnificent works. The hoped-for grace of the aspirant man of medieval mentality is replaced by sanctifying *virtù*. *Virtù* makes a man great: "All'animo grande, ben constituito, non può parer gran cosa alcuna sopra quella che fa lui esser grande: la virtù."[30] It is with *virtù* alone that man can perform properly his role in society, for *virtù* is nothing more than "nature itself, complete and well-formed."[31]

The *animo grande, ben constituito* must also be a *constitutore*, and it is with this in mind that we see Leon Battista's hero operating from an extra-moral perspective as a *speculatore e operatore delle cose*[32] who is "suited and able to make good use of the world."[33] His primary goal is to achieve happiness through *essercizio*.[34] The rules for picking an *essercizio* are simple and completely amoral:

> To decide which is the most suitable career for himself, a man must take two things into account: the first is his own intelligence, his mind and his body, everything about himself; and the second, the question requiring close consideration, is that of outside supports, the help and resources which are necessary or useful and to which he must have early access, welcome, and free right of use if he is to enter the field for which he seems more suited than for any other.[35]

Here, precisely, is the attitude of the *homo faber* as Thomas Aquinas presents him, but now turning his artful eye upon himself. The external matter becomes the self objectified before the producing agent, and the thing made by art is not external to man as it is for Aquinas. Alberti's two rules conform to Aquinas' judgement that "art does not require of the craftsman that his act be good, but that his work be good (*Summa*, I–II, 57, 5)." One examines the intellect and the body to determine if they are suitable, much as the craftsman selects his materials to make a good knife, in order to produce a work of art *ben constituito*. Like a well-made knife, this well-crafted man needs only to be able to act well as an instrument; as such he must be useful: "Man was born to be useful to himself, and no less useful to others."[36] In the *De Iciarchia* he says again that man was born to be useful to man, and that whoever spends too much time, study, and effort on useless ventures is to be condemned.[37] The system is one in which failure to be useful and productive is the only sin, and in which one's essence is defined by his activity, since, according to Alberti, a man who is idle renders himself unworthy to be called a man, and cannot be considered worthy of being alive.[38] The individual must, like an individual part of nature (*natura naturata*), be *utile* not only to himself (praise, wealth, etc.) but also to the family and city, the former having the same relationship to the latter that the individual has to the family:

> From what I can discern of its nature, it seems to me that the city, just as it is made up of many families, so does it in itself

35

seem to be like one large family. Likewise, the family seems to be like a small city. If I am not mistaken, the existence of both was due to the joining together and uniting of many out of necessity and for the advantage of all.[39]

Just as the parts of nature strive to conserve themselves as nature seeks its own perfection, so man's "artificial" reproduction, in imitation, seeks to maintain itself at all cost, adopting whatever means are necessary (*qualunque elle siano*).[40] The preservation of the health of the city and family is no less "scientific" a problem than that of caring for an animate creature, which is what these structures resemble for Alberti:

> One ought to think of the family as a body similar to a republic, composed of you and this one and all these others: and to the family you are like natural instruments [*innati instrumenti*] and members of this body. The first obligation of whoever may be a part of the family, will be to be industrious and studious so that together all can truly become a well-formed body, in which the whole, as in an animate body, feels the movements of each of the separate parts.[41]

Frequently, if not always, in discussing such matters, Leon Battista plays, like Machiavelli, the role of *homo sciens* advising *homo faber*, not only when addressing a member of the "casa Alberta" but when addressing any citizen. The impersonal *chi*-plus-verb-of-volition construction used by Machiavelli is also used by Alberti, for the same purpose of offering amoral advice and for the opening the way to productivity to whoever would desire to follow it.[42]

Alberti as *homo sciens* addresses the youth of the Alberti family in the *Libri della famiglia* in order to instruct them on how to make themselves craftsmen whose aesthetic and pragmatic preoccupations will be the primary motivation for their activity. They will be makers of themselves, of their families, and finally of society by following the directives of the *speculatore* — the social theorist who guides them toward their extra-moral rewards. For Leon Battista the first principle of social theory is an aesthetic principle; it is the principle of unity or integrity of form. The perfection of man and his world is identical to the perfection found in nature; it is the presence of *virtù*, the artistic ability to impose a correct form on whatever matter the artificer handles. It is that power which for Machiavelli has been defined as "the power essentially to make, to impress a form upon matter, durably — or as durably as possible. *Virtù* is the power of the sculptor, of the forger."[43] Even the qualification "as durably as possible" has validity for Alberti if we recall the boat race: "Perhaps a fourth place might also give you if not the supreme prize at least some reputation and remembrance." *Virtù* orders and structures the material, or in Alberti's terminology, it removes *vizio*, which is nothing more than disorder and unstable lack of form: "l'animo de' viziosi sempre sta disordinato e infermo."[44] The *animo* of the man of *virtù* is *ben constituito* and he is, consequently, *di forte e intero animo*.[45] Alberti expects the same integrity of form from the state and explains how Italy, once divine, fell through lack of unity.[46] The goal which he sets for the man of *virtù* is that of being, and then appearing to be, virtuous.[47] *Virtù*, however, offers only extra-moral rewards such as magnificence, dignity, grace, splendor (a word which recurs incessantly, as P.-H. Michel rightly points out), and glory, first for the individual, then for the family and *polis*.

Alberti sees glory as a goal naturally desired by intelligent persons.[48] If Machiavelli wrote his treatise *The Prince* with hopes of gaining employment, Alberti the advisor also hopes to profit from his writings, as he admits in his treatise on painting, saying that those who find his remarks on painting useful can acknowledge their gratitude to him by portraying him in their pictorial creations.[49]

To the young men of the Alberti family he says he will always do whatever results *in bene e utile* for the family, and counsels them to do likewise, always heeding the voice of the Alberti ancestors, who, he says, were very studious, literate, and civil.[50] Obviously including himself among the honored patriarchs, he ends his Prologue to the *Libri della famiglia* with the imprecation "Leggetemi e amatemi." It is a perfect Albertian replacement for the "Tolle, legge" of Saint Augustine, and similar to the recommendation of at least one other educator (Ser Brunetto Latini) promoting himself saying "Sieti raccomandato il mio Tesoro,/ Nel qual io vivo ancora; e più non cheggio."

But like Machiavelli, Alberti, who accepted the bourgeois structure and its rewards, was genuinely interested in seeing every man of "animo intero" make a respectable and rewarding place for himself in the world. John White has already explained that in his treatise on painting Alberti uses artificial perspective as

> a lever with which to ease the humble craft of painting into the lordly circle of the liberal arts. With this accent the formerly humble, but now scientific, painter was to move into the sphere of the princely patrons and attendant men of letters. Social

and economic pressures were combined with the aesthetic and the practical.[51]

This combination of "pressures" is a permanent aspect of Alberti's system, a system in which these forces are naturally united and virtually indistinguishable. His view of life is always that of a practical craftsman, reflecting the mentality of *Della pittura*: "In all this discussion, I beg you consider me not as a mathematician but as a painter writing of these things."[52] He sees life as a framed "slice of life," so to speak, a section through the plane formed by the bases of two identical visual pyramids placed base to base, fixed by artificial perspective, and viewed from the "central point" of art as myth to its re-creator, the artist,[53] and from the "central point" of history as the raw material of the *homo faber*. The importance of *istorie* in painting, emphasized in *Della pittura*, is one half of a vision which also sees the importance of art in life as well. If the painter-Narcissus is the model of the new terrestrial god who captures the divine creative power of nature, it is the architect in real life who becomes the supreme demiurge controlling the force in a highly ordered and practical manner. The architect for Alberti is the *raggio centrico* of society, the *principe dei raggi*, as he says of the central ray in his explanation of perspective. As the central ray of the city-state the architect is the first among many *semidii* and *dii*, giving form to life through *virtù*.

The question of which of the two arts, painting or architecture, is supreme is difficult to answer. Painting is the mistress of things, because it shows how life can be structured to accept *artificial* form as *artificium*, but architecture is the fullest embodiment of the union of the "social and economic pressures . . . with the aesthetic and the practical." Narcissus' story is appropriate to painting, the "flower of all the arts," since he was the first to find man himself to be the most fascinating source of beauty in nature, after which discovery man was able to resume a rightful place in the scheme of nature, symbolized by the transformation of Narcissus into a flower. The divine force which Narcissus recovered is thus a unifying principle. In a social context, however, the architect must rise above the painter. In his intensely practical world view Alberti is willing to concede discovery of the divine force to the painter, but the architect is responsible for man's ultimate triumph. The painter's *summa opera*, he says, is *la istoria*, which is to say a re-creation of life, of all those things "worthy of being seen."[54] But the architect, who is applying his art directly to life, lends dignity to man in history itself. The seeming contradiction between Professor Garin's assertion that for Alberti architecture is "the art of all arts"[55] and Professor Birkmeyer's statement that Alberti considered painting as "the first and foremost art" of the times[56] is only part of the dialectical dynamism of Alberti's order, in which society is seen as a malleable *bonum exteriorum.* The "dialectic of Being and Becoming"[57] which Eugenio Donato finds in Alberti is that of a *homo faber* trying to discover the productive and unifying power of nature which gives to reality rational integrity, and which explains the passage from the divine One (Individual) to a multiple reality (Society). It is the dialectic between life as myth and life as history. For the artificer, to be divine means to have unity of being (the *rational* which is the source of *virtù*) which can impose itself on the external world as well as on man himself. Narcissus, the father of painting, first saw the reflection of himself in nature, which "seems to abolish both time and history,"[58] and it is painting that first mythologized life through *istorie.* But it is the structured society (*structura structurata*) acting with divine force (*structura structurans*), with the architect at the head, which frees man from the bonds of time and history. Of the intensity of historical consciousness in the Renaissance we are well aware.

That Alberti would honor the intellect and its products as divine is not surprising.[59] Nor is it strange that he would expect the architect to be very nearly omniscient, for, as Eugenio Garin says in explaining that the treatise on architecture is something more than a study of architectural matter: "l'architetto deve riunire in sé ogni dote umana per essere a pieno *homo faber.*"[60] Painting too is a product of the intellect with practical applications. The relationship of painting to life is that of Alberti to *homo faber.* It is a relationship between master and pupil, *homo sciens* the advisor and *homo faber* the maker, or between *speculatore* and *operatore delle cose,* to use Alberti's names. It is not pushing Alberti too far to suggest, as J. R. Spencer has, that painting has an ambitious didactic aim involving all citizens. As Spencer says of the painter:

> His rôle is to create an art that will touch learned and unlearned alike by the universality of its appeal. Such an art surely will move all men and leave a mark on their soul. It is in this respect that Alberti and Cicero wish to educate, to raise the level of each man's life and consequently of all mankind. . . . The painting he desires would seem to have the same end he advocates in his *Della famiglia* . . . the acquisition of *virtù.*[61]

Narcissus, then, is not only the father of painting but also the father of humanistic education. It is as a *maestra* in the educational sense that his discipline holds first place over the others.

The ultimate aim of the individual and of society for Alberti is not only to possess the divine force of nature but to apply it in a practical way. *Edificare* is nature's final cause and society's as well. Man must be able to withstand the tides of opposition just as nature does; like nature man should be able to surpass whatever force hinders or opposes him. Indeed, "adversities are the material of which character [*virtù*] is built."[62]

In the Preface to his *De Re Aedificatoria* Alberti says that the urge to create is not only useful and necessary, but also natural to man. He also states that men organized into social groups out of the need for protection against the elements, and that it was man's natural inclination to construct shelters which served as the primary stimulation for the creation of society.

Later the author, in his own Latin text, says that "facere quidem aliquid certa cum ratione artis est."[63] This, as Santinello points out, is a definition not far from the medieval definition of art as *recta ratio factibilium*, the right reason about certain works to be made. It is a definition of an extra-moral operative habit which Alberti directs toward the *materia* of the self, the family and the state, as well as to architecture. Santinello says:

> L'accento batte anzitutto sul *facere*, a maggior ragione per il fatto che tale definizione viene data a proposito dell'architettura, che per l'Alberti è arte molto meno manuale e molto più intellettuale delle altre come la pittura, la scultura. Vi è dunque un fare, un aspetto poietico, anche dell'ingegno e dell'intelletto, se è vero che l'architetto non è fabbro o manovale, e che è possibile tracciare con l'animo e la mente forme complete a prescindere della materia . . .[64]

Professor Garin has also stated that for Alberti *edificare* has a very wide range of meaning, adding that there is no separation between circulation of goods and ideas for Alberti.[65] Thus Alberti's thought again resembles that of Aquinas, who saw something in common between the operative habit of Art and the speculative habits insofar as "neither art nor speculative habit makes a good work as regards the use of the habit, which is the property of a virtue that perfects the appetite, but only regards the aptness to work well."[66] Furthermore,

Aquinas sees that speculative matters reflect an operative process, which accounts for calling the *liberal* arts by the name *arts*.

For Alberti, then, the model man of *virtù*, in a public sense, is the architect, for as Garin says:

> A city in its physical being, in its buildings, is the civic community made real and concrete and fully manifest. For this reason the architect is the universal man. Or, if one prefers, the governor becomes architect and the politician a theoretician of architecture precisely at the point that science becomes practical and is joined to political wisdom.[67]

In a private sense he is an *animo intero* whose clear reasoning makes him a *speculatore*. And the family of *virtù* is the one which has been formed into an aesthetic unity which reveals no disordered part or aspect which Alberti terms *bruttezza*. It is a family like the "casa Alberta," which never showed any sign of *bruttezza*, including the disfigurement of poverty.[68] The choice of terminology is consistent with Alberti's notion, like that of Cusanus, that beauty is directly proportional to unity. *Virtù* is the principle which lends form and evokes a natural formative impulse: "Let us agree, then, that man was not born to languish in idleness but to labor and create magnificent and great works."[69] This understanding of the *homo-Deus artifex* brings us close to the definition of Alberti's acquaintance Cusanus of God as *forma formarum* and *forma formante*.[70] In Alberti's hierarchy of *semidii* and *dii*, if it is the painter-Narcissus who rejoins man to nature, it is the architect who unifies all human activities and joins man to man. It is interesting to note also that Cusanus was almost disposed to deny form to what was simply formed and not formative.[71] Such a notion applied to Alberti would offer an explanation for his obvious insistence that all forms (painting to society) be efficient (instructive or productive).

In his treatise on sculpture Leon Battista Alberti states that nature is the source of principles which will guide man in all of his disciplines, recalling his assertion that nature is mistress of all things.[72] Because *edificare* in all its meanings is the final goal of all creation, the one principle which will apply to all disciplines is the principle of creativity. Badaloni rightly points out that at the heart of the Albertian position there is an accent on the creative aspect of productive activity.[73] This is precisely the point, as life and art, or politics and architecture, become completely intertwined.[74] Thus, for example, what is the painter's primary creation is not a material artifact, but a world recreated in perspective, a world of *istorie* which edifies the observer. This educative goal blends with society's goal, the glorification of man, the deification of man through *virtù*. The last of Alberti's *Sentenze pitagoriche* advises: "Ultimo, stima certo dell'animo tuo ch'ello è cosa divina e immortale." [75] Just as nature seeks perfection through unity and conservation of its parts so must man dominate the forces of deterioration, such as time, which Alberti classifies with the body and mind as one of man's possessions [76]— something the medieval mind would not comprehend, but which was consistent with the new *Geistesgeschichte*.

By understanding what nature is, how it operates and toward what end its energies are directed, man in effect repeats the process of generation which nature embodies. The notion of "edificare" employed by Filarete is equally valid for Leon Battista Alberti: "Building is a voluptuous pleasure, as when a man is in love." [77] What is more appropriate to Alberti, however, is an inversion of Filarete's maxim, that is, the idea that the "voluptuous pleasure" is the introduction to a form of *constructive* activity. The *inamorato* is, in fact, what Pompanazzi might have called the simple instrument of natural necessity.[78] Being also a "speculatore," he sees that "voluptuous pleasure" has a practical purpose, since nature "labors to make everything that is procreated preserve itself." [79] Man too has a natural necessity "to have and to raise children and afterward to take delight in seeing them express his very image and likeness." [80] Once Alberti convinces his audience that the individual can and must make himself *di forte e intero animo* he proceeds to show that the union of individuals (ultimately as a society) must be guided by natural laws and structured by the formative power of *virtù*, which brings with it the corrective capabilities of reason. Whereas in his treatise on architecture Alberti states that man is by nature an artificer and supplied with a set of natural principles to guide him in all disciplines, in the *Libri della famiglia* he adds to the picture in such a way as to indicate that procreation is a discipline to be guided by such principles and that the procreator is an artificer.

The analysis of the construction of a family begins with the assertion that companionship is a natural necessity, and Alberti quickly adds that marriage was instituted by divine nature: ". . . fu il coniugio instituito dalla natura ottima e divina maestra di tutte le cose." [81] The *homo sciens* then takes over and proceeds to tell the *homines fabres familiarum*, the young men of the Alberti family, how to choose a wife with whom to build a family. This he does much as he tells the architect how to choose his materials, but not before confirming that "for the procreation of children, no one can deny that man requires woman."[82] Then he turns to the selection of the materials themselves assisted by the wisdom of poets:

> It is a well-known saying among poets: "Beautiful character dwells in a beautiful body." The natural philosophers require that a woman be neither fat nor very thin. Those laden with fat are subject to coldness and constipation and slow to conceive.[83]

The natural philosophers know also how new the material should be and when is the best time to begin laying the family foundation:

> [The natural philosophers] always have a preference for youth, based on a number of arguments which I need not expound here, but particularly on the point that a young girl has a more adaptable mind. Young girls are pure by virtue of their age and have not developed any spitefulness. They are by nature modest and free of vice. They quickly learn to accept affectionately and unresistingly the habits and wishes of their husbands.[84]

As to how long the main pillar of the family should be aged and allowed to mature Alberti says that men should wait until they are at least twenty-five years old before marrying. "Let men wait for solid maturity" — "Aspettasi adunque la virilità matura e soda."[85] At the same time that we are thinking that *sodo*, as a substantive, means foundation, and as an adjective firm or well-grounded, we cannot help but recall the analogy in the *De Re Aedificatoria* between edifice and human body, and that in Book Three of the *De Iciarchia* between family and republic and living body. We understand why no individual, family or city can admit of any *bruttezza* whatsoever, for such a *bruttezza* would be to society or family what a deformity would be to the body. The aesthetic principle underlying this theory is that

> no Man beholds any Thing ugly or deformed, without an immediate Hatred and Abhorrence. . . . Beauty, Gracefulness, and the like Charms consist in those Particulars which if you alter or take away, the Whole would be made homely and disagreeable. . . . For every Body consists of certain peculiar Parts, of which if you take any one, or lessen, or enlarge it, or remove it to an improper place; that which before gave the Beauty and Grace to this Body will at once be lamed and spoiled.[86]

This, as Wölfflin has said, is the "classic definition of the perfect in L. B. Alberti," [87] and it was with the perfect that he was especially concerned.

Then, with the arrival of children at the proper time, Alberti steps back to view the results much as an architect might admire a new structure: "Now we have filled the house with people." [88] Once the family begins to grow, the *paterfamilias*, because nature makes him guide his family to good fortune, will direct the development of the children. In accord with natural principles, also, the family tends to conserve its parts and fortunately, unlike a building, it can be moved if this will prolong the life of its members: "How shall we keep men alive a long time? I think we had better follow the example of the wise shepherd as he preserves his flocks." [89] Just as the shepherd knows that goats thrive best in rough, barren places, so the father should know how to pasture his family in the most suitable place. If the air in Florence is too thin, Alberti says, for any member of the family, he should be sent to Rome; if Rome is too warm, then Venice; if Venice is too humid, then elsewhere. It is better to have the children far from home and strong, than close and weak.

One of the most important choices for the child is that of choosing an *essercizio*, an activity which will give meaning to his life. All *essercizi*, as we have said, are judged by Alberti to be of some merit and deserve to be well executed. In the end, of course, it is the architect who becomes the "governor and co-ordinator of all civic activities." [90]

If Alberti does not advocate open opposition to nature, his desire to appropriate the creative power of nature opens the way to a new gnostic heresy pointing toward the divinization of man through his intellect. Setting up an order created *ab ingenio* in a world ruled by nature can only invite comparison. If Alberti says that nature is still master, his disciple Leonardo will say that the painter is the new lord and that mastery of the Self becomes a mastery of nature. For Alberti, as for Cusanus, man is divine because he is a creator whose creation is an actualization of divine intellect. Man as his own creator tries to surpass nature and equal the Christian Divinity in whom there is a coincidence of art and artificer in the form of the divine Word. At best, however, he can be a demiurge or a Magus, which is, to say with Giordano Bruno, *homo sapiens cum virtute agendi.*" Like God viewing the results of his creation the *homo faber* can say that the *bonum exteriorum* is good, while his own goodness, except as a craftsman, is never questioned. The artificer in Alberti's world sees himself as good only when he sees himself as the actualization of his amoral intellect, as a *bonum exteriorum*, when *faber fabricans* sees *faber fabricatus*.[91]

NOTES

1. Anthony Blunt, *Artistic Theory in Italy: 1450–1600* (Oxford, 1940), p. 21.
2. Giuseppe Saitta, *Il pensiero italiano nell'umanesimo e nel rinascimento*, 3 vols. (Florence, 1961), I, 432.
3. Badaloni, "La interpretazione delle arti nel pensiero di L. B. Alberti," *Rinascimento*, seconda serie, 3 (1963), 59–113, p. 72.
4. Paul-Henri Michel, *Un idéal humain au XVᵉ siècle. La pensée de L. B. Alberti: 1404–1472* (Paris, 1930), p. 533. See also Carroll W. Westfall, "Society, Beauty, and the Humanist Architect in Alberti's *De Re Aedificatoria*," *Studies in the Renaissance*, 16 (1969), 61–79, which discusses thoroughly the importance of nature as a model of *concinnitas* (congruity) and as a source of "perfect forms" for the humanist architect. Professor Westfall does say that for Alberti "*concinnitas* is a part of every action of man's life" (p. 66). This is said with reference to a passage in the *De Re Aedificatoria* (IX.V.815), but without further elaboration, and the article (which deals primarily with Alberti's treatise on architecture, as the title clearly indicates) makes only one reference to the *Libri della famiglia* (plus a reference to Cecil Grayson's prologue.)
5. For another recent discussion of the relationship between art and nature in Alberti's thought see Joan Gadol, *Leon Battista Alberti: Universal Man of the Early Renaissance* (Chicago, 1969), esp. Chapter Three. See reviews of Professor Gadol's study by Cecil Grayson in *Renaissance Quarterly*, 24 (1971), 51–53; by J. H. Whitfield in *Italian Studies*, 26 (1971), 97–102; and by Lawrence V. Ryan in *The Neo-Latin News*, 19, No. 1 (1971), 30, in and published jointly with *Seventeenth Century News*, 29, No. 1 (1971). I share Professor Gadol's view that there is an "inner logic" (p. 19) in Alberti's thought which results in a "steady clarification of one intellectual perspective, an outlook in which the theoretical and the experiential penetrate each other" (p. 234). This view is at variance with those of P.-H. Michel, whose abstract analysis (cited above) emphasizes the inconsistencies and lack of unity in Alberti's thought, and of Santinello (cited below, note 64), who also suggests that Alberti was not systematically consistent. It also differs from the views of Cecil Grayson ("The Humanism of Alberti," *Italian Studies*, 12 [1957], 37–56, and his review cited above), who focuses on the "apparent inconsistencies" of Alberti and sees the "opposition of moral idealism and reality" as the element which "constitutes the principle crux of his thought" (p. 54). I am not entirely convinced, however, that Professor Gadol, who concentrates more on the artistic and technical aspects of Alberti's thought than on his literary-humanistic side, has fully succeeded in finding the "inner logic" which "clarifies the relationship of the various phases of Alberti's work" (L. V. Ryan, review cited above). Professor Whitfield also feels that the book does not get "Alberti whole,"

partly because it is "in the form of an apologia, with a technical slant" (review cited above, p. 98). My view is that the crux of Alberti's thought, found also in his moral writings, is his aesthetic preoccupation (at times only implicit) with the dialectical relationship between life and art, or, as Eugenio Donato has suggested (*op. cit.*, note 21 below, p. 40), the "dialectic of Being and Becoming [in which] the dialectical relationship between myth and life begins to acquire a dynamic element." No rupture exists between Alberti's artistic views and his ethical views. In fact, they are closely interwoven, since the latter are equally founded upon a "natural" inclination toward perfection. In spite of surface contradictions, an "inner logic" is to be found even in Alberti's humanistic writings. Alberti's moral idealism (an appreciation of the beauty of proper conduct) and his artistic vision are both the logical results of his seeing the world around him consistently through the eyes of a craftsman seeking to approximate that evasive perfection. Cecil Grayson is, of course, right in saying that Alberti's ideals of perfection "can scarcely be said to achieve complete and systematic expression in the corpus of his moral and literary works," and that they "find instead their full realization in architecture" (p. 55). It is true, nevertheless, that the same "inner logic" guides Alberti the humanist as guides Alberti the architect and art theorist. Professor Grayson has rightly spoken of Alberti as a "moral architect."

The reader is referred to Professor Gadol's Introduction for critical evaluations of the studies of Michel and Santinello.

6. Leon Battista Alberti, *On Painting*, trans. John R. Spencer (New Haven, 1966), p. 39. For the Italian text I have used the critical edition by Luigi Mallè: *Della pittura* (Florence, 1950), p. 53. Reference will be made to both editions.

7. *Summa Theologica*, II-II, 134, art. 2.

8. Leon Battista Alberti, *The Family in Renaissance Florence*, trans. Renée Neu Watkins (Columbia, S.C., 1969), p. 49. This edition is hereafter referred to as *The Family*. Reference is also made to the Italian edition of *I libri della famiglia* in *Opere volgari*, ed. Cecil Grayson, 2 vols. (Bari, 1960), p. 32, hereafter referred to as *Opere*. All references to Volume One are to *I libri della famiglia*, while, unless otherwise specified, all references to Volume Two are to Alberti's *De Iciarchia*.

9. *The Family*, p. 49; *Opere*, I, 32.

10. *The Family*, pp. 139–40; *Opere*, I, 138–39.

11. L. B. Alberti, "Fatum et Fortuna," in *Prosatori Latini del Quattrocento*, ed. Eugenio Garin (Milan, 1952), pp. 644–57.

12. *The Family*, p. 140; *Opere*, I, 139.

13. Matteo Palmieri, *Della vita civile* (Bologna, 1944), p. 127.

14. *The Family*, p. 138; *Opere*, I, 136.

15. *The Family*, p. 142; *Opere*, I, 141.

16. Professor Garin notes that for Alberti man "is most human when he is an architect" (Eugenio Garin, *Science and Civic Life in the Italian Renaissance*, trans. Peter Munz [Garden City, New York, 1969], p. 41; referred to hereafter as *Science*).

17. *Op. cit.,* I, 412.
18. *The Family,* p. 133; *Opere,* I, 131.
19. See Charles S. Singleton, "The Perspective of Art," *Kenyon Review,* 15 (1953), 169–89. Aristotle's distinction between *making* and *doing* is the beginning of a line of thought which divides action into two distinct categories — that which passes into outward matter, and that which abides in the agent. This cardinal distinction is taken up, among others, by Thomas Aquinas, who treats it in the *Summa Theologica* under the question "Utrum prudentia sit virtus distincta ab arte" (I-II, 57, 4). Aquinas establishes Art as an activity which is not concerned with rectitude of the appetite. The activity of man as maker (*homo faber* or *homo artifex*) is seen as having its focus on outward things. This externally directed action, totally independent of the category of Prudence, is consequently independent of moral restraints (I-II, 57, 4). The *homo artifex* is therefore operating with limited or partial vision. The result is that the maker is engaged in his activity in what Professor Singleton calls the "perspective of art," and which he defines as "a mode of action passing into external matter, and consequently viewed as having its end and its good in that external goal; a mode of action, in short, which is extra-moral, amoral. . . ." It is my view that Alberti, like Machiavelli (whom Singleton discusses), and like the artificer whom Aquinas has in mind, also operates from this amoral perspective. The intention of this paper is not to show the influence of Thomas Aquinas on Alberti, but to point again to a "pattern of thought" (Singleton, p. 188) which is found in Aquinas and recurs at least in Alberti and Machiavelli.
20. A good, succinct explanation of the distinction between these two aspects of nature is offered by R. G. Collingwood, *The Idea of Nature* (Oxford, 1957), p. 94: "The naturalistic philosophy of the Renaissance regarded nature as something divine and self-creative; the active and passive sides of this one self-creative being they distinguished by distinguishing *natura naturata,* or the complex of natural changes and processes, from *natura naturans,* or the immanent force which animates and directs them." My own parallel terms *homo fabricans, homo fabricatus, structura structurans* and *structura structurata* are also used to distinguish between the active, generative side and the passive, receptive side of the same being.
21. Eugenio Donato, "Death and History in Poliziano's *Stanze,*" *MLN,* 80, No. 1 (1965) 27–40, p. 40.
22. *Della pittura,* p. 53; *On Painting,* p. 39.
23. *On Painting,* p. 64; *Della pittura,* p. 77.
24. *Ibid.*
25. *The Family,* p. 134; *Opere,* I, 132.
26. Georg Weise, *L'ideale eroico del rinascimento e le sue premesse umanistiche,* 2 vols. (Naples, 1961), I, 84.
27. *Della pittura,* p. 76; *On Painting,* p. 63.
28. Saitta, I, 427–28.
29. *Opere,* I, 45; *The Family,* p. 60.
30. *Opere,* II, 227.
31. *The Family,* p. 75; *Opere,* I, 63.

32. *Opere*, I, 132; *The Family*, p. 133.
33. *The Family*, p. 136; *Opere*, I, 134.
34. *The Family*, pp. 134–36; *Opere*, I, 132–34.
35. *The Family*, p. 137; *Opere*, I, 135–36.
36. *Opere*, II, 198.
37. *Opere*, II, 243.
38. *Opere*, II, 198.
39. *Opere*, II, 266.
40. *Opere*, II, 266–67.
41. *Opere*, II, 267. By "scientific" I mean a point of view which excludes moral considerations. The "perspective of art" is in this sense a "scientific" perspective. *Cf.* Rocco Montano, *L'estetica del rinascimento e del barocco* (Naples, 1962), pp. 52–53: "Nelle *Artes* medievali la posizione dei trattatisti è proprio quella di chi insegna una *scienza* e fa appello a una *virtus* che non hanno a che fare con i fatti morali e religiosi. L'affermazione di S. Tommaso: 'All'arte non si richiede che l'artista operi secondo il bene ma che faccia un'opera valida' vale per tutti i trattatisti medievali."
42. *Cf.* Professor Singleton's reference to such constructions in Machiavelli in the article cited above.
43. Singleton, p. 178.
44. *Opere*, I, 66; *The Family*, p. 78.
45. *Opere*, I, 25; *The Family*, p. 43.
46. *The Family*, pp. 28–29; *Opere*, I, 7–8.
47. *The Family*, p. 43; *Opere*, I, 25.
48. *The Family*, pp. 79–80; *Opere*, I, 67.
49. *On Painting*, p. 98; *Della pittura*, p. 114.
50. *The Family*, p. 32; *Opere*, I, 12.
51. John White, *Birth and Rebirth of Pictorial Space* (London, 1957), p. 126.
52. *Cf.* Donato, p. 40, who speaks of Alberti as having "best expressed the relationship of the work of art as myth to its creator."
53. Donato, p. 40.
54. *On Painting*, p. 95; *Della pittura*, p. 111.
55. *Science*, p. 40.
56. Karl Birkmeyer, "Leon Battista Alberti and Jan van Eyck on the Origin of Painting," *Italian Quarterly*, 2, No. 2 (1958), 35–54, p. 46.
57. Donato, p. 40.
58. *Ibid.*, p. 39.
59. *Opere*, II, p. 241.
60. In *Prosatori Latini*, p. 635.
61. John R. Spencer, "Ut Rhetorica Pictura: a Study in Quattrocento Theory of Painting," *Journal of the Warburg and Courtauld Institutes*, 20 (1957), 26–44, p. 44.
62. *The Family*, p. 43; *Opere*, I, 25.
63. Leonis Baptistae Alberti florentini viri clarissimi, *Libri De Re Aedificatoria Decem* (Paris, 1512).
64. Giovanni Santinello, *Leon Battista Alberti: Una visione estetica del mondo e della vita* (Florence, 1962), p. 240.

65. *Science*, p. 42.
66. *Summa*, I-II, 57, art. 3.
67. *Science*, p. 42.
68. *The Family*, pp. 143–44; *Opere*, I, 142–43.
69. *The Family*, p. 135; *Opere*, I, 134.
70. Giovanni Santinello, *Il pensiero di Nicolò Cusano nella sua prospettiva estetica* (Padova, 1958), esp. Part 2, Chapter 2.
71. *Ibid.*, p. 84.
72. Leon Battista Alberti, *Della statua*, in *Della pittura e della statua* (Milan, 1804): p. 110.
73. *Op. cit.*, p. 73.
74. *Science*, p. 42.
75. *Opere*, II, 300.
76. *The Family*, p. 165; *Opere*, I, 168–69.
77. *Science*, p. 43.
78. Saitta, II, 330.
79. *The Family*, p. 49; *Opere*, I, 31.
80. *The Family*, p. 47; *Opere*, I, 30.
81. *Opere*, I, 106; *The Family*, p. 112.
82. *The Family*, p. 111; *Opere*, I, 105. For a modern feminist view of Alberti's attitude toward women see Kate Millett, *Sexual Politics* (Garden City, New York, 1970), p. 74.
83. *The Family*, p. 116; *Opere*, I, 111.
84. *Ibid.*
85. *The Family*, p. 114; *Opere*, I, 109.
86. Leon Battista Alberti, *Ten Books on Architecture*, trans. James Leoni (London, 1955), pp. 194–95. This is a reprint of the 1755 edition, which is an English translation of Cosimo Bartoli's Italian version.
87. Heinrich Wölfflin, *Principles of Art History*, trans. M. D. Hottinger (New York: Dover Publications, n.d.), p. 185.
88. *The Family*, p. 123; *Opere*, I, 120.
89. *The Family*, p. 124; *Opere*, I, 120.
90. *Science*, p. 40.
91. The research for this and other studies on attitudes toward nature in the Renaissance was initiated during my tenure of a Fulbright Grant for study in Italy. I am happy to acknowledge my gratitude to the Bureau of Educational and Cultural Affairs and the American Commission for Cultural Exchange with Italy. I am also indebted to Professor Eugenio Garin for listening to my thoughts, while to Professor Ulrich Middledorf of the Deutsches Kunsthistorisches Institute in Florence I owe thanks for his kind permission to use the facilities of the Institute, and for offering me use of his 1512 edition of Alberti's *Libri De Re Aedificatoria*. I would also like to thank Professor Marvin L. Trachtenberg of the New York University Institute of Fine Arts for stimulating conversation and for professional courtesies extended to me in Florence.

Pierre de Langtoft's Chronicle

AN ESSAY IN MEDIEVAL HISTORIOGRAPHY

Robert Stepsis

SURPRISINGLY LITTLE scholarly work has been devoted to the important field of later medieval historical theory. Interest in what the medieval historian or chronicler may have intended his work to be, what concepts of human nature or society he might be taking for granted, or what shape he wanted to give to the human actions he recorded is recent, and the methods of investigation still experimental.[1] The fact is that we have very little evidence about contemporary medieval attitudes toward history with which to verify conclusions, and yet have a serious need to understand this important aspect of the medieval mind. This essay is an attempt to broach the subject of medieval historiography through the study of the early fourteenth century Anglo-Norman chronicle of Pierre de Langtoft.[2]

Langtoft's chronicle is interesting for this purpose because it is one of the first histories of England written in French and because it was fairly popular throughout the fourteenth century. Sixteen manuscripts have survived.[3] Also the last two-thirds of Langtoft's work was translated into English by Robert Mannyng of Brunne,[4] and through him became the source for the history of the reign of Edward I in the English prose *Brut*. From the point of view of his attitude toward the events of history, Langtoft's chronicle is also interesting because it demonstrates characteristics found in both contemporary "clerical" Latin histories and "aristocratic" vernacular works.[5]

The chronicle itself is written in alexandrine rhyming couplets and is divided into three parts. The first, beginning with the exploits of Brutus and his settling of Britain, concludes with the defeat of the Britons and the establishment of English hegemony over the island. It is simply an abridgement of Geoffrey of Monmouth's *Historia Regum Britanniae*. The second part encompasses the history of Anglo-Saxon and Anglo-Norman kings from Ine to Henry III. It is a com-

51

pilation derived from the works of William of Malmesbury, Henry of Huntingdon, Florence of Worcester, and some other, unknown sources.[6] The final part is a history of the reign of Edward I derived from contemporary events, eyewitness accounts, or hearsay. The chronicle ends with the death of Edward in 1307, although there are recensions which end earlier at high points of Edward's Scottish wars.[7] We are interested here, however, in the complete chronicle, ending in 1307, which shows Langtoft's most mature work.

Langtoft both reflects certain trends in contemporary historical writing and diverges in several respects. Except for the chronicle of Matthew Paris, the thirteenth century in England was a relatively barren period for historical writing. Nothing comparable to the spate of histories written during the reigns of Henry II and Richard I, under the pressures of Henry's dispute with Beckett and Richard's crusade, was produced until late in Edward's reign. The stimulus this time was Edward's protracted war with Scotland and the struggle over the relationship between the English and Scottish crowns.[8] All parts of England contributed historical arguments to this debate, but Langtoft's Yorkshire was preeminent in both the quantity and passion of its contribution.[9]

All of the English writers, like Walter of Guisborough, Walter of Coventry, Robert of Gloucester, the anonymous compilers of the Bury St. Edmunds chronicle and the *Short English Metrical Chronicle*, and Langtoft were clerics and wrote from the perspective of their monasteries. Langtoft, however, seems to have had a more extensive acquaintanceship with the larger political world than most of his contemporaries, since from 1271 to 1286 he was procurator of his Priory of Bridlington and acted as attorney for his prior on business as far away as Westminster. In 1293 he was absent without leave from the Priory while travelling "in Southern parts." [10] Also, Langtoft presumably had a patron outside his monastery, as his chronicle was written at the request of someone named Schafeld. The fact that Langtoft chose to write in Anglo-Norman when most of his contemporaries were writing their chronicles in Latin may indicate that Schafeld was not a cleric. In any event, his chronicle appealed to a wider audience than the normal monastic chronicle did [11] and seems to have been written with a slightly different focus than theirs. This difference, which I will attempt to illuminate, was not, strangely, in the direction of a wider and more objective historical perspective. His exposure to the secular and political world does not seem to have mitigated an intense national feeling and a violent hatred of the Scots. In a sense these passions determine the shape of Langtoft's history.

Langtoft shared with his contemporaries an interest in the national past stimulated by Edward's wars[12] and an interest in history as a body of moral lessons.[13] But he differs from them in the way in which he defines significant national events and in the precise moral and didactic aim he has for his work. I will note, as I proceed in this essay, similarities of detail between Langtoft and other English chronicle writers of the late thirteenth and early fourteenth centuries, but it is important to be clear about the difference in Langtoft's particular conception and procedure. For instance, the first part of Walter of Coventry's chronicle, which was compiled at St. Mary's Priory in York and is the only part of that chronicle written during Langtoft's lifetime, is a short history of England from Brutus to 1293.[14] It is almost exclusively a propaganda piece intended to prove Edward's claim to the overlordship of Scotland by detailing instances of Scottish kings doing homage to English kings. It is much like Edward's letter to Pope Boniface VIII written in 1301 to refute the pope's claim of Scottish sovereignty.[15] Langtoft was interested in this question — in fact there is an Anglo-Norman version of Edward's letter, which Wright tentatively assigns to Langtoft since it is written in alexandrine rhyming couplets, the same meter that Langtoft uses for his chronicle[16] — but this matter is really only a minor concern in the chronicle itself. Langtoft, as we will see, was occupied with a broader question than Anglo-Scottish relationships. Walter of Guisborough's chronicle, which shows some borrowings from Langtoft,[17] nevertheless confines itself to the history of England from 1066 to 1305. Within this framework Walter's intention is to detail the events of history for posterity: "successoribus nostris brevem margaritam relinquo . . . ab ipso conquestore Willelmo Bastarde seriatim prosequi et compilare propono."[18] While there are some moral judgments implied in his choice of events,[19] basically he is interested simply in notable incidents as they follow one another in the flow of time. He includes official documents and set speeches in his work to give substance and depth to the events he records, devices Langtoft rarely uses since he is less interested in the event itself and more interested in the meaning of collections of events. The Guisborough chronicler has none of Langtoft's didactic intent and no apparent notion about the overall movement of English history, which may be why "his outlook on northern affairs was more moderate than that of many of his contemporaries."[20] Robert of Gloucester's chronicle is, like Langtoft's,

written in a vernacular, in this case English, and begins with the settling of England by Brutus.[21] However, the notices of Edward's reign
at the end of the chronicle are short and annalistic; the relationship
between past history and contemporary affairs is clearly not the focus
of Gloucester's work, as it is for Langtoft. It is difficult to tell just what
Robert's focus is, since through the bulk of the chronicle he merely
transcribes his sources — Geoffrey of Monmouth, William of Malmesbury, Henry of Huntingdon, Roger of Howden, etc.[22] — and simply
takes over their differing attitudes towards the events they record. One
detail that does stand out, although it is difficult to say whether it is
Robert's point of view or that of the earlier generations of historians
that he is copying, is the interrelationship between the moral life of
the English people and historical events or between historical events
and phenomena of nature. Thus the invasions of the Danes and Normans are attributed to the moral laxity of the inhabitants of England,
and the death of William Rufus causes a series of strange natural occurrences.[23] Langtoft, as we will see, works from a different basis of
historical causation and rarely mentions events of nature in connection
with events of history. Finally, Langtoft's chronicle has little or nothing in common with the other types of histories produced during this
period. The universal chronicles of Ranulph Higden and Nicholas
Trivet treat the history of the world beginning with creation.[24] Langtoft deals with the history of only one country, England, beginning
with its mythical settlement; there is nothing in the chronicle that
does not in some way relate to the history of England. Matthew Paris
and the St. Albans school were indiscriminate collectors of information;
the only organizing principle that informs their work is a rough chronological order.[25] While Matthew professes some didactic intent,[26] nowhere does he show the moral and thematic coherence that in Langtoft
is an implicit shaping force of the work. Langtoft's chronicle is an
historical poem, not an encyclopedia.

But what is Langtoft about? Some attempts have already been made
to establish a controlling theme in the chronicle. More than a hundred
years ago Wright suggested that, "Pierre de Langtoft like a true North-
country man, proposed to write a popular history of England, which
should show the justice of king Edward's Scottish wars, by proving
his right to sovereignty over Scotland, and by detailing the long series
of provocations which the Scots had given to England" (I, xix–xx).
M. Dominica Legge, a more recent student of Langtoft's work, pro-

poses a complementary but extended theory for the composition of the work:

> The poem . . . was designed as an epic, an epic whose hero
> was Edward I, just as the hero of Geoffrey of Monmouth's
> prose epic was Henry I. From time immemorial English his-
> torians looked for the coming of a second *Brut*, who would
> reunite the three parts of the original Britain. . . . Langtoft at
> one time had hopes of Edward I. There is something tragic
> in Langtoft's misgivings about the character of Edward II,
> which he expressed in an epilogue to his work, written after
> Edward I had died in the midst of a failure caused by what
> seemed to Langtoft a particularly black piece of treachery. To
> him the Scots were not only savages of whom he was frankly
> terrified, but stubborn heretics refusing to recognize the com-
> ing of a Messiah.

Miss Legge goes on to point out that Langtoft's "old fashioned style . . . the monorhymed *laisse* in alexandrines" reminds one of a twelfth-century *chanson de geste*.[27]

Both these theories point up the problem of this study; for despite their similarities, Wright and Legge are, in fact, ascribing to Langtoft two different, although not necessarily mutually exclusive, theories of history. For Wright, Langtoft's concerns are purely political — the his-tory was a way of justifying, by means of precedent, a series of con-temporary political actions. Legge, on the other hand, suggests a re-ligious and even, by her metaphor of the messiah, an eschatological purpose behind Langtoft's work — all English history points to its ful-fillment in this moment of time and anyone who opposes the fulfill-ment should be destroyed as a theological adversary. The fact that there is support for both these views in the chronicle — that Langtoft has a very strong anti-Scottish bias, that he details many instances of the tradition of Scottish kings doing feudal homage to English kings, that after Edward's victory at Dunbar Langtoft recalls Merlin's proph-ecy about the reunion of the island (II, 264–66), that Edward's reign is certainly the focus of the whole work — does not, however, exhaust the possibilities of Langtoft's history. Wright and Legge are not wrong in their statements as to particular facets of the chronicle. Their ex-planations are just not adequate to account for the overall direction and shape of the work, since there is more purpose here than simply a story of English-Scottish relations. We must take a wider view of Langtoft's history.

There are three elements in the chronicle which affect either Langtoft's choice of events to narrate, the shape which he gives to events, or his attitude toward historical happenings. The first of these elements are the many instances of warning, pleading, or criticism aimed at Edward I in the last part of the chronicle. That is, far from being the fulfillment of kingship, Langtoft sees Edward as a king periodically in need of advice and criticism. Particularly, the lessons of the past provide Langtoft with a fertile source of example and admonition on the pitfalls of kingship and the requirements of rule. When Edward delays in his attempts to win back Aquitaine, which had been treacherously seized by Philip of France, Langtoft says,

> Et li rays Arthur surpris par tricherye,
> Et Mordred demaglé pur sa reverye;
> Kaduualdre pur poverte wayna Brettaynye,
> Par poer l'enchacaint les genz de Germenye;
> Après à tort le tynt Haralde le fiz Godwye,
> Ke en sun an primer perdist seygnurye;
> William le Conquerour le conquist par espeye.
> Le ray Jon de Balliolf ad perdu par folye,
> Pur li et pur ses heirs, le regne de Albanye.
> Allas! ke nul homme par altre se chastye.
> O riche rays Eduuard, pur Deu, eyez mercye;
> Ne suffrez poynt perir la graunt genturye
> De cels ke sunt remys conquere Aquytanye.
> [II, 284]²⁸

When Edward's nobles refuse to follow him on an expedition to Flanders, Langtoft reflects that history shows how such disunity can be avoided,

> En gestes aunciens trovoums-nous escrit
> Quels rays et quels realmes ly rays Arthur conquist,
> Et coment sun purchace largement partyst.
> Roys suz ly n'avoit ke ly countredist,
> Counte, duc, e baron, qe unqes li faillist,
> En guere n'en bataille ke chescun ne suyst.
> Ly rays sir Eduuard ad doné trop petyt;
> Par quai à sun aler, quant en mer se myst
> Vers ly roys de Fraunce, fet ly fu despit,
> Ke nes un de ses countes of ly le aler emprist.
> [II, 296]²⁹

In other words, the purpose of recalling the past is as much to teach the present how to rule, to urge Edward to emulate the success and avoid the failures of the past, as it is to glorify or justify Edward.³⁰

The second element conditioning Langtoft's view of history is the framework within which he places the human events he narrates. He begins his chronicle with an invocation to, "Deus le tot pussaunt, ke ceel e terre crea,/ Adam nostre pere homme de terre fourma,/ Naturaument purvyst quant il ordina/ Ke homme de terre venuz en terre revertira" (I, 2).[31] And just before reporting the death of Edward I at the end of the work he says,

> O Sire tutpuissant ke Cristien ahure,
> Ton overe est chescon terrene creature.
> En fesaunt le mounde fu taillé la figure,
> Qe homme, femme, e beste deit morir par nature.
> Pus le tens Adam unqes fut nul hure
> Ke prince pur nobley, ne baroun pur baudoure,
> Ne marchaund pur avoyr, ne clerk pur lettrure,
> Par art ne par engine la mort peut eschure.
> [II, 378–80][32]

These are not expressions of contempt of the world or of the events of history which Langtoft has narrated, but rather the attempt to place those events within the perspective of the inevitable end of every individual human life and to see history and earthly affairs as part of the human journey and not the end. These are medieval commonplaces but bear repeating, if only to show that, although Langtoft may have had high hopes for the achievement of Edward I, especially after his victory at Dunbar (II, 260–68) and regarded him as the best ruler in the British Isles since Arthur (II, 380), he had no illusions about Edward being a messiah or his reign being the goal of English history. Edward, like Arthur, like every king before him, like every son of Adam, is caught in the vortex of an endlessly repeated cycle of history larger than the affairs of state. He comes from the earth and returns to the earth. It is within this cyclic vortex of birth and death that we must look for meaning in Langtoft's chronicle and for the shape he gives to human history.

The final conditioning factor of Langtoft's work is that it is a national history of England. That is, it is not a universal history dealing with the eschatology of the human race — the birth of Christ, for instance, is mentioned almost as an aside (I, 62). Nor is it, like William of Malmesbury's work, a history of the kings of England. Although Langtoft is interested in each successive ruler, he is interested in them exclusively as rulers of England and passes over in silence anything about them that does not concern that rule, such as details of personal

57

history before they became kings or contemporaneous events in the world outside of England that have no bearing on the kings.[33] The only exception to this concentration is Brutus, whose background is related, following Geoffrey of Monmouth, in order to show where the Britons came from. The early life of William the Conqueror, which Langtoft could have easily gotten from William of Malmesbury, is ignored, except for his meetings with Edward the Confessor and Harold which established his claim to the throne. Richard I is barely mentioned before he is crowned king, and even the events of Edward I's youth are related only as they pertain to his father's struggle with the barons (II, 136, 142, 144, 150, 152) or, briefly, his crusading experience (II, 154–60). The point is that not only do we have a continuation of that nationalistic interest which was stimulated by Geoffrey of Monmouth and fostered by Edward I for his own purposes,[34] but we have what is, psychologically, the natural extension of this concern, an emphasis on the country itself as the scene of the history. The land, England as place, as continuing center and locus of action, can just as easily be designated the "hero" of Langtoft's chronicle as Edward I, or Arthur, or any of the kings whose actions and reigns constitute the history of the land.[35]

So it is within the confines of birth and death, and of the land, that the human actions which Langtoft records take place; actions which have some bearing on the way the land has been ruled. In fact, through most of the chronicle, Langtoft's "history" is little more than an account of successive kings and how they exercised jurisdiction over the land, with comments on the quality of their rule. A passage which is typical of Langtoft's concerns, and useful for its condensed presentation of those concerns, is the description of three successive pre-Christian British kings and their reigns. The information is from Geoffrey of Monmouth but the details are severely abridged by Langtoft:

> En tens le ray Morvyder en Brettayne aryvayt
> Un rays de graunt poer, de Moryan estayt,
> Ke tut Northumberlande destrut e wastayt.
> Ly Morvyder le approche cors al cors tut drayt;
> Le ray soul en bataylle mout plus là fesayt
> Ke la mayté de gens ke ouf ly menayt.
> Les Morryans sount morz, les cors comaundayt
> De tut arder en poudre, trop cruel se moustrayt.
> Un monstre de la mer, ke la terre dotayt,
> Cum il soul par meschaunce assaylir volayt,
> Le monstre si se leve, ly rays tranglotayt.

Cestuy ray Morvyder V. fiz engendrayt;
Garbodyon, le aynez, après ly regnayt
E draiture e pees sour totes choses amayt.
Les temples en Brettayne par tut renovelayt,
Plus ke nul rays an aver abundayt,
Les gaygnours de terre par tut honurayt.
Dys aunz vesquyt rays, soun frere ly entoumbayt
En Trinovaunt le bele, cum mesmes devisayt.
Artygallus son frere reteent le regne après,
Feel e orguyllus, contrarius al pees.
Si malement se content, sa terre myst à destrès.
Le pople de Brettayne ne vout suffrir tel fees,
Li tollent la corune, ly chacent hors de dees.
[I, 52–54][36]

Details in Geoffrey which Langtoft leaves out are: a summary of Morvidus' character, the mustering of his army, an extended description of his slaughter of the Moriani, the fact that the monster came from the Irish sea and preyed on the sailors of the area, a short description of the battle with the monster, Gorbonianus' protection of the farmers against their landlords, a statement about his generosity to his soldiers, and an indictment of Arthgallo for avarice. Eliminated are facts or details which are peripheral to Langtoft's main concern here, which is the qualities or characteristics the men possessed as rulers. Morvidus was a strong warrior but overly cruel and so suffered an appropriate fate by being swallowed by the sea monster. Gorbonianus was a beloved king because he promoted justice, peace, the cultivation of the land, and religion. His brother, who is an anti-type of true kingship, was felonious, proud, a destroyer of peace and of the land, and, as such, was driven from the throne by the people.[37]

Again and again, as he enumerates the succession of kings, Langtoft returns to these qualities of successful rule. Good kings, like Belinus, Arthur, Alfred, Athelstan, William the Conqueror, or Richard I are courageous warriors. Under them justice, both in terms of the enforcement of law in the country and of the kings' own observance of traditional laws,[38] peace, and the prosperity of the land and religious institutions obtain.[39] Likewise, unsuccessful kings, like Vortigern, Ethelred, or John, are pusillanimous warriors and, under them, laws are broken, either by unpunished outlaws or by the kings themselves, the country is involved in chaotic warfare, and the land and religious establishments plundered.[40] Most often these characteristics of rule are interrelated, so that a king who is a weak warrior is unable to control outlaws, rebels, or invaders who destroy the land, churches, and monasteries; while a good king promotes peace, justice, prosperity, and religion because he is a strong warrior.[41] However, Langtoft's vision of the kingly character, although it tends to be static in this way, is not necessarily so. At one point in his subjugation of England William the Conqueror's brutalities in the north became so intense that Langtoft, following Malmesbury and Florence of Worcester[42] in details about the ravaging of the lands, adds a moral indictment that is not in his sources:

> Molt fist le Conquerour cel houre graunt pechez
> Kaunt il prist vengaunce sur les ordinez,
> Ke ren avaynt mesfet dedenz ses regnez.
> De Everwik à Dureme n'est nul leu habitez,
> Ne nule terre overte, ne greyn de blé semez.
> [I, 416–18][43]

However, the bishop of Durham convinces William to mitigate his cruelty and to restore the ecclesiastical property. Immediately thereafter William's rule becomes praiseworthy, as he also establishes peace and sends justices throughout the country to enforce the law (I, 424–26). William *became* a good king by eventually combining all the necessary aspects of kingship into an interrelated whole. He arrived as a great warrior, but he had to acquire a respect for religious institutions and the prosperity of the land. Likewise, his son, William Rufus, who continued to possess his father's martial prowess, eventually *falls* from true kingship when he disregards the other imperatives of rule:

> Kant le rays William ad fet sun talent
> En Gales et en Escoce, ne fet force de gent,
> As ryches et as povers se porte estraungement.
> Clers et saynt eglyse charge trop sovent,
> Xvii mousters abbate nettement,
> Et joint à la foreste terre et tenement,
> Ke unkes eynz ne fust en tens de nul parent.
> Cele vye pur veirs dura longement,
> Xiiii aunz molt près avayt governement
> De tut Engleterre le jours ke mort ly prent.
> Du secle est passez, escotez ore coment.
> [I, 444–46][44]

Langtoft proceeds to relate a story about William Rufus having a dream in which he devours a religious image. The next day he is accidentally killed while hunting. The story of the dream, only one of three such stories tentatively offered by Malmesbury,[45] and the one most unfavorable to the king, is presented by Langtoft as an epitome of Rufus' later life and a fitting prelude to the death of a king who, while being a great warrior and subduing the rebellious Scots and Welsh, nevertheless destroyed churches, taxed the clergy, "conducted himself strangely" towards the rich and the poor, and violated the traditional forest laws of the land.

Of course, these criteria of kingship against which Langtoft measures each reign are not principles invented by him. In fact, whether or not he is consciously shaping his chronicle according to these principles, Langtoft reflects, very conservatively, traditional medieval thinking on the functions and duties of kingship. From at least the fourth to the thirteenth century, Christian philosophers had defined true kingship in terms of the maintenance of peace and dispensing of justice in the land.[46] What we find in Langtoft's chronicle are these philosophical principles of kingship shaping his narrative and providing the basis on which he judges contemporary events, particularly the reign of Edward I. Edward is praised for his reform of the coinage and for the Mortmain statutes (II, 174–76), which facilitate the prosperity of the land; for his punishment of men who abuse the administration of justice (II, 184–86); for his attempts to impose justice and law in Scotland (II, 260); and for his vigorous efforts against those who disturb the peace or destroy churches (II, 248–50, 256–58, 312, 360–66, 378). But Edward is criticized as well, for his tardiness in preventing Philip of France from ravaging Gascony (which is considered part of the English domain)[47] and destroying the law and order established there (II, 202, 216); for his illegal attempt to tax the clergy (II, 270); and for his delays in performing the promised perambulations of his lands, an act that serves to alienate, for a time, the loyalty of the nobility to the crown (II, 318–32). Significantly, Langtoft does not see this difficulty with the barons as part of the struggle for power between the crown and the nobility, but rather as a mistake on Edward's part which, by losing the service of his nobles, prevents him from carrying out his kingly duties of suppressing the Scottish outlaws (II, 320, 326–28). None of Langtoft's contemporaries judge Edward's reign on the basis of all of these factors.

If, however, these requirements of kingship are the grounds on which Langtoft organizes the events of the past and judges contemporary affairs, we are still left with the crucial question for a medieval historian of the operation of divine power in earthly affairs and the related problem of the purpose of human action within the earth-to-earth cycle of life. The operation of the power of God in the history of man is a complex problem in Langtoft. There is no explicit sense in this chronicle that God is directing the whole course of human history toward some predestined fulfillment, as there was in the historians of the early Middle Ages.[48] There are, however, several references to the "fall of Britain" theme that forms the substance of the histories of Gildas, Bede, and Geoffrey of Monmouth.[49] God has punished the Britons for their manifold sins by allowing the pagan Saxons to conquer them (I, 248, 258). Yet, these are part of the abridged translation of Geoffrey and, perhaps, should be considered as reflections of his historicism rather than Langtoft's. There is no other indication in the chronicle that any general pattern or sweep of history is directed by God or that a national malaise or sinfulness brings on a divine punishment. When quoting Henry of Huntingdon's list of the five wounds, or invasions, suffered by England, Langtoft leaves out Henry's statement that they are wounds inflicted by God in retribution for the continuous moral turpitude of the inhabitants of the island. Instead, he presents them as morally neutral "events" which afflict the land, not the people.[50] The Danes ravage, and subsequently rule over England, because of the treachery, stupidity, and weakness of one man — Ethelred. Following Malmesbury, but removing all his direct references to God,[51] Langtoft has St. Dunstan predict, at Ethelred's coronation, a reign of warfare and eventual foreign domination; but it is specifically Ethelred, not the English people, being punished, because he gained the throne by a murder. Although God is not mentioned in Langtoft's passage (I, 344), it is undoubtedly a divine vengeance that Ethelred suffers by having his reign poisoned in this way, but by muting the divine presence Langtoft conveys the impression that there is also a natural, human connection between usurpation and a calamitous reign. Langtoft's account of the causes of the English defeat at Hastings lacks even this minimal flavor of divine intervention. In summarizing Harold's reign he attributes the Norman victory to a combination of impersonal political circumstances and personal moral flaws:

Si [Harold] travaillez avaunt en bataylle n'eust esté,
Ne perduz ses genz, ne fet falseté,
Ne sun serement enfraint pur la regalté,
Le duk William uncore n'eust gayné playn pé
De terre sur Englays, ne nul de sa mesné.
[I, 406][52]

Ultimately we must assume it is God who is punishing Harold, as he did Ethelred, in this case for his personal treachery in breaking his oath to William, an act that has national consequences. But it is remarkable that Langtoft should confine himself to this statement of causation, in which divine agency is, at best, only implicit, since his source explicitly emphasizes God's role in the change of sovereigns.[53] Malmesbury even echoes the "fall of Britain" theme by attributing the Norman victory to the generally shabby moral character of the English people, of which Harold's treachery is only one example.[54] Langtoft deliberately submerges the divine and national to the personal and kingly responsibilities.

There are, however, a few instances in which Langtoft reports the operation of divine power in human affairs, either in the form of a miracle or of a particular political event which came about by the "grace of God." This reliance on direct, divine agency as an explanation of events is far less frequent here than in the Latin chronicles and appears only in the second and third sections of the history; but the instances are worth noting: two early victories over the Danes are attributed to the showing of the Cross and the help of God (I, 302, 314); the miracle of the martyred St. Edmund's head is reported (I, 312); Sweyn, the Danish king who is threatening St. Edmund's shrine, is shocked to death by a vision of the saint (I, 358); Robert Courthose dies ignominiously because he refused the crown of Jerusalem after a voice from heaven had proclaimed his election (I, 460); punishments are meted out by God to certain men who plunder church property during Stephen's reign (I, 490–92); some of Richard I's crusaders are miraculously saved from a storm at sea (II, 39); Edward I is twice saved from treason by God's grace (II, 228, 294); and several of Edward's victories over the Scots are attributed to God's grace and to His vengeance on those who destroy church property (II, 238, 312, 362, 378). There is no pattern or consistency in these reported intrusions of divine power into human affairs, they remain simply intrusions; that is, haphazard reminders of the omnipresent, if mainly quiescent, power ruling above human history. Sometimes God will interfere directly in the events of this world, to punish or to reward in specific instances, but on the whole, Langtoft conceives of the individual human will as having a generous latitude in solving the problems of political order and in suffering the consequences of abusing that order.

Rather than human history being a field on which the operation of divine power is seen in a direct and obvious way, there is the unmistakable sense in Langtoft that God's will inheres in right rule, in justice, peace, and the prosperity of the land and religious institutions. It is the function of Langtoft's history to reveal this inherent, latent, and continuous pressure of the divine will which is manifested in right rule, just as it is the function of kings to constantly try to achieve that right rule and thereby fulfill the will of God.[55] Langtoft shows this tense interrelationship between divine will and human action when he says, commenting on events during Edward's reign, "Si li rays volt Deu servir,/ La lay ly covent mayntenir,/ Si noun, il pecche et molt mesprent" (II, 258) and

> Sur cil ke Deu mayns ayme cherra l'acravaunte.
> En guere et en bataylle Deu dona jadye
> Honur et victorye al fiz Mathatye;
> Ausint le fet à tuz ke plus ly sunt amye.
> Le Prince ke morust en mount de Calvarye
> Ayme li rays Eduuard et sa baronye.
> [II, 286][56]

God aids those He loves, and He loves those who exercise their human wills in the fulfillment of the imperatives of the law and right rule. God's judgement, then, operates continuously throughout the history that Langtoft is recording, but because it is a judgement based on the exercise of the human will regulating itself, His punishments are seen as merely outgrowths, or inherent results, of the misuse of that will. Morvidus is devoured by a sea monster; Arthgallo is deposed by "le pople de Brettayne"; Ethelred has a long, unhappy and chaotic reign; Harold is defeated by William; William Rufus is killed while hunting; and Stephen has another unhappy and chaotic reign, because God did not love them. But He did not love them because they misused their human will and failed to fulfill the divine requirement of right rule.[57]

Ultimately, the implicit subject of Langtoft's chronicle is the exercise of the human will in the political history of the land. The references to Adam at the beginning and the end of the history (I, 2 and II, 380) are superfluous reminders that the human will, within the cycle of birth and death, is infected, restless and unstable, yet capable of being directed towards a harmony with the divine will. Langtoft's work itself is an attempt to indicate the right direction, and the archetypal story of Brutus, the first focus of this as well as of innumerable other chronicles of medieval England, is the initial statement of the theme.[58] The story, taken from Geoffrey of Monmouth, says that Brutus, the product of an incestuous relationship, was the accidental cause of the death of both his mother and father, yet went on to found a great and honorable kingdom. One can only see this strange narrative of Brutus' origin as symbolic of the inherently flawed quality of any human endeavor.[59] But Brutus, as is the duty of every man, turned that flaw into a positive good — he settled in Britain and established peace and justice in a unified land (I, 4–22).

But, just as the human will is subject to the contradictory impulse of harmony with the divine will in right rule and capricious instability and misuse, so the land, the explicit subject of Langtoft's chronicle, wavers constantly between stability with justice and disunity with chaos. Wright and Legge are surely correct when they indicate that the unity of the island is one of Langtoft's dominant preoccupations, but not simply because he supported Edward's territorial rights or because he saw Edward as a second Brutus. Rather, the unity of the land was for Langtoft, both in historical fact and in philosophical concept, a necessary precondition of right rule.[60] Not only did unity have a happy way of interacting with peace and justice, but it was the inherent and natural condition of the land as established by Brutus, after he disposed of the giants who had controlled the country.[61] The story of Langtoft's history is not simply, as Legge suggests, an attempt to *return* to this unity and harmony of the land, a search for a *second* Brutus, but the attempt to *maintain* the condition of unity and peace established by Brutus. The distinction between returning and maintaining may be a small one, but it is of the utmost importance in determining Langtoft's conception of human history.

What Langtoft saw in Geoffrey of Monmouth, and what he emphasizes in his abridgement, is the periodic dismemberment of the kingdom, beginning with Brutus' sons Locrine, Camber, and Albenac, whose names became the mythological representations of the three separate parts of the island, continuing with Lier, the brother combinations of Ferrex-Porrax and Belinus-Brennius, and finally Vortigern, and the civil war that attended each partition. The subsequent reunifications of the island, under Dunwallo, Constantine, and, most notably, Arthur bring greatness and prosperity; but it is always a fragile unity and, at the end, the victorious Saxons divide the country into seven kingdoms. The Anglo-Saxon period, also, shows the long attempt to unify, reaching a peak of success under Athelstan and Edgar,[62] only to be dissipated again by the crimes of Ethelred and the

Danish partitions. William the Conqueror presented his heirs with a unified country, but according to Langtoft, that unity was constantly threatened by the uprisings of the Welsh and the Scots, and by the rebellious and disorderly activity of the barons, particularly under Stephen, John, and Henry III. Under Edward, the forces of fragmentation, in the guise of an independent nobility and rebellious Welsh and Scots chieftains, were continuously active, and his whole reign, as Langtoft eventually came to see it, was a struggle to preserve the integrity of the land.[63]

This view of human history as a struggle to maintain an initially established condition of the land, a struggle that goes on constantly since it is, in essence, a battle against the forces let loose by the fall of man — instability, restlessness, disunity, and evil — is, I suggest, the central preconception of Langtoft's chronicle and what separates him from other, contemporary, historians to whom this unity was of only peripheral concern. If the larger allegory of a return from earth to earth dominates the framework of history, within the framework, in the history itself, the dominant concept is one of stability and preservation. The human race, as a Christianized entity, may be in the process of returning to an original state from which it has departed, but British history, as presented by Langtoft, is a condition (rather than a process) of man's trying to keep things together, of holding on, of retrieving that which has been temporarily lost,[64] of attempting to maintain a stability as he waits for his return to Eden-Paradise.

As a consequence of this controlling perception, the actions of human history which Langtoft records are events which, from a moral point of view, never should have occurred.[65] They are painfully necessary responses to a disturbance of the stasis which was first established by Brutus. It is for this reason that Langtoft insists so strongly on the quality of rule of the successive kings of England. The extent to which they maintain justice, peace, and the prosperity of the land and of religious institutions determines the degree of stability the land will enjoy under them. It is also for this reason that Langtoft insistently refers to usurpers of the throne and disturbers of the peace, particularly the Scots, as "fols" — fools or madmen.[66] To him only an aberrant mind or one deficient in judgement could think of jostling the stability which is the end of right rule and the inherent mark of the proper functioning of the human will as it seeks a harmony with the divine will.

This innately conservative substance in Langtoft's chronicle grows out of the perception that the world, defined as a collection of human actions, is not going anywhere, but merely waiting for the ultimate eschaton. However, while waiting, man had a moral duty to maintain himself in a condition of peace and justice and religious stability, a stability that enabled the human will to conform itself with the divine.

NOTES

1. Some recent, very interesting, books to which I am much indebted are: William J. Brandt, *The Shape of Medieval History: Studies in Modes of Perception* (New Haven, 1966); Robert W. Hanning, *The Vision of History in Early Britain* (New York, 1966); John Taylor, *The Universal Chronicle of Ranulf Higden* (Oxford, 1966); and R. Vaughan, *Matthew Paris* (Cambridge, 1958).

2. Ed. Thomas Wright, Rolls Series, 47, 2 vols. (London, 1866). All references to Langtoft's chronicle are from this edition. Since there is no line numbering, each quotation will be followed by volume and page numbers only. Wright translates the chronicle on facing pages of this edition, and the translations given here are his, although I have silently modernized some of the punctuation and smoothed out some of the phrasing.

3. M. Dominica Legge, "A List of Langtoft MSS., with notes on MS. Laud Misc. 637," *Medium Aevum*, IV (1935), 20–24 and *Anglo-Norman in the Cloisters* (Edinburgh, 1950), pp. 72–73. Wright uses as his base text MS. Cotton Julius A.V., which is certainly the best manuscript and, except for a few minor additions, the fullest. My analysis is based on this text.

4. An early edition of Mannyng is entitled *Peter Langtoft's Chronicle, As Illustrated and Improved by Robert of Brunne, From the Death of Cadwalader to the End of King Edward the First's Reign*, ed. Thomas Hearne, 2 vols. (Oxford, 1725).

5. The distinctions "clerical" and "aristocratic" are from Brandt, p. xviii. In general, according to him, "clerical" chronicles reveal an essentially static world view, in which historical human actions are seen as disturbances of the natural and inherent stasis of the world or, at best, as reactions to a disturbance with a view to restoring the initial stasis. "Aristocratic" chronicles tend to concentrate on the actions of great men, actions which had their foundations in a particular expression of the human will. Brandt classifies Langtoft as an "aristocratic" chronicler. I hope to show, among other things, that he fits both categories.

6. Thomas Duffus Hardy, *A Descriptive Catalogue of Manuscripts Relating To The Early History of Great Britain*, Rolls Series, 26, III (London, 1865), 302.

7. Legge, *Cloisters*, pp. 73–74.

8. John Taylor, *Medieval Historical Writing in Yorkshire* (York, 1961), pp. 13–14.

9. Besides the obvious proximity to the scene of the conflict with the Scots, York was an important political center during this period. "The Exchequer was at York from 1298 to 1304–5" (Legge, *Cloisters*, p. 72).

10. Legge, *Cloisters*, p. 70.
11. Taylor, *Yorkshire*, p. 30.
12. "The war with Scotland and secular politics predominate in the narratives of most chronicles [at the end of the thirteenth century]. Though the chroniclers of this period were all ecclesiastics, and in the majority of cases members of religious houses, it is clear that their work was done against the background of the emergent national state. . . . Already in the fourteenth century there was a growing awareness of a 'national' past and an awakening interest in forms of 'national' history" (Taylor, *Yorkshire*, p. 14).
13. Cf. Taylor, *Higden*, p. 48, and Vaughan, p. 151.
14. *Memoriale Fratris Walteri de Coventria*, ed. William Stubbs, Rolls Series, 58 (London, 1873), I, 1–19.
15. Reprinted in *Anglo-Scottish Relations 1174–1328: Some Selected Documents*, ed. E. L. G. Stones (Oxford, 1965), pp. 96–109.
16. Wright, II, Appendix I, pp. 402–20.
17. *The Chronicle of Walter of Guisborough (previously edited as the Chronicle of Walter of Hemingford or Hemingburgh)*, ed. Harry Rothwell, Camden Series, 39 (London, 1957), pp. 102, 105, 106, 108, 116, 127. Rothwell's statement (Introduction, p. xxvi, note 3) that Walter, like Langtoft a Yorkshire Austin canon, is the borrower seems valid to me. The Guisborough chronicle was probably written between 1300 and 1305 (Introduction, p. xxxi).
18. Pp. 1–2.
19. Particularly in the manner of treating the death of William Rufus, pp. 21–22. Most medieval chroniclers saw this as an unmistakable moral *exemplum*. See below, note 45.
20. Taylor, *Yorkshire*, p. 17.
21. *The Metrical Chronicle of Robert of Gloucester*, ed. William A. Wright, Rolls Series, 86, 2 vols. (London, 1887). The chronicle was written about 1300 (Introduction, p. xi).
22. W. A. Wright gives an exhaustive study of the relationship between the chronicle and its sources in his Introduction, pp. xv–xxxii.
23. Danes: lines 5905–15; Normans: lines 7503–13; William Rufus: 8612–13. Cf. Matthew Paris, *Chronica Majora*, ed. H. R. Luard, Rolls Series, 57 (London, 1872–84), IV, 85, 568, 603; also Vaughan, p. 150.
24. See Taylor, *Higden*, pp. 38–39, 49, and for Trivet, M. Dominica Legge, *Anglo-Norman Literature and Its Background* (Oxford, 1963), pp. 299–301.
25. Vaughan, p. 143.
26. *Chronica Majora*, V, 580–81; also, Vaughan, p. 151.
27. *Cloisters*, pp. 71–72.
28. "And king Arthur surprised through treachery,/ and Mordred slaughtered because of his madness;/ Cadwallader through poverty lost Britain,/ By force the people of Germany drove him from it;/ Afterwards Harold, son of Godwin, held it wrongfully,/ Who in the first year lost the lordship;/ William the Conqueror acquired it by the sword./ King John de Baliol has lost by folly,/ For himself and his heirs, the kingdom of Albany./ Alas! that no man corrects himself by the example of another./ O rich king

Edward, by God, have mercy;/ Suffer not to perish the great nobility/ Of those who are left to conquer Acquitaine."

29. "In ancient histories we find written/ What kings and what kingdoms king Arthur conquered,/ And how he generously shared his gain./ There was not a king under him who contradicted him,/ Earl, duke, or baron who ever failed him/ In war or in battle, but each followed him./ The king sir Edward has given too little;/ Whereby at his departure, when he put to sea/ Against the king of France, the affront was shown him/ That none of his earls undertook the expedition."

30. See also II, 178, 202, 216, 256–58, 268, 274–76, 326–28. One has the sense that this is the implicit purpose of most medieval histories, although Taylor, *Higden*, p. 48, denies that it is Higden's aim. However, none of Langtoft's contemporaries, to my knowledge, are as explicit in this connection as he is.

31. "God the almighty, who created heaven and earth,/ Who formed our father Adam a man out of earth,/ Provided according to nature when he ordained/ That man, having come from the earth, shall return to the earth." This passage is Langtoft's addition; it is not found in Geoffrey of Monmouth.

32. "O Lord almighty, whom the Christian adores,/ Every earthly creature is thy work./ In making the world the law was formed/ That man, woman and beast must die by nature./ Since the time of Adam there never was any hour/ In which a prince for nobility, or baron for splendor,/ Or merchant for wealth, or clerk for learning,/ By art or by genius could escape death."

33. Among contemporary chronicles, only the *Anonymous Short English Metrical Chronicle*, ed. Ewald Zettl, E.E.T.S. O.S. 196 (London, 1935), which was compiled shortly after 1307 in the South Midlands (Introduction, p. ciii), observes this restriction with the same rigor that Langtoft does.

34. See G. H. Gerould, "King Arthur and Politics," *Speculum*, II (1927), 33–52; and R. S. Loomis, "Edward I, Arthurian Enthusiast," *Speculum*, XXVIII (1953), 114–27.

35. Shortly after the opening of the second part of the chronicle (I, 286–90), Langtoft quotes Henry of Huntingdon's division of English history into five periods corresponding to five "wounds" inflicted on the people by the invasions of the Romans, Picts, Saxons, Danes, and Normans. However, where Henry specifically refers to the wounds as punishments visited on the English people for their periodic sinfulness, Langtoft leaves out all reference to human sinfulness and divine retribution and emphasizes that it is the land, a morally neutral entity, that is the recipient of the wounds. Cf. *Historia Anglorum*, ed. Thomas Arnold, Rolls Series, 74 (London, 1879), p. 8. Guisborough, p. 1, mentions the five wounds in the same morally neutral way, and both *Gloucester*, ll. 1–5, and the *Anonymous . . . Chronicle*, ll. 7, 15 begin with references to the "land" of England, as if that is to be the "subject" of each work. Neither, however, retains this focus with any consistency.

36. "In the time of king Morvidus there arrived in Britain/ A king of great power, he was from Morian,/ Who destroyed and laid waste all Northumberland./ Morvidus encounters him directly, body to body./ In battle the

king alone did much more/ Than half the people that he led with him./ The Moriani are killed, he ordered their bodies/ To be all burnt to powder; he showed himself too cruel./ A sea monster, which terrorized the land,/ As he alone, by misfortune, wished to attack,/ The monster rose upon him and swallowed him up./ This king Morvidus begat five sons./ Gorbonianus, the eldest, reigned after him/ And loved above all things justice and peace./ He repaired the temples in Britain,/ He abounded in wealth more than any other king./ He everywhere honored the cultivators of the land./ He reigned king for ten years, his brother buried him/ In fair Trinovant, as he himself willed./ Arthgallo his brother received the kingdom next./ Wicked and proud, hostile to peace,/ He behaves so malevolently that he brought the land to decline./ The people of Britain will not suffer such a burden,/ They take the crown from him and drive him from power." Cf. *Historia Regum Britanniae*, ed. Acton Griscom (London, 1929), Bk. III, Chaps. 14–17.

37. Although Langtoft, in the later portions of the chronicle, is an implicit supporter of the inviolability of kingship, he does so because this seems to him the most efficient means of promoting the peace, justice, and prosperity he wants, not from any principle of divine right. He quotes approvingly many instances of kings being deposed when they do not live up to the requirements of their office, e.g., I, 88, 104, 116, 252, 291, 336. In this respect Langtoft reflects the dominant theory of medieval political philosophy which held that the king ruled only for the good of the people. See R. W. and A. J. Carlyle, *Medieval Political Theory in the West* (London, 1903ff.), II, Chap. 7; III, Chap. 4; V. Chaps. 3, 7; Fritz Kern, *Kingship and Law in the Middle Ages*, trans. S. B. Chrimes (Oxford, 1968), pp. 81–133; Fritz Schultz, "Bracton on Kingship," *English Historical Review*, LX (1945), 153. Bracton, who died in 1268, provides a convenient gloss on many of the themes found in Langtoft. His dictum on this point is: "Dicitur enim rex a bene regendo et non a regnando, quia rex est dum bene regit, tyrannus dum populum sibi creditum violenta opprimit dominatione." *De Legibus et Consuetudinibus Angliae*, ed. George Woodbine (New Haven, 1915ff.), II, 305.

38. For the medieval theory of the relationship between the king and the law, which again Langtoft accurately reflects, see Kern, p. 69–79 and Ernst H. Kantorowicz, *The King's Two Bodies* (Princeton, 1957), pp. 143–64.

39. Belinus: I, 42–50; Arthur: I, 146–226; Alfred: I, 316–18; Athelstan: I, 322–32; William: I, 410–34; Richard: II, 26–122.

40. Vortigern: I, 98–116; Ethelred: I, 342–64; John: II, 122–34.

41. "Ad hoc autem creatus est rex et electus, ut iustitiam faciat universis, et ut in eo dominus sedeat, et per ipsum sua iudicia discernat, et quod iuste iudicaverit sustineat et defendat, quia si non esset qui iustitiam faceret pax de facili posset exterminari, et supervacuum esset leges condere et iustitiam facere nisi esset qui leges tueretur. . . . Potentia vero omnes sibi subditos debet praecellere." Bracton, *De Legibus*, p. 305.

42. *Gesta Regum Anglorum*, ed. Thomas Duffus Hardy, *English Historical Society*, 5 (London, 1839), 422–24; and *Florence of Worcester's Chronicle*, trans. Thomas Forester (London, 1854), pp. 173–74.

43. "The Conqueror at this time committed a very great sin/ When he took vengeance on the ecclesiastics,/ Who had done no wrong in his kingdoms./ From York to Durham no place is inhabited,/ Nor is any land worked, nor seed of wheat sown."

44. "When king William had done his will/ In Wales and in Scotland, he makes no account of people,/ Conducted himself strangely to the rich and to the poor./ Too often he taxes clergy and holy church,/ Destroys entirely seventeen minsters,/ And joins to the forest land and lordship,/ As was never before in the time of any of his kindred./ This life, in truth, lasted a long time,/ Nearly fourteen years he had the government/ Of all England on the day when death took him./ He is departed from the world, now listen how."

45. *Gesta*, pp. 507–8. *Gloucester*, ll. 8628–39, reports a similar dream and presents William's death as a product of divine justice. *Guisborough*, pp. 21–22, also sees a moral fitness in the event. He goes on to implicitly connect it with a freak of nature: "Ante mortem uel *casum* Willelmi regis contigit in pago qui Barrukeschire nominatur mirabile quoddam, quod sanguis scilicet emanauit a fonte quodam ibidem tribus septimanis continuis," p. 22; emphasis added.

46. Carlyle, I, Chaps. 14, 18; III, chaps. 2, 3, 5. Also, for specific twelfth- and thirteenth-century theory, see: John Dickinson, "The Medieval Conception of Kingship as Developed in the *Policraticus* of John of Salisbury," *Speculum*, I (1926), 319–20; Kantorowicz, pp. 97–143; Gaines Post, "Two Notes on Nationalism in the Middle Ages," *Traditio*, IX (1953), 295; and above, note 41.

47. Kantorowicz, pp. 166–68.

48. Hanning, pp. 1–43.

49. *Ibid.*, pp. 44–172.

50. See above, note 15.

51. Cf. Malmesbury, *Gesta*, p. 262.

52. "If [Harold] had not been previously engaged in battle,/ Nor lost his men, nor done falsehood,/ Nor broken his oath for the royalty,/ Duke William would not yet have gained a foot/ Of ground on the English, nor any of his family."

53. Malmesbury, *Gesta*, pp. 387, 416. *Guisborough*, pp. 2–5, goes into great detail on the background to the Norman invasion. He, too, emphasizes Harold's personal folly rather than the hand of God in the developing crisis.

54. *Gesta*, pp. 414, 417–19. *Gloucester*, ll. 7503–13, also attributes the English defeat to the moral flaws of the people.

55. The concept is analogous to the Scholastic definition of law, in that the different categories of law — eternal, natural, human — are said to be inherent in the human conscience and in reason. They are implanted in man by God, but it is the function of man to recognize and fulfill the requirements of law. See Thomas Aquinas, *Summa Theologiae*, 2a 2ae, question 91, arts. 1–3. I do not mean to imply by this that Langtoft is a Scholastic philosopher, only that he shares the same intellectual atmosphere as the philosopher. Bracton also says much the same thing: "De sacramento quod rex facere debet in coronatione sua: Imprimis se esse praecepturum et

pro viribus opem impensurum ut ecclesiae dei et omni populo christiano vera pax omni suo tempore observetur. Secundo, ut rapacitates et omnes iniquitates omnibus gradibus interdicat. Tertio, ut in omnibus iudiciis aequitatem praecipiat et misericordiam, *ut indulgeat ei suam misericordiam clemens et misericors deus*, et ut per iustitiam suam firma pace gaudeant universi." *De Legibus*, p. 304; emphasis added.

56. "If the king wishes to serve God,/ He must maintain the law,/ If not, he sins and acts wrong." And, "Upon him whom God loves least will the ruin fall./ In war and in battle God gave in the past/ Honor and victory to the son of Matathias;/ So he does to all who are most loved by him./ The prince who died on the mount of Calvary/ Loves king Edward and his barons."

57. Historians contemporary with Langtoft are only fitfully and haphazardly concerned about the relationship between the human will and right rule. Matthew Paris, consistently pessimistic, sees human history as chaos and calamity. At times this is attributed to God's punishment of the evil will of human beings (*Chronica Majora*, V, 134, 165, 170–72, 625; also Vaughan, *Matthew Paris*, p. 150), but it rarely has anything to do with a question of rule. Robert of Gloucester, who is most like Langtoft in this respect, has God frequently interfering in human history (ll. 5897–5920, 7503–13, 7705–08, 8550–59, 8612–13, 8824–28, 9150), but the interference is almost always in response to the personal, moral qualities of the king. Robert mentions God more often than Langtoft does, and it is obvious that he is less interested in right rule than Langtoft is, but it is possible to see the seeds of Langtoft's idea in Gloucester. Guisborough, interested in events and not the quality of rule, confines his moral judgements to obvious cases, like William Rufus (pp. 21–22) and Stephen (pp. 41–42, 53–54).

58. Since the story, beginning with Geoffrey of Monmouth, became traditional and rather set, it is impossible to tell whether Langtoft or any of his contemporaries were conscious of its exemplary value. But see Laura Keeler, *Geoffrey of Monmouth and the Late Latin Chroniclers, 1300–1500* (Berkeley, 1946), pp. 47–61, for the political use the story had in Langtoft's time.

59. This may also be one of the implications of the opening stanza of *Sir Gawain and the Green Knight*, ed. J. R. R. Tolkien and E. V. Gordon, rev. N. Davis (Oxford, 1968), ll. 13–17, in which Brutus is mentioned as having founded Britain "wyth wynne," but "Where werre and wrake and wonder/ Bi sythes hatӡ wont therinne."

60. Although he is talking about the advantage of monarchy over other forms of government, rather than the condition of the land as Langtoft is, Thomas Aquinas expresses an analogous idea: "Bonum autem et salus consociatae multitudinis est, ut eius unitas conservetur, quae dicitur pax, qua remota, socialis vitae perit utilitas, quinimmo multitudo dissentiens sibi ipsi sit onerosa. Hoc igitur est ad quod maxime rector multitudinis intendere debet, ut pacis unitatem procuret." *De Regimine Principum*, ed. Joseph Mathis (2nd. rev. ed., Turin, 1948), Bk. 1, Chap. 2. See also Kantorowicz, *The King's Two Bodies*, p. 240.

61. Aside from this reference to non-human giants as the original inhabitants of the island (I, 20), which is straight from Geoffrey of Monmouth (Book

I, Chap. 17), there is no implication of a primitive or pre-social state of man. The arrival of people, Brutus and his followers, means the arrival of unity, peace, and justice, which is the natural condition of the country. Any pre-existent state is irrelevant to human history.

62. For a similar notion about Anglo-Saxon history see *Anonymous . . . Chronicle*, line 391.

63. This idea was very much alive during the later part of Edward's reign. His early martial successes prompted such expressions amongst Langtoft's contemporaries as: "Hic monarcha [Edward I] effectus et totius insulae dominus, Walenses saepius rebellantes devicit, Scotos subvenit, et accepit homagium de magnatibus Scotiae, et omnia castra accepit in manu sua, et omnes insulas, anno Domini MCCXC primo." *Memoriale Fratris Walteri de Coventria*, p. 18. And, under the year 1296: "Rex igitur Anglie omne regnum Scocie dominacioni sue dubdidit et regimini. Unde ex Anglia, Scocia et Wallia monarchiam quondam tocius Britannie per multa tempora decisam et truncatam occupauit." *The Chronicle of Bury St. Edmunds, 1212–1301*, ed. Antonia Gransden (Oxford, 1964), p. 133. This from chroniclers from whom the question of unity receives no other notice.

64. This would apply particularly to the Holy Land, a sacred Christian place temporarily lost to the pagan Saracens. Langtoft's interest in the crusading experiences of Robert, Earl of Normandy, Edward I, and particularly Richard I, can be attributed to the special place the Holy Land held in the medieval imagination. See Kantorowicz, pp. 236–42.

65. This, as Brandt points out, p. 79, was the controlling perception of history for the Latin "clerical" chronicle.

66. II, 140, 146, 184, 220, 230–32, 238, 300, 366, 372.

Clerical Judges in English Secular Courts

THE IDEAL VERSUS THE REALITY

Ralph V. Turner

St. PAUL advised Christians that "no man that warreth for God entangleth himself in the things of this world,"[1] and councils of the Church constantly legislated against involvement of the clergy in worldly affairs, concerned that time would be taken from a cleric's chief concern, the care of souls. Yet throughout the Middle Ages, lay rulers relied upon members of the clergy to serve them as judges, secretaries, and other administrative agents. Bishops were also barons, dual personages in the eyes of twelfth and thirteenth century canonists and theologians. The result was an intermingling of the two orders — laity and clergy — that confronted ecclesiastical leaders with a conflict between their ideal and the reality of medieval society. There was the ideal of St. Paul's advice, and there was the reality that the Church was deeply entangled in secular affairs, with its clergy holding powerful posts at the courts of princes.

The revolution in government of the twelfth and thirteenth centuries with growth of bureaucracies made the mingling of clerics in secular matters more common than ever. Henry II and his sons in England needed civil servants who could only come from the clergy. Bishops, abbots, and lesser clergy served the Angevin kings as clerks, itinerant justices, and more rarely, sheriffs.[2] The royal administration was largely staffed with clerics, not only because they were literate, but also because the king could be certain that their ecclesiastical benefices would provide them an income. This situation posed a number of problems.

Under the circumstances, pluralism and absenteeism were obvious consequences.[3] Rectors of some rural churches and archdeacons of some dioceses were constantly absent in the king's service. Other royal clerks were not priests or deacons, but though only in minor orders

75

were eligible for lucrative benefices, and appointed poorly paid deputies to perform their ecclesiastical duties. The most convenient benefices for royal servants were cathedral prebends, since they provided a good income yet according to canon law were without care of souls. This meant that the holder, if in higher orders, could lawfully hold another benefice with care of souls.[4] C. N. L. Brooke has estimated that about a quarter of cathedral prebendaries were regularly absent in the king's service in the twelfth century, although in some cases the number could rise higher.[5] Although popes, councils, and bishops inveighed against pluralism throughout the Middle Ages, the pluralists' consciences seem to have been little troubled.

Another problem was possible conflicts of interest for clerics obliged to serve both Church and king. Which would receive their first loyalty in case of conflict? Perhaps medieval men did not see conflict as necessary, since both Church and monarchy served the same end, the security of the *Respublica Christiana*. Yet the problem could arise for bishops who held high office in the royal government. The chancellor was traditionally a member of the clergy who could look forward to appointment to a bishopric, and who might then resign his office, as did Thomas Becket, or who might continue to hold it.[6] Possibly some sought papal dispensation before accepting appointment to secular posts. William of Malmesbury wrote in his *De Gestis Regum Anglorum* that Roger of Salisbury, Henry I's justiciar, had shunned the king's courts until three different Archbishops of Canterbury and the pope had allowed him to share in the work of secular justice. William then noted that Roger's secular responsibilities did not cause him to neglect his ecclesiastical duties.[7] Nigel Wireker, a satirical writer of the late twelfth century, hinted that bishops sometimes sought papal "indulgences" before serving as secular judges.[8] But no more direct evidence of such papal dispensations survives.[9] Lesser royal clerks who shifted back and forth from ecclesiastical to royal duties must have had a blurred sense of distinction between the two spheres, as had their episcopal masters. As Sir Frank Stenton wrote of one of them, "We may doubt whether Jocelin, archdeacon of Chichester, deliberately assumed a new habit of mind when he passed from a session of the king's court to sit in that of his own archdeaconry."[10]

The Church could condone the employment of these clerics in the civil service in the hope that they were helping to improve standards of government, softening with Christian teaching the harshness of barbarian and feudal custom. But at the same time, the Church was trying to draw a sharper distinction between clergy and laity. Clergy in the twelfth century were being encouraged to dress in a distinctive way, to remain celibate, to refrain from hunting and hawking; in short, to stress their status as a superior order apart from the world at large.[11] St. Bernard enveighed against those clerics who insisted on imitating the lives of the laity, writing in *De consideratione*, "Indeed, in dress they are soldiers, in profession clergy, in conduct neither. For they neither fight like soldiers nor preach like clerics. To which do they belong? In wishing to belong to both, they desert both, confuse both."[12]

The ideal of the Church that clergy should stand apart from worldly concerns placed clerics in the royal service in an awkward position. If they were to continue to serve the king, they could not avoid violating certain ecclesiastical canons. Councils from the time of the early Church had constantly legislated against involvement of members of the clergy in worldly affairs, particularly as advocates in the law courts. The Apostolic Canons, a collection made sometime before the mid-fourth century, included the decree, "Let not a bishop, priest, or deacon undertake worldly business; otherwise let him be deposed," while the canons of other early councils included similar measures.[13] Gratian summarized the canons in his great twelfth-century collection of canon law, adding a warning to bishops that they ought not to involve themselves in secular causes in the courts.[14]

Gratian, aware that some service by the clergy in government offices was unavoidable, sought to define the types that would be acceptable. He wrote that priests could act as judges, provided that they had gained a dispensation for the swearing of oaths; but he warned that should they be involved in the shedding of blood, they would be degraded.[15] In a further discussion of clerics involved in sentences of death or mutilation, Gratian repeated a canon of the Council of Toledo in 675 which declared that those who handle the sacraments of the Lord were not to be permitted to participate in blood-judgments, and those priests who ignored this precept were to be degraded and punished with perpetual imprisonment.[16] Although Gratian recognized the Church's opposition to the shedding of blood, he also recognized the need for capital punishment; elsewhere in the *Decretum*, he gave examples from the law of the Old Testament as evidence of divine sanction for the death penalty. Following St. Augustine's teaching, he added that those who executed the wicked by authority of the law and

77

not by their own authority could not be considered in violation of the Church's commandments.[17]

All these canons plus those of ecclesiastical councils held since the appearance of Gratian's *Decretum* were summarized in 1234 in Pope Gregory IX's *Decretales* under the title "That neither clerics nor monks ought to involve themselves in secular affairs."[18] The chief canons to be added were those of the Third and Fourth Lateran Councils, 1179 and 1215. Pope Alexander III at the Third Lateran Council demanded that clerks hand over their offices held of secular princes, including the office of judge (*justiciarius*);[19] and Pope Innocent III prohibited clerks from pronouncing or carrying out sentences of blood, from writing or dictating letters directing capital punishment, from participating in trials by ordeal or combat.[20]

Throughout the twelfth and thirteenth centuries, provincial and diocesan synods legislated against clerical involvement in secular affairs. In 1138, an ecclesiastical council at London prohibited clerics from acting as tax collectors (*exactores*) or stewards (*praepositi*) for laymen;[21] and in 1172 a council at Avranches, Normandy, barred clergy and Jews from exercising secular jurisdiction, threatening clerics who did so with loss of their benefices.[22] The Council of Westminster in 1175 once more pointed out the prohibitions against the clergy's participation in judgments of blood and against their holding the secular offices of sheriff or steward.[23] The same prohibition against priests in secular offices was among the canons of a council held by Walter of Coutances, Archbishop of Rouen, in 1189.[24] Yet Walter's whole career was a violation of this canon. He was an Englishman from Cornwall, prominent for years in the chamber and chancery, Keeper of the Seal, and King Richard's justiciar, 1191–93. As justiciar, he went on judicial eyres and presided over the exchequer and the bench at Westminster. His ecclesiastical career rose with his administrative career: he was Archdeacon of Oxford, then Bishop of Lincoln, translated to Rouen in 1184.[25]

In 1213 and 1214, Archbishop Stephen Langton held a council which enacted statutes to regulate the conduct of the clergy in the diocese of Canterbury. They included prohibitions against priests participating in secular administration, acting as advocates in judgments of blood, or in any secular cases unless their own or those of poor people.[26] These prohibitions appear among the articles adopted by a number of English diocesan synods in the thirteenth century: statutes of Bishop Richard Poor for the diocese of Salisbury, 1217–19, reissued for Durham, 1228–36; statutes of Bishop William of Blois for Worcester, 1229; *Constitutiones cuiusdam episcopi*, 1225–30(?); statutes of Richard de Wich for Chichester, 1245–52; and statutes of William of Bitton for Bath and Wells, 1258(?).[27]

The Fourth Lateran Council's action in denouncing clerical involvement in blood-judgments is reflected in the canons of some English councils. A council of the province of Canterbury in 1222 adopted an article prohibiting any beneficed clerk or anyone in holy orders from writing or dictating letters inflicting a penalty of blood, or from being present where a judgment of blood was being handed down or carried out.[28] Similar articles were included in the legislation of Bishop Walter de Cantilupe for Worcester, of William Raleigh for Norwich and, after his translation, for Winchester, and later of John Gervais for Winchester.[29] Bishop Robert Grosseteste was strong in his opposition to clerics who served in secular offices. He was more specific in statutes that he issued for his diocese of Lincoln in 1239, stating that clerics should not serve as sheriffs or secular justices or hold offices (*ballivas*) that obliged them to be accountable to laymen.[30] This measure was borrowed by Bishop William Raleigh for his statutes of Norwich and Winchester.[31] His issuing such statutes shows that they were not taken too seriously in thirteenth-century England, for he had a long career on the bench, rising to the rank of senior justice of the court *coram rege* in 1234, before becoming a bishop in 1239. All the time that he was a justice of the king's court he was also rector of a village church, treasurer of Exeter, and a canon of St. Paul's.[32] As C. R. Cheney, an authority on the legislation of the medieval English Church, admits, the synodal statutes largely "represented unattained ideals."[33]

Attempts by the episcopate to enforce the canons in England could take more positive forms than legislation by diocesan synods. Serving as sheriff was a more outrageous violation of the canons than occasional service on the bench, and few clerics served in the office under Henry II and his sons. Among those who did was Hugh de Nonant, Bishop of Lichfield and Coventry and Sheriff of Warwick, Leicestershire, and Staffordshire about the end of the twelfth century.[34] Baldwin, Archbishop of Canterbury and a former Cistercian abbot, threatened action against Hugh in 1190, pointing out that such work was "against the dignity of the episcopal office." But Hugh was "crafty, bold, and shameless," a cleric who had served for years at the court of Henry II. Although he promised to resign the shrievalties, he did not, and Baldwin had to make preparations for his trial.[35]

One of those who most strongly opposed the participation of clerics in secular government was the saint and former Carthusian monk Hugh of Avalon, Bishop of Lincoln at the end of the twelfth century. His monastic biographer noted that when he became bishop, many of the canons of Lincoln were also "members of the king's council and household, and were distinguished politicians and scholars."[36] Hugh soon set to work to change this situation, for in his view royal clerks holding cathedral prebends "devastate and plunder all the churches like rapacious birds of prey."[37] His biography records his policy: "It was exceptional for him to make either royal clerks or the clergy of any other cathedral canons of his church, because he expected those on whom he conferred the revenues of the canonries of his church to reside at Lincoln."[38] His policy soon caused a crisis, for Henry II expected to continue his practice of maintaining his clerks with ecclesiastical appointments. When the king demanded that the bishop grant a prebend to a royal clerk, Hugh refused, stating his reasons strongly:

> Ecclesiastical benefices should not be conferred on royal officials, but on ecclesiastics, since their holders should not serve at court, at the treasury or the exchequer, but as the Scripture enjoins, at the altar. The lord king has the wherewithal to pay his own servants, he has the possessions with which to reward those who transact secular business for him. It is only right for him to let those who are serving the King of Heaven enjoy the provision made for their needs, and not allow them to be deprived of the salary due to them.[39]

Fortunately, Hugh could speak freely to the king, since they were friends. This one firm refusal freed the bishop from any future requests from Henry II for prebends for his clerks, but he had to fight the battle again with Richard I in 1197. Richard tried to force twelve of the Lincoln canons to serve him abroad at their own expense, but St. Hugh refused to permit it, telling the king, "I have never constrained my clerks to serve the king, nor will I do so."[40]

King Richard's agent in this affair was Hubert Walter, a prime illustration of the clerical preoccupation with secular affairs that St. Hugh so strongly opposed. Hubert Walter seems to have had little awareness of any distinction between his two roles as an officer of the Church and a servant of the king; he once said that he "had both swords committed to his custody."[41] Hugh tried to be certain whether his instructions from the archbishop came in his capacity as head of the

English Church or as the king's representative. As his biographer wrote, "Wherever he [Hubert Walter] ordered or advised anything which pertained rather to the material than to the spiritual sword, the man of God [Hugh] had no scruples about saying to him as we read in Acts that the apostles did to the high priests, 'It behooves us to obey God rather than men.' "[42]

Hubert Walter had no scruples about using the clerks of his and other bishops' households to assist him in his duties as justiciar and chancellor, so that a number of them also served at the exchequer and on the bench at Westminster.[43] A letter written for him by Peter of Blois about 1195 reflects his feeling that he could call freely upon the cathedral clergy to staff the civil service, and that their service to the king exempted them from the usual rules of residence. The letter requested that the chapter of Salisbury Cathedral permit the absence of one of their canons because he was needed for the king's service:

> Since reverence is everywhere due to the great ones of the earth and especially and above all to the king, the exchequer account and the necessities of the state exempt from the general rule those who do the business of the king or kingdom; for in all walks of life he sufficiently fulfills his duties, although absent, who devotes himself to the welfare of all. Therefore, because the faithfulness and industry of Master Thomas of Hurstbourne in the public business of the king is abundantly proved, we do not wish you to compel him to reside as long as he is so occupied.[44]

The attitude toward secular service by clerics of a later Archbishop of Canterbury, Master Richard Grant, contrasts with Hubert Walter's complacency. Richard Grant's appointment to the archbishopric in 1227 came from the pope, not the king; and unlike Hubert Walter, he had no background in royal administration.[45] When Richard visited Rome in 1231, he protested to the pope against the involvement of English clergy in secular government. He complained that bishops "were sitting at the king's exchequer, bringing forward secular causes, and giving judgments of blood to the neglect of their pastoral cares." He added that they were encouraging beneficed clergy and priests to follow their example, "mixing themselves in secular cares and judgments of laymen."[46] Although the pope promised his aid in ending these abuses, Richard died soon; and apparently nothing came of his complaint.

Perhaps the strongest opponent of the employment of clerics as royal judges was Robert Grosseteste, mid-thirteenth century scholar-bishop of Lincoln. In 1236, he challenged Henry III's appointment of the abbot of Ramsey as an itinerant justice, complaining to Edmund Rich, Archbishop of Canterbury.[47] He pointed out in his letter that the canons and constitutions of councils forbade any cleric, much less a Benedictine abbot, to sit in judgments of blood, and he asked the archbishop to counsel the king to withdraw his appointment.[48] In a second letter, Grosseteste stated his dissatisfaction with the archbishop's response to his first request. The archbishop had twice replied that it would be better to await a council's discussion, but Grosseteste cited Scripture, canon law, and a letter of Gregory the Great to prove that clerical participation in secular justice was already clearly labelled a sin. Bishops who have clerics in their care themselves sin, therefore, by allowing them to sin in this way.[49]

Later the Bishop of Lincoln wrote a long letter to the archbishop, actually a treatise considering six areas of conflict between the crown and the Church.[50] He cited the royal writs appointing abbots as itinerant justices, and then he made his first point that "it can be shown infallibly that abbots assuming by their command the burden of judicial office sin gravely."[51] He continued, saying that they sin not only because they will be drawn into judgments of blood but also because they will be drawn away from spiritual things toward lower ones, citing the usual passages from St. Paul in support.[52] Also, he stressed the separation of the tasks of the two powers with judgment in secular matters clearly belonging to the temporal sphere.[53] Grosseteste anticipated that some clerics who were also barons owing feudal services might cite Christ's words, "Render unto Caesar . . ." But he answered that they need not perform personally their judicial responsibilities any more than they performed personally their military service.[54]

Grosseteste, like St. Hugh of Lincoln, was preoccupied with the clergy's responsibility for the care of souls, and he feared that secular duties would divert them from their first duty. He fought against presentation of clerics holding posts in the royal government to benefices having care of souls, causing him to oppose some of the ablest men in the kingdom.[55] But his fellow-bishops did not share his concern. They were like Hubert Walter, finding no harm in having substitutes to fulfill the functions of cathedral canons who were absent in the royal service. Grosseteste held to a stricter view, however, maintaining that prebends had care of souls and that appointment of absentee royal clerks endangered those souls.[56] The tradition of royal service was so strong that he had little success in winning the support of the archbishop or the other English bishops. Grosseteste did gain, however, the support of Pope Gregory IX, who authorized him to proceed against the clergy of his diocese who were sheriffs and justices.[57]

The bishop refused to admit Robert Passelewe, a longtime royal clerk, to a church to which the king had presented him because he had been a justice of the forest. In a letter to Henry III, Grosseteste again attempted to define the distinction between the temporal and spiritual spheres, so that each might attend to its proper sphere. He advised that "spiritual things be dealt with by ecclesiastical and spiritual men, secular things by secular men; namely military things by military men, and corrections and reforms of excesses and defects in those things that touch the commonwealth of the kingdom to be dealt with by secular persons. . . ."[58] His position involved him in another quarrel with the Archbishop of Canterbury, for Passelewe appealed to Boniface of Savoy and gained admission to the church. Grosseteste wrote still another letter to the archbishop, complaining of his action and repeating his arguments against the mingling of secular and spiritual responsibilities.[59] Grosseteste, then, saw clearly the conflict between the Church's teaching on the clergy's withdrawal from secular government and their actual involvement. He so feared the consequences for the care of souls that he was willing to contend against Henry III himself, but his struggle did little to change conditions in thirteenth-century England.

Several moralists and satirists in twelfth- and thirteenth-century England complained of the employment of clerics as royal judges. The most learned of all these was John of Salisbury in the time of Henry II. John's close association with two archbishops of Canterbury, Theobald and Thomas Becket, acquainted him well with Henry's clerical courtiers. Certainly he knew many of them as his associates in the archbishop's household.[60] He came to despise royal courtiers, as he made clear throughout his *Policraticus*, complaining of their venality, avarice, and sycophancy. He wrote to a petitioner who was seeking a position for a friend in the royal household, warning that he would be torn between loyalty to the Church and obedience to the king: "If you act rightly and defend the liberty of the Church, the authority of the king bars the way; whereas if you act ill, the authority of the law of God cries out against you on every side." And he asked, "What could be more filthy, more shameless and unscrupulous than an old priest turned informer? Will he do such outrage to his conscience and his reputation merely to please the satellites of the court?"[61]

Typical of the curialist clerks whom John of Salisbury condemned was Walter Map, a clerk of Henry II's household, who often served as an itinerant justice and who collected ecclesiastical benefices as a reward for his royal service. He held prebends at St. Paul's and Lincoln, was named Chancellor of Lincoln, and finally Archdeacon of Oxford.[62] He was known as a wit, the author of *De nugis curialium*, a sharp satire on conditions in the Church and at court. Even though he served as a royal judge, he opposed the employment of clerics, but for reasons far different from John of Salisbury's. His opposition was based on snobbism. He noted that clerical judges were often harsher than lay ones, which he explained by their base birth, citing the Roman poet Claudian, "Nothing is harder than the lowly whenever he riseth to high degree."[63] Then he told a story to illustrate his point:

> It came to pass recently, moreover, that a certain abbot took upon himself to become one of the justices, and he more cruelly than any layman, spurred on the spoiling of the poor, hoping perchance to win a bishopric through the favour gained from his spoils; upon him, however, after a few days, vengeance came, and made him turn his teeth upon himself, and to die gnawing off his hands.[64]

Another satirist who commented unfavorably on the secular activities of clerics was Nigel Wireker, a monk of Canterbury toward the end of the twelfth century, who wrote the popular poem *Speculum stultorum*. He was a kinsman or countryman of William Longchamp, Bishop of Ely, chancellor, papal legate, and briefly justiciar under Richard I.[65] He wrote his only prose work, *Contra curiales et officiales clericos*, in 1193–94 to convince Longchamp of the incompatibility of the offices of chancellor and bishop. His fifth point concerned the bishop's activities at the exchequer. He asked, "Whatever does sitting at the king's exchequer and hearing these accounts and conversations from dawn to dusk have to do with divine matters?" And he answered that there, "The concern is for securing coins, not for salvation of souls, for collecting coppers, not for rescuing souls of sinners from the devil."[66]

A writer who shared Nigel Wireker's views about the impropriety of bishops serving at the exchequer was Gerald of Wales, a harsh critic of Hubert Walter. His pique at the archbishop's opposition to his promotion to the bishopric of St. David's may have colored his opinion.[67] He made outrageous accusations to the pope, charging that Hubert Walter had ordered a *Te Deum* sung to celebrate the killing of 3000 Welshmen in battle against the English in 1198. He added, "So on that occasion he made an evil use of both the swords committed to him, and to speak the truth, it was an evil thing that he should at that time have had both swords at once in his grasp."[68] Again Gerald complained to the papal court of the archbishop's background of secular offices and his continuing concern for them. He asked, from where was Hubert called to be archbishop? And he answered:

> From the Exchequer; and what is the Exchequer? It is the seat of the public Treasury in England, a sort of square table at London, where royal dues are collected and accounted for. This was the academy, this the school, in which he has already grown old, from which he was summoned to all the grades of his dignities, like nearly all the English bishops. . . . A year ago he was Justiciar, and when that office was taken from him by the Court at Rome, he managed at once to get himself appointed the king's Chancellor. And when of late he lost that honor he spared no effort till he recovered it. . . . For as a fish cannot live out of water, so he cannot live without his Court and worldly cases, since he is either wholly ignorant of the words of the Apostle or conceals the fact that he has ever read them, to wit "no man that warreth for God entangleth himself in the things of this world."[69]

Was Hubert Walter required to resign the justiciarship by the pope, as Gerald maintained? Certainly as the chief of the king's justices he could not avoid violating the prohibitions against clerical participation in judgments of blood.[70] But the only confirmation of Gerald's statement comes from the chronicler Roger Howden, who states that Innocent wrote Richard I in 1198, asking him to release the archbishop from his secular duties and warning him not to appoint any other prelates or priests to secular offices.[71] The lack of any confirmation of Innocent's letters from other English sources or from papal records makes the accuracy of Howden's account doubtful.[72] It seems, then, that the reasons given in Richard's letter accepting the archbishop's resignation — the burdens of work and poor health — are the real reasons for his leaving the justiciarship.[73] Additional doubt is cast upon Innocent's role in Hubert Walter's removal from the justiciarship by the lack of any papal complaint in 1199, when he became King John's chancellor.

Although writers in England were concerned about clerics serving secular rulers in judicial and financial posts, they rarely treated the question in theoretical terms. It was theologians and canonists on the Continent who wrote the formal treatises. A significant group of theologians at Paris around the end of the twelfth century was the circle of Peter the Chanter. He and his pupils manifested in their writings "a passionate interest in practical morality," [74] which caused them to consider the role of the clergy in secular government. Several members of the Chanter's circle were Englishmen. The best known is Stephen Langton, from Lincolnshire, a master of theology at Paris before he became Archbishop of Canterbury.[75] But there was also Master Robert de Courson, author of a *Summa* that demonstrates knowledge of Roman and canon law as well as theology, and later a legate for Pope Innocent III.[76] Master Thomas of Chobham, who returned from Paris to serve the Bishop of Salisbury in various posts, wrote a popular penitential, the *Summa confessorum.*[77]

Peter the Chanter and his pupils tended to follow Gratian and the canonists in treating the problem of the clergy's participation in secular judgments.[78] They tended to lose sight of the basic objection that time spent on worldly matters was time that could be better spent on spiritual concerns, splitting hairs over what a cleric who served the king could or could not do to avoid the taint of shedding blood. Their discussion of clerical participation in judgments of blood can be separated into two topics: first, the problem of bishops as secular lords exercising jurisdiction over their tenants; second, the problem of "curialist" clerks, serving as secretaries at princely courts.

Gratian, in his *Decretum*, had recognized that there were bishops "who — not content with tithes and first-fruits — possess lands, towns, castles, and cities," and that these bishops owed certain secular services to the prince of whom they held such properties.[79] Peter the Chanter, like Gratian, recognized that bishops had a dual character.[80] Their secular character obviously required them to hold courts where opponents fought duels, suspects underwent ordeals, and convicted criminals were hanged. Yet Peter advised against prelates' participation in passing sentences of death.[81] Stephen Langton, Thomas of Chobham, and Robert of Courson also recognized that bishops sometimes had police powers through their positions as agents of the secular prince, and they felt that the bishops had such powers rightfully.

But all three agreed that their power to punish criminals should be exercised only through lay officers.[82] Clearly, they were following the twelfth-century canonists who had considered the problem of bishops with *regalia*. They had recognized that bishops sometimes had jurisdiction over cases involving death or mutilation, but had recommended that they appoint lay representatives to pass judgment and execute sentence in such cases.[83] Robert of Courson compared the bishop's situation to that of a lay ruler lacking a hand who orders his servant to do what he himself cannot do; that is, he has the right to judge and to execute, but not the force.[84]

Peter the Chanter also discussed the problem of lesser clerics assigned various tasks by the secular ruler whom they served. One duty which was arousing debate in the late twelfth century was the blessing of the instruments of proof used in ordeals. Peter forbade clerics to participate in ordeals, for those convicted by such proof were subsequently executed or mutilated, possibly involving them in the shedding of innocent blood.[85] He did admit that a clergyman could give advice to judges outside of court, if he gave it in such general terms that he could not be identified with any individual decision.[86] His solution, allowing clergymen to give general but not specific advice, was adopted by Thomas of Chobham, Robert of Courson, and Stephen Langton.[87]

The Chanter discussed "curialist" clerics, who might be involved in judgments of blood through service as secretaries to princes. Gratian in his *Decretum* had considered the case of one who drafted a legal document ordering a sentence of death, and he had concluded that the drafter working at the command of a secular official was free from guilt.[88] Another canonist, Huguccio, concluded that if the secretary was a cleric, he sinned by involving himself in a judgment of blood, and that such sinful clerics were to be barred from advancement in holy orders.[89] His view was incorporated into canon law with the Fourth Lateran Council's decrees. Peter the Chanter and his pupil Robert of Courson followed Huguccio, advising secular rulers to assign the drafting of such documents to literate laymen.[90] The Chanter returned to his distinction between general and specific advice, however, allowing clerics to draw up general decrees concerning punishment of criminals but forbidding them to draft individual death sentences.[91] Robert did feel it necessary to point out that the pope often granted dispensations to royal clerks barred from advancement by canon law.[92] Yet he must have known that employment of clerics in posts that technically barred them from advancement was so common that they rarely bothered to seek dispensations.

Discussions such as those centering on what documents clerics could and could not draft illustrate the approach of the canonists and theologians. Such an approach could have little influence on the practice of clerics at princely courts, and it overlooked the basic question of their presence at court at all. Yet the canons of councils from earliest times had urged the clergy to avoid the courts of princes.[93] It is difficult to detect any results from the speculations of the Chanter and his circle, other than influence on the decrees of the Fourth Lateran and of some diocesan synods.

The only member of Peter the Chanter's school to deal directly with the question of ecclesiastics as royal justices was Thomas of Chobham, who wrote his *Summa confessorum* about 1216 in England with English priests in mind. He recognized that it is meritorious for secular judges to condemn the wicked, but he warned that clerics must not participate in any way in sentencing men to death or mutilation.[94] He wrote, "So great is the dread of human blood that even a judge who justly slays the wicked, if he enters the religious life or wishes to be made a cleric, cannot be promoted to holy orders."[95] Chobham did concede, however, that clerics could participate in judgments of blood if the prince assured them of the security of the accused's life and limb.[96]

Since the opposition to the king's use of clerics in courts and chanceries was so ineffective, there was little need for theoretical defenses of the practice. Some supporters and servants of Henry II, however, did comment favorably on his employment of ecclesiastics in government. Richard fitz Neal, author of the *Dialogus de scaccario*, illustrates the increasingly important role that clergy played in royal administration as a result of the bureacratic revolution of the twelfth century. He served Henry II as a clerk of the exchequer, treasurer, judge of common pleas, and itinerant justice. At the same time that he was rising in the royal administration, he was rising in the ecclesiastical hierarchy; he was archdeacon of Ely and Colchester, a canon of St. Pauls, and finally Bishop of London, succeeding Gilbert Foliot.[97] The statements that he made on the royal power could have come from the period before the Investiture Contest; the Church's efforts at a sharper separation between the two spheres made no impression on him. In the *Dialogus*, he wrote:

For there is no power but of God. There is clearly, therefore, nothing incongruous, or inconsistent with the clerical character in keeping God's laws by serving kings as supreme and other powers, especially in those affairs which involve neither falsehood nor dishonour. And we ought to serve them by upholding not only those excellences in which the glory of kingship displays itself but also the worldly wealth which accrues to kings by virtue of their position.[98]

Peter of Blois expressed views also reminiscent of theocratic concepts. He is typical of the new academically trained men who sought careers as civil servants in the twelfth century. His work as secretary to two archbishops of Canterbury brought him into contact with Henry II's courtiers, and he possibly hoped to join them in the king's service, gaining ecclesiastical preferment as a reward.[99] In one of his letters, Peter defended the clerks of the household of the Archbishop of Canterbury from the criticism of a grammarian that their lives as courtiers should be most harshly condemned.[100] He recognized that many members of the archbishop's household also served the king, but he saw nothing wrong in this, for their higher standard of right and justice meant that they could help solve all the knotty problems of the kingdom. Surely such work was more valuable than grammatical exercises!

In another letter, addressed to the clerks of the royal household in 1180, Peter of Blois stated more clearly his view that service to the king need not conflict with Christian duties.[101] First, he apologized for his criticisms of courtiers in an earlier letter,[102] explaining that he had been in bodily distress and danger of death when he wrote it. He wrote that while it could be dangerous to linger at court, he did not condemn civil servants, "who even if they cannot have leisure for prayer and contemplation, are nevertheless occupied in the public good and often perform works of salvation." He recognized that "those who are admitted into the sanctum of royal familiarity can do and say much by which the need of the poor is lessened, religion is fostered, justice is done, and the Church is expanded."[103]

These views seem to have been shared by Peter's master, Archbishop Richard of Canterbury. In 1179, the same year that the Third Lateran Council legislated against clerics serving as secular judges, Henry II named three bishops as royal justices.[104] Peter, as the archbishop's secretary, drafted a letter to the pope for his master, making the point he would later make in his own letter: it was useful to have bishops in important positions in the king's council, where they could protect ecclesiastical liberties, monastic property, and the interests of widows, orphans, and the poor.[105] He made no attempt to deny directly the charge that the bishops were guilty of sharing in judgments of blood. Probably the archbishop would not have gone as far as Peter would in his letter to the royal clerks. He made a statement about the sanctity of kingship much like those that had been made in the midst of the Investiture struggle. He wrote, "I admit that it is a holy thing to aid the king, for he is holy and the Anointed of the Lord: neither did he receive in vain the sacrament of royal unction, the power of which, if anyone is ignorant or doubtful, is made fully evident by the disappearance of inguinal plague and the cure of scrofula."[106]

Sometimes Peter had less favorable feelings toward ecclesiastics in the king's service. His feelings were partly due to genuine doubts about their secular preoccupations, but possibly also due to bitterness at his own failure to gain any post higher than archdeacon. Once he wrote to his friends in the king's service, reminding them that the life of a courtier is "death to the soul," and quoting with approval *Ecclesiasticus*, "Seek not of the Lord pre-eminence, neither of the king the seat of honour. . . . Seek not to be judge. . . ."[107] Peter recognized the temptation to put professional advancement ahead of spiritual growth that the king's service presented to clerics. He urged one of Henry II's clerks to turn away from study of law, the key to advancement in the civil service, and take up theology and devotional literature. He wrote, "There are two things which drive men strongly to the study of law, ambition for honors and vain appetite for glory."[108]

Master Ralph de Diceto, dean of St. Paul's, began writing his histories about the time that Peter of Blois was writing his letters. A secular cleric like Peter, he had studied at Paris and knew many leading figures of the royal court, and was in a position to produce capable historical work.[109] He had great respect for Henry II, and he wrote favorably of his judicial reforms. He also commented on the king's selection of three bishops as royal judges in 1179. As might be expected from an intimate of Bishop Gilbert Foliot of London, Ralph praised his prince for turning to the "sanctuary of God" to find judges who would not oppress the poor or favor the rich, and he excused the prelates for violating canon law by accepting the posts.[110] He wrote, "If then these prelates should occupy themselves in secular business, contrary to the ordinances of Canon Law, and should be called to account for this, let them instantly oppose to the rigour of the canons the importunity of the king, his good intentions, and his actions pleasing to God and meet for the praise of men."[111] Ralph did recommend that the bishops follow the example of Roger of Salisbury, who would not serve as Henry I's justiciar until he had a dispensation from the pope and the Archbishop of Canterbury.[112] As noted above, there is no evidence that the bishop of Salisbury had troubled himself to secure such dispensations.

As Ralph de Diceto indicated, Henry II frequently called on bishops and abbots to serve him as itinerant justices.[113] Then in 1178, when he took a step toward creating a permanent professional court, he specified that two justices should be clerics and three, laymen.[114] By the early 1240's, the professional judicature had grown large enough to staff entirely the eyres, but many of these professionals continued to be clerics.[115] Three of the greatest judges of the thirteenth century — Martin Pateshull, William Raleigh, and Henry de Bracton — were clerics holding benefices with care of souls.[116]

No particular effort seems to have been made to prevent these judges from hearing judgments of blood. Henry II's Constitutions of Clarendon in 1164 did release bishops present at the king's court as royal vassals from participation in judgments of blood. Article 11 noted that they should sit in judgment with the king's barons "until a case shall arise of judgment concerning mutilation or death."[117] Yet they must have continued to participate in such judgments, for the Archbishop of Canterbury's consistory in 1179 declared that bishops might "with tranquil spirit" decide cases involving a penalty of blood, if they were acting in their capacity as barons.[118]

Although little is known of how the royal justices did their work, nothing indicates that those who were clerics took care to absent themselves when judgments of blood came before the panel. Doris M. Stenton suggests that the itinerant justices may have held concurrent courts,[119] which might have allowed the clerics to concern themselves with civil pleas, while the laymen heard criminal cases. The rolls themselves rarely offer any clues concerning which judges heard which pleas, for they record judgments only as "*judicium est . . . ,*" "*consideratum est. . . .*" But sometimes a justice's name creeps into the account of a case; for example, two appeals of felony in 1232 were postponed for hearing before William Raleigh.[120] Certainly ecclesiastics as late as the middle years of Henry III did not hesitate to accept appointments as justices of gaol delivery trying accused criminals, which would have required them to impose the death penalty.[121]

An examination of the published *curia regis* rolls and numerous assize rolls has revealed only one case in which it is recorded that an ecclesiastic absented himself from a judgment of blood. In this case in 1219, the judge — Jocelin, bishop of Bath and Wells — may have wanted his absence recorded because he disagreed with his colleagues' treatment of the case.[122] It is not certain that his clerical status had any connection with his absence. In 1230, the bishop of Bath did not hesitate to witness a command that prisoners be brought before justices of gaol delivery, even though he must have known that hanging would be the fate of many of them.[123]

The first legislation that indicates any real attempt to guard against clerical participation in judgments of blood came only in 1299. The Statute of Fines stated that the justices sent to the counties to take the assizes should also be justices of gaol delivery. If one of the justices should be a cleric, the statute provided that the other justices should select some knight of the shire to replace him for the hearing of criminal cases.[124] By the end of the thirteenth century, however, far fewer clerics were acting as royal judges. The peak period for clerical justices had been the late twelfth century, when Henry II had called upon his abbots and bishops to make judicial circuits. T. F. T. Plucknett considers 1300 to have marked a turning point in the recruitment of royal justices. According to him, royal clerks and administrative agents supplied most of the judges before that date; but by then, a group of laymen — professional attorneys — had grown up to supply them.[125] It was the growth of a group of laymen learned in the law, then, that ended the appointment of clergymen as secular judges, not the canons of the Church.

It is clear that the Church's opposition to clerical participation in judgments of blood had little effect on secular rulers' appointments of judges. A great gap separated the ideal expressed in decrees of councils, complaints of moralists, and commentaries of canonists and theologians from the practice of the Angevin kings. About the only men who tried seriously to bring the reality into conformity with the ideal were bishops of a monastic or scholarly background, a minority of the English episcopate, such as St. Hugh of Lincoln or Robert Grosseteste. Not even the canonists and theologians questioned the rulers' right to the service of the clergy; they were aware of the intermingling of the two orders, and they only tried to limit through technicalities anything that would leave blood on the hands of clerics.

Certainly, the entanglement of ecclesiastics in secular affairs had the effect of reducing their pastoral care to secondary importance, and it encouraged men of little or no spirituality to seek clerical careers. Yet something can be said for the benefits to both Church and monarchy that came from cooperation. Clerical judges who had some training in Roman and canon law, who had at least some concept of Christian charity, did much to aid the growth of English common law. F. W. Maitland wrote of Henry II, "His most lasting triumph in the legal field was this, that he made the prelates of the church his justices."[126] Peter of Blois and Ralph de Diceto recognized that if the Church wished to lead society toward Christian goals, then the clergy had to take positions of leadership in secular government.

NOTES

1. II Timothy 2:4.
2. According to C. R. Cheney, *From Becket to Langton, English Church Government, 1170–1216* (Manchester, 1956), pp. 24–25, seventeen bishops, or a third of the episcopate, served as royal justices, while at least two served as sheriffs. Marion Gibbs and Jane Lang, *English Bishops and Reform, 1215–1272* (Oxford, 1934), p. 167, list seven bishops and eleven abbots who served Henry III as itinerant justices.
3. On the question of pluralism, see A. Hamilton Thompson, "Pluralism in the Medieval Church; with notes on Pluralists in the diocese of Lincoln, 1366," *Lincolnshire Architectural and Archeological Society, Reports and Papers*, XXXIII, 35–73.
4. Thompson, p. 62; Kathleen Edwards, *The English Secular Cathedrals in the Middle Ages, a Constitutional Study with Special Reference to the Fourteenth Century* (Manchester, 1949), pp. 37–38.
5. C. N. L. Brooke, "The Composition of the Chapter of St. Paul's 1068–1163," *Cambridge Historical Journal*, X (1951), 120.
6. Cheney, p. 22: Geoffrey Ridel, named Bishop of Ely, and Geoffrey Plantagenet, named Archbishop of York. Gibbs and Lang, *English Bishops and Reform*, p. 165: the bishops of Durham, Chichester, Bath and Wells, and Worcester were also chancellors; the bishops of Coventry and Lichfield, Carlisle, Ely, London, and York resigned the office of chancellor on being raised to their bishoprics.
7. William of Malmesbury, *De Gestis Regum*, ed. William Stubbs (Rolls Series [London, 1887–89]), II, 484.
8. *Anglo-Latin Satirical Poets of the Twelfth Century*, ed. Thomas Wright (Rolls series [London, 1872]), I, 219.
9. Cheney, p. 24.
10. "Acta Episcoporum," *Cambridge Historical Journal*, III (1929), 9.
11. Cheney, pp. 104–6.
12. Jacques Paul Migne, *Patrologia Latina, cursus completus* (Paris, 1844–64), CLXXXII, cols, 771–72, *De consideratione*, lib. iii, cap. v.
13. Giovanni D. Mansi, *Sacrorum concilorum nova et amplissima collectio*

(Florence and Venice, 1758–98), I, col. 30, canon vi, trans. Philip Schaff and Henry Wace, eds., *A Select Library of Nicene and Post-Nicene Fathers of the Christian Church* (second series), *The Seven Ecumenical Councils* (New York, 1900), XIV, 594. The Council of Chalcedon, 451, decreed that no cleric should be involved in worldly business except the guardianship of minors, care of widows, orphans, and the defenseless (Mansi, VII, col. 359, canon iii); *Nicene and Post-Nicene Fathers*, XIV, 269.

14. *Decretum*, P. I, dist. lxxxviii, c. 3, 4, in E. A. Friedburg, ed., *Corpus iuris canonici* (Graz, 1959), I, col. 307.

15. *Decretum*, P. II, causa xxiii, quest. viii, c. 29, cols. 963–64. For views of other canonists, see Robert L. Benson, *The Bishop-Elect, a Study in Medieval Ecclesiastical Office* (Princeton, 1968), pp. 321–23.

16. *Decretum*, c. 30, col. 964; Mansi, XI, col. 141, canon vi.

17. *Decretum*, P. II, causa xxiii, quest. v, c. 7, col. 932. For Augustine's teaching see *Pat. Lat.*, XXXIII, *epistola* xlvii, cols. 184–87; *epistola* cliii, cols. 653–65; *De Civitate Dei*, xix, 6.

18. *Decret. Greg. IX*, lib. III, tit. 1, in *Corpus iuris canonici*, II, cols. 657–60.

19. *Ibid.*, cap. iv, col. 658.

20. *Ibid.*, cap. ix, cols. 659–60. For the full text, see Mansi, XXII, cols. 1006–7, canon xviii.

21. David Wilkins, *Concilia Magnae Britanniae et Hiberniae* (London, 1837), I, 418; cited in Cheney, p. 21.

22. Roger Howden, *Gesta Regis Henrici Secundi*, ed. William Stubbs (Rolls Series [London, 1867]), I, 34.

23. *Gesta Henrici Secundi*, I, 85; also Mansi, XXII, col. 148, canon iii.

24. Mansi, XXII, col. 583, canon x.

25. Francis West, *The Justiciarship in England, 1066–1232* (Cambridge, 1966), pp. 74–78.

26. F. M. Powicke and C. R. Cheney, *Councils and Synods with Other Documents Relating to the English Church* (Oxford, 1964), pp. 25–27, articles 1, 10.

27. *Ibid.*, pp. 60, 63–64, articles 1, 11, Salisbury; p. 180, article 61, Worcester II; pp. 186–87, articles 32, 40, *Constitutiones cuiusdam episcopi*; p. 456, article 25, Chichester; p. 607, article 34, Bath and Wells.

28. *Ibid.*, p. 110, article 13.

29. *Ibid.*, pp. 310, 314, articles 57, 75, Worcester, 1240; p. 348, article 16, Norwich, 1240–43; p. 406, article 19, Winchester II, 1247; p. 712, article 51; Winchester III.

30. *Ibid.*, p. 271, article 16; repeated in a list of rules for priests, no. 16, p. 276. Another rule forbade priests to study civil law, p. 277, no. 37.

31. *Ibid.*, p. 348, article 17, Norwich; p. 406, article 20, Winchester II.

32. For Raleigh's career, see C. A. F. Meekings, "Martin Pateshull and William Raleigh," *Bulletin of the Institute for Historical Research*, XXVI (1953), 157–79.

33. Cheney, "Statute-Making in the English Church in the Thirteenth Century," *Proceedings of the Second International Congress of Medieval Canon Law* (*Monumenta iuris canonici*, series C, I [Vatican City, 1965]), p. 414.

34. Charles L. Kingsford, "Hugh de Nonant," *Dict. Nat. Bio.*, ed. Sidney Lee (London, 1900), XIV, 545–48; Cheney, *Becket to Langton*, p. 25. Others were Hilary, Bishop of Chichester and sheriff of Sussex, 1154–55 and 1160–62, Henry Mayr-Harting, "Hilary, Bishop of Chichester (1147–1169) and Henry II," *Eng. Hist. Rev.*, LXXVIII (1963), 213, 216; and Geoffrey Plantagenet, illegitimate son of the king, Archbishop of York, also sheriff of York, 1194, Cheney, p. 25.

35. Ralph de Diceto, *Opera Historica*, ed. William Stubbs (Rolls Series [London, 1876]), II, 77; *Dict. Nat. Bio.*, XIV, 547.

36. *Magna Vita Sancti Hugonis*, ed. and trans. Decima L. Douie and Dom Hugh Farmer (London, 1961–62), I, 92.

37. *Ibid.*, p. 119.

38. *Ibid.*, pp. 119–20.

39. *Ibid.*, p. 115. A similar view is expressed on p. 120: "He said emphatically that, as they who served at the altar were rightly partakers with the altar, it was unjust that the endowments of the altar should go to those who never served there. This seemed to him a species of robbery. . . ."

40. *Ibid.*, II, 111–13; see also Introduction, I, xix.

41. *Ibid.*, II, 28.

42. *Ibid.*, 29; Acts 5:29.

43. C. R. Cheney, *English Bishops' Chanceries, 1100–1250* (Manchester, 1950), pp. 17–19; Charles R. Young, *Hubert Walter, Lord of Canterbury and Lord of England* (Durham, N.C., 1968), pp. 58–59.

44. *Pat. Lat.*, CCVII, cols. 403–4, *epistola* 135; C. R. Cheney, trans., *Hubert Walter* (London, 1967), p. 158.

45. William Hunt, "Richard Grant," *Dict. Nat. Bio.*, VIII, 401–2.

46. Roger Wendover, *Flores Historiarum*, ed. H. G. Hewlett (Rolls Series [London, 1886–89]), III, 14.

47. *Letters of Robert Grosseteste*, ed. H. R. Luard (Rolls Series [London, 1861–63]), I, 105–8, *epistola* xxvii. Later, in 1239, he sought removal of the abbot of Croyland from the list of itinerant justices, p. 262, no. lxxxii.

48. For a discussion of the letter, see J. H. Srawley, "Grosseteste's Administration of the Diocese of Lincoln," in D. A. Callus, ed., *Robert Grosseteste, Scholar and Bishop* (Oxford, 1955), p. 165; Francis S. Stevenson, *Robert Grosseteste, Bishop of Lincoln* (London, 1899), pp. 171–72.

49. *Letters*, p. 111, no. xxviii; Callus, p. 166; Stevenson, p. 172.

50. *Letters*, pp. 205–34, no. lxxii. For a list of the six points, see Stevenson, pp. 173–74.

51. *Letters*, p. 205.

52. *Ibid.*, p. 206. I Cor. 6:4; II Tim. 2:4.

53. *Ibid.*, pp. 208–10.

54. *Ibid.*, p. 213.

55. A protégé of William Raleigh, *ibid.*, p. 63, no. xvii; Hugh Pateshull, p. 97, no. xxv; Robert Passelewe, pp. 349–50, no. cxxiv; Ralph Neville, pp. 188–90, no. lxii.

56. W. A. Pantin, "Grosseteste's Relations with the Papacy and the Crown," in Callus, pp. 179–83.

57. *Entries in the Papal Registers relating to Great Britain*, ed. W. H. Bliss

(Public Record Office [London, 1894]), I, 155, July 1236. In 1247, Innocent IV sent Grosseteste a similar letter, *ibid.*, p. 230.

58. Grosseteste, *Letters*, p. 349, no. cxxiv; Pantin, in Callus, p. 199.

59. *Letters*, pp. 353–56, no. cxxvi.

60. For biographical information, see W. J. Millor and H. E. Butler, *Selected Letters of John of Salisbury* (London, 1955), I, introduction, xii–xvi.

61. *Ibid.*, pp. 144–45, no. 94, undated, to an unknown petitioner.

62. Charles L. Kingsford, "Walter Map," *Dict. Nat. Bio.*, XII, 994–97.

63. Walter Map, *De nugis curialium*, ed. Thomas Wright (Camden Society, L [London, 1850]), p. 9.

64. *Ibid.*, trans. Frederick Tupper and Marbury Bladen Ogle (London, 1924), p. 8.

65. John A. Herbert, "Nigel Wireker," *Dict. Nat. Bio.*, XIV, 507–8.

66. *Anglo-Latin Satirical Poets*, I, 202.

67. F. M. Powicke, *The Christian Life in the Middle Ages* (Oxford, 1935), "Gerald of Wales," pp. 126–29.

68. Giraldus Cambrensis, *Opera*, ed. J. S. Brewer *et al.* (Rolls Series [London, 1861–91]), III, 25; cited in Young, pp. 120–21.

69. Giraldus Cambrensis, III, 28, *De Invectionibus*; trans. H. E. Butler, *The Autobiography of Giraldus Cambrensis* (London, 1937), p. 215.

70. See Cheney, *Hubert Walter*, pp. 93–94, and Young, pp. 128–29, for a flagrant violation, the case of William fitz Osbert.

71. Roger Howden, *Chronica*, ed. William Stubbs (Rolls Series [London, 1868–71]), IV, 47–48.

72. C. R. and Mary G. Cheney, *The Letters of Innocent III concerning England and Wales (a Calendar)* (Oxford, 1967), p. 10, nos. 47–48, include the letters, although their only source is Howden. Cheney, *Becket to Langton*, pp. 25–26, accepts Howden with some reservations. West, *Justiciarship*, p. 96, and Young, pp. 129–30, reject his account.

73. *Foedera, conventiones, litterae*, ed. Thomas Rymer (Record Commission [London, 1816]), I, pt. 1, 71; cited in Young, p. 130.

74. John W. Baldwin, *Masters, Princes, and Merchants: The Social Views of Peter the Chanter and his Circle* (Princeton, 1970), I, 17.

75. *Ibid.*, pp. 25–26.

76. *Ibid.*, p. 19.

77. *Summa confessorum*, ed. F. Broomfield (Analecta mediaevalia Namurcensia, 25 [Paris and Louvain, 1968]), xxviii–xxxviii.

78. Baldwin, I, 178.

79. *Decretum*, P. I, causa XXIII, quest. viii, c. 20, 25, cited in Robert L. Benson, "The Obligations of Bishops with 'Regalia': Canonistic Views from Gratian to the early Thirteenth Century," *Proceedings of the Second International Congress of Medieval Canon Law*, pp. 125–26. See also his book *The Bishop-Elect* on the whole question of the dual character of bishops.

80. Peter the Chanter, *Verbum abbreviatum*, MS. cited by Baldwin, I, 186.

81. *Pat. Lat.*, CCV, col. 220; cited by Baldwin, I, 188–89.

82. Baldwin, I, 187–88. Chobham, *Summa confessorum*, p. 424. The prelate's

seneschal could hang malefactors by the authority of the law or of the prince.

83. Benson, "Obligations of Bishops," pp. 129–30.
84. Courson, *Summa*, MS. cited in Baldwin, I, 188.
85. *Pat. Lat.*, CCV, cols. 226–27; John W. Baldwin, "The Intellectual Preparation for the Canon of 1215 against Ordeals," *Speculum*, XXVI (1961), 631–32.
86. Peter the Chanter, *Summa de sacramentis et animae consillis*, ed. Jean-Albert Dugauquier (Analecta mediaevalia Namurcensis, 4, 7, 16, 21), par. 324: III (2a) 386, cited by Baldwin, I, 185, 189.
87. Baldwin, I, 189; citing Chobham, *Summa*, p. 305, Courson, *Summa*, MS., and Langton, *Questiones*, MS.
88. *Decretum*, P. II, causa XXIII, quest. iv, c. 46, col. 924.
89. Huguccio, *Summa*, MS., cited by Baldwin, I, 185.
90. Chanter, *Summa de sacramentis*, par. 162: III (2a), 36; Courson, *Summa*, MS.: cited by Baldwin, I, 185.
91. Chanter, *Summa de sacramentis*, par. 332: III (2a), 401; Baldwin, I, 185. Clerics could draft sentences imposing only fines.
92. Courson, *Summa*, MS.; Baldwin, I, 178.
93. Council of Sardica, canon vii, *Nicene and Post-Nicene Fathers*, XIV, 422; repeated by Gratian, *Decretum*, P. II, causa XXIII, quest. viii, c. 28, col. 963.
94. *Summa confessorum*, pp. 304–5, 422–25.
95. *Ibid.*, p. 423.
96. *Ibid.*, p. 425.
97. *Dialogus de Scaccario*, ed. Charles Johnson (London, 1950), introduction, pp. xiv–xvi.
98. *Ibid.*, p. 1.
99. For his career, see J. Armitage Robinson, *Somerset Historical Essays* (London, 1921), pp. 100–40; R. W. Southern, *Medieval Humanism* (New York, 1970), pp. 105–30.
100. *Pat. Lat.*, CCVII, *epistola* vi, cols. 16–18; response to Master Ralph of Beauvais.
101. *Ibid.*, *epistola* cl, cols. 439–42; R. W. Southern, *The Making of the Middle Ages* (London, 1953), pp. 212–13, partial trans.
102. *Pat. Lat.*, CCVII, *epistola* xiv.
103. *Ibid.*, *epistola* cl, col. 440.
104. Cheney, *Becket to Langton*, pp. 22–23: the bishops of Ely, Norwich, and Winchester.
105. *Pat Lat.*, CC, *epistola* xcvi, cols. 1459–61.
106. *Ibid.*, CCVII, *epistola* cl, col. 440.
107. *Ibid.*, *epistola* xiv, col. 43; for similar views, see *epistola* xlii, cols. 122–25. Ecclesiasticus 7:1–7.
108. *Pat. Lat.*, CCVII, *epistola* cxl, col. 416.
109. R. L. Poole, "Ralph de Diceto," *Dict. Nat. Bio.*, V, 217–19.
110. Diceto, *Opera*, I, 435; trans. David Douglas, ed., *English Historical Documents*, II, *1042–1189* (Oxford, 1953), pp. 481–82.
111. Trans. *English Historical Documents*, II, 482.

112. Diceto, I, 435.
113. E.g. eyre of 1179, Doris M. Stanton's list of justices, *Pleas before the King or his Justices, 1198–1212*, III (Selden Society, 83 [London, 1966]), pp. lxi–lxii. For King John's appointments, see her table, pp. lxxix–ccxciv.
114. Howden, *Gesta Regis Henrici Secundi*, I, 207–8; trans. Douglas, *English Historical Documents*, p. 482.
115. C. A. F. Meekings, *Crown Pleas of the Wiltshire Eyre, 1249* (Wilts Archaeological and Natural History Society, XVI [Devizes, 1961]), p. 11.
116. Meekings, "Martin Pateshull and William Raleigh," *Bulletin of the Institute for Historical Research*, XXVI (1953), 157–79; H. G. Richardson, *Bracton, the Problem of His Text* (Selden Society, Supplementary Series [London, 1965]), pp. 1–3. For another example, see Meekings, "Robert of Nottingham, Justice of the Bench, 1244–6." *Bulletin of the Institute for Historical Research*, XLI (1968), 132–38. Robert was only a subdeacon, but he held benefices worth 150 pounds. See also Meekings, "Roger of Whitchester (d. 1258)," *Archeologia Aeliana*, 4th series, XXXV (1957), 100–28. He was rector of two churches.
117. William Stubbs, ed., *Select Charters and other Illustrations of English Constitutional History* (rev. ed.: Oxford, 1913), p. 16; trans. *English Historical Documents*, II, 721.
118. Diceto, I, *Ymagines*, p. 436.
119. *Pleas before the King*, III, xxxi.
120. *Curia Regis Rolls* (Public Record Office [London, 1923–]), XIV, 456, no. 2133; 507, no. 2351. Also evidence that Raleigh did not hesitate to hear criminal cases is an abjuration of the realm, p. 92, no. 464.
121. Appointment of Martin Pateshull, 1225, *Rotuli Litterarum Clausarum* (Record Commission [London, 1844]), II, 76b; Stephen Segrave, 1228, *Close Roll, 1227–31* (Public Record Office [London, 1902]), pp. 104–5; 1229, p. 227; William Raleigh to give counsel to laymen appointed, 1232, *Patent Roll, 1225–32* (Public Record Office [London, 1903]), p. 516; William of York, 1235, *Close Roll, 1234–37* (Public Record Office [London, 1908]), p. 159; and *Calendar of Patent Rolls, 1232–47* (Public Record Office [London, 1906]), p. 442: appointment to hear pleas of the crown, 1244.
122. *Curia Regis Rolls*, VIII, 80–81. For a discussion of the case, see Ralph V. Turner, *The King and His Courts* (Ithaca, N.Y., 1968), pp. 193–95.
123. *Close Roll, 1227–31*, p. 388.
124. *Statutes of the Realm* (Record Commission [London, 1810–28]), I, 129–30.
125. Plucknett, "The Place of the Legal Profession in the History Of English Law," *Law Quarterly Review*, XLVIII (1932), 328–40. The change did not come suddenly, however; seven of the fifteen justices of King's Bench under Edward I were clerics; *Select Cases in the Court of King's Bench under Edward I*, ed. G. O. Sayles (Selden Society, LV [London, 1936]), I, lxiii.
126. F. Pollock and F. W. Maitland, *A History of English Law* (2nd ed.: Cambridge, 1898), I, 132.

Medieval Poems
and Medieval Society

Donald R. Howard

Do WE READ medieval poems for their social significance? Most literary critics would answer "No, we read them for their artistic merit." I wish to inquire how far this is so.

The problem at first does not seem difficult. We read the great medieval poems — *The Divine Comedy* or *The Canterbury Tales* or *Troilus and Criseyde* — because they are classics. This does not mean they couldn't one day pass out of fashion; it only means that so far they have "stood the test of time." Scarcely anyone denies that such poems had social significance in their own age and that we need to understand that significance in order to understand the poems. But we do not read them *for* it, we read them *with* it. And we read some poems without it. *Beowulf* and *Sir Gawain and the Green Knight*, both resurrected in the nineteenth century, have come to be reckoned masterpieces, even classics; yet we know nothing about the author of either and little about the milieu in which either was written. We can extrapolate from the poems themselves some notion of the audience they were intended for and can bring to them from cultural and social history some guesswork about the society which produced them. Aside from this, we have scarcely a clue about their social milieus or historical circumstances. In some degree we understand the significance of both against the larger traditions of medieval culture, but their immediate social significance, if they had one, is largely a riddle.

The case is different with Chaucer, about whose life, times, and circle we know a good deal. Stacks of articles and books have tried to demonstrate a social significance of the occasional or timely kind — that Chauntecleer stands for Bolingbroke, or Sir Thopas for Richard II, or Theseus for John of Gaunt.[1] But such "discoveries" are always downed by rival ones. The enterprise, now chiefly a dead issue, has

99

not really helped us understand Chaucer. It is, I suppose, a help to have one bit of pictorial and a few bits of internal evidence that Chaucer read his poems aloud at court;[2] much has been made of it. It is similarly a help to know that *The Book of the Duchess* is an elegy for the Duchess Blanche of Lancaster. But how big a help? *The Book of the Duchess*, which I admire, always moves me deeply, but not because I grieve for the Duchess of Lancaster. In the poem she is a conventional abstraction, an ideal of womanhood, a memory; that is partly what makes it so moving when we come to the bald statement at the end, "She is dead." The immediate social significance which makes the poem an "occasional" poem does not make it any more or less successful as a poem. Its success depends on its tact and elegance, its style, its mastery of convention, its depth of feeling, its human or religious sentiments. Nor would it have any more or less artistic merit if it had *not* been read aloud at court or was not meant to be. We do not demote *Areopagetica* because Milton never got to give it as a speech before an audience, any more than we read *Paradise Lost* for its remarks about the Restoration. We do not normally read *The Fairie Queene* for its relevance to Elizabethan politics, or *The Divine Comedy* for its contribution to Florentine affairs. Certainly we do not read *The Book of the Duchess* because it is about John of Gaunt's first wife.

From such ordinary evidence about what we read poems *for*, one could derive two principles. But, as I will try to suggest, neither is wholly valid:

(1) *Social significance, when it involves merely what is timely or occasional, is not relevant — it fades out of sight in a generation or so and becomes an antiquarian's toy.* As a rule of thumb this is an acceptable proposition. But, at least with some modern poems, it cries out for exceptions. *The Rape of the Lock* would be a puzzle if we did not know something about the occasion for its being written; we do not need to know much about Arabella Fermor and Lord Petre, but we do need to know that they existed and that the incident satirized really happened. If we had had to interpret the poem with no knowledge of this "background," as we sometimes have had to do with medieval poems, imagine what a weight of rival hypotheses would have mounted up! Such topical or personal elements are scarcer in medieval poems than in modern ones, but they occur. More often than not, when they do occur, we have no information to explain them.

100

Hence many medieval poems which may or may not have a topical or personal element are *suspected* of having one. The digression addressed to governesses at the beginning of the Physician's Tale is sometimes thought a topical allusion — two or three court scandals have been proposed[3] — but, without startling new evidence, no one can prove such an "explanation," and the tale can be understood without one. Still, we would understand *Pearl* a little better if we knew something about the author and his deceased female relative, real or imagined. We would understand Andreas Cappellanus' treatise a great deal better if we knew who he was, who "Walter" was (if he was anyone), and what kind of audience the work was written for.[4] We could — and I have heard respected Dantisti say we should — read *The Divine Comedy* without a running dictionary of medieval biography at the bottom of the page; but we would be at a disadvantage if we had to read the work (as Chaucer probably did) without such information available when we wanted it. We could read *The Book of the Duchess* as an allegory of Death in the abstract, or of bereavement and consolation, but I am not sure it would be so effective, at least to the modern reader, without the personal or topical occasion in the background.

(2) *Social significance and artistic merit are unrelated; we can tell a good poem even when its social significance is a mystery.* As a rule of thumb this is also an acceptable proposition. I have cited *Beowulf* and *Sir Gawain* as examples. But it is a matter of degree. The *De contemptu mundi* by Bernard of Morval, because it is a satirical diatribe in the Juvenalian tradition, has social significance aplenty. This gives it interest of a historical kind, but does not contribute to — if anything, detracts from — its artistic value: anyone not taken up in the disputes of Bernard's day will find it too bombastic and too long. The same might be said about "moral Gower." Still, these are matters of taste; if the next generation were to acquire (as they seem to be doing) a taste for explicit moralizing, one might witness a renewed interest in Bernard of Morval, or Gower, or Pope Innocent III. But it would have to be accompanied by a taste for history, because the moral vision of these writers is tied to specific matters quite different from those which seem to be the objects of moral vision today.

All the same, a good poem is a good poem even if its significance, social or otherwise, is in doubt. Let me quote in full a medieval Latin lyric of acknowledged merit, affixing an unambitious translation of my own:[5]

101

Levis exsurgit Zephirus,	*Light Zephirus arises,*
et sol procedit tepidus,	*the warm sun comes forth,*
iam terra sinus aperit,	*now earth bares her bosom*
dulcore suo diffluit.	*and pours forth her sweets.*
Ver purpuratum exiit,	*Purple Spring comes out*
ornatus suos induit,	*and puts its finery on,*
aspergit terram floribus,	*scatters the earth with flowers,*
ligna silvarum frondibus.	*the trees in the woods with leaves.*
Struunt lustra quadrupedes,	*Animals build their lairs*
et dulces nidos volucres,	*and the sweet birds their nests;*
inter ligna florentia	*among the blossoming trees*
sua decantant gaudia.	*they sing their happiness.*
Quod oculis dum video	*I see this with my eyes,*
et auribus dum audio,	*I hear it with my ears,*
heu pro tantis gaudiis	*but alas, for so many joys*
tantis inflor suspiriis.	*I am filled with as many sighs.*
Cum mihi sola sedeo	*When I sit, a woman alone,*
et hec revolvens palleo,	*and think of these things, I pale,*
si forte capud sublevo,	*and if I chance to raise my head*
nec audio nec video.	*I do not hear, I do not see.*
Tu saltim, Veris gratia,	*You at least, for Spring's sake,*
exaudi et considera	*hear and care about*
frondes, flores, et gramina;	*the leaves and flowers and grass;*
nam mea languet anima.	*for me, my spirit languishes.*

I cannot imagine anyone with a taste for poetry who would not find this a haunting and moving lyric. But what does it mean? The speaker, a lady, complains of a "languishing" spirit while Spring bursts all about her. The "you" she addresses is unidentified — it may be the reader, or someone she knows or loves, or (if you translate *Veris gratia* "grace of Spring") Spring itself. The cause of her mood must be guessed; the only way to guess it is to assume the poem involves a literary convention familiar to the society in which it was written. Yet the one manuscript of it was copied in the mid-eleventh century by an Englishman from a Rhenish original now lost, so we cannot tell what social milieu it came from. A reliable scholar thinks it a Latin imitation of a Mozarabic *kharja*, whence he interprets it as the springtime lament of a woman whose lover has left her.[6] But one can imagine another scholar arguing that it is an allegory of Winter's defeat by Spring; or still another arguing that it is an allegory of a

102

lost soul. One scholar thinks it an ambiguous personal utterance: "Her love, or her baby, or her faith is dead."[7] Another thinks poems like it are male fantasies about female desire.[8]

The poem *had* a social significance, doubtless; but it is lost. And yet after almost a thousand years we find it elegant and subtly disturbing in spite of this loss. Possibly the loss itself bequeaths to the poem the haunting "ambiguous" tone which has come to be admired in modern times, so that we are touched by it for the wrong reason — or rather, what would have been at the time it was written no reason at all. Still, the fact that we *do* respond to it is socially significant. A critic could explain why it is a successful poem now, in the twentieth century, by pointing to its balanced structure; to the controlled contrast between its lustrous visual images of the external world in springtime and the tactile and kinesthetic images with which it expresses an unspeakable interior desolation; to its extraordinary repetitions and progressions of vowel sounds; to the effective contradiction or irony by which the woman languishes as the world comes alive, sees and sees not, hears and hears not. None of this quite explains what the poem says; it explains why it startles and impresses us. That is already quite a lot: that it can be alive in a society so different from its own is a striking fact, one which calls for explanation as much as the poem itself. My imagined critic would address himself to this fact, and would have something to say about his, or our, emotions. A "historical" critic would want to ferret out the authentic response to it in its own time. And that is where the trouble starts.

Poems are made of words, and words get their meaning from the society in which they are used; from this linguistic point of view we read everything for its social significance. Some words mean now pretty much the same thing they meant in the fourteenth century — "April," "showers," "drought," "March," "root," "flower"; others, like "liquor" and "virtue," mean something different. These differences can be very subtle: "courtesy" denotes now much the same type of conduct it denoted then, but the rules and values governing that conduct have changed utterly, so that the connotation or feeling-tone of the word is altogether different. What is true of words is, I suspect, true of poems. Some mean now what they meant then, are funny or sad for pretty much the same reasons; others have lost their meaning, or mean something similar but with subtle differences about which we must be cautious. English society of the fourteenth century was different from English or American society of the present century, but not in *all* respects. We are bound to it by a cultural tradition and share with its members more, say, then we share with the Japanese; we probably understand the death of Becket better than the death of Mishima. In *The Canterbury Tales*, when the Knight, just returned from a crusade, goes on pilgrimage without even changing his clothes, we need to have his behavior explained; but when Alisoun of Bath says, "Allas! allas! that evere love was synne," or when Alisoun in the Miller's Tale says "Tee-hee," we manage to understand.

This shouldn't need to be said except that so many medievalists, especially in literary studies, oversell the strangeness of medieval culture. If nothing is what it seems, we can all "discover" what it is. I will offer one example. In the Miller's Tale the hapless clerk Absolon, having kissed Alisoun in the wrong place, drops his artificiality and sets off bent on revenge — he was, Chaucer says, "heeled of his maladie." He applies to the local smith, Gerveys, who is busy sharpening the blades of plows (shares and colters). The clerk and the smith have a brief and amusing conversation, Absolon single-minded and close-lipped in his purpose, Gerveys all high spirits and playful innuendoes:

> This Absolon knokketh al esily,
> And seyde, "Undo, Gerveys, and that anon."
> "What, who artow?" "It am I, Absolon."
> "What, Absolon! for Cristes sweete tree,
> Why rise ye so rathe? ey, *benedicitee*!
> What eyleth yow? Som gay gerl, God it woot,
> Hath broght yow thus upon the viritoot.
> By seinte Note, ye woot wel what I mene."
> This Absolon ne roghte nat a bene
> Of al his pley; no word agayn he yaf;
> He hadde moore tow on his distaf
> Than Gerveys knew, and seyde, "Freend so deere,
> That hoote kultour in the chymenee heere,
> As lene it me, I have therwith to doone . . ."
> [I. 3764–77]

Everyone knows what Absolon does with the hot colter, and to my knowledge no one has proposed any hidden meaning for the famous "branding." But lately Professor Reiss has had a close look at Absolon's brief conversation with the smith.[9] The smith swears a great deal, he notes, and his odd word *viritoot* might etymologically mean "true devil." Absolon has sworn "My soule bitake I unto Sathanas" that he will be revenged. Blacksmiths, Professor Reiss shows with a display of citations, symbolized creators *in bono* and devils *in malo*; they were associated with Vulcan, who signified hellfire and the devil. Thus Chaucer might have seen smiths as associated with violence and destruction. The same was true of millers, who were, like smiths, associated with hammering; and Professor Reiss reminds us that the tale is being told by the Miller, "who is described in terms of demonic colors, red and black, and who has a mouth as large 'as a greet forneys.'" Furnaces symbolized Hell. The smith's constant swearing is sinful, so it is ironic that he is sharpening plowshares, which are symbols of peace and forgiveness (Isaiah 2:4, on turning swords into plowshares), and it is ironic that Absolon turns a plowshare into a weapon.

This is interesting as information, but what does it mean? Professor Reiss grants that "the scene operates in terms of plot requirements, making us aware of how Absolon obtains the instrument of his revenge," and that "such an interpretation is not to deny the humor of either the *Miller's Tale* as a whole or the final branding scene in particular." "But," he adds, "at the heart of Chaucer's *mirthe* there is frequently a *doctryne* that is revealed through parody and comic irony." He does not say what this *doctryne* is; I assume it is that Absolon should have turned, or in his case kissed, the other cheek. If Chaucer meant this for a *doctryne* he managed to bury it in a most entertaining transition. Others have found similar echoes of Christian symbolism buried elsewhere in the tale,[10] and I agree that they are there. But why? They were associations indigenous to medieval culture which Chaucer could have brought into the tale without conscious motives, or for fun. They let Christian ideas reverberate in the background, as they did all the time in the Middle Ages anyway. To say more than this, to say they are there to teach or prove anything, requires a great deal of special pleading, and little taste for a funny story.

What gets forgotten in such discussions is the opposite kind of reverberation. If it does not surprise us to find religious ideas reverberating in a secular context, it should not surprise us to find secular ideas reverberating in a religious context. But some medievalists look for the one and avert their eyes from the other. We have lost our religion, and we want so badly to have it back, or to have a substitute, that some of us turn to the Christian past with insatiable longing and see Christianity in every stone or plowshare. Yet it *does* work both ways. If it is true that St. Bernard of Clairvaux crossed the Alps with his eyes upon the ground to shut out the glories of the world, he must

105

have felt an attraction to those glories. Another kind of saint, or a saint living in another kind of society, might have peered at their snow-capped glories with lackluster eyes, or might have divined in them evidence of the Creator's majesty or ingenuity. Recently Professor Constable has discovered that in the twelfth century the old monastic "angelism," by which monks fancied themselves living in imitation of the angels, was supplanted by the idea of revering and imitating the human Christ. He quotes one monk who tells in the most effusive language how in transport he climbed weeping upon the altar, embracing and kissing the Corpus upon the crucifix. In somewhat this spirit Richard Rolle of Hampole, echoing the Song of Songs, writes "The wisdom of God comes as one beloved; she embraces and kisses the one she loves just as a sister would, and he is filled with joy," or, "When we are wounded [by love], we sigh and groan; and when we are cut off from the world, we languish for love; languishing, we are lifted up, and when we are lifted up, we are amazed." So Walter Hilton writes "Ah! burning love that maketh the inly substance of my soul soft and easy, hot and clear and nesh and sharp."[11] When we find the language of sexuality applied this way to religious feeling, we do not explain away the religious feeling; only some obsessed Freudian would see in such passages no more than sublimated or repressed sexuality. Yet a whole school of critics, when they find in the erotic poetry of the Middle Ages language normally applied to religious devotion, explain away the eroticism and interpret the poems as ironic condemnations of cupidity. Alas, alas, that ever love was sin!

I have some doubts that we can know exactly how Chaucer's contemporaries would have responded to such reverberations. I think some would have responded one way and some another. That is how Chaucer tells us the pilgrims responded to the Miller's Tale:

> Whan folk hadde laughen at this nyce cas
> Of Absolon and hende Nicholas,
> Diverse folk diversely they seyde,
> But for the moore part they loughe and pleyde.
> [I. 3855–58]

Perhaps we can guess "for the moore part" how people would have responded to a medieval literary work and how the author meant them to respond, but it is never going to be more than guesswork — it's hard enough to calculate the average or the intended response to a work written in our own time. And anyway, is this what we want?

An analogy with musical performance has come to be fashionable in discussions of this problem.[12] Surely we want to hear Bach the way he meant to be heard, not to hear him performed — worse, rewritten — so that his music takes on the romantic style of the nineteenth century or the post-romantic styles of the twentieth century. Obviously Tschaikowsky did his own thing better than we could make Bach do it; so we ought to let Bach's music be what it was meant to be. The trouble is, we can never wholly succeed. We can reconstruct the instruments of the day and study the scores, recapture the musical spirit of the time, its dynamics and tonal colorings; but the enterprise stops there. An authentic performance of Bach as performed in his own time might be a very bad performance by our standards — Bach himself complained of bad musicians. And we can never *listen* as men of his time did. What sounds "baroque" to us sounded modern to them; they did not have to put Tschaikowsky out of mind. Then, too, Bach's reputation since the nineteenth century makes us hear him with the awe and reverence due what is classical and old, an advantage he did not enjoy in his own day. What we really want is a *good* performance of Bach, not a historically authentic one. If our musicians are better trained, our acoustics improved, our experience of music wider, and our reverence for those sublime works greater, do we not do Bach a service he might have longed for while alive?

And can we hope to recapture the social significance of his music? We need program notes about the Leipzig coffeehouses to understand the *Coffee Cantata*, but all the "background" in the world would never make it seem as funny as it must have seemed to *some* of the Leipzig burghers when it was first performed. Yet it is still a skillful piece of music and an amusing trifle. We can be transported by "Jesu du der meine Seele" even if we do not espouse Christianity as a religion, even if we have only a foggy notion of the social or religious purpose a cantata was supposed to have, and know little about the specific character of religious observations in the churches where Bach was employed. It is up to the music historian to supply these "ifs" and up to us to accommodate them into our frame of reference if we want to understand Bach in a historical way. It is up to the critic to find out what values in Bach have made him outlive his unknown contemporaries (and to find out if some of his unknown contemporaries don't deserve better acquaintance). And it is up to the performer too. Bach did not write for electronic instruments; but isn't it possible — Glenn

Gould thinks so — that performing some of his works on electronic instruments has helped us hear things in Bach that are really there?

This analogy with performance is useful because when we read or interpret a poem we *are* doing something like performing it.[13] When critics talk about "the text itself" it is like musicians talking about a score. "The work" remains so many marks on a page until we engage ourselves with it; it is by itself only a potential cause of experience, a structure of norms. Rival performances of a piece of music can be different from one another but equally valid as performances. We may long for verifiable "validity" in interpretation, but could we ever establish so much about Bach's intentions that all performances would have to be the same? And would we want this? Assuming we could establish historically verifiable intentions, would we do violence to Bach if we verged from them? If he heard us transpose a key or speed up a tempo, who is to say he might not approve, or merely shrug?

It strikes me that this leeway allowed to the performer is exactly the circumstance of literary criticism, even when "valid" historical interpretation is its goal. Some find it an unbearable circumstance — they want so badly to have in the humanities something comparable to "scientific truth" that they try to turn the historical study of literature into a science complete with a "methodology" and a theory of theories. One would expect their impatience towards "currently fashionable theories of criticism" to be matched with impatience towards currently fashionable theories of history, but they seem to reckon history a science. And yet it is in the nature of history to puzzle us, to recommend polysemous interpretations, to leave questions open. The ultimate defeat of "scientific" history was the investigation which followed President Kennedy's assassination: with mountains of evidence, hosts of eye-witnesses, even a film, the questions of guilt and motive were never determined. What happened, in the broadest sense, remains a puzzle. So it is in literary history: with some modern writers we have journals and drafts, reviews, letters, interviews, pronouncements, all kinds of source material, and still we cannot settle matters of interpretation in a scientific way. Even textual criticism never got to be a science: when all the *stemma*'s and genealogies have been drawn up and all the variants and *durior lectio*'s put down, the editor makes his choices the way such matters so often get decided even in the sciences — by going on instinct and taking a chance.[14]

If this sounds like the beginning of an argument for human values or universal human nature, I hasten to assure the reader it is no such thing. We will never get closer to the Middle Ages by assuming that we have "human nature" in common with the medievals; but neither will we get closer to them by denying it. From what evidence behavioral scientists have, it appears that most behavior is culturally determined. Yet the one great finding of anthropology has been that there *is* a universal human nature. What we do not know is the precise linkage between the two. We have, then, in common with the medievals whatever we have in common with all other tribes and nations of men. In addition, we can find some *cultural* continuity between medieval and modern. Let us take as an example, after the manner of anthropologists, an artifact. We inherit from the Middle Ages certain musical instruments. That is not to say a medieval viol wasn't different from its modern descendents and didn't have a different "role" in medieval society; but we are in a better case when it comes to hearing horsehair scraped across gut than the member of some culture where such music-making never has been heard.

As for literary artifacts, there is no doubt a "deep structure" yet to be discerned in all literature, but most literary norms and expectations vary from one culture to another. For this reason, we can understand most medieval European poems better than we can understand, say, Oriental or African ones of any period. But some medieval European poems can *not* be compared with the anthropologist's shards newly dug up and ready for the whiskbroom. Some, like Chaucer's works or Dante's, have been read continuously since their own time; they have helped *create* a literary and cultural tradition. We read them to understand that tradition as much as to understand the society which produced them. And because they belong to that tradition, they belong to *our* society as well as to their own. Their social significance goes back beyond their own society to its historical antecedents and forward to its posterity. We read them because our society still thinks they are good. For this reason the freshman who looks up from the Miller's Tale and laughs out loud at the ludicrous contrast between ebullient Gerveys and purposeful Absolon has grasped something about the social significance of the passage which may escape the specialist hung up on Vulcan and Isaiah 2:4.

We read many medieval poems for their social or historical significance which we would not read if we were interested in artistic merit alone. We read *Gamelyn* as one of Shakespeare's sources, *Sir Launfal* as an example of what *Sir Thopas* parodies, and both of these because they reveal something about the bourgeois mentality of the fourteenth century. No one in his right mind would class either of these drab romances with *Sir Gawain*. But if we read *all* medieval poems only for this antiquarian or archeological kind of reason, and argue that doing so broadens our horizons, gives us equanimity and detachment, makes us see how our own attitudes are contingent upon our own age and culture, we might as well be studying poems from Samoa or Korea. We might as well study Chaucer the way he was understood in the seventeenth or the nineteenth century as study him the way he was understood in his own time. If you study the past only for its strangeness, you might as well study one thing as another.

The antiquarian cult of the present day is as much a product of our time as anything else is, and ought to be viewed with as much equanimity and detachment. There is such a lot in our own day to lead us to despair — while Professor Robertson cries out, in a splendid Freudian image, against "that rancid solipsistic pit into which the major tendencies of post-romantic thought have thrust us,"[15] others are crying out against mass society, or the loss of community, or depersonalization, or pollution, or poverty, or power. In such a time, equanimity and detachment are hard to come by, and there's a whole school that wants involvement and "relevance" instead. I suppose we are all searching for something we can feel sure of and be devoted to. But the great literature of the past disappoints us in this search — it always reminds us of the complexity, the incomprehensibility of life, its variousness, terror, absurdity. If we ask why grown men should be teaching the young to read poems, the answer *ought* to be that the poems have something to say or do to us. And yet why haven't they said or done more? Literature is thought to have a humanizing effect, but its effects are not evident — certainly not in English departments. Perhaps we should forget it, should be studying human behavior, studying exotic cultures, studying man himself in a factual, scientific way. It has such a lure: if poems have not shown the power to uplift or illuminate which we thought they had, how tempting it is to retreat into historical relativism and say that it was never there — that the emotions we feel when reading them are the products of post-romantic sentimentality; that the interest we find in the characters is owing to a modern cult of personality; that the human insight we admire must be ascribed to our post-Freudian preoccupations; that what we take for their wisdom is only our own; that we enjoy the works for the wrong reasons; that

110

they are really all technique and symbol, all part of a "system" or a "structure"; and that we can put on white coats and study all this objectively, get a factual, historical truth, and have something to teach which isn't open to question or subject to taste.

This may happen to the study of medieval literature and perhaps to literary study in general. Classics, philosophy, and history have all had their fling at imitating the sciences; one can imagine specialists in the Middle Ages and the Renaissance trying to turn their subject into a behavioral science modelled on anthropology, or sociology, or "area" studies. And why not? We make graduate students learn the whole spectrum of English and American literature, but when they become professionals we tell them "Stick to your field." Perhaps every historical period should *be* a sort of island lying in wait for its Margaret Mead, or a Troy for its Schliemann. Literary study could profit from the methods of the behavioral sciences. Some of the things we don't know about poetry would be answered that way. We still don't know to what extent poetry is characteristic of all advanced civilizations, or of primitive ones; don't know much about its origins or its relation to the development of language or other culture traits. We don't really understand the "function" of poetry in various civilizations, or even at various periods of our own; and don't know why men write or read poems, not even why we do ourselves. As a species characteristic of man, if it is that, poetry is understood and studied less than sexuality, or aggression.

But if we go in the direction of social science this way, we ought to retain and cultivate those kinds of historical inquiry which are not synchronic and "archeological." The historical method tries to understand a phenomenon by understanding its past; as a method it came into being at about the time the scientific method did, in the seventeenth century, and its work is by no means complete — not as near complete as science's. The historical method is interested, among other things, in process — in change, continuity, "drift," evolution, decline. This calls for the differentiation of historical periods, entities, or phenomena, and for diachronic study of them. In the humanities some of the most successful historical work has fallen into this category — Lovejoy's studies in the history of ideas, Auerbach's and Spitzer's studies in the history of style, Curtius' *European Literature and the Latin Middle Ages*, C. S. Lewis' *The Allegory of Love*, Georges Poulet's *Studies in Human Time*, Ralph Cohen's *The Art of Discrimination*, Roy Harvey Pearce's *The Continuity of American Poetry*, the

111

studies of allegory and iconography by Erwin Panofsky, D. W. Robertson, and Don Cameron Allen. Some of these books sweep from the ancient world to the present day, others isolate significant periods of development or change. It is silly and trivial to complain that such scholarship "frequently oversimplifies or distorts the actual situation before us in the historical evidence, since it tends to neglect the shifting position of the ideas being studied within the social structure as a whole."[16] Oversimplification and distortion is a pitfall of all scholarship. We are always out to understand the whole, but how to do so without studying the parts? In medieval studies one of those parts which scholars are only just beginning to study is the history of medievalism itself, that is, the *idea* of the Middle Ages since it was discovered or invented in the eighteenth century.[17] Though some students of medieval literature fancy that our own age has found true keys to knowing medieval poems as they were intended when written, historians of the future will likely find in our searches for tension, allegory, and *doctryne* amusing material of social significance to the study of the twentieth century — may see our labors as an extension of the rival medievalisms of the Victorian and Edwardian eras, or a reflection of our discontents or fantasies. The current taste for historical objectivity, hidden symbolical meaning, a unified medieval culture, and an omnipresent *doctryne* is comparable in kind to the tastes of previous generations for political allegory, cyphers, and topical allusions, or for chivalric virtues tarnished and the old order changing.

Perhaps we would do best to let our own tastes come out in the open where they can be seen, to forget objectivity and "methodology," read the poems we like with care, and put down on paper what we really think. It is hard to know what to call this method, if it is a method, so I suppose one might as well call it humanism. Humanism has always been critical and faddish (it has always been philological, scientific, and historical as well); we admire many humanists who wrote about literature — Petrarch, or Dr. Johnson, or Matthew Arnold — largely for their personalities, their style, and their idiosyncrasies. It doesn't seem to bother us that they were all characteristic of their ages, so why should we shrink from being characteristic of our own? For instance, just at the moment "consciousness" is much in the air. Everybody is raising, expanding, or exploring his consciousness — or somebody else's. Inevitably, there is a school of criticism which fastens attention upon consciousness.[18] This sounds very trendy, but it is no more so than any other trend. Criticism of this kind is often called "phenomenological," though its practitioners usually tip-toe away from the word — wisely, because one can find such criticism appealing and effective without having any interest in phenomenology as a philosophical position, or any temperamental affinity for Hüsserl, or Merleau-Ponty, or Sartre, or Gaston Bachelard. Criticism of this kind might have developed independently, out of stylistics or in re-action against the "new" criticism. I suspect in part it did. It will all go out of fashion like everything else, but the best of it will outlast its faddishness. Its way of thinking about literature is appealing, to me at any rate, because it seems to square so precisely with what happens when we read a literary work and when we interpret one.

Reading a literary work is after all an act of awareness; it may en-gage the unconscious, or the affective, or the volitional aspect of the mental life, but picking up a book and experiencing it means grasping with awareness something which existed in the author's consciousness. This leap or overlap of minds is the unique event which happens when-ever a work is read; so if we think of poems as a force in society, they are such a force for this reason and no other. When we read a poem we enter, in some measure, the author's consciousness and his "world"; that is not to say the world of the *Troilus* isn't different from the world of *The Canterbury Tales*, but the worlds of these poems make up part of the world of Geoffrey Chaucer, a world different (though the two share a "universe of discourse") from the world, say, of John Gower. We may theorize that personality and individual differences are modern categories which we wrongly impose upon the "unified" culture of the Middle Ages, but there is no escaping the fact that the two poets are vastly different, and our experience of them different. We cannot really get at these differences without getting at our experience of them; and yet your experience of either is sure to be a shade different from mine. On this account critics of consciousness grant that "an in-definite number of valid critical essays could be written on the same writer,"[19] a fact which one always supposed anyway since it was always true. If we write about this shared consciousness we *are* writ-ing about the text and its language, about the author, and about his society; we are also willy-nilly writing about ourselves and our own society. Since this state of affairs governs most criticism which pur-ports to be objective, the recent trend seems to me a healthy one: it is always nice to have the truth out in the open. We read and interpret some medieval poems more willingly than others, and the medieval society we are best in touch with is the "world" of that society ap-

113

propriated by the author's experience of it. Medieval society lives in our own consciousness this way more vibrantly than when it is put together "objectively," and its significance is plainer. We read medieval poems for the same reason we read any poems, for this leap or overlap of minds: their significance is always to be discovered — again.

NOTES

1. A copious account of such notions will be found in F. N. Robinson's *The Works of Geoffrey Chaucer* (2nd ed., Cambridge, Mass.: Houghton-Mifflin, 1957), the text used for quotes and citations below. The latter two identifications are in George Williams, *A New View of Chaucer* (Durham, N.C.: Duke Univ. Press, 1965), pp. 154–55, 145–51.

2. See Margaret Galway, "The 'Troilus' Frontispiece," *Modern Language Review*, 44 (1949), 161–77; Ruth Crosby, "Oral Delivery in the Middle Ages," *Speculum*, 11 (1936), 88–110, and "Chaucer and the Custom of Oral Delivery," *Ibid.*, 13 (1938), 413–32; Bertrand H. Bronson, "Chaucer's Art in Relation to his Audience," *Five Studies in Literature* (Berkeley: Univ. of California Press, 1940), pp. 1–53.

3. Robinson, p. 727, n. 72ff.

4. Some good sense is applied to this last matter by E. Talbot Donaldson, *Speaking of Chaucer* (New York: Norton, 1970), pp. 158–61.

5. I have treated this poem as a kind of case study in an essay called "Lexicography and the Silence of the Past," to appear in *New Aspects of Lexicography*, ed. Howard D. Weinbrot (Carbondale, Ill.: Southern Illinois University Press). The Latin text is that of Karl Strecker, *Die Cambridger Lieder*, Monumenta Germaniae Historica (Berlin: Weidmannsche Verlag, 1926), No. 40, p. 95.

6. Peter Dronke, *Medieval Latin and the Rise of European Love-Lyric*, 2 vols. (Oxford: Oxford Univ. Press, 2nd ed., 1968), I, 271–77, and *The Medieval Lyric* (London: Hutchinson University Library, 1968), pp. 92–94.

7. Philip Schuyler Allen, "Mediaeval Latin Lyrics," *Modern Philology*, 5 (1908), 431.

8. Leo Spitzer, "The Mozarabic Lyric and Theodor Frings' Theories," *Comparative Literature*, 4 (1952), 1–22.

9. Edmund Reiss, "Daun Gerveys in the *Miller's Tale*," *Papers in Language and Literature*, 6 (1970), 115–24.

10. E.g., Paul E. Beichner, "Absolon's Hair," *Mediaeval Studies*, 12 (1950), 222–33, and R. E. Kaske, "The *Canticum Canticorum* in the *Miller's Tale*," *Studies in Philology*, 59 (1962), 479–500.

11. Giles Constable, in an unpublished paper on the idea of the imitation of Christ; *The Contra Amatores Mundi of Richard Rolle of Hampole*, ed. and trans. Paul F. Theiner (Berkeley and Los Angeles: Univ. of California Press, 1968), pp. 148–49; Walter Hilton, *The Goad of Love*, trans. Clare Kirchberger (London: Faber and Faber, 1952), p. 129.

12. See the remarks of D. W. Robertson, Jr., in "Some Observations on Method in Literary Studies," *New Literary History*, 1 (1969), 29–30, possibly ticked

off by my own in *The Three Temptations* (Princeton: Princeton Univ. Press, 1966), p. 9.

13. Cf. Morton W. Bloomfield, "Generative Grammar and the Theory of Literature," *Actes du Xe Congrès International des Linguistes*, 3 (1970), 57–65.

14. Donaldson, *op. cit.*, pp. 102–130, documents an editor's experience of this fact.

15. *Op. cit.*, p. 31.

16. Robertson, *op. cit.*, p. 24.

17. E.g., the excellent book by Lionel Gossman, *Medievalism and the Ideologies of the Enlightenment: The World and Work of La Curne de Sainte-Palaye* (Baltimore: Johns Hopkins Press, 1968). In English studies the only work I know being done in this area is that of Robert Ackerman, who is preparing a biography of Sir Frederic Madden. We need to know more about the medievalists and medievalism of the eighteenth and nineteenth century and whatever legacy we have accepted from them unawares.

18. See Sarah Lawall, *Critics of Consciousness: The Existential Structures of Literature* (Cambridge, Mass.: Harvard Univ. Press, 1968), and J. Hillis Miller, "The Geneva School," *The Virginia Quarterly Review*, 43 (1967), 465–88.

19. Miller, "The Literary Criticism of Georges Poulet," *Modern Language Notes*, 78 (1963), 476.

"Bachelor" and Retainer

J. M. W. Bean

IN RECENT YEARS historians of late medieval England have devoted a great deal of attention to the structure and influence of "bastard feudalism." There is now substantial information about its basic character — a relationship between lord and man based, not upon the tenure of land, but upon the payment of a money fee to a retainer.[1] In current explanations of the origins of this practice two influences are generally stressed: the rise of the contract system of military service, beginning in the Welsh and Scottish wars of the late thirteenth century, and the effects of the statute of *Quia Emptores* (1290) which by abolishing subinfeudation made it impossible for a lord to reward a man with land held of himself by military tenure. But some doubts now exist about this picture. On the one hand, there is much evidence to show that "bastard feudalism" was already well, if not fully, developed by the opening years of the fourteenth century. There is enough documentation from the reign of Edward II to show that great lords were then rewarding men with money fees[2] and retaining them by indenture of retinue.[3] In fact, this period was "the first age of turbulent bastard feudalism."[4] But difficulties obviously arise in relating this evidence to the conventional picture of the origins of "bastard feudalism." If the effects of the rise of the contract system of military service were so decisive, it is odd that retaining by indenture was so well developed and, even more, deliberately employed as a means of raising men for rebellion within a few years of the death of Edward I. On the other hand, the view that the promulgation of *Quia Emptores* had decisive effects is unsound.[5] Life-grants of land held of the grantor were still possible after the statute, while money fees drawn from landed revenues were known before 1290.

The present state of knowledge thus imposes the task of deeper investigation into the origins of "bastard feudalism." Yet this is extremely difficult, since scarcely any of the financial or administrative records of great landed families before the close of the thirteenth century have survived. Without such evidence we have to rely on

117

stray remarks in chronicles and occasional references in government records, both often imprecise in meaning. The purpose of the present study is to approach this problem by analysing the meaning of the term "bachelor" in the late thirteenth and the fourteenth centuries. It was used a great deal by magnates to describe dependents. By investigating this practice the author hopes to elucidate one aspect of the origins of "bastard feudalism."

I

Historians of feudal institutions have always been aware of the "bachelor." In the generally accepted view the word denotes a young man who was already a knight or would soon become one.[6] The emphasis is on his youth, and in Latin texts, the word, found in various spellings in French sources, is translated as *tiro* or *juvenis*. With this goes the assumption that the man so described is unmarried — lacking, because of his youth, the resources to provide for a wife and family. By the beginning of the twelfth century — for example, in the *Song of Roland* — the word already describes a youthful member of the knightly class. And in this sense it can be found in many literary sources of the thirteenth and fourteenth centuries, in both its Latin and French forms. But the type of social status it describes has a much longer history, with its origins in the chieftain-led warrior bands of the early Middle Ages[7] — for example, in the young warriors who followed Beowulf or those for whose morals Bede expressed fears in his letter to Archbishop Egbert of York when he deplored the connivance of Northumbrian rulers in fraudulent grants of bookland, thus depleting the lands available for the kingdom's youth.[8]

When we meet the word in thirteenth-century England, it contains more than one strand of meaning, the context determining which is dominant. The term "bachelry" can be used to describe a large body of the country's knightly class. The Burton annalist's account of the *Communitas bachelerie Anglie* and their demands in 1259 is well known.[9] A century later the Chandos Herald told how the Black Prince's expedition of 1355, which culminated in the victory of Poitiers, set off from England as "the flower of chivalry and right noble bachelry [*bachelrie*]."[10] The great council summoned by the government of Richard II in 1382 on hearing of the French invasion of Flanders contained "a great number of the more sufficient bachelors of the realm."[11] At the deposition of Richard II in 1399, proctors met him on behalf of the "bachelors and commons" of the north and south.[12] But two chroniclers of the mid-thirteenth century used the word in two somewhat different senses — Matthew Paris quoting it as the term which the English knights used for themselves at the Brackley tournament of 1249, and Wykes to portray the rash and youthful element in the London mob of 1263.[13]

From our standpoint the record sources are more important. At the beginning of the thirteenth century we find the word used in both the singular and plural by King John. In 1200–1201 he wrote to the seneschals of Poitou and Normandy commanding that they seize the lands given to "bachelors" of his household who had not done fealty and homage for them.[14] In 1216 he used the term to describe a knight who was to be paid an annual fee out of his chamber until provided with land.[15] On these occasions the word is applied to a king's knight. But in 1260 we find it employed for the future Edward I.[16] On this occasion we see a reversion to another kind of meaning, since the heir to the throne was presumably so described because he was young and unmarried. However, this usage is rare in record sources, where in the late thirteenth and fourteenth centuries the word generally denotes the follower of a great lord. The pardons issued to followers of the Earl of Gloucester in 1267 employed it as a definition of status.[17] A number of those who fought in the Scottish wars of Edward I used the term to describe individual followers.[18] We also find it employed in the same way during the reign of Edward II by a number of leading magnates — Thomas, Earl of Lancaster, Humphrey Bohun, Earl of Hereford, and Hugh Despenser the younger,[19] and in that of Edward III by Henry, Earl of Lancaster, Henry, Duke of Lancaster, and Humphrey Bohun, Earl of Hereford.[20] The most copious illustrations are to be found in the Registers of the Black Prince[21] and his brother John of Gaunt, Duke of Lancaster.[22] Both used the term in administrative warrants or indentures of retinue as a means of addressing individual retainers.[23] This practice was followed in the same period by Roger Mortimer, Earl of March,[24] Thomas, Earl Marshal of Nottingham,[25] and Thomas Beauchamp, Earl of Warwick.[26] Occasionally indentures of retinue made by leading magnates with knights of some importance specify that the retainer will bring a "bachelor" with him to his lord's service.[27] The term "bachelor" thus has a continuous history through the fourteenth century as a means of designating the relationship between lord and man.

From these details it is, of course, quite clear that the term in itself in some way implied knighthood. In fact, the available evidence indicates that an individual who was described as a "bachelor" in the late thirteenth and fourteenth centuries had already taken knighthood. For example, in an agreement with the Earl of Pembroke in 1309 it was arranged that John Darcy would only become one of his "bachelors" when he had assumed knighthood.[28] But a careful investigation shows that the terms "knight" and "bachelor" are not exactly interchangeable. If they were, it is odd that both terms, instead of one only, are used to describe the followers of the Earl of Gloucester in 1267.[29] In the agreement made with John Darcy in November 1309 the Earl of Pembroke promised to increase the land or rent with which he was to be enfeoffed on his taking knighthood and Darcy agreed in his turn to become one of the earl's "bachelors."[30] But in another agreement, made the following April, in return for a larger grant, he simply bound himself to take up knighthood.[31] If we search the Registers of the Black Prince and John of Gaunt, we find that, while some individual retainers are singled out for description as "bachelors," for many others the term "knight" suffices, both usages sometimes occurring in the same document.[32] When the Black Prince rewarded those of his retinue who had distinguished themselves on the field of Poitiers, some were named as "bachelors," others as "knights."[33]

II

What, then, did a lord mean when he described a knight as his "bachelor"? The answer can only be discovered by a painstaking analysis of the ways in which the term was used. But this task is difficult for two reasons. First, it is not enough to glance at documents in which the simple term occurs without any details to assist in tracing its meaning. Evidence which throws light upon the functions of a "bachelor" can only be found in indentures of retinue which list the duties imposed upon a retainer. But, second, the number of such documents naming the retainer as a "bachelor" is not large. Apart from a few in the Black Prince's Register and elsewhere,[34] most are to be found in the Registers of John of Gaunt and in letters patent confirming some of his indentures issued by the Crown. The only means of solving our problem is to examine these and interpret the remainder of our evidence in this light.

If we exclude those that do not mention the word "bachelor" at all, the rest of John of Gaunt's indentures of retinue fall into two groups.

In the first are those in which the knight retained is merely described as a "bachelor" and there are no details to help elucidate the word's meaning.[35] In the second there are those in which the retainer is simply described as a knight but given benefits, in peace or war, defined as those available to other "bachelors" of his condition.[36] The key to the problem lies in the discovery of the nature of these benefits. There is considerable variety in the terms of indentures of retinue, the knight sometimes receiving an annual fee of the same amount in both peace and war, sometimes taking a fee in time of war only, or an increased fee then, sometimes receiving wages in war over and above his fee. But there is nothing in details of this sort peculiar to those described as "bachelors." One feature which is almost always found in common is *bouche de court* whenever the knight was summoned to the lord's household in time of peace — that is, the provision of free meat and drink while he remained there.[37] Was the "bachelor," then, a knight provided with free board by his lord? There are, however, indentures containing this feature which confer such other benefits as are available to "knights of his condition" but do not employ the word "bachelor" at all. In a number of other indentures the normal perquisites of the rank of "bachelor" include not merely *bouche de court* but also wages when serving in the household in time of peace. Nevertheless, we cannot say that those two benefits together form the distinguishing marks of the "bachelor" status, since there are three indentures [38] in which wages only, without *bouche de court*, are given to knights who thereby obtain the rank of "bachelor."

In the light of this discussion we must conclude that a "bachelor" in the retinue of John of Gaunt was a knight paid when he attended his lord in the household. Such knights formed a special group in association with the organization of the household, since one indenture refers to the "bachelors of the duke's chamber." [39] It is fortunate that enough indentures of John of Gaunt have survived to permit the development of these arguments. In the case of those of the Black Prince, there are too few to allow detailed comparisons between them. But the terms of those we have [40] do fit the conclusions from the indentures of John of Gaunt. In one, "bachelors" are described as belonging to the prince's chamber,[41] and in another the "bachelor's" fee was to be paid from the prince's wardrobe.[42]

From these details there emerges a picture of the "bachelors" as an inner group within the magnate's household, enjoying a position of closeness to their lord.[43] A number of them were accompanied in time of peace by one or more esquires and a chamberlain.[44] They administered their lord's affairs, helping to direct the central administration of his estates, acting as stewards of lordships, or holding the constableships of castles.[45] It is abundantly clear that they were a distinct group of retainers in whom their lord reposed a special trust. Occasionally they were knights of some wealth and importance — for instance, one of the Black Prince's "bachelors" was Sir William Shareshull, so described when a justice of the Common Pleas and then as Chief Justice of the King's Bench.

These conclusions are based on evidence from the fourteenth century. Do they also apply to those occasions in the previous century when lords used "bachelor" to describe a retainer? The difficulty here is that the necessary details as they appear in the Registers of the Black Prince and John of Gaunt are lacking. There is certainly compelling evidence in support of the view that the "bachelor" was a household knight. Some of this relates to the royal household. When in 1200–1201 King John wrote to the seneschals of Poitou and Normandy about the "bachelors" who had not done homage and fealty for their lands, he described them as being *de familia nostra*.[46] We also have a glimpse of their role in his household in the verse *History of William Marshal*. When in 1205 the Marshal refused to fight against Philip Augustus on the ground that the French king was his lord in Normandy, the English king sought the advice of his "bachelors," after failing to get the support and encouragement of his barons.[47] Clearly, he regarded his "bachelors" as a special group of followers who were under a duty to think only of his interests.[48] When the Crown pardoned the followers of the Earl of Gloucester for their rebellion in 1267, they were described variously as the earl's knights, "bachelors," esquires and yeomen.[49] If they had not been members of his household, it would not have been necessary to specify their connection with the earl, since the pardons were prefaced with the statement that they were granted at his request.

But does the word "bachelor" in these contexts possess precisely the same technical meaning as can be observed in the Registers of the Black Prince and John of Gaunt? There is some evidence to suggest that the "bachelor" was a knight serving at wages in the household. In 1216 a "bachelor" of King John was paid out of his chamber.[50] At the beginning of the fourteenth century Edward I was petitioned by one of his "bachelors," who told how, when he was knighted, Alexander I of Scotland had granted him a yearly fee out of his chamber and that he had received the payment since then.[51] On the other hand, an indenture between the Earl of Hereford and Sir Bartholomew Denefeud does not mention the payment of wages or fee within the household among the benefits he is to receive in common with the earl's other "bachelors."[52] The thirteenth-century evidence, therefore, is not as precise in meaning as that we find in the Registers of the Black Prince and John of Gaunt. Both these magnates employed the term "bachelor" in a technical sense of those knightly retainers who drew wages for their period of service in the household. We cannot be certain that other magnates who so described their retainers in the fourteenth century used the term in precisely the same sense. There is even less clarity about the situation in the thirteenth century, though there are indications that the king and at least some magnates followed practices similar to those of the Black Prince and John of Gaunt. But it is quite clear from all our evidence that throughout the thirteenth and fourteenth centuries the "bachelor" was a special kind of retainer associated, whatever the precise provenance of the payments made to him, with service in the household, and enjoying a more intimate relationship with his lord than did other knightly retainers who did not have his status.[53]

It is not difficult to reconstruct the links between this idea of the "bachelor" and the origins of the term. Its roots lay back in the time when kings and lords were little more than chiefs of war bands, followed by warriors eager for the rewards and booty which successful leadership could bring them. During the period when feudal tenures were emerging, it must have become increasingly necessary to differentiate between those followers who had been endowed with land and those who remained in their lord's company waiting for the same reward. At this stage the word "bachelor," hitherto employed to describe a poor rural proprietor, came to be transferred to the landless warrior. Someone in this position, of course, was generally young and unmarried; and it is this which accounts for one strand in the word's meaning.[54] At the same time, when the status of knighthood came to be defined, it was natural to regard the "bachelor" as a young warrior recently knighted or aspiring to knighthood. By the thirteenth century there are three distinct elements of meaning in the word — unmarried youth, nearness to the ceremony of knighthood, and membership in a close group within the lord's household. Which strand was dominant depended upon the identity of the person who was using the term. For a great lord the important fact was the "bachelor's" dependence on his favour and hence in this context the essential feature of the word is that it connotes membership in a lord's permanent following — that is, his household. Indeed, within this context this aspect of the word's meaning came to overshadow its other connotations: a "bachelor" might well be married and possess a landed estate. But, because he was a knight attending on his lord within the household, he was still called a "bachelor."

III

From this discussion there emerges some sort of continuous history of the household retinue throughout the Middle Ages. There appears to be an underlying similarity among the practices of Anglo-Saxon warlords, great Norman barons, and those of the Black Prince and John of Gaunt. In one sense this conclusion is not remarkable. Lordship was bound to gather a body of dependents. But, if we take this view, we face an important problem. Does it mean that the relationships of "bastard feudalism" were essentially endemic throughout the Middle Ages, rather than peculiar to the last two-and-a-half centuries of that era?

The answer to this question can only be approached by means of a careful elucidation of the meaning of "bastard feudalism." The bonds between lord and man were there expressed in three ways — the indenture of retinue which arranged for the payment of a fee or wages, the grant of an annnuity from landed revenues, and the wearing by a man of his lord's livery. The last was in a very real sense an extension of the practices of the household, since the lord was giving a man what his household attendants already wore. The grant of a fee from landed revenues was always possible and may well have existed to an extent greater, and at a time earlier, than the extant sources permit us to assert.[55] The real problem lies in the indenture of retinue. The conventional explanation for its appearance is that it arose out of the contract system of military service in the Welsh and Scottish wars, and then the larger operations in France in the fourteenth century. But this does not go deep enough. Our discussion of the term "bachelor" has shown how great lords already possessed household retinues in the thirteenth century. Why, then, did they not provide the leaders of the contingents they supplied the King by exploiting the resources of their households? The obvious answer is that, if they had tried to do so, as the King's wars outside England increased in scale, his needs could only have been met by an expansion, perhaps an enormous one, of household retinues. To attach a much larger number of knights and esquires to the household would have placed its finances under considerable strain, especially since, in order to ensure that the lord always had a call upon a man's services, it was necessary to retain him for life.

The solution was found in the variety of financial arrangements permitted in an indenture of retinue which made it possible to achieve some sort of compromise between the need of a lord for service and his retainer's expectation of financial reward. In the Registers of John of Gaunt, for example, we can see a diversity of such indentures. In some he gave fees out of landed revenues to those who were already "bachelors"; in most he retained knights and esquires for the first time. But, when he did this, the benefits conferred were tailored according to the status, need, and availability for service of the man retained. To some he gave wages in the household when summoned there in time of peace; some received *bouche de court* in addition, and others this alone. What thus emerged was an adaptable system, differing from the existing structure of the household. In time of peace some financial strain might still be felt, since the lord had to pay the fees due from landed revenues to those retained for life. But the effort to provide contingents in time of war through the enlargement of a paid household retinue would have been more difficult to administer. The result would have been an increase in the size of the peacetime establishment, and this would have raised the complicated problems of housing, and therefore of building, as well as those of fees and wages. There was, moreover, another reason why, from the late thirteenth century onwards, lords should decide to construct their retinues in some measure outside the household. Had they not done so, it might well have become more difficult to recruit dependents. The rules enforced in the courts of law placed serious practical obstacles in the face of an individual who had been granted a fee or annuity out of another's chamber and had not been paid.[56] If he wished to sue out a writ against a great lord who might have a number of seats throughout England, some probably remote from his own neighborhood, he had to take care to do so in the shire where the lord was resident at the time.

To treat "bastard feudalism" as the mere extension of relationships existing in an earlier period is thus to oversimplify. The expansionist wars of the late thirteenth and fourteenth centuries were bound to lead to restructuring of the relationships between lord and man. Household elements survived, however, and throughout the fourteenth century a great lord regarded the household as the core of his following. Knights and esquires who were granted fees out of landed revenues were given the opportunity to participate in the household, at least to the extent of receiving their keep when commanded to their lord's side. Above all, every leading magnate had a group of knights — his "bachelors" — who formed both part of the household and an inner ring within his following as a whole.

It is, of course, important to remember that the term "bachelor" is found in the fourteenth century only in the records of leading magnates. Indeed, most of our examples come from the Registers of the Black Prince and John of Gaunt. In those cases where the term was in use, we are dealing with households which maintained administrative traditions which must have gone back into the thirteenth century — that of the Black Prince, for example, linking up with the earlier royal household and that of John of Gaunt with those of Edmund and Thomas of Lancaster. The scraps of information that have survived in the case of other leading magnates at this time do not justify the assumption that they were surrounded by "bachelors" to the same extent as the Black Prince and John of Gaunt. Still less can we be certain that all great lords, whether in the thirteenth or the fourteenth century, used the term with precisely the same meaning. Nor did the term "bachelor" in the sense of a household knight have a currency outside the records of a leading magnate's administration. By the end of the fourteenth century in government records it had come to designate an ordinary knight who was not a banneret.[57] And Chaucer used it to denote a young unmarried man of the knightly class,[58] thus paving the way for the present-day meaning of the word.

The fact remains, however, that leading magnates still used "bachelor" during the fourteenth century, thus updating a concept which ultimately went back to the warrior bands of the early Middle Ages. Although there was an element of anachronism in this practice, it nevertheless gives us a glimpse into their attitudes toward the bonds which bound them to their retainers. In "bastard feudalism" new forms of the relationship between lord and man were created; but an older one, commemorated in the "bachelor," was incorporated within the new. In order to help provide for the military needs of the Crown, a magnate entered into indentures of retinue with knights and esquires who were not members of his household; but there were still some dependents organised within his household and paid out of its financial resources, among whom his "bachelors" formed a chosen inner group.

Through this discussion we obtain a valuable insight into the forces which bound both lords and men together in the mutual obligations of "bastard feudalism." Historians encounter little difficulty in documenting the main features of retaining by indenture, and the practices that went with it. But in explaining the wider social and political repercussions of what began as military arrangements, they are forced to fall back on "lordship" — the notion that a man was obligated to support his lord, and his lord him, by virtue of the grant and receipt of a money fee. The mutual obligations thus created were moral ones: there is no record of either lords or men endeavouring to enforce the terms of indentures of retinue in a court of law. We know, of course, that a man might take fees from more than one lord and that in actual fact the loyalties of "bastard feudalism" were fickle ones. Without their existence, however, and the general acceptance of the mutual obligation of loyalty on the parts of both lord and man, "bastard feudalism" would not have been feasible. It was in the war band that the duty of such loyalty first emerged, moving with more settled times into the baronial household. In "bastard feudalism" we see this transferred out of the household into the area of a lord's territorial influence. But the values on which this process depended for the effective maintenance of a lord's following remained those of a much earlier time. At the close of the fifteenth century the poet John Skelton lamented the cowardice of followers who had allowed their lord, the Earl of Northumberland, to be murdered:

> Alas! his gold, his fee, his annual rent,
> Upon that sort was ill-bestowed and spent.[59]

But did the standards of conduct by which he was judging them differ in any real sense from those we find in Wiglaf's speech before going to the help of Beowulf: "I remember that time at which we drank the mead, how in the beer-hall we pledged ourselves to our lord, who gave us the rings, that we would repay him for the war-equipments, the helmets and hard swords, if any need like this befell him." [60] Enormous as were the differences between the world of Beowulf and that of Skel-

127

ton, the basic nature of the bond of loyalty between lord and man remained the same. The Anglo-Saxon lord was the "bread-giver" (*hlaford*) for his retainer: the fourteenth-century magnate was the source of money. The two were linked by the "bachelor" and by the retainer who, though not paid out of the household, sometimes ate at his lord's table. Fourteenth-century magnates clung to the concept of the "bachelor," partly because their households had a contribution to make to the recruitment of men for the King's wars side by side with retaining by indenture, partly because they knew full well that the enlarging of their retinues which this entailed required the transference outside the household of values which had hitherto been confined within its limits. The concept of the "bachelor" was inherited from an earlier and more primitive age; but, in one sense, the "bastard feudalism" of fourteenth-century England was fashioned in its image.

NOTES

1. The standard account is still K. B. McFarlane, "Bastard Feudalism," *Bulletin of the Institute of Historical Research*, XX (1945), 161–80.
2. The Earl of Gloucester was paying money fees from his landed revenues before the end of the preceding reign (M. Altschul, *A Baronial Family in Medieval England, 1217–1314* (Baltimore, 1965), pp. 237, 279).
3. G. A. Holmes, *The Estates of the Higher Nobility in XIVth Century England* (Cambridge, 1957), Ch. 3.
4. *Ibid.*, p. 82.
5. J. M. W. Bean, *The Decline of English Feudalism, 1215–1540* (Manchester and New York, 1968), pp. 306–9.
6. P. Guilhiermoz, *Essai sur l'Origine de la Noblesse en France au Moyen Age* (Paris, 1902), pp. 244–47, esp. n. 8. Cf. L. Gautier, *Chivalry* (ed. J. Levron, trans. D. C. Dunning (New York and London, 1965), pp. 83–84, where it is argued that the "bachelors" of the legends of the eleventh and twelfth centuries were always knights.
7. The etymology of the word lies outside the confines of the present study. The examples supplied by Du Cange show that, when first met in Latin sources, it denotes a poor but free rural proprietor, and that this sense can be found contemporaneously with that discussed above. It is tempting to look for a connection between "bachelor" and the late Roman and Byzantine *buccellarius*. But this is dismissed by Guilhiermoz (*op. cit.*, pp. 110–15). The problem is worth further investigation.
8. Bede, *Opera*, ed. C. Plummer, 2 vols. (Oxford, 1896), I, 415.
9. The discussion by T. F. Tout, "The 'Communitas Bacheleriae Angliae'," *English Historical Review*, XVII (1902), 89–95 is now superseded by E. F. Jacob, *Studies in the Period of Baronial Reform and Rebellion, 1258–1267* (Oxford Studies in Social and Legal History, ed. P. Vinogradoff [Oxford, 1925]), pp. 126–43.

10. *Life of the Black Prince by the Herald of Sir John Chandos*, ed. M. K. Pope and E. C. Lodge (Oxford, 1910), p. 18. For similar language, see also p. 91.
11. *Rotuli Parliamentorum* (London, 1767–77), III, 144b.
12. *Ibid.*, III, 424a.
13. For discussions of these passages see Tout, *op. cit.*, pp. 91–92. That from Matthew Paris is also discussed by A. Tomkinson, "Retinues at the Tournament of Dunstable, 1309," *Eng. Hist. Rev.*, LXXIV (1959), 86, where it is suggested that the "bachelors" on this occasion may have been "a social grouping distinct from any division for combat." Paris' language, however, argues against this view. He states that one side consisted of "multi de militibus universitatis regni, qui se volunt bachelarios appellari." *Bachelarios* should surely be taken in conjunction with *universitatis regni*. They thought of themselves as representing the knighthood of England, combatting the aliens who formed the opposing side. This interpretation certainly fits with Paris' comment on the ill-repute occasioned by the conduct of the Earl of Gloucester, who fought against his fellow-countryman.
14. *Rotuli Chartarum* (Record Comm.), 59a and 102b.
15. *Rotuli litterarum patentium* (Record Comm.), I, 190b–191a.
16. N. Denholm-Young, *Collected Papers* (Cardiff, 1969), p. 130, n. 2.
17. *Calendar of Patent Rolls, 1266–72*, pp. 145–47.
18. *Calendar of Documents relating to Scotland*, ed. J. Bain, II, 255 (no. 995), 307 (no. 1205), 324 (no. 1274), 346 (no. 1346), 372 (no. 1418), 480 (no. 1789). In a number of cases an individual described himself as the King's "bachelor" (*ibid.*, 311 [no. 1225], 434 [no. 1630], 469 [no. 1737]). In the contemporary Song of Caerlaverock the word in its plural form is generally used to denote a body of knights (*The Roll of the Princes, Barons and Knights who attended King Edward I to the Siege of Caerlaverock in 1300*, ed. T. Wright [London, 1864], pp. 5 and 28). But, since the writer is commenting upon the composition of retinues, the term may also denote membership of a lord's following. On two other occasions the author definitely employs it in this sense (*ibid.*, pp. 24, 27).
19. Holmes, *op. cit.*, pp. 72–73 and 81, n. 8.
20. *Ibid.*, pp. 66–67, 70.
21. *Register of the Black Prince*, 4 vols. (London, 1930–33).
22. *John of Gaunt's Register, 1372–76*, ed. S. Armitage-Smith, 2 vols. (Royal Historical Society, Camden Third Series, Vols. XX, XXI [London, 1911]); *John of Gaunt's Register, 1379–1383*, ed. E. C. Lodge and R. Somerville (Royal Historical Society, Camden Third Series, Vols. LVI, LVII [London, 1937]). Indentures of retinue of John of Gaunt which have survived in the form of confirmations by the Crown enrolled on the Patent Rolls are printed by N. B. Lewis in *Camden Miscellany*, XXII, 87–112 (Royal Historical Society, Camden Fourth Series, Vol. I [London, 1964]).
23. John of Gaunt's son employed it in the case of one retainer shortly after his accession to the throne as Henry IV (*Sir Christopher Hatton's Book of Seals*, ed. L. C. Loyd and D. M. Stenton (Oxford, 1950), p. 340, no. 492).
24. *Cal. Pat. R., 1396–99*, p. 457; *Cal. Pat. R., 1399–1401*, p. 196.
25. *Cal. Pat. R., 1405–8*, p. 29.

26. T. Blount, *Nomo-Lexicon: A Law Dictionary* (London, 1670), *sub* "Bouche of Court."
27. N. Denholm-Young, *Seignorial Administration in England* (Oxford, 1937), p. 167; *Cal. Doc. Scot.*, II, 362–63 (no. 1407); *Black Prince's Register*, I, 128; Lewis, *op. cit.*, p. 89.
28. Public Record Office, Ancient Deeds, A. 11547.
29. *Cal. Pat. R., 1266–72*, pp. 145–47.
30. Public Record Office, Ancient Deeds, A. 11547.
31. *Ibid.*, A. 6404.
32. E.g., "a nostre tres cher bacheler monsire Walter Blount et a nostre cher et tres ame monsire Thomas Ponynges" (*John of Gaunt's Register, 1372–76*, II, 132).
33. For a convenient list see H. J. Hewitt, *The Black Prince's Expedition of 1355–1357* (Manchester, 1958), pp. 160–62.
34. See notes 19–20, above.
35. Lewis, *op. cit.*, pp. 105–6 (no. 27); 108–9 (no. 33); 111 (no. 38).
36. *John of Gaunt's Register, 1372–76*, I, nos. 782, 788, 819, 822, 832; *John of Gaunt's Register, 1379–83*, nos. 24, 29, 31, 32, 38, 39, 40, 41, 46, 49, 50.
37. Blount, *Nomo-Lexicon*, *sub* "Bouche of Court"; Denholm-Young, *Seignorial Administration*, p. 167, n. 2.
38. *John of Gaunt's Register, 1373–76*, I, nos. 835, 849, 855.
39. *John of Gaunt's Register, 1379–83*, I, no. 40.
40. *Black Prince's Register*, I, 83, 128–29; II, 45–46; IV, 12, 80, 83.
41. *Ibid.*, II, 45–46.
42. *Ibid.*, IV, 12. Another "bachelor" was on the rolls of array of the prince's household (*ibid.*, IV, 83).
43. In his description of the death-bed of the Black Prince, the Chandos Herald (*op. cit.*, p. 128) tells how the prince "made all his men come who had served him in his life and still gladly served him." All those then present are described as "earls, barons, and bachelors."
44. Denholm-Young, *Seignorial Administration*, p. 167; *Cal. Doc. Scot.*, II, 362–63 (no. 1407); *Black Prince's Register*, I, 128; Lewis, *op. cit.*, p. 89.
45. For the role of two of the Black Prince's "bachelors" in the administration of his estates, see T. F. Tout, *Chapters in the Administrative History of Mediaeval England* (Manchester, 1920–33), V, 387–89. A list of his "bachelors" (*ibid.*, V, 344, n. 7), which names fourteen of them, is badly defective, since over sixty can be traced in the Register.
46. *Rotuli Chartarum*, pp. 59a and 102b.
47. *L'Histoire de Guillaume le Marechal*, ed. P. Meyer, 3 vols. (Societé de l'Histoire de France [Paris, 1891–1901]), II, 110.
48. For a discussion of this incident and of the meaning of "bachelors," see S. Painter, *William Marshal* (Baltimore, 1933), pp. 142–43: "Apparently in this context the bachelors were men in the king's pay as semi-permanent members of his household as distinct from the barons who were present in fulfilment of their obligations as tenants-in-chief." But no reason is adduced for describing them as semi-permanent.
49. *Cal. Pat. R., 1266–72*, pp. 145–47.
50. *Rot. litt. pat.*, I, 190b–191a.

51. *Cal. Doc Scot.*, II, 469 (no. 1737).

52. *Ibid.*, 505 (no. 1899). He did, however, receive robes and saddles as the earl's other "bachelors" did, while his three grooms had wages. It is quite possible that the features of this indenture were exceptional, since it was made in occupied Scotland and, in return for his service, Sir Bartholomew was given land in Annandale for life.

53. The conclusion of this argument agrees broadly with that of the late Professor E. F. Jacob (*op. cit.*, pp. 127–33), although there is no evidence to support his suggestion that any of the "bachelors" of the Earl of Gloucester whom he discusses had been enfeoffed with land in return for service in that capacity (*ibid.*, pp. 132–33). The evidence discussed above certainly makes it impossible to accept the view of Mr. Denholm-Young that the "bachelor" was simply a knight who was not a banneret (see his *Collected Papers*, pp. 129–30; *History and Heraldry, 1254–1310* (Oxford, 1965), pp. 20–23; *The Country Gentry in the Fourteenth Century* (Oxford, 1969), *passim*.

54. Out of this, of course, developed its use, first in common usage and then as a formal term, in the universities to describe any senior student shortly intending to proceed to the doctorate (H. Rashdall, *The Universities of Europe in the Middle Ages*, 2nd ed. by F. M. Powicke and A. B. Emden, 3 vols (Oxford, 1936), I, 207, esp. n. 2).

55. Bean, *op. cit.*, pp. 308–9.

56. W. S. Holdsworth, *A History of English Law*, 4th ed., III (London, 1935), p. 152, esp. n. 6.

57. E.g., *Rot. Parl.*, III, 58a, where the term defines status for the graduated poll-tax.

58. Geoffrey Chaucer, *Complete Works*, ed. W. W. Skeat, 6 vols. (Oxford, 1894), I, 132 and 155 ("The Romaunt of the Rose," II, 918, 1469); IV, 3 ("The Prologue to the Canterbury Tales," I, 80). But the emphasis is on youth rather than knighthood, especially in "The Romaunt of the Rose."

59. John Skelton, *The Complete Poems*, ed. P. Henderson, 2nd ed. (London, Toronto, 1948), p. 7.

60. *Beowulf*, trans. J. R. Clark Hall; new ed. revised by C. L. Wren (London, 1950), p. 152.

The Medieval Lyric and Its Public

Stephen G. Nichols, Jr.

IN TWO RECENT ARTICLES on troubadour lyrics, I have explored several aspects of the role of the poet's consciousness in the language of this lyric tradition. The first article[1] was concerned with the nature of the emotional experience recounted by the speaker and which the reader is solicited to share. The second article[2] explored the way in which the troubadours' awareness of language and their role as creators transformed the rhetorical tradition they inherited from antiquity into a highly self-reflexive rhetoric. The explorations of these studies do help us to understand something of the nature of the troubadour lyric as personal expression, as individualistic art, but if left to stand alone, uncompensated, might well run the risk of falsifying our image of the medieval lyric. For medieval poetry, indeed medieval literature as a whole, was neither primarily created nor enjoyed privately, as is the case today,[3] but was, almost invariably, a public act with specific social implications. Morton Bloomfield has recently reminded us that:

> The changeover from a social to an individualistic art began, no doubt, in the West with the Renaissance of the twelfth century, but the process was long; it was not until the late eighteenth and early nineteenth centuries that it was widely victorious, although never perhaps completely so, for we still have occasional coronation odes and poems of that sort. The arts were primarily useful socially, and the emergence of nonuseful, purely decorative and expressive art which began in the twelfth century . . . was a long, slow process.[4]

That process had scarcely begun during the period which concerns us, and, indeed, there was little impetus for it to do so.

As we know from the various names by which poets were designated — bard, *fili*, skald, *scop, troubadour, trouvère,* even *jongleur* — the poet was not regarded as an individual who composed, but as a quasi-public official; bard, *fili*, skald: these are not neutral or descriptive terms like our poet, artist, novelist, essayist, but rather terms con-

133

noting a specific rank in society, a definite place in the carefully stratified hierarchy of medieval life. As Frank P. Chambers pointed out,
"The first purpose of art, of which the medieval mind was fully self-
conscious was usefulness";[5] accordingly, the poet had a definite social
function to perform, and his titles tended to reflect his status in society. Indeed, even within the *métier*, distinctions of a hierarchical
nature were drawn; the terms denoting rank were not judgments upon
the work of a given individual, but rather levels of achievement traditionally defined by the profession itself, to which a given individual
might aspire and ultimately attain by serving an apprenticeship. In
other words, distinctions of rank among *littérateurs* tended to be determined by the social process of the craft, rather than by individual
achievement, at least in the first instance. Thus Eleanor Knott defined
the difference between bard and *fili* hierarchically, in terms of the different levels of social usefulness each performed:

> . . . according to the early metrical tracts, the bard was sim-
> ply a poet and versifier; the *fili* a poet, but also a scholar and
> guardian of traditional knowledge; he is especially a prophet
> and a seer and can wield supernatural powers. In short, he
> somewhat resembles in his functions the druid of pre-Christian
> Gaul.[6]

Something of the same observation may be made regarding Old Norse
poetry. Little or nothing is known of the poets responsible for eddic
poetry (the oldest known old Norse verse), but its function is unmis-
takably that of preserving and glorifying the traditions prized by Norse
society; mythology, heroic legend, and folk wisdom. To the extent that
it reflects a heritage common to all in the society, it is anonymous,
like much early Irish poetry. The eddic poet (*fornskald*) was not considered the author of his poem, but rather a skilled functionary trained
in the preservation and oral composition of traditional material. His
talent lay in giving a skillful rendition of poems evolved over many
generations; the emphasis fell upon performance and accuracy, rather
than innovation.

In the ninth century, a new and more complex poetry suddenly
sprang into existence, a poetry which drew upon eddic for its source
material, but which differed profoundly from it in form and purpose.
From the ninth to the fourteenth century, Skaldic poetry flourished
as one of the most complex verbal art forms ever developed. Unlike
eddic poetry, Skaldic or court poetry was not anonymous. A well-

made Skaldic poem could mean fame and honour to the skald who composed it, so the more than two hundred skalds known to us by name took pains to associate their creation with their name. But the skalds were not primarily professional poets; they were mainly of good family, Icelandic Vikings who sought to make their fortune in the world before settling down to farm and raise a family in Iceland. Icelanders had a reputation as good poets as well as good fighters, so they were much in demand throughout Europe, especially to serve in the personal guard of kings and emperors. But even if their purpose was trading, the protection of king, prince, or chieftain could mean the difference between success or failure, as many incidents in the sagas testify.

Our knowledge of the mode of being of the Anglo-Saxon *scop* is far less complete than is the case for skald, bard, or *fili*. While some scholars have refused him any social importance at all, I tend to follow Morton Bloomfield's assessment that he did indeed perform an important social function, whatever his relative rank in society.[7] Like the skald, the *scop* was close to his lord, addressing him freely when the need arose, and exhibiting the same kind of fierce personal pride we have seen in the skald. Their art was an aristocratic one, composed in court to celebrate events important to the aristocratic milieu: victories, heroic deeds, funerals, acts of largesse. Most significant for our purposes is Bloomfield's assertion that "the Anglo-Saxon *scop* performed various important functions in his society and was attuned to the needs of his audience."[8] Furthermore, his social status and function was determined by his relationship to that audience, his ability to respond to its needs in a satisfactory manner.

The position of Guillaume IX as the first troubadour has tended to lend an aristocratic aura to the troubadour *métier* as a whole. In fact, the majority of troubadours — as Jeanroy long ago pointed out — were professional poets who earned their living by their wits and their talent, and who were forced to live the life of the mendicant vagabond, wandering from one court to another looking for sustenance that could only be temporary. This by no means presupposes inferior social origins on the part of the troubadours: many were of the nobility or the bourgeoisie. In fact, all social classes, with the exception of the peasant class who had neither the means nor the freedom to acquire the requisite learning, were represented among the troubadours. Rather, it is a commentary on the fact that the poetry, more than the poet, was prized, at least in the Midi.

The *trouvères* of the north were more fortunate than the troubadours, perhaps because of the generally more favorable economic conditions prevailing there. The thirteenth century saw many minstrels comfortably established as a matter of course in the courts of wealthy patrons, both bourgeois and aristocrat. Adenet le Roi, Henri d'Andeli, Jean de Condé, and a host of other *trouvères* occupied established positions in the hierarchy of courtly life. We know from the records of these courts that the *trouvères* were, at times, overseers of a number of lesser literary functionaries: secretaries, jongleurs, and minstrels. When a lord like Guy de Dampierre, Adenet le Roi's patron, travelled, he was sure to include his minstrel in his retinue. Contemporary texts recount how well fêted minstrels found themselves at the courts where their lords stopped along the way. The northern *trouvère* who had the good fortune to be employed in this way occupied a position much more analogous to the bard or skald than that of his southern counterpart. This does not mean that all *trouvères* were comfortably situated court poets. The testimony of a Rutebeuf or a Villon all too frequently conveys the fact that in the north, as in the Midi, poetry was not the most secure of trades.

The condition of the troubadour or the *trouvère* cannot be discussed without reference to that thorny question of the distinction between troubadour/*trouvère* and *jongleur*. Even in the Middle Ages, the terms were loosely enough employed to be synonymous at times. Strictly speaking, troubadour signified "creator" in the musical and poetic sense of the term. *Jongleur*, on the other hand, designated an acrobatic entertainer purely and simply. In the eighth century, when the term was created (med. Latin **joculare*), it almost certainly signified nothing more than an acrobatic entertainer of no social stature.[9] However, just as the *scop* had to respond to the needs of his audience, or the bard to his, so the *jongleur* ultimately had to supplement his acrobatic repertoire by singing lyric poetry composed by troubadours. Gradually, it was his ability to sing such poems well that guaranteed a *jongleur* access into the most desirable châteaux, with the result that the terms *jongleur* and troubadour became almost interchangeable. There were, of course, *jongleurs* who continued to specialize in animal acts, juggling, tight-rope walking, and the rest, just as there were *jongleurs* who excelled in playing and singing. Nonetheless, a number of texts of the twelfth and thirteenth centuries make quite plain the social distinction between *jongleur* and troubadour. Troubadours did not appreciate being confused with *jongleurs*, who were socially déclassé, and considered disreputable.[10] Particularly gifted *jongleurs* aspired to be troubadours in their own rights, and there is evidence to suggest that troubadours would, for a price, train talented *jongleurs* in the fine art of composition. More than one well-known troubadour started his career as a *jongleur*.[11]

What is important for us, however, is the fact that, from the viewpoint of the audience, the talent of the singer was at least as appreciated as that of the poet,[12] and the strictures of Guillem de Cabrera to his *jongleur* contain references to the performance of poems, but little comment which we could term literary criticism, properly speaking. Thus the *jongleur* as well as the troubadour had a hand in forming the poetic taste of the audience. But ultimately, it was the troubadour rather than the *jongleur* who had the authority, training, and inspiration to develop the poetic tradition which has come down to us.

More significantly, if the aristocratic patrons prized the singing of the song as highly as the creation, they nonetheless were cognizant of the need for a creator, and rewarded the troubadour accordingly. However fine a distinction might be drawn in practice between *jongleur* and troubadour, it was the troubadour who occupied the more enviable position, the troubadour who left his name to posterity. *Jongleurs* could hope to better their situation only by becoming troubadours, but troubadours could occasionally, and in fact did rise to positions of authority and fortune, although few had so meteoric a career as Foulquet de Marseilles, who became Bishop of Toulouse.

A common phenomenon that was true throughout the period covered in this brief sketch of the social situation of medieval poets was a two-step evolution of poets from anonymous guardians of and spokesmen for the mythopoeic "historical" tradition of society as a whole — generally preserved in epic poetry — into highly skilled, publicly known creators of conventionalized lyric for the aristocratic or ruling class. In this evolution, their art ceases to be a reflection of the traditions of society as a whole, and turns progressively to reflecting the tastes and aspirations of a specific, elite minority: a minority which is flattered to fill its leisure time seeing itself reflected in the quasi-magical authority of poetic language, which was still viewed with the awe that nascent societies accord to the "written" word.[13] More important still, we have seen that the livelihood of bard, *fili*, skald, *scop*, troubadour, or *trouvére* increasingly depended upon his ability to compose lyric poetry for this purpose, even though he might still be required to maintain the earlier kind of poetry as part of his repertoire.

In the context of these societies as a whole, what takes place on the literary scene may be understood as a reflection of the kind of transformation that was occurring generally as the earlier tribal constellations gave way, in the High Middle Ages, to a more sophisticated socio-theological order based upon monarchy or rule by a divinely ordained elite. In place of the earlier heroic society of Celtic and Germanic antiquity there emerged a highly stratified and hierarchical concept of world order. This theocratically oriented society based itself squarely upon "the Church, which itself, however, was governed on the monarchic principle, according to which original power was located in one supreme authority, from which all power in the public sphere was derived — a system which, for want of a better name, [may be called] the descending or theocratic theme of government and law." [14]

This system was predicated upon the subjection of all Christians to higher authority, not in so far as they were natural men, but in their condition as Christians. Since every Christian was baptized, and baptism bore the ontological meaning of regeneration from the condition of natural man into the condition of a Christian "who moved, so to speak, on a level different from that of naturalness," [15] the Christian had to be ready to accept the authorities God had placed over him. As Saint Paul says, "because whatever power there is comes from God, every soul should be *subjected* to the higher authorities, from which follows that it is a necessity for the sake of good functioning of the body that individual Christians should be *subjects* of princely power." [16] Faith thus became synonymous with obedience, obedience not only to divine authority, but also to what in this system was the same thing, i.e., secular authority: "the element of obedience presupposed the existence of faith." [17]

Obviously, such a doctrine stressed the inequality of men, vesting a divine aura in constituted authority. By virtue of holding public rank, some members of society were superior to others, while within the ranks of authority there were descending degrees of importance from the king on down. As Ullmann points out: "the individual's standing within society was based upon his office or his official function: the greater it was, the more scope it had, the weightier it was, the more rights the individual had." [18] Thus, as the power structure crystallized around the courts, the role of the poet became one of reflecting the needs of this restricted audience. And, though the aristocrats had difficulty in focussing on the *personae minores,* the poets — *personae minores* though they were — found it natural to share the perspective of their patrons. Each lord, no matter how minor a role he played in the large scale of things, exercised supreme authority on his own domain, and it became the function of the court poet to celebrate this authority and the tastes it affected, just as earlier the poet had been charged with renewing and propagating the mythopoeic origins and "history" of society.

The world of the court and cloister, then, was the world for and in which the poets of the High Middle Ages lived and composed. If we accept, as I think we must, the responsiveness of the court poets to the tastes and needs of the elite audience for whom they wrote, we may come to understand something of the imaginative life of these societies by looking at the lyric poetry they encouraged. In particular, let us look at poems of life and death, two of the essential experiences faced by men in any society, and traditionally, the experiences that poets have consistently tried to plumb in western literature.

The worlds of court and cloister were, according to all indication, extremely circumscribed, limited in terms of individual freedom of movement and perhaps even expression. Love and death, as represented in the Celtic, Germanic, and Romance lyric traditions, share a common bond of close converse with the Other World, a milieu uncircumscribed by the harsh reality of space and time, and recommending itself to the unrestricted play of the imagination by its very vagueness. Almost all the literary traditions which here concern us expressed the need to evoke the unrestricted emotional life of the Other World. I use the term "vagueness" with regard to the boundaries of this world, and indeed, by comparison with the closed world of the court, it could not be specifically fixed in space or time. This does not mean that the Other World was understood as an unreal, purely imaginative, place. On the contrary, the Other World was potentially all around medieval man, and seems to have been consistently identified with nature, as opposed to the world of everyday life centered in the court.

"To seek out and watch and love Nature, in its tiniest phenomena as in its grandest, was given to no people so early and so fully as to the Celt," wrote Kuno Meyer. He recognized that the sensitivity to nature was one of emotional identification rather than the conventionalized description found in classical antiquity:

It is a characteristic of [early Irish] poems that in none of them do we get an elaborate or sustained description of any scene or scenery, but rather a succession of pictures and images, which the poet, like an impressionist, calls up before us by light and skillful touches. Like the Japanese, the Celts were always quick to take an artistic hint; they avoid the obvious and the commonplace; the half-said thing to them is dearest.[19]

For an anonymous Irish monk of the ninth century, the solitude to be found in nature is seen as a means of purifying himself from the defilement of social existence before going to meet death:[20]

1   All alone in my little cell, without a single human being along with me: such a pilgrimage would be dear to my heart before going to meet death.

2   A hidden secluded little hut for forgiveness of all evil; a conscience unperverted and untroubled directed towards holy Heaven.

3   Sanctifying a body trained in good habits: trampling like a man upon it, with eyes feeble and tearful for the forgiveness of my passions.

. . . .

8   Dry bread weighed out — let us carefully cast our faces down — ; water from a bright and pleasant hillside, let that be the draught you drink.

To the secular spirit, however, nature has quite a different connotation. In the "Lament of the Old Woman of Beare,"[21] nature is precisely the state from which age now excludes her, much as *vieillesse* is forbidden entry into the *Garden of Delight* of Guillaume de Lorris. When she was young, the Old Woman seemed a part of nature; now she grows old and decays, unable to regenerate herself as nature can:

1   Ebb-Tide has come to me as to the sea; old age makes me yellow; though I may grieve thereat, it approaches its food joyfully.

2   I am Buí, the Old Woman of Beare; I used to wear a smock that was ever renewed; today it has befallen me, by reason of my mean estate, that I could not even have a cast-off smock to wear.

. . . .

8   When my arms are seen, all bony and thin! — the craft they used to practise was pleasant: they used to be about glorious kings.

9   When my arms are seen, all bony and thin, they are not, I declare, worth raising around comely youths.

10   The maidens are joyful when they reach May-day; grief is more fitting for me: I am not only miserable, but an old woman.

    . . . .

15   The wave of the great sea is noisy; winter has begun to raise it: neither nobleman nor slave's son do I expect on a visit today.

    . . . .

17   Alack-a-day[?] that I sail not over youth's sea! Many years of my beauty are departed, for my wantonness has been used up.

    . . . .

34   It is well for an island of the great sea: flood comes to it after its ebb; as for me, I expect no flood after ebb to come to me.

The most poignant part of the Old Woman of Beare's lament is her recognition that her exclusion from the Other World of nature and love, the world of her youth, is itself a part of the natural order in which all things age and decay. Unlike Jean de Meung's *La Vieille* or Villon's *La Belle Heaulmière*, however, the Old Woman of Beare finds greater consolation in looking forward to death, than in looking back to life. Lest her vision of the Other World of death be distracted by gazing too long on this world, she has sacrificed her sight:

26   My right eye has been taken from me to be sold for a land that will be for ever mine; the left eye has been taken also, to make my claim to that land more secure.

Running throughout the Old Woman's lament is a quiet pride in the man she has loved. It is typical of Old Irish poetry that the man and not the woman is the primary love object. This explains why so many Irish love lyrics take the form of women's laments. Thus the ninth-century poetess Líadan laments her love Cuirithir. She herself renounced the life they shared together by entering the closed world of the convent. Religious fervor could not however overcome her passion for Cuirithir; the communion of needing and being needed; of giving and taking; of comforting and being comforted. Trying to express what she has walled up by taking the veil, she gives us one brief, but graphic glimpse of their previously shared freedom:

> 7   Forest music used to sing to me beside Cuirithir, together with the sound of the fierce sea.[22]

Her vocation bids her love all men equally, but her passion exalts Cuirithir above all others; her religion commands her to live for Christ, but her love obliges her to die for Cuirithir:

> 9   Conceal it not: he was my heart's love, even though I should love all others besides.

> 10   A roar of fire has split my heart; without him for certain it will not live.

Occasionally, we find poems directly soliciting lover or mistress to come to the Other World. In such poems, the emphasis falls less upon the natural world as such than on an idealized *paradis terrestre*. Physical perfection, perfect union, harmony, and plenty are cited among the attractions of this paradise. Such poems are precious, for they undoubtedly helped to reinforce the idea of the Other World as tangible and attainable: [23]

> 1   Fair Lady, will you go with me to a wondrous land where there are stars? Hair there is as the primrose top, and the whole body the colour of snow.

> 2   In that land "mine" and "thine" do not exist; teeth are white there; brows are black; all our hosts there are a delight to the eye; every cheek there is the color of foxglove.

> 3   The surface of every plain is purple[?]; a blackbird's eggs are a delight to the eye; though fair the prospect of the plain of Ireland, it is desolate after familiarity with the Great Plain.

> 4   Though you think the beer of Ireland intoxicating, more intoxicating is the beer of the Great Land; a wonderful land is the land of which I speak; the young do not die there before the old.

> 5   Gentle sweet streams water the earth there; the best of mead and wine is drunk; fine and flawless are the inhabitants of that land; conception there is without sin or guilt.

> 6   We see everyone on every side, and no one sees us: it is the darkness caused by Adam's sin which hides us from those who would count us.

7   O woman, if you come to my firm folk, a crown of gold
will be on your head; fresh pork, ale, milk and drink shall
you have with me there, Fair Lady.

From the fourteenth century on, the Irish love lyric fell under the influence of Provence, thereby evidencing, as one might expect, a slightly different orientation from that we have seen above.[24] Now it is the man who sings of hidden or unattainable love, and the emphasis is less upon the Other Worlds, than upon courtly forms of address in this.

There is another kind of continuity besides that of form and attitude toward the Other World in Early and Middle Irish love lyric. This is the continuity of the audience: all of the poems discussed evoke the emotional life of those in court and cloister who could afford the luxury of indulging their passions; of riding out to the forest and sea. The lyric creates another world from that of reality, a world which could be shared and appreciated only by those who by birth and education could both understand the intricacies of the poetic language that expressed it and empathize with the emotional experience which motivated it. The poetry was more than entertainment. It demonstrated a meta-world to which comparatively few could aspire, but those who shared it derived a sense of difference, of superiority to other men, even stronger than that accorded by the tangible perquisites of the aristocracy. The love poet's main function resided in his ability to create and perpetually renew this meta-world of emotion, thereby confirming, if not widening, the gulf which separated court and cloister from the rest of society.

No matter how important a social role the Irish lyric may play, it claims always to represent the subjective emotional experience of the poet, who predicates the possibility of communication with the reader on the presupposition that the reader can share the emotional experience on the basis of his own life. Old Norse poetry relies to a far lesser extent than Irish or Romance upon such subjective interplay. Eddic poetry, especially, eschews the private emotional world of a knowing poet-subject, in favor of imaginative re-creation of the experience of characters equidistant from poet and audience. Often the characters inhabited a mythical or legendary world. It is the task of the poet, nevertheless, to take these Other World characters and make them participate realistically in a world which the audience could recognize as its own. The Other World of Celtic and Romance does

143

not figure in Old Norse poetry, perhaps because the attitudes toward nature are so different.

Since the Eddic poems are primarily narrative, their treatment of love and death is consonant with the tenor of the narrative setting. Given the subject matter of the great heroic legends, love and death intermingle in complex patterns of lust and vengeance. Love, more often than not, is expressed as a lament for a slain hero, or else serves as motivation for a bloody act of revenge. Death must be faced stoically, and frequently embraced joyfully, as the only possible alternative to life with dishonor. In all cases, emotions of any sort are understated. Situations of great emotional potential require filling-in by the audience, so low-keyed do they appear in the text. Very frequently, their effectiveness is the greater for the dramatic understatement. So with the *Atlakviða*, when Gunnarr and Hogni have been ambushed at Attila's court. Gunnarr wants his brother's heart cut out of his breast as a guarantee that the secret of the Nibelung hoard will die with them. Attila tries to trick Gunnarr by bringing in the heart of a lesser man. Both Gunnar's and Hogni's behavior, as drawn with extreme reticence by the poet, in the face of death tell us much about the Old Norse emotional ethic: [25]

> 20   They asked the brave one
> if he would for his life,
> lord of Goths,
> pay with gold.

> 21   "Hogni's heart
> must lie in my hand,
> cut bleeding from the breast
> of the brave knight,
> with cruel-slitting knife
> from the king's son."

> 22   They cut the heart
> from Hialli's breast
> bleeding, and laid it on a platter
> and brought that before Gunnarr.

> 23   Then Gunnarr said,
> leader of men,
> "Here I have the heart
> of Hialli the coward,
> unlike the heart
> of Hogni the brave:
> it quivers much

144

as it lies on the platter —
it quivered twice as much
when it lay in his breast."

24   Hogni laughed then
as they cut to the heart
the living sculptor of scars —
to cry out never entered his thoughts.
Bleeding, they laid it on a platter
and brought it before Gunnarr.

25   Glorious, Gunnarr spoke,
spear-skilled Niflung:
"Here I have the heart
of Hogni the brave,
unlike the heart
of Hialli the coward:
it hardly quivers
as it lies on the platter —
it quivered not even so much
when it lay in his breast."

Poems of this sort celebrate a particular kind of ethic; aside from re-creating in a dramatic fashion a legendary setting, they make a value judgment of a way of life: Gunnarr and Hogni are more than heroes, they are exempla for a way of life which should be emulated by those who hear and appreciate the poem. Skaldic poetry, on the other hand, strikes the modern reader as much less concerned with problems of the heroic ethic, much more oriented toward commentary on the skald's own experience, or that of the person to whom the poem is dedicated. Although the source material for the poetic tropes and figures is often drawn from mythological or heroic lore, the immediate occasion for a Skaldic poem almost invariably springs from present experience, the poet's or his patron's.

This in no way means to suggest that Skaldic verse is subjective in the sense that Celtic and Romance lyric may be understood as subjective. On the contrary, the Skaldic tends to be highly formalistic, even when treating subjects of great emotional content. The formalism lends itself to *drápa*,[26] like the *Ragnarsdrápa, Hautslong,* or *Husdrápa* which try to transpose into poetic *tours de force* the magnificence of decorated presentation shields or newly built halls. In the case of encomniastic poems, visions, or laments, the formalism tends to objectify the emotional components, to the point where they may be accepted with that dignity so highly prized by the Norse.

So for example, in the *Gisli Saga*, when Gisli wishes to express his love and confidence in his wife's fidelity, having been told that she seems on the verge of betraying him, he says:

"Put your mind at rest, for it will not be treachery from
Aud that will be the cause of my death." And he spoke a verse:
> "Loud they tongue my lady,
> Lords of masted fjord-elks;
> Hoards she, say they, hard thoughts
> Heart deep for her partner.
> I have seen that single
> Sorrow keeps she, mourning;
> True drops, never traitor
> Tears fall from my dear one."

The stanza contains little of the conscious obscurity so beloved of skalds, containing, in fact, but one kenning. Nonetheless, Gisli carefully couches it in descriptive terms, concentrating on Aud's situation, and letting us infer his confidence in her from the almost dispassionate image he evokes of the sorrowing woman.

An even more striking example of the objectivity with which skalds treat emotion may be seen in the most famous lament in all Skaldic poetry: the poem composed by Egill Skallagrímsson on the death of two of his sons. The *Sonatorrek* was composed in *kviðuháttr*, one of the simpler, more popular Skaldic measures, and yet it still seems strangely formal to our ears.

Could we but read the entire poem, and other samples of Skaldic verse, it would become strikingly apparent that in the last analysis, the verse itself occupies the central focus of attention (and in this respect it is not unlike troubadour poetry). Egill's first concern is that his grief may prevent him from composing a song worthy of his subject. Indeed, the first three stanzas refer to the poetic act, and half of stanza two consists of a kenning for poetry. Again and again in reading Skaldic verse, our attention is diverted from the subject by the necessity of solving the riddling kennings. In a poem like Braggi's *Ragnarsdrápa*, the poetry itself becomes the subject to the extent that Braggi tries to outdo by the splendor of his verse the magnificence of the presentation shield he describes. The feat of re-creating this shield in verse renders the gift even more noteworthy, thereby doubly flattering its donor. Reading these poems in English, we can never be fully cognizant of their formal virtuosity, for the English translation is already in large measure a transposition of the order and a resolution of the allusive obscurities.[27] Indeed, one might well speak not of translating Skaldic verse, but of solving it. So intricate were the complexities of this verse in fact that late night or early morning hours, when the poet could work without distraction, were preferred for creating this art.

Thus, despite the many differences in form and content between the Old Norse and Irish treatment of love and death in the lyric tradition, the place of the poet in society and the audience to which he appealed were analogous. To appreciate the formal intricacies of Skaldic verse required training and education available only to the better families in Iceland. We have already seen, in the first part of the paper, that good birth was a prerequisite for recommendation to the courts abroad where the best reward for the skald's art might be expected. Finally, it required the leisure and social training of a courtier or wealthy landowner to devote an evening's drinking and entertainment to the appreciation of a Skaldic poem. These were not simply recited, but discussed technically and critically by an audience highly skilled in the interpretation of such poems. Viewed as social acts, composing and interpreting a Skaldic poem were conscious assertions that Skald and audience possessed attributes of birth and education which united them as a class and set them above ordinary men, just as surely as the heroic feats of Gunnar of Hliðerend, or Egill Skallagrímsson, or Gisli set them apart from the common run of men.

Provençal and Old French lyric were formalistic arts, too, but unlike Skaldic poetry, they were practised by professional poets, men who owed their admission to court to their art rather than to social equality with their audience. The professionalism of the troubadour and *trouvère* is an important consideration to bear in mind when considering their work. As professionals, they possessed specialized training in the effects language could produce and had, as apprentices, been initiated into the mysteries of when and how to use these effects. As court "functionaries," they were conscious of the degrees of rhetoric appropriate for a given subject or occasion. Indeed, their language can be viewed — in its social setting — as another of the many systems of signs of which court life consisted, along with heraldic devices, court dress, etiquette, forms of address, and so on.

In this connection it is beneficial to keep in mind that Old French and Provençal lyric were not only in the court, but *of* the court. Edmond Faral and Roger Dragonetti, to name but two literary historians who have studied this question, remind us of the extensive formal consistency of this work, a formalism concerned less with the intrinsic complexity of the poetry, than with assuring harmony of language, theme, and setting.[28] This in part explains the repeated assertions by troubadour and *trouvère* alike of the appropriateness of a given *chanson* to the subject treated:

> Le vers est simple, et je le vais affinant, sans mot grossier, impropre ou postiche: il est tout entier bâti de telle sorte que je n'y ai employé que des termes élégants; et toujours il va s'améliorant s'il se trouve quelqu'un qui le chante et le présente bien.[29]

These theories of stylistic appropriateness presume some critical analysis of the subject matter even before the song was composed. Thus it is that Romance lyric fostered such a wide range of genres. Even within the bounds of a single genre, variations of mood, tone, and form may be observed. Indeed, considering only the songs devoted to love, we find that the genres and sub-genres, in themselves, constitute a wide-ranging analysis of the multiple facets of this complex subject. *Pastourelles* generally affect the light, lively rhythms of the dance, rhythms appropriate to the inconsequence of the subject:

> L'autrier jost'una sebissa
> Trobei pastora mestissa,
> De joi e de sen massissa,
> Si cum filla de vilana,
> Cap' e gonel' e pelissa
> Vest e camiza treslissa,
> Sotlars e caussas de lana.[30]

Cansos, on the other hand, concerned with graver metaphysical implications of love, affect a proportionately weightier tone and often a more complex formal structure.

But the concern to find an appropriate style for the particular mood or facet of life to be sung does not mean that troubadours or *trouvères* had their attention focussed solely upon technical matters. Formal concerns do not prevent the troubadours from turning their gaze to nature with as much, or more, sensitivity as the Irish bards. Indeed, the troubadours go even further than their Irish counterparts in developing a metaphysical identification with nature. In both the songs quoted, the poet finds in the natural world the meaning and motivation for his song. Nature itself is the meta-world in which he can seek solace; there he can evoke the spiritual presence of the *domna* if her physi-

148

cal presence be denied him. The song itself becomes her being, keeping him company through enforced separation. It is always in a natural setting that a Bernart de Ventadorn or a Jaufré Rudel desire to lie with their *domna*; and of course, orchard and field are the traditional venues of the alba. In the longer lyric genres, particularly the *lai*, nature assumes overtly the form of the Other World, the Celtic realm of faery which, as in Marie de France's *Lanval*, stands in bold relief to the closed milieu of the court. Such an extensive contrast cannot be achieved in short lyrics, although the opposition of closed and open worlds is at least implicit in most troubadour and *trouvère* lyric. Whether the irony be conscious or unconscious, the lyrics, no matter how much they may claim to identify with the open-ended natural world, are by virtue of their form, inspiration, and setting very much products of the closed society of the court. Perhaps, like Mallarmé's *Brise marine*, the poems recognize the listeners' desire to contemplate an imaginative escape to exotic parts, knowing full well the impossibility of realizing the ideal, but accepting the need to overlay the flat certainties of everyday life with the mystery of another world, elusively tangential to this. Put another way, the Romance love lyric had the effect of removing love from the world of everyday commerce, where it ran the risk of being accessible to anyone with adrenaline glands, and of placing it securely in a world accessible only to those possessing the sensitivity, intellect, and breeding to appreciate the poems which gave access to it.

A paradoxical, but nevertheless healthy, counter to the flight of love lyric away from the world was effected by poetry devoted to visions of death. From the late thirteenth century on, the poetry of death turned a fascinated eye upon the horrors of death-in-life, paying special attention to everything transient and vulnerable. All that seemed to epitomize power, opulence, privilege in the world — in short church and court — served as fair game for ecstatic visions of imminent corruption and putrefaction. Great comfort seemed to be derived from the assurances of the *ubi sunt* theme, employed with endless variation, that no living thing had ever escaped the end common to prince and serf alike. In light of the sense of hierarchy so strongly ingrained in medieval life, one of the greatest shudders — not wholly unpleasurable we must imagine — felt when contemplating death must have been the novel realization that one's partner in the dance of death might well be a commoner. Integration of social classes, unthinkable in life, was one of the novelties of death. "While it reminded the spectators of the frailty and the vanity of earthly things, the death-dance at the same time preached social equality as the Middle Ages understood it. Death levelling the various ranks and professions." [31]

The recognition of death as a social equalizer, perhaps more than any other aspect, separates this treatment of death from the Old Norse. The death of Hogni, quoted earlier, expresses the belief, common to heroic codes, that far from abolishing social and ethical distinctions, death confirms them once for all. Hialli was a base-born coward in life — coward, in part because he was base-born — and in death his quivering heart could not possibly be mistaken for that of Hogni. The manner of one's death confirmed the quality of a hero's life; death meant apotheosis, particularly if it became the subject of a song. The Old Irish tradition preserves examples of the *ubi sunt* theme, like the "Lament of the Old Woman of Beare," as well as ascetic hymns to death on the order of the anonymous hermit's song we began with. Even so, the emphasis in the Irish lyrics of death in no way approaches that which we find developing on the continent.

In the Old Irish, as in the Old Norse, death's dominion is clearly separated from this world. What is at once so fascinating and so repellent about the death esthetic developed in France and the Netherlands in the fourteenth and fifteenth centuries is the ease and plausibility with which it is implanted on the world of reality. Death becomes a mode of life while, conversely, all life is viewed in terms of death. Huizinga's description of the Parisian crowds flocking to the charnal houses of the Cemetery of the Holy Innocents makes this point all too clearly:

> Day after day, crowds of people walked under the cloisters, looking at the figures and reading the simple verses, which reminded them of the approaching end. In spite of the incessant burials and exhumations going on there, it was a public lounge and a rendezvous. Shops were established before the charnal-houses and prostitutes strolled under the cloisters. A female recluse was immured on one of the sides of the church. Friars came to preach and processions were drawn up there. A procession of children only (12,500 strong, thinks the Burgher of Paris) assembled there, with tapers in their hands, to carry an Innocent to Notre Dame and back to the churchyard. Even feasts were given there. To such an extent had the horrible become familiar. [32]

No single lyric exemplifies these aspects of the death esthetic so well perhaps as *L'épitaphe de François Villon*, known also as the *ballade des pendus.* Taking his cue from the macabre spectacle — so much a part of medieval landscape — of the rotting corpses of criminals left dangling on their gibbets as a warning to would-be malefactors, Villon speaks, in this poem, as such a hanged man:

> Frères humains qui après nous vivez
> Vous nous voyez ci attachés cinq, six:
> Quant de la chair que trop avons nourrie,
> Elle est pieça dévorée et pourrie,
> Et nous, les os, devenons cendre et poudre.[33]

By establishing a we-you relationship between the hanged men and the audience, Villon transforms the experience of the poem into a *danse macabre* in which the poet and his fellow *pendus* link hands, metaphorically speaking, with the living audience.

The immediate and desired result is to awaken the audience's awareness of its own involvement in the acts of condemnation and atonement the hanged undergo. Villon insists that the poet, the anonymous *pendus*, and audience are brothers — the fact that the ones were condemned and punished while the others have not been is irrelevant. As humans we are all potentially guilty, and the *pendus* differ from us only in having preceded us; they are potential extensions of ourselves.

The graphic imagery used by Villon derives at once from his characteristic realistic perception and from the surrealistic horror school of painting then coming into vogue:

> La pluie nous a tués et lavés,
> Et le soleil dessechés et noircis;
> pies, corbeaux, nous ont les yeux cavés,
> Et arraché la barbe et les sourcils.
> Jamais nul temps nous ne sommes assis;
> Puis ça, puis la, comme le vent varie,
> A son plaisir sans cesser nous charrie,
> Plus becquetés d'oiseaux que dés a coudre.

Villon's astuteness lies in perceiving that dessicated, blackened, and maimed corpses ceaselessly swaying to and fro at the pleasure of the winds do constitute a *langage*, an act of social expression, just as surely as the more palatable panache and bustle of a court tourney. The fact that Villon's message — the equality of all men in frailty and sin — and his world — the sordid and squalid demi-monde of Paris — differ from the world and world-view of a Bernart de Ventadorn or a Marie de France, simply demonstrates the range of social commen-

151

tary provided by medieval lyrics of love and death in France. It is not a question of contradiction, but rather of the force of poetry in defining and expressing the variety and vitality of medieval thought.

NOTES

1. "Towards an Aesthetic of the Provençal *Canso*," in *The Disciplines of Criticism*, ed. Demetz, Greene, and Nelson (New Haven: Yale University Press, 1968), 349–74.
2. "Rhetorical Metamorphosis in the Troubadour Lyric," in *Mélanges Pierre LeGentil*, to be published in the winter of 1972.
3. See George Steiner, "A Note on Literature and Post-History," in *Festschrift zum achtzigsten Geburtstag von Georg Lukács*, ed. Frank Benseler (Berlin: Neuwied, 1965).
4. Morton Bloomfield, "Understanding Old English Poetry," in *Essays and Explorations* (Cambridge, Harvard University Press, 1970), p. 61.
5. *The History of Taste, An Account of the Revolutions of Art Criticism and Theory in Europe* (New York: Columbia University Press, 1932), p. 10.
6. Eleanor Knott and Gerard Murphy, *Early Irish Literature* (London: Routledge and Kegan Paul, 1967). p. 21. The element of magic and foresightedness of the *fili* is graphically described in the introduction to an anonymous 9th-century poem from the Finn cycle: "Finn learnt the three arts which establish a poet in his prerogatives, namely . . . prophetic marrow-chewing, . . . divination which illuminates . . . and incantation from heads" (*ibid.*, p. 157).
7. *Op. cit.*, p. 63ff.
8. *Ibid.*, p. 64.
9. See Alfred Jeanroy, *La poésie lyrique des troubadours* (Toulouse: Edouard Privat, 1934), I, 135–36.
10. "Le métier de jongleur fut de tout temps extraordinairement décrié. Le bon frère mineur Matfré Ermengau se faisait certainement l'écho de l'opinion publique quand il les définissait ainsi: 'Ils s'adonnent nuit et jour aux vanités du siècle, à toute folie, à tout péché. Pourvu qu'on leur donne robes et deniers, il repaissent les gens de bourdes propres à decevoir les sots; médisants, mal appris, déloyaux, menteurs, débauchés, ivrognes, vrais piliers de tavernes' " (*ibid.*, p. 139).
11. For Jeanroy's account of the confusion between the terms *jongleur* and *troubadour*, see *ibid.*, pp. 137–39.
12. *Ibid.*, p. 137.
13. For a good description of the special aura attendant upon "the word" in early societies see Ernst Cassirer, *Language and Myth*, trans. Susanne K. Langer (New York: Harper Bros., 1946). Mircea Eliade and Claude Lévi-Strauss have also commented upon the same phenomenon.
14. Walter Ullmann, *The Individual and Society in the Middle Ages* (Baltimore: The Johns Hopkins Press, 1966), p. 9.
15. *Ibid.*, p. 8.
16. *Ibid.*, p. 10.

17. *Ibid.*, p. 12.
18. *Ibid.*, p. 17.
19. *Ancient Irish Poetry*, quoted by James Carney in his Introduction to Knott and Murphy, *op. cit.*, p. 5.
20. *Early Irish Lyrics*, ed. Gerard Murphy (Oxford: Clarendon Press, 1956), p. 21.
21. *Ibid.*, p. 75ff.
22. *Ibid.*, p. 85.
23. *Ibid.*, pp. 105–7.
24. For an analysis of the troubadour influence in late medieval and early modern Irish poetry, see the anthology of Irish love poetry, *Dánta Grádha*, ed. T. F. O'Rahilly (2nd ed., 1926), especially the long introduction by Robin Flower. This essay was reprinted in part in Flower's posthumous book *The Irish Tradition* (Oxford, 1947).
25. *The Poetic Edda*, ed. Ursula Dronke (Oxford: Clarendon Press, 1969), pp. 7–8.
26. "Where special stateliness was desired, groups of stanzas of the same pattern were articulated by a burden (*stef*) of two or more half-lines at set intervals, so as to constitute an organic whole, with Introduction, Body of the Discourse, and Conclusion. This form was called a *drápa*. It was designed more particularly for ambitious encomniastic purposes. If without the *stef*, and shorter, the poem was a *flokkr* — and to dedicate such a slight effort to a powerful lord was considered a studied insult. Needless to say, no such architectonic forms are found elsewhere in Old Germanic poetry." Lee M. Hollander, *The Skalds* (Ann Arbor, Mich.: University of Michigan Press, 1968), pp. 10–11.
27. "Still another, and perhaps the most singular feature of all in Skaldic poetry is the steady propensity to partition a sentence (and occasionally even a word) into syntactically unrecognizable parts, which are then intertwined with the parts of another sentence so partitioned" (*Ibid.*, p. 18).
28. See Dragonetti, *La technique poétique des trouvères dans la chanson courtoise* (Bruges: "De Tempel," 1960), Chapter I.
29.   Plas es lo vers, vauc l'afinan
                Ses mot vila, fals, apostitz,
                E es totz enaissi bastitz
                C'ap motz politz lo vau uzan,
                E tot ades va·s meilluran
                S'es qi be·l chant ni be·l desplei.
Cercamon, "Assatz es or' oimai q'eu chan," Stanza VI, ed. Jeanroy (Paris: Champion, 1922).
30. Marcabru, quoted in Hill and Bergin, *Anthology of the Provençal Troubadours* (New Haven: Yale University Press, 1957), p. 17.
31. J. Huizinga, *The Waning of the Middle Ages* (New York: Doubleday Anchor, 1954), p. 146.
32. *Ibid.*, p. 149.
33. "L'épitaphe de Villon en forme de ballade," in François Villon, *Oeuvres*, ed. André Mary (Paris: Garnier, 1959).

Simon of Saint-Quentin as Historian of the Mongols and Seljuk Turks

Gregory G. Guzman

PRIOR TO THE mid-thirteenth century, the Latin West was dependent on vague oral rumors for its information about the rising Mongol Empire; no reliable eye-witness accounts written by Westerners were available to the peoples of Europe until after the Mongol expansion became rather extensive. In 1247 the Franciscan John of Plano Carpini wrote the earliest western history of these Central Asian conquerors;[1] Simon of Saint-Quentin supplied the second in 1248. Because a good portion of each was incorporated into Vincent of Beauvais' famous encyclopedia, the accounts of John and Simon became not only the first, but also the most widely read and influential, Western documents about the Mongols. William of Rubruck's narrative,[2] which was written a little later (*c.* 1255) and which is generally considered to be more accurate and informative, did not have the circulation and prestige that the earlier reports of John and Simon had. While the *Ystoria Mongalorum* of John is well known to scholars of Medieval Europe, the *Historia Tartarorum* of Simon is seldom mentioned in Western historiography.

Simon of Saint-Quentin was a member of one of the four missions which Pope Innocent IV sent to the Mongols in 1245.[3] He was a traveling companion of Ascelin, the leader of the Dominican embassy sent to make contact with the first Mongol army which it could find in the Near East.[4] Simon's account, *Historia Tartarorum*, has been lost save for considerable excerpts which Vincent of Beauvais preserved in the last three books of his *Speculum historiale*. The problem of extracting the *Historia Tartarorum* text from the *Speculum historiale* is complicated by the fact that Vincent of Beauvais combined Simon's Mongol material with that of John of Plano Carpini, the Franciscan

155

who traveled to the Great Khan in Karakorum. However, the existence of complete manuscripts of the latter delegation[5] enables one to separate the accounts of Simon and John by comparing the *Speculum historiale* excerpts with the unabridged text of John. The *Historia Tartarorum* has been neglected by historians and paleographers for centuries; they have repeatedly put aside Vincent's abridged text in the hope that a complete manuscript of the original might eventually be discovered. None has been found.[6]

The much needed study of Simon of Saint-Quentin's account was started by two distinguished French scholars, Edgar Boutaric and August Molinier. Neither investigation was completed or published; the manuscripts of both are in the archives of the Académie des Inscriptions in Paris.[7] Although these early works have been superseded by later research, they laid the groundwork for all subsequent inquiries on the subject.

Simon and the Papal Missions to the Mongols also attracted the interest of Paul Pelliot, probably the most respected Western orientalist of the last generation. During the 1920's he published a series of three articles on the Mongols and Papacy in *Revue de L'Orient chrétien*;[8] offprints of these articles have subsequently been bound together in book form in many libraries.

Another French scholar, Jean Richard, has continued the research initiated by his eminent predecessors. In the only recent book dealing with Simon's history Richard extracted and published the text of Simon's *Historia Tartarorum*. He focused on the textual problems, since his primary intent was to make Simon's work available to other scholars;[9] he made no attempt to interpret or evaluate any historical information contained in the Latin text. His comments on the content of Simon's account were limited to identifying people and places.

This investigation supplements Richard's work, since it deals with the substance and quality of Simon's history. The objective is to study and analyze the *Historia Tartarorum* material that deals with the Mongol conquest of the Near East[10] in order to determine precisely what the account contains concerning the Mongol arrival in that part of the world. Simon's narrative will also be briefly compared to other records of the same conquest[11] in order to ascertain the accuracy and reliability of the *Historia Tartarorum* and to discover how much Simon added to what the West already knew.

Very little is known about Simon. The *Historia Tartarorum* is the only source of information about him,[12] and even that contains surprisingly little about its author. As his name indicates, he was probably from the town of Saint-Quentin.[13] Richard believes that Simon was a Dominican missionary in the Levant and that he was probably selected as one of Ascelin's companions en route because of his knowledge of Oriental languages.[14] The *Historia Tartarorum* contains a reference to the fact that the papal letters were translated from Latin into Persian and then into Mongol, and that the translations were then read back to Greek and Turkish interpreters and also to the friars. This implies that some of the friars could understand the Oriental languages, and by the process of elimination Richard concludes that Simon was one of the two friars who most likely had a command of those languages. At any rate, while the evidence to substantiate Simon's knowledge of Oriental tongues is not conclusive, the degree of probability that he had such skills is high.

Simon possessed a flair for writing engaging history. His account may be characterized as a colorful travelogue describing interesting places and persons encountered in the Near East. On occasion he is suspected of having sacrificed accuracy to his penchant for producing a lively narrative. In a few instances, Simon gives detailed coverage to dramatic events and all but overlooks what are today considered to have been major occurrences and important people.[15] Simon was merely an on-the-spot eyewitness, lacking complete historical records screened by centuries of critical scholarship.

To date, Simon has been generally regarded as a less trustworthy and valuable reporter than John of Plano Carpini, who was considered to have been more precise and objective [16] because he was specifically sent as a spy to observe, record, and bring back all the information he could gather on the Mongols, especially in regard to their intentions and military tactics.[17] Simon, on the other hand, was not personally commissioned by the Pope but was merely a traveling companion of Friar Ascelin.[18] Simon's report thus lacks the official purpose and order found in that of John; it is more anecdotal in tone and less structured in organization.[19] Simon was recording the experiences of himself and his mission, not analyzing the complete spectrum of Mongol society; however, his narrower scope or frame of reference does not mean that he is any less reliable or trustworthy an historian than John. Moreover, in specific cases the *Historia Tartarorum* is more accurate than the *Ystoria Mongalorum*. For example, John's account contains the usual list of Eastern wonders — i.e., underground people, men with hooves and dog faces, cyclopedes, etc.; Simon's short history does not contain these typical medieval legends about the East. Further-more, John's story of Prester John's victory over a Mongol army is a mixture of historical truth overlaid with Alexandrian romance.[20] Simon, on the other hand, makes Prester John the Khan of the Keraits,[21] and reports that Chinggis Khan married the Christian daughter of King David (the granddaughter of Prester John). Actually Chinggis Khan did marry a Nestorian Christian; she was the daughter of the Khan of Kerait.[22] In this instance, Simon's description is better and more accurate than that of John.

Returning to Simon and his account, the *Historia Tartarorum* is largely a collection of interesting episodes acquired from a variety of sources. Guichardus of Cremona,[23] who was a member of the mission for five months, and the other friars at Tiflis undoubtedly furnished Simon with much information on Mongol customs and on the religious beliefs and practices of the Georgians and Armenians.[24] As a result, Simon goes into considerable detail concerning the ecclesiastical organization of Georgia and what he considers to be the corrupt clerical practices of both the Georgians and Armenians.

The Latin mercenaries in the armies of the Sultan of Iconium were another major source of information for Simon.[25] Like most soldiers of fortune, they boasted constantly of their exploits;[26] Simon includes several reports which recount their deeds of incredible bravery.[27]

But Westerners living in the Levant were not Simon's only sources; part of his material came directly from the native peoples with whom he had contact. If he could indeed speak some Oriental languages, as is highly probable, he may have been able to by-pass interpreters completely. The most obvious example of information which Simon received from the Mongols, either directly or through on-the-spot interpreters, concerns his detailed account of the enthronement of Güyüg Khan.[28] Simon's most likely source for this information was Anguthan, the Khan's official whose late arrival delayed the friar's departure from Baiju's camp.[29] Since Anguthan had come directly from Karakorum, he undoubtedly took part in the recent ceremony itself. Only one who had participated in the actual dialogue between the new Khan and his noblemen could have provided Simon with the series of questions and answers involved in the enthronement ritual. The *Ystoria Mongalorum* of John of Plano Carpini, who had witnessed the enthronement while in Karakorum, does not mention this dialogue or contain any part of the question-and-answer ritual.[30] The Mongol chiefs held their conferences and elected Güyüg inside a large tent;

guards prevented all others from entering. Thus John did not witness the dialogue between the newly elected Khan and his nobles, and since there is no mention of it in his account, he probably was unaware of the series of questions and answers. Yet this interesting aspect of the Khan's enthronement is recorded by Simon.

Despite his divergent sources, Simon's account is not free from bias; all epochs and all men have their prejudices. As a member of a medieval religious order, Simon apparently felt that he was an exemplary representative of Latin Christianity. In keeping with the traditional religious views of the age, he was intransigent in all matters of dogma and practice, rejecting all deviations from Western tradition and condemning all forms of Eastern Christianity.[31]

In addition to possessing the attitudes of his religious milieu, Simon also had a rather low opinion of the Mongols. He records most Mongol activity in a very unfavorable manner, tends to dramatize their less praiseworthy qualities,[32] and fails to mention the commendable attributes of the Mongols: that they were tolerant of all Christians,[33] that they allowed the Dominicans to establish a house in Tiflis in 1240, and that they were not altogether merciless in their treatment of prisoners.[34]

Simon could hardly be faulted for not loving the Mongols; few of his contemporaries did. In addition, Simon had a traumatic personal experience which could easily be the source of the bitterness that he felt toward the Mongols. Simon's personal dislike of them can be traced back to fear and wounded pride. The Dominican party was in territory controlled by the Mongols for over one year and spent nine weeks in Baiju's camp.[35] During this time, Simon and the other friars were made to suffer humiliation and want, treated as prisoners rather than envoys, and sentenced to death no less than three times.[36] Simon thus had good reason for personally disliking the Mongols.

A general outline of the Mongol conquest of the Near East emerges from the *Historia Tartarorum*. Simon's account of the Mongol invasion, as presented in the *Speculum historiale*, is not systematic; however, a coherent chronological and geographical framework may be reconstructed from his narrative. In addition to recording the westward progress of the Mongol armies, the *Historia Tartarorum* includes a description of their invasion tactics and practices.

Cruelty was only one aspect of the military tactics employed by the Mongols, who, according to Simon, were exceedingly cold-blooded toward conquered peoples. Only rarely did they spare the civilian male population of those who opposed them. They even resorted to cannibalism,[37] sometimes out of necessity,[38] and sometimes out of a desire to strike fear into the hearts of their enemies. Cannibalism was directed particularly against those peoples whom the Mongols considered rebels. Simon dramatizes the cruelty of the Mongols in his description of their invasion of Derbend[39] where he records the various methods used to massacre the inhabitants of that city.

Deceitfulness was another weapon in the tactical arsenal of the Mongols.[40] Simon contends that the Mongols preferred to win battles by trickery rather than by valor; since this was diametrically opposed to the traditions (if not always to the practices) of Western chivalry, it was viewed with abhorrence by the Dominican friars. The Mongols were a people whose word could not be trusted.[41] Repeatedly they slaughtered those who surrendered, despite their promise to spare them.[42] Brave resistance and courage in their opponents struck fear in the Mongols, who made a virtue of deceit.[43]

Mongol deceit is also exemplified in their method of surrounding and besieging fortified cities and castles. If they could not overcome a fortress, they would retreat not far from it and hide.[44] When the besieged believed that the Mongols had withdrawn, they would open their gates. Immediately, the Mongols would rush in and capture the city. In similar manner, when they could not subdue Spapham by force of arms, they flooded the city in order to seize it.[45]

Simon also discusses the method of invasion utilized by the Mongols.[46] Entering a region by night, they hid in the surrounding mountains, and, in the morning, raiders were sent to attack the people on the plain. The unwary natives would then flee to the hills for safety, where they were ambushed and killed by the Mongols who had previously hidden themselves there.[47]

After discussing Mongol military tactics, Simon turns attention to the various stages of their territorial expansion. His account of their conquest of southern and central Asia is brief.[48] The invasion of India, one of the first Mongol victories under Chinggis Khan, is the only early conquest recorded by Simon.[49] He treats the subjugation of the rest of central Asia by briefly stating that Chinggis Khan began to attack neighboring regions and soon extended his control over most of central Asia. The Mongols conquered numerous kingdoms and by 1248, when Simon wrote, had spread from China in the east to the Black Sea in the west.

The only central Asian invasion that Simon reports in considerable detail is the Mongol attack on the Khorezmians.[50] After their initial victories, the Mongols were so filled with pride and self-confidence that they made plans to conquer the entire world. Their envoys arrogantly ordered the Khorezmians, their powerful neighbors to the west, to become subservient and tributary to them. The Khorezmians were so enraged at the manners and commands of the Mongol delegates that they killed them;[51] this, in turn, angered the Mongols. They collected a large force and invaded the vast Khorezmian empire, slaughtering all whom they found and putting the rest to flight. The Khorezmian state was conquered between 1220 and 1222; those who managed to escape fled to Persia and Georgia.[52] In Tiflis, the capital of Georgia since 1122, the Khorezmians killed seven thousand people.[53] The Mongols pursued them into Georgia and forced them to flee again. This time they hid in the land of the Sultan of Iconium.[54] In 1244 the Khorezmians were invited into Palestine by the Aiyūbīd Sultan of Egypt; they defeated the Christians at Gaza and burnt the Church of the Holy Sepulchre in Jerusalem.[55] Subsequently the Khorezmians disappeared as a nation.[56]

Simon becomes progressively more specific as he records the Mongol conquest of the countries and peoples in western Asia and the Near East. He gradually increases his coverage, devoting one chapter to the Mongol attack on Persia, two chapters to their invasion of Georgia, and three chapters to the destruction of Armenia.[57] Turkey, more commonly known as the Sultanate of Rum or Iconium in the mid-thirteenth century,[58] receives the major share of Simon's attention; he devotes no less than fourteen chapters to this westernmost Asiatic kingdom. However, not all of the fourteen chapters pertaining to this Turkish state deal with its invasion and conquest by the Mongols; some give the Latin West its first description of Turkish greatness, riches, and its nobility, while others deal with its political history, especially its revolts and conflicts over succession.[59]

The Mongol invasion of Persia,[60] as recorded in the *Historia Tartarorum*, is not very detailed. After reporting the Mongol capture of the two Persian cities of Spapham and Derbend,[61] Simon spends the rest of this chapter discussing the Iron Gates of Alexander and the people who were reportedly imprisoned in the Caspian Mountains by them.[62]

In his description of the invasion of Georgia,[63] Simon stresses the methods which the Mongols employed. He begins by recording that they entered Georgia in 1220, initiating their sporadic conquest of that country.[64] He then goes into a detailed account of how a great Georgian baron and his family were captured and killed (except the wife) as they tried to flee to the mountains.[65] More than one half of the chapter is devoted to this one incident, which was undoubtedly characteristic of the Mongol tactics utilized in conquering mountainous Georgia. When they destroyed Tiflis, they hung seven men upside down as a sign that seven thousand had been slaughtered in the capture of that city.[66]

After subjugating that country, the Mongols attacked and defeated Greater Armenia.[67] The noble city of Ani, which had, according to Simon, one thousand churches and one hundred thousand families, was captured by the invaders in twelve days.[68] Since Mongol military operations in Greater Armenia brought complete victory within two weeks, Simon spends the rest of the chapter discussing the location of Noah's ark in the Armenian mountains and the local legends that grew up around this sacred relic.[69]

Simon concentrates almost exclusively on the political and military history of Lesser Armenia,[70] also known as Cilicia. He locates Cilician Armenia between Turkey and Syria and indicates that Tarsus is its leading city. After thus setting the scene, he devotes the remainder of the chapter to tracing this state's chief political events. At this time, Hetcum[71] was the king of Cilician Armenia. His father Constantine[72] sent another of his sons[73] to the Mongols. The purpose of this embassy was to submit their tribute and to make an alliance with them.[74]

After discussing the alliance between Cilician Armenia and the Mongols, the *Historia Tartarorum* delves into the political and dynastic history of that state. Understandably, considering Simon's sources, some events, dates, and obscure dynastic relationships are blurred.[75] At the end of the chapter, Simon again returns to the reign of Hetcum I. In order to gain the favor of the Mongols, Hetcum I committed an unpardonable crime. He sent the mother and sister of the Sultan of Iconium[76] to the Mongols even though the Sultan had sent his family to his vassal Hetcum I for safety from them. To avenge this outrage, the Sultan invaded Cilician Armenia and besieged Tarsus;[77] the attack ended with the death of the Sultan shortly thereafter.

And finally, Simon turns his attention to Armenia's Turkish neighbors to the west. He begins his report of the conquest of the Seljuk Sultanate by recording that the Mongols had often invaded that country[78] before their armies crushed it decisively in one battle.[79] These opposing forces clashed repeatedly along the western border of the Sultanate of Iconium, particularly in the area of Khilat.[80] To illustrate these raids, Simon relates two events which occurred in the year preceding the Mongol destruction of the Turkish Sultanate, i.e. in 1242.

The first of these two incidents was the Mongol conquest of the city of Erzerum,[81] which withstood a twenty-day siege before capitulating. Erzerum was a vassal state of the Sultan of Iconium,[82] but it received no aid from its overlord. The inhabitants of that city decided to surrender to the Mongols with the provision that none of them would be killed, that all would be spared and held as servants and slaves. They then sent the leader of the city[83] to make such an agreement with the enemy. The Mongols consented to the petition, and, as was their custom, they promised and swore they would faithfully observe all of its provisions. On entering Erzerum, the Mongols broke their word and slaughtered all of the citizens.[84]

Simon also reports General Baiju's massacre of two thousand women from Erzerum. These women had gone a short distance from the city to bathe. After they had finished bathing, they saw the Mongol army approaching. Realizing that escape was impossible, they offered themselves to Baiju and his men in perpetual servitude. Even their music and singing was not able to mitigate the ferocity of Baiju, who ordered the women killed on the spot.

The Mongols also captured two Franks in 1242.[85] One was an Italian named William of Brindisi; the other was a Frenchman from the Midi called Raymond Gascon.[86] While they were held captive, one of the Mongols, who had heard that the Latins were excellent fighters, suggested to his leaders that the two fight each other. This would enable the Mongols to observe western fighting techniques and would result in the prisoners being killed by each other and not by their captors. While arming themselves, William and Raymond agreed to attack the Mongols rather than each other. Feigning close combat, they suddenly turned on the Mongols; they killed fifteen and seriously wounded thirty before they themselves were cut down. Because of this and other exploits like it,[87] Simon records that the Mongols had a deadly fear of the Latins.

In 1243, when the Mongols heard of the victories of Baba Isḥāq's small rebel band,[88] they realized how weak the Turks were and invaded Asia Minor with a large army. They decisively crushed the Sultan of Iconium at Köse Dagh.[89] Simon does more than merely record the outcome of the battle itself; he also enumerates the reasons for the Seljuk defeat. According to the *Historia Tartarorum,* Sultan Kai Khusrau II had been drunk the previous night and was still dizzy when the initial military contact took place. Secondly, the Sultan's army was engaged in battle before it was fully assembled and prepared to fight.[90] And finally, the Sultan's neighbors wanted to join in the Mongol victory over the Seljuks.[91] A Turkish defeat was the only outcome possible under these conditions.

Sultan Kai Khusrau II was not a brave man; he elected not to lead his troops personally, but to remain a safe distance from the actual fighting. He soon fled, leaving his tents and treasures behind. However, the Mongols feared that this was some sort of a trick and felt that Turks were hidden in the seemingly deserted tents. So they left them untouched until the evening of the next day when they were certain that the Turkish retreat was not a trick, but real.[92]

Simon then lists the treasure and booty that the Mongols found in the baggage of the Sultan of Iconium. Kai Khusrau II had abandoned about three thousand pack loads of his household goods and forty cart loads of leather cuirasses. The Mongols also found a very large amount of precious metal in the Sultan's deserted tents;[93] thirty camel loads of gold pieces (each as thick and wide as a palm), each load being worth about one hundred Muslim bezants; three hundred pack loads of Muslim bezants, each load containing forty thousand bezants; three thrones, two of silver and one of gold;[94] and one tent full of gold and silver vases and vessels.

Most of this vast treasure of the Sultan of Iconium had been confiscated from defeated enemies. The Seljuks had appropriated one thousand cart loads of gold and silver from the Byzantine Emperor Manuel Comnenus after defeating him in battle in 1176.[95] Likewise, the Sultan of Egypt had lost a large amount of booty and treasure when he was crushed by the Turks in 1234.[96] In addition to the conquered hoards from these two rulers, the Sultan of Iconium had a sizeable income from his rich lands and vassals.

After annihilating the Sultan's army at Köse Dagh, the Mongols continued their invasion of Asia Minor, pillaging and looting at will. The city of Erzinjan[97] made a surrender agreement or peace treaty with the Mongols, but, on entering that city, they killed all of the inhabitants. Sebaste's[98] citizens were not massacred because they voluntarily approached the Mongols and offered them the keys to the city. However, the Mongols destroyed the city and enslaved the people.[99] Turning southward, the invaders next attacked Caesaria in Cappadocia.[100] When they arrived before the city, they demanded an oath of loyalty from its citizens. Those inhabitants who went out to declare their allegiance to the Mongols[101] were slaughtered. Hearing that the king of Cilician Armenia was coming to the aid of Caesaria, the Mongols withdrew, even though their vast army outnumbered the small force which King Hetᶜum I supposedly led. The Mongols returned after learning that the rumor was not true.[102]

In 1245 the Mongols signed a treaty with the Turks,[103] who sent fourteen camel loads of Byzantine bezants, three hundred loads of silk and scarlet, and many precious garments to the Great Khan. According to the terms of this pact, the Seljuks submitted to the Mongols and became tributary to them. Every year they were to send the Mongols one million two hundred thousand Byzantine bezants, five hundred silk garments, five hundred horses, five hundred camels, and five thousand rams.[104] The Turks had to transport all this to the Plain of Mughan on the western coast of the Caspian Sea. In addition to the above terms, the defeated Seljuks also had to provide all Mongol envoys throughout Turkey with horses and supplies. The Sultan's notary totaled the expenses of the Mongol delegates at Iconium[105] for two years and found that, not counting bread and wine, the Turks had spent sixty thousand Byzantine bezants. A similar study was made at Sebaste, but Simon does not give the amount it cost to supply the Mongol envoys there.

To conclude, Simon's coverage of the Mongol conquest of Asia improved as the Mongols advanced westward. He began with rather general accounts of the early Central Asian conquests, and he ended with a more detailed description of the Mongol conquest of the Near East, and especially of the Seljuk Sultanate of Iconium. Simon's history may not be lengthy, but it represents a more detailed version than John's *Ystoria Mongalorum*, which merely lists Persia, Georgia, Armenia, and Asia Minor under the areas conquered by the Mongols.[106] Thus Simon's account is significant because it was the earliest and most complete Western report of the Mongol conquest of the Near East to reach Europe.

While the *Historia Tartarorum* may not be as detailed a narrative as historians desire, nevertheless, portions of it contain new data on the Mongol advance into the Near East. In particular, Simon records some facts about the conquest of the Seljuk Turks that are not found in any other records; he is the only source that reports such things

165

as the Mongol massacre of the two thousand bathing women at Erzerum, the reasons for the Turkish defeat at Köse Dagh, and the most complete listing of the tribute which the Mongols imposed on the Seljuks.

In evaluating Simon as a source for Turkish-Mongol history, one must bear in mind that, although his sources may have exaggerated and although he himself had no love for the Mongols, he, nevertheless, produced a primary account of Seljuk-Mongol history. Its chief significance lies in the fact that much of the Turkish history recorded by Simon in 1248 was, at that time, entirely new to the Latin West, since most Near Eastern reports received in Europe dealt with the Latin states in Syria and Palestine. This is illustrated by Matthew of Paris, who collected a considerable amount of information about the Mongols in his *Chronica Majora*,[107] but who referred to the relations between the Turks and Mongols only once.[108]

The fact that Vincent incorporated so much of Simon's Turkish material into his *Speculum historiale* is a further indication that this information was previously unknown to Western Christendom.[109] The erudite scholar Vincent indicated his opinion of the worth and value of the *Historia Tartarorum* by the fact that he used John's narrative to supplement that of Simon.[110] This is significant because one would expect that an embassy to the Great Khan himself would take precedence over one to an army general; one would ordinarily expect Simon's history to supplement that of John.[111] Vincent also shows his preference for the *Historia Tartarorum* by the fact that the bulk of his Mongol material is derived from Simon; a linear count reveals a 1700:1250 ratio in favor of Simon.

However, some scholars may be hesitant to accept Simon's additional information unless it can be verified by other primary sources. To be sure, the *Historia Tartarorum* does contain some incorrect information, but there is always the possibility that the compiler Vincent, not the author Simon, is responsible for these inaccuracies. The most glaring dating error in the *Historia Tartarorum* concerns the granting of a crown to Leo II of Cilician Armenia by the Holy Roman Emperor; this event occurred in 1198, not in 1242. But there is evidence to support the suggestion that this may be Vincent's error rather than Simon's, as Vincent was not infallible in copying dates: Vincent wrote "eighty" instead of "forty" twice in selections that he otherwise copied word-for-word from John of Plano Carpini.[112] The fact that Simon received most of his material orally from eye-witnesses must also be taken into account; occasional discrepancies and the confusing of issues and events inevitably result from this type of oral transmission. Rather than dwelling on the fact that Simon's unique information is not confirmed by other records, scholars should take a more positive approach and be grateful that he preserved materials which would otherwise have been lost permanently. Without Simon's diligence in preserving primary evidence, Western knowledge of the Mongol advances into Asia Minor would be much poorer.

Thus Simon's *Historia Tartarorum* is important in the development of Western historiography because it made available to Europe some of the dramatic events that occurred during the Mongol conquest of the Near East, and particularly of the Turks in Asia Minor. Thereafter, until the late seventeenth century, the Turks were to loom ever larger in the consciousness of Europe.

NOTES

1. The West was so eager for information on the Mongols that parts of Plano Carpini's *Ystoria Mongalorum* circulated before the final draft was finished. See Jean Richard, "The Mongols and the Franks," *Journal of Asian History*, III (1969), 47.

2. William of Rubruck, *Itinerarium*, ed. by Anastasius van den Wyngaert, in *Sinica Franciscana* (Quaracchi, 1929), I, 147–332. This is the most recent Latin text of Rubruck's journey to the Great Khan in Karakorum. The older English translation, *The Journey of William Rubruck to the Eastern Parts of the World, 1253–55*, trans. and ed. by W. W. Rockhill (London, 1900), has now been superseded by that in *The Mongol Mission*, trans. by a nun of Stanbrook Abbey and ed. by Christopher Dawson (New York, 1955), pp. 89–220. All references to Rubruck's Latin text will be cited as *Itinerarium*.

3. Two of these deputations were entrusted to the Franciscans and two to the Dominicans. The Franciscan missions were led by Lawrence of Portugal and John of Plano Carpini, while Andrew of Longjumeau and Ascelin were in charge of the Dominican counterparts. See Gregory G. Guzman, "Simon of Saint-Quentin and the Dominican Mission to Mongol Baiju: A Reappraisal," *Speculum*, XLVI (1971), 232–49, for the history of Ascelin's embassy; Berthold Altaner, *Die Dominikanermission des. 13. Jahrhunderts* (Habelschwerdt, 1924), 52 and 122; and Paul Pelliot, "Les Mongols et la Papauté," *Revue de l'Orient chrétien*, 3rd series, IV (1924), 270. Hereafter Guzman will be cited as *DM* and Pelliot as *MP*.

4. *DM*, pp. 240–41 and 248–49, and Vincent of Beauvais, *Speculum historiale*, Johann Mentelin edition (Strasbourg, 1473), XXXII, 46–47. All references to the *Speculum historiale* will be to this Mentelin edition, as it is the most reliable of the early printings; see Berthold L. Ullman, "Classical Authors in Certain Mediaeval Florilegia," *Classical Philology*,

XXVII (1932), 13, note 1, and Jean Richard, *Simon de Saint-Quentin: Histoire des Tartares* (Paris, 1965), p. 10. These two works will be cited as *SH* and *HT*.

5. For the most recent and only complete Latin edition of John of Plano Carpini, see *Ystoria Mongalorum*, ed. Anastasius van den Wyngaert, in *Sinica Franciscana* (Quaracchi, 1929), I, 27–130. The text of John will be cited as *YM*.

6. If, in effect, all of Simon's account was incorporated into the *Speculum historiale*, this may be the reason why his work was not copied as a unit, and ultimately the reason why no manuscripts of it survived. In *MP*, IV, 272, note 1. Pelliot cites two reports that a little book on Mongol history existed in the 1250's; if this little book was the *Historia Tartarorum*, this is the last known reference to it.

7. Edgar Boutaric, "Recherches sur les sources du Speculum historiale," 1863, and August Molinier, "Études sur les trois derniers livres du Miroir historial," 1905. Each of these studies was awarded the Académie's prize for research on the sources of Vincent's *Speculum historiale*; for a more complete and detailed analysis of these two old French works, see *MP*, IV, 274–80.

8. See *MP,* 3rd series, III (1922–23), 3–30; IV (1924), 225–335; and VIII (1931–32), 3–84.

9. *HT*, p. 18.

10. The *Historia Tartarorum* contains other interesting information, i.e., the history of Ascelin's mission and a rather extensive narrative on Mongol customs and habits. Since the Latin West received its first description of Mongol life and society from John of Plano Carpini, only that material which refers to the Mongol expansion will be extracted and discussed here. The Mongol conquest will be followed only to June of 1247 since that is the last date covered by Simon's history; see *SH*, XXXII, 53.

11. George Altunian, *Die Mongolen und ihre Eroberungen in Kaukasischen und Kleinasiatischen Ländern im XIII Jahrhundert* (Berlin, 1911) synthesizes the basic Armenian sources of this period, but a more recent collection of Armenian texts will be found in A. G. Galstian, *Armianskie Istochniki o Mongolakh* (Moscow, 1962). While Persian and Arabic sources were thoroughly and critically evaluated by Bertold Spuler, *Die Mongolen in Iran: Politik, Verwaltung und Kultur der Ilchanzeit, 1220–1350* (Leipzig, 1939), it is still necessary to look at 'Ala-ad-Din 'Ata-Malik Juvaini, *The History of the World-Conqueror*, trans. from the text of Mirza Muhammad Qazvini by John Andrew Boyle (Manchester, 1958), and Rashid al-Din Tabib, *Sbornik letopiseĭ* (Moscow, 1946). Rashid has overshadowed Juvaini in the West because large parts of his work were translated into the Western languages while Juvaini was accessible only to Persian scholars until Boyle's recent translation. A. C. Mouradja d'Ohsson, *Histoire des Mongols depuis Tchinguiz-Khan jusqu'à Timour Bey ou Tamerlan* (Hague and Amsterdam, 1834) represents the first Western account that used Juvaini; this nineteenth-century work, which is based on both Persian-Arabic and Western sources, is still considered one of the best and most readable surveys of the whole Mongol period. Turkish

history is best treated in the two following works by Claude Cahen: "The Turkish Invasion: The Selchükids," in *A History of the Crusades*, ed. Kenneth M. Setton, 2nd ed. (Madison, 1969), I, 135–76, and "The Turks in Iran and Anatolia before the Mongol Invasions," *ibid.*, II, 661–92. However, the main Seljuk source Ibn Bibi should not be neglected; see Herbert Duda, *Die Seltschukengeschichte des Ibn Bibi* (Copenhagen, 1959). In order to see what the Mongols were saying about themselves at this time, one should look at the only Mongol source of this period, which has been adequately translated by Erich Haenisch, *Die Geheime Geschichte der Mongolen* (Leipzig, 1948). The Setton work will be cited as *HC*.

12. Simon is mentioned in Vincent's editorial comments in *SH*, XXXII, 2 and 25, but this can not be considered another source.

13. *MP*, IV, 291.

14. *HT*, p. 13.

15. The most frequent examples of what may be called misplaced emphasis occur in *SH*, XXXI, 139–47 and 150–51, and XXXII, 26–29; these references contain Simon's discussion of internal Turkish history and Mongol-Turkish relations.

16. See D. -M. Daunou, "Simon de Saint-Quentin," *Histoire litteraire de la France*, XVIII (1835), 402, and Leonardo Olschki, *Marco Polo's Precursors* (Baltimore, 1943), p. 31.

17. *YM*, pp. 10–11 and 27–28. See also Richard, "The Mongols and the Franks," p. 47.

18. *DM*, pp. 236 and 240–41.

19. Simon's failure to present his divergent source material in a more organized fashion may not have been due to lack of interest on his part. He may not have had time to structure his various notes; furthermore, one cannot rule out the possibility that Vincent shuffled the order found in the *Historia Tartarorum*. In *HT*, p. 51, note 3, Richard cannot help but wonder whether *SH*, XXX, 87 (*De nationibus quas Tartari post necem domini sui subiugarunt*) immediately followed after XXX, 69 (*De interfectione David Indiae regis a Tartaris*) in Simon's original text; in *HT*, p. 16, he states that it is impossible to know whether the *Speculum historiale* reflects the plan of Simon or of Vincent.

20. See Vsevolod Slessarev, *Prester John: the Letter and the Legend* (Minneapolis, 1959), p. 5, note 5.

21. *HT*, p. 27, note 3.

22. Juvaini is the only primary source which reports that Güyüg was brought up as a Christian. Juvaini, I, 259.

23. See *DM*, pp. 240–41 and 246, for the relationship of Guichardus to Ascelin's mission.

24. Richard, *HT*, p. 14, also believes that Guichardus and the other Dominican friars at Tiflis were Simon's primary source for his detailed discussion of the Georgian and Armenian churches in *SH*, XXX, 96 and 98.

25. There were many Latin mercenaries in the Turkish army at this time; see Jean Richard, "An Account of the Battle of Hattin Referring to the Frankish Mercenaries in Oriental Moslem States," *Speculum*; XXVII (1952), 171–75. Hereafter cited as Richard, "Frankish Mercenaries." At

the end of *SH*, XXXII, 28, Simon names a Latin mercenary, Provençal, as one of his chief sources; he provided Simon with most of the information concerning Mongol-Turkish relations.

26. Richard, "Frankish Mercenaries," pp. 173–74.

27. *SH*, XXXI, 140 and 145–47.

28. *SH*, XXXII, 32, is entitled *De solennitate qua fuit intronizatus.*

29. *SH*, XXXII, 50, and *DM*, p. 237. See *MP*, IV, 304–6, for Pelliot's discussion of the proper spelling of this Mongol general's name. He argues that the correct spelling is *Baičhu*, as this is the form favored by the Armenian and Syrian sources. Pelliot himself uses the Muslim form of *Baĩju* as it is more prevalent. Here the form *Baiju* will be used without the diacritic as this is the accepted English transcription for historical writing. In the Latin sources the name usually appears as *Baiothnoy* or *Baiotnoy.*

30. See *YM*, pp. 117–18.

31. Simon accuses both the Georgian and Armenian clergy of practicing simony and usury; he also lists the differences in doctrine and practice that existed between the Armenian and Roman churches and between the Armenian and Georgian churches. See *SH*, XXXI, 96 and 98.

32. *SH*, XXX, 77, is entitled *De crudelitate ipsorum et fallacia*; see pp. 159–60 of this article.

33. Leonardo Olschki, *Guillaume Boucher: A French Artist at the Court of the Khans* (Baltimore, 1946), p. 16.

34. Frenchmen and skilled craftsmen usually escaped the terrible treatment which the Mongols generally inflicted upon all whom they conquered; see Olschki, *Guillaume Boucher*, pp. 5–7 and B. Vladimirtsov, *Le régime social des Mongoles; le feodalisme nomade*, trans. M. Carsow (Paris, 1948), p. 53.

35. *DM*, pp. 237 and 243.

36. *SH*, XXXII, 44.

37. The Mongols are called cannibals in *SH*, XXX, 77–78. John of Plano Carpini and Matthew of Paris also describe the Mongols on several occasions as man-eaters; see *YM*, pp. 47–48, and Matthew of Paris, *Chronica Majora*, ed. Henry R. Luard, in *Rerum Britannicarum Medii Aevi Scriptores* (London, 1872–83), LVII (in seven parts), Part IV, pp. 76, 273, 388, and Part VI, p. 77. Hereafter cited as *CM*. These three Western accounts of the Mongols are the only sources which accuse the Mongols of cannibalism; most non-Western sources, e.g., Juvaini, Rashid ad-Din, the Armenian historians etc., do not associate cannibalism with the Mongols.

38. Both Simon and John report that the Mongols sometimes practiced cannibalism out of necessity; see *SH*, XXX, 77 and *YM*, pp. 47–48. However, only John clarifies his statement by means of a specific example. He claims that while besieging a certain city, the Mongols ran short of food, and rather than lift the siege, they ate one out of every ten of their own men. Since it was imperative to continue the siege, it was necessary for the Mongols to resort to cannibalism to sustain their attack without interruption.

39. The citizens of this city were massacred by the Mongols in 1239; see *HT*, p. 38, note 3, and d'Ohsson, II, 118. This account of the destruction of

Derbend appears in two different places, *SH*, XXX, 83 and 89; see also *HT*, p. 39, textual note b, for evidence that it is inserted in a third place in some manuscripts of the *Speculum historiale*. Richard attributes this repetition to Vincent's reorganization of his source material.

40. Mongol deceit is mentioned twice in the Simon extracts in *SH*, XXX, 77 and 82. Also see *SH*, XXXII, 18, where Vincent copies the same thing from John, but in slightly different words. The latter reference lends support to the theory that Vincent, not Simon, is the source of some of the repetition in the text.

41. *SH*, XXX, 77.

42. After promising the inhabitants of Erzerum and Erzinjan mercy, the Mongols massacred them when they surrendered; see *SH*, XXXI, 147, and pp. 162–63 and 164–65 of this article.

43. As a result, the Mongols feared the courageous Franks more than any other people. This fear appears twice in the text; see *SH*, XXX, 87, and XXXII, 41. By Franks, the Mongols and the whole of Asia meant all Western Christians, not merely those from France.

44. *SH*, XXX, 82.

45. The capture of Spapham is recorded twice; see *SH*, XXX, 82 and 89; see also note 61.

46. *SH*, XXX, 81, is entitled *Qualiter regiones invadere solent*.

47. The Mongol invasion tactics described here by Simon are undoubtedly those used in conquering mountainous Georgia; see *SH*, XXXI, 95. The Mongol vanguard which defeated the Georgian king, George IV Lascha, in 1221 was light-armed and small in number, about 20,000–25,000. The mountainous terrain of Georgia was not suited to operations by large armies. The Mongols first overran the open rural areas and then turned against the cities and population centers. See Altunian, *Die Mongolen und ihre Eroberungen*, pp. 20–21 and 34.

48. *SH*, XXX, 87, is given the all-inclusive title *De nationibus quas Tartari post necem domini sui subiugarunt*.

49. For the legendary Mongol conquest of David, son of Prester John and King of India, see *SH*, XXX, 69, and Richard Hennig, *Terrae Incognitae*, 2nd ed. (Leiden, 1953), III, 11–23. Prester John is usually identified with Yeh-lü Ta-Shih, the Qarā-Ktitāyan leader who, in 1141, defeated the Seljuk sultan Sanjar at Qatwan near Samarkand. For a more detailed discussion of the historical Prester John, see Slessarev, *Prester John*, pp. 80–92, and Charles E. Nowell, "The Historical Prester John," *Speculum*, XXVIII (1953), 435–45. For the popularity of the Prester John legend in Western Europe in the twelfth and thirteenth centuries, see Slessarev, pp. 3–8.

50. See *SH*, XXX, 88 and Claude Cahen, "The Turks in Iran and Anatolia before the Mongol Invasions," in *HC*, II, 668–74. Hereafter cited as Cahen, "Turks in Anatolia." Cahen uses the form Khorezmians in his English account of these peoples; his spelling will be adopted here for the sake of consistency, even though the form Khwarazmian is also prevalent in English. His article is the best concise treatise on the Khorezmians, but Altunian, pp. 26–31, should also be consulted.

171

51. Simon's summary confuses two different episodes here. The initial Mongol envoys to the Khorezmians were not killed; those sent a little later to demand justice for the death of certain Mongol merchants were the ones who were executed. For additional references, see *HT*, p. 53, note 1. Since the killing of envoys was an unpardonable crime, Mongol fury against the Khorezmians knew no bounds; see Vladimirtsov, *Le régime sociale des Mongoles*, p. 72. The Khorezmian shah, Muhammad, was a hunted man until he died on an island in the Caspian Sea; see Altunian, pp. 27–28, and Cahen, "Turks in Anatolia," p. 672. Muhammad's son, Jalāl-ad-Din Manguberti, was in turn pursued by the Mongols; Ögödei Khan was so anxious to destroy Jalāl-ad-Din that he sent Chormaghan after him with thirty thousand men. See Altunian, p. 27.

52. Simon does not give the names of the Khorezmian shahs, their military activities, or their escape routes; for these additional details, see Altunian, pp. 22–29, and Cahen, "Turks in Anatolia," pp. 670–73.

53. The Khorezmians destroyed Tiflis in 1226. Simon is the only source who gives seven thousand as the number of casualties in Tiflis. This figure appears twice in the text; see *SH*, XXX, 88, and XXXI, 95. In *HT*, p. 53, note 2, Richard mentions a Georgian chronicle that speaks of one hundred thousand dead in Tiflis, but such a large number is hard to accept; see also note 66.

54. Sultan 'Alā'-ad-Din Kai Qobād I and his allies defeated the Khorezmians near Erzinjan in 1230; shortly afterward (in 1231) Jalāl-ad-Din was killed. The leaderless Khorezmians hired themselves out to the highest bidder; they served in upper Mesopotamia until Sultan Kai Qobād I enlisted them to defend his Armenian border against the Mongols. But they had no stomach for the job, so the Sultan had to divide them and deploy them alongside his own troops throughout his kingdom. The Khorezmian mercenaries left after a quarrel with Kai Qobād I's successor, Ghiyāth-ad-Din Kai Khusrau II, and spent the years 1237–43 in the service of the Sultan of Jazira before accepting an offer from the Sultan of Egypt. See Cahen, "Turks in Anatolia," pp. 673–74, and *HT*, p. 54, note 1.

55. The Sultan of Egypt, aṣ-Sālih Aiyūb, hired the Khorezmians to help him against a coalition of Syrian Muslim princes and the Latin Christians of Palestine. For additional detail, see   Joseph R. Strayer, "The Crusades of Louis IX," in *HC*, II, 489, and in that same volume, Steven Runciman, "The Crusader States, 1243–1291," p. 561; Sir Hamilton A. R. Gibb, "The Aiyūbīds," pp. 709–10; and Cahen, "Turks in Anatolia," pp. 673–74. Simon has the Christian defeat at Gaza and the burning of the Church of the Holy Sepulchre in reverse order. The Khorezmians captured Jerusalem on August 23, 1244; they then sacked the city and burnt the Church of the Holy Sepulchre. An Egyptian army from the south joined the Khorezmians at Gaza; this united force defeated the Syrian-Christian coalition on October 7, 1244. See Strayer, p. 489; Gibb, pp. 709–10; and Cahen, "Turks in Anatolia," pp. 673–74.

56. The princes of Homs and Aleppo decisively defeated the Khorezmians near Homs in 1246; the latter were almost annihilated. The survivors found service where they could, but this defeat was the end of the Khorezmians

as an important military force in the Near East. See Cahen, "Turks in Anatolia," p. 674, and Gibb, p. 710.

57. For the Mongol invasion of Persia, see *SH*, XXX, 89; for Georgia, see *SH*, XXXI, 95–96; and for Armenia, see *SH*, XXXI, 97–98, and XXXII, 29.

58. This Turkish state was at the peak of its power under 'Alā'-ad-Din-Kai Qobād I (1220–37), and Ghiyāth-ad-Din Kai Khusrau II (1237–45). For the Seljuk defeat by the Mongols, in 1243, see *SH*, XXXI, 150, Robert Lee Wolff, "The Latin Empire of Constantinople, 1204–1261," in *HC*, II, 223–24, and pp. 163–64 of this article.

59. *SH*, XXXI, 139–47, 150–51, and XXXII, 26–28. See *SH*, XXXII, 141, 146–47, 150, and XXXII, 28, for the Mongol conquest of the Seljuks; *SH*, XXXII, 142–44 for a description of Turkish wealth and society; and *SH*, XXXI, 139–40, 145, 151, and XXXII, 26–27 for Seljuk political affairs.

60. *SH*, XXX, 89, is entitled *De destructione Persarum*. For a detailed account of the Mongol conquest and occupation of Persia, see Spuler, *Die Mongolen in Iran*.

61. The Mongols captured Spapham by flooding the city in 1227. For additional references, see *HT*, p. 54, note 2, and note 45 of this article. For the fall of Derbend, see note 39 of this article and *HT*, p. 55, note 1.

62. Matthew of Paris, *CM*, Part IV, 77–78, also discusses the legend of Alexander's Gate in reference to the Mongols. See *HT*, p. 55, note 3, for a discusison of the bibliography of Alexander's Gate; see the review of A. R. Anderson, *Alexander's Gate: Gog and Magag and the Inclosed Nations* (Cambridge, Mass., 1932) by Phillips Barry in *Speculum*, VIII (1933), 264–70, for a short but excellent summary of various aspects of this legend.

63. *SH*, XXXI, 95, is entitled *De Georgianorum destructione*.

64. The Mongol vanguard entered Georgia in the winter of 1220–21. King George IV Lascha opposed them, but was defeated in 1221. This was not a decisive battle, but a preview of the future. Georgia was conquered and occupied by the Mongol general Chormaghan between 1232–38. Richard, *HT*, p. 57, note 1, suggests that reporting these two separate attacks as one long Mongol invasion may have been the work of Vincent and not Simon. See also Altunian, pp. 20–21 and 40–41; *HT*, p. 56, note 1; and Spuler, p. 36.

65. For the invasion tactics of the Mongols see notes 46–47.

66. Tiflis fell to Chormaghan in 1238; see Spuler, p. 37, and d'Ohsson, III, 76. Shortly before the Mongols arrived, Simon records that the Khorezmians had also killed seven thousand when they destroyed Tiflis in 1226; see note 53. Simon is the only source which records the figure seven thousand in reference to the capture of Tiflis. Since he gives the same number of dead for the conquest of Tiflis by both the Khorezmians and the Mongols, one suspects that he is applying the number of casualties of one battle to the other as well.

67. *SH*, XXXI, 97, is entitled *De vastatione Armeniorum*.

68. Chormaghan himself captured and plundered Ani in 1239. It was the residence of the Bagratid dynasty of Armenia, and thus the medieval

capital of that kingdom. The Armenian sources confirm Simon's description of Ani by recording the same figures for that city in the eleventh century. See Altunian, p. 35, note 12, and p. 36; Spuler, p. 37; d'Ohsson, III, 76–77; and *HT*, p. 59, note 1. William of Rubruck confirms only the one thousand churches; see *Itinerarium*, pp. 325–26.

69. Simon and William of Rubruck record essentially the same legends about Noah's ark, but they differ in some of the details. Compare the last half of *SH*, XXXI, 97, with *Itinerarium*, p. 323. The *Chronica Majora* of Matthew of Paris also has sporadic references to the Armenians scattered throughout its pages; see *CM*, Parts III, 163, and V, 341, for specific mention of Noah's ark.

70. *SH*, XXXII, 29, is entitled *Qualiter rex minoris Armeniae Tartaris se subdidit.*

71. Hetᶜum I ruled from 1226–69. Hetᶜum is the preferred transcription of this name although the form Hethum is also used rather extensively. Kirakos of Gandzak wrote an account of Hetᶜum I's later trip (1254–55) to Mongolia; see also Emil Bretschneider, *Medieval Researches from Eastern Asiatic Sources* (London, 1910), I, 164.

72. Constantine of Lambron was the founder of the powerful Hetᶜumid house. The Hetᶜumids and their opponents, the Rubenids, were the two most powerful Cilician Armenian feudal families. Beginning in 1221, Constantine ruled as regent for Isabel, the heir of Rubenid king Leon II who had died in 1219. Constantine married Isabel to Philip of Antioch in 1222; in 1224 he led a revolt against Philip, who was captured and poisoned. He then married Isabel to his son Hetᶜum in 1226. This marriage united the rival Rubenid and Hetᶜumid houses; this meant internal peace for Cilician Armenia. See Sirarpie Der Nersessian, "The Kingdom of Cilician Armenia," in *HC*, II, 651–52, and Mary N. Hardwicke, "The Crusader States, 1192–1243," pp. 540–41 in the same volume. Also see W. H. Rüdt-Collenberg, *The Rupenides Hethumides and Lusignans: the Structure of the Armeno-Cilician Dynasties* (Paris, 1963), *passim.*

73. Smbat, the military commander of Cilician Armenia and the brother of King Hetᶜum I, was sent to Güyüg Khan at Karakorum as Hetᶜum I's official envoy; he left in 1247 and returned in 1250 (after the termination of Simon's *Historia Tartarorum*) with documents which guaranteed the integrity of Cilician Armenia. Smbat was well received and honored by Güyüg. See Der Nersessian, p. 652, and Grigor of Akanc, "History of the Nation of Archers," trans. and ed. R. P. Blake and R. N. Frye, in *Harvard Journal of Asiatic Studies*, XII (1949), 309.

74. After the Mongol victory over the Sultan of Iconium in 1243, Hetᶜum I realized that only an alliance with the Mongols could save his kingdom from destruction, so he voluntarily submitted to Baiju. This victorious Mongol general welcomed and accepted the voluntary submission of Cilician Armenia; a treaty of friendship, which made Hetᶜum I a vassal of the Khan, was concluded between the Mongols and Cilician Armenia in 1243. See Altunian, p. 40. Richard suggests that it may have been Vincent rather than Simon who confused this 1243 treaty of submission with Smbat's later embassy to the Mongols in 1247–50; see *HT*, p. 86, note 3.

None of the other sources connect Smbat with the 1243 treaty. On the other hand, Grigor of Akanc, p. 313, specifically distinguishes between the two embassies, reporting that after Het^cum I had made a pact of friendship and submission with Baiju, he sent his brother Smbat to Güyüg Khan.

75. This chapter, *SH*, XXXII, 29, is not precise or totally correct concerning the fine-line relationships between Ruben III, his brother Leo III, Leo's daughter Isabel, Leo's grand-nephew Raymond Ruben, Constantine of Lambron, Philip of Antioch, and Het^cum I. See Der Nersessian, pp. 630–59, and Hardwicke, pp. 522–54. The coronation of Leo II took place in 1198, not in 1242 as recorded in the *Historia Tartarorum*. See Der Nersessian, p. 648, Hardwicke, p. 529 and p. 166 of this article.

76. This was Sultan Kai Khusrau II who ruled from 1237–45. According to Simon, the Sultan's mother and sister were turned over to the Mongols by King Het^cum I. However, the secondary sources do not agree with Simon or with each other on this point. According to Der Nersessian, p. 652, it was the Sultan's wife and daughter; according to Altunian, p. 40, it was the Sultan's wife, mother, and daughter; and according to d'Ohsson, III, 87, it was the Sultan's children. While it is uncertain as to exactly who was given to the Mongols, both primary and secondary sources agree that they were members of Kai Khusrau II's immediate family. This treacherous act was against all of the laws of hospitality and chivalry, but it was the wise thing for Het^cum I to do from the political viewpoint. By this act he saved his kingdom from the invading Mongols.

77. Kai Khusrau II invaded Cilician Armenia in 1245. Constantine II of Lambron revolted against Het^cum I and joined the Turks. They captured a few of the cities and forts in western Cilicia. The Mongols made the Seljuks return the captured areas later; the document which Smbat brought back from Karakorum in 1250 contained the Khan's orders to this effect. These directives were executed by Baiju. See Der Nersessian, p. 652 and d'Ohsson, III, 91.

78. Simon twice records that the Mongols had been attacking and raiding Seljuk territory for about twenty years; see *SH*, XXXI, 141, entitled *De longa Turcorum a Tartaris impugnatione*, and XXXI, 147, entitled *De destructione quarundam Turquiae civitatum*. Sultan Kai Qobād I had refused to go to the Khan in 1232–34, so he was regarded as an enemy and was, therefore, subject to Mongol attacks. See Spuler, p. 43.

79. For Kai Khusrau II's defeat at Köse Dagh on July 2, 1243, see *SH*, XXXI, 150, and the discussion of it on pp. 163–64 of this article. This Mongol victory broke the power of the Seljuk state; it never recovered its former prestige and glory. See also Wolff, "The Latin Empire of Constantinople," pp. 223–24; Gibb, "The Aiyūbīds," p. 708; Cahen, "Turks in Anatolia," pp. 691–92; and Cahen, "The Mongols and the Near East," in *HC*, II, 717. Hereafter cited as Cahen, "The Mongols."

80. *SH*, XXXI, 141. Khilat or Akhlat is situated at the northwest corner of Lake Van; its masters controlled one of the chief routes into Asia Minor. See Cahen, "Turks in Anatolia," p. 673, and *HT*, p. 65, note 2. For Khilat's capture by the Mongols, see Altunian, 41.

81. *SH*, XXXI, 147. The Mongols sacked this rich commercial city and massa-

cred its inhabitants in 1242; see Cahen, "Turks in Anatolia," p. 691; Altunian, pp. 38 and 39, note 2; and *HT*, p. 75, note 1.

82. *SH*, XXXI, 142.

83. In *HT*, p. 75, note 2, Richard states that the *civitatis baiulum* was the commander of the garrison rather than a civil leader.

84. In addition to *SH*, XXXI, 141 and 147, see Altunian, pp. 38–39, and Spuler, p. 43.

85. See note 25 for information on Latin mercenaries in Turkey, and *SH*, XXXI, 146, for the account of these two captured Western knights.

86. *HT*, p. 74, note 1.

87. Simon follows the adventures of William and Raymond with another episode which illustrates the bravery of the Latins and the cowardice of the Turks.

88. *SH*, XXXI, 139–40, deal with the revolt of Baba Isḥāq. See also Cahen, "Turks in Anatolia," p. 691.

89. *SH*, XXXI, 150, is entitled *De vastatione regni Turcorum*; also see note 79.

90. Sultan Kai Khusrau II's army was not well organized. He was so busy with his wars in Diyār-Bakr that he had made no provision for repelling a Mongol invasion in the north. He hastily collected a large force, including a contingent of Latins, and met the Mongols at Köse Dagh on the traditional invasion route between Sebaste and Erzinjan. See Grigor of Akanc, p. 309, Cahen, "Turks in Anatolia," p. 691, and d'Ohsson, III, 80–81.

91. See *HT*, p. 78, note 3.

92. This is confirmed by Grigor of Akanc, p. 311. See also d'Ohsson, III, 81.

93. In *HT*, p. 79, note 1, Richard discusses the differences between the various coins named by Simon. Apparently he refers to the Muslim bezants as *solidi* or *soldani* and to the Byzantine bezants as *hyperpera*.

94. The Latin word *scalae*, usually translated as ladders, does not make any sense here, unless it is translated as thrones, which is the meaning suggested by the context. One of the silver thrones had six steps (*gradus* in the Latin) and the other had four. The gold throne had only three steps.

95. Emperor Manuel Comnenus was defeated in 1176 at Myriokephalon Pass. See Joan M. Hussey, "Byzantium and the Crusades, 1081–1204," in *HC*, II, 140–41, and Cahen, "Turks in Anatolia," p. 679. See also George Ostrogorsky, *History of the Byzantine State* (New Brunswick, N.J., 1957), p. 347.

96. Simon's Sultan of Babylon is al-Kāmil Muhammad, the Aiyūbīd Sultan of Egypt; he was defeated by the Seljuk Sultan Kai Qobād I at Khartpert in 1234. See also Gibb, p. 704.

97. For the fall of Erzinjan, see *SH*, XXXI, 147, and d'Ohsson, III, 83–84.

98. Sebaste (modern Sivas) was one of the important commercial crossroads of the Near East; it was located northwest of the source of the Halys River. See Cahen, "Turks in Anatolia," p. 687.

99. On the contrary d'Ohsson, III, 81–82, asserts that the people of Sebaste escaped both death and captivity because of their prompt submission.

100. *SH*, XXXI, 147; two Franks at Caesaria regretted that there were not more Latins present to defend the city against the Mongols.

101. Simon reports that one hundred thousand were killed according to some and three hundred thousand according to others. The conquest and sack of Caesaria was very bloody according to Altunian, p. 39; d'Ohsson, III, 82; and Grigor of Akanc, pp. 311 and 313. The last author records that Caesaria's nobles were massacred and its common people led into captivity.

102. King Het^cum I was a vassal of the Sultan of Iconium; he owed Kai Khusrau II three hundred lances for four months according to *SH*, XXXI, 144. Cilician Armenia also had to pay tribute to the Sultan of Iconium after Kai Kobād I invaded that country in 1237. Since Het^cum I owed Kai Khusrau II military service, he should have gone to the aid of his lord against the Mongols. After promising to send an Armenian corps to Kai Khusrau II, Het^cum I withheld his troops. He decided to look to his own safety first; this resulted in the treaty of peace and alliance between Cilician Armenia and the Mongols. See Der Nersessian, p. 652, d'Ohsson, III, 86, and notes 74 and 76 of this article.

103. *SH*, XXXII, 28. According to d'Ohsson, III, 82–83, Sultan Kai Khusrau II did not authorize the treaty between Baiju and the Turks; one of his generals agreed to the conditions in the name of the Sultan whom he supposedly represented. The Sultan first found out about the treaty after it had been signed. Kai Khusrau II fled toward the Greek frontier according to Cahen, "Turks in Anatolia," p. 692. It was his vizir, Muhadhdhib-ad-Din, who went to the Mongol general Baiju, and with him to Batu Khan, whom Baiju served. With Batu, Muhadhdhib-ad-Din arranged a peace treaty which permitted the Seljuk state to continue in return for tribute and, undoubtedly, a promise of troops whenever called for.

104. Matthew of Paris also lists the tribute which the Turks had to pay to the Mongols; he records Andrew of Longjumeau's report that the Sultan of Iconium sent to the Mongols one thousand Byzantine bezants and one mounted knight every day. *CM*, Part VI, 114, reads, ". . . et singulis diebus pro tributo mittit ei mille perperos aureos et unum Quiritem [sic] in dextrario." For the meaning of the unusual phrase *Quiritem in dextrario*, see C. D. Du Cange, *Glossarium Mediae et Infimae Latinitatis*, new ed. by L. Favre (Noirt, 1883–87), *s.v. dextrarii* and *Quirites*. In regard to the precious metal, Matthew's yearly rate of 365,000 Byzantine bezants is considerably less than Simon's yearly rate of 1.2 million Byzantine bezants. Both d'Ohsson, III, 83, and Spuler, p. 326, record the figure 400,000 dinars as the amount of the Turkish tribute. According to Friedrich Risch, *Geschichte der Mongolen und Reisebericht 1245–1247* (Leipzig, 1930), p. 156, note 6, one dinar is equal to one *hyperperum* or one Byzantine bezant. There is no basis on which to decide which of the above tribute figures is correct. Simon's figure, which appears very oppressive, was obviously not beyond the Turk's ability to pay, especially if his figures on the Sultan's income in *SH*, XXXI, 143, are correct. But this tribute made effective Turkish government impossible and thus led to the gradual disintegration of the Seljuk state. See Cahen, "The Mongols," p. 725.

105. For the Mongol conquest of the city of Iconium, see Altunian, p. 39, and Wolff, p. 223.

106. *YM*, pp. 74–76, 88–91, and 111–12.

107. Richard Vaughan, *Matthew Paris* (Cambridge, 1958), p. 144. It should also be noted that while Matthew of Paris collected numerous eye-witness accounts of those having contact with the Mongols, he never mentions the reports of Simon, John of Plano Carpini, and William Rubruck. See J. J. Saunders, "Matthew Paris and the Mongols," in *Essays in Medieval History Presented to Bertie Wilkinson*, ed. T. A. Sandquist and W. R. Powicke (Toronto, 1969), pp. 128 and 130.

108. *CM*, Part VI, 114 and note 104.

109. Richard, *HT*, pp. 15–18, is of the opinion that Simon recorded more information on Georgia, but that Vincent did not include it because he had discussed Georgia in considerable detail elsewhere in his encyclopedia.

110. See *SH*, XXXII, 2 and 25.

111. See *DM*, p. 238.

112. Compare *SH*, XXX, 73 and 80 to *YM*, pp. 64–65 and 81 respectively. In *HT*, p. 88, note 2, Richard also attributes this dating error to Vincent.

Quest in Query and *the* Chastelaine de Vergi

Emilie P. Kostoroski

THE TIME HAS PASSED when *La Chastelaine de Vergi* (herein-after, the *ChV*), an anonymous and very popular poem of the thirteenth century, could be admired in a superficial and somewhat saccharine way as a "joli et touchant petit poème."[1] Contemporary criticism has both deepened appreciation of the narrative's psychological finesse and sharpened awareness of the poet's technical skill: "Nous sommes là en présence d'une oeuvre extrêmement savante, voulue et dont aucun détail n'est abandonné aux hasards de l'inspiration ou des redondances."[2]

One modern critic, F. Whitehead, admits the poet's skill but ex-presses reservations about the coherence of the poem as a whole. Sen-sitive to the *ChV*'s challenging ambiguities, Whitehead has produced within seven years two radically differing interpretations. In the first, he saw the story as an integrated whole, its unity being provided by an idealistic system of values derived from medieval *courtoisie* and manifested in a consistent, compact, and highly reasoned plot.[3] The Châtelaine's death was not an incredible solution, but the affirmative answer of the poem to the ultimate question posed by the value system: in love, disinterestedness had no limits; love *could* make the greatest sacrifice without any hope of return.

This interpretation was based on a broad notion of courtly love. In Whitehead's second study, however, the earlier flexibility gave way to a more rigid acceptance of traditional courtly love (i.e., with the characteristics of Provençal love lyrics).[4] While still speaking of "the perfectly integrated character of the narrative and the almost mathe-matical rigor with which the plot is developed" (II, xviii), Whitehead now discerned serious discrepancies or artificialities in plot and char-acterization. The major incongruity stemmed from a change in the heroine's attitude: originally the haughty *dompna* (cf. the Guenièvre

179

of Chrétien's *Chevalier de la Charrette*), she was in her monologue and death a much more romantic figure (in the sense of being truly in love), animated by feelings of enthusiastic selflessness and loving submission quite at variance with the concept of loyalty implicit in her previous status as courtly mistress. Whereas the ideal system of values had produced unity in the first interpretation, in the second this unity was something of an illusion or deception obtained through masterly handling of narrative techniques.

The purpose of this study is to demonstrate briefly that Whitehead's first interpretation is more consistent with the *données* of the poem, and then to carry this explanation a step further, from quest for the perfect love to query about the system within which that love could exist. These two notions are the substance of the poem's meaning. If, as Whitehead said originally (I, xvi), "we believe in the design because, for the time being at least, we have been induced to accept the very idealistic system of values that lies behind it," there are numerous indications that, once we have contemplated with sympathy and pleasure the extreme of this ideal, we are also being invited to examine it objectively and even critically.[5] If this be true, then the poem's contradictions cease to have a negative value. The insertion of a true love relationship in a context of false love (i.e., traditional courtly love)[6] will not appear to be a source of defects; rather it will be seen as a device by which the poem questions the value of the ideal so poignantly illustrated and also as evidence of the poet's consummate art.[7]

Whitehead's second interpretation emphasizes three incongruities and artificialities: 1) lack of communication between hero and heroine on the subject of the Duchess' importunities and the Duke's demand that the knight justify himself; 2) the credulity and precipitous conclusion of the Châtelaine that her knight has ceased to love her, notwithstanding her extraordinary precautions against *losengiers* or evil-intentioned gossips; 3) discrepancies in the Châtelaine's attitude at the beginning and end of the story. Although the third criticism is the most serious, all three demand attention. Rather than simply accept these "improbabilities" and heighten incongruities, particularly by minimizing plot in favor of its lyrical or descriptive components, one should ask whether the radical contradictions really exist. Rehabilitating the plot will contribute to that end and pose further questions about the meaning of the poem.

Both the narrative content of the *ChV* and its development are entirely credible within the frame of reference supplied by the poem.

180

The tale consists structurally of a series of interpersonal relationships involving initiation by one character and response by another. This structure may be expressed in the following manner:

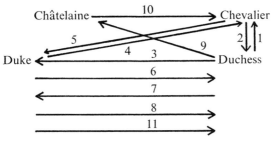

Each arrow represents one of the relationships and one stage of the unfolding action. By following the arrows, one can easily reconstruct the story: 1) the Duchess' advances to the Chevalier; 2) his negative response; 3) her reaction: the Phaedra-like accusation of the Chevalier before her husband, inspired by hatred and a desire for revenge; 4) the Duke's confrontation of the Chevalier in response to his wife's charges; 5) the Chevalier's response to the Duke (including the positive proof of the rendezvous with the Châtelaine); 6) the Duke's reply to the Duchess and subsequent behavior (satisfaction, increased affection for the knight, dismissal of his wife's charges as groundless, thereby adding to her humiliation and hatred); 7) the Duchess' efforts to wheedle the truth from her husband; 8) the Duke's betrayal of his vassal's secret; 9) the Duchess' confrontation of the Châtelaine; 10) the Châtelaine's death, which brings about the Chevalier's suicide; 11) the Duke's final act of justice, i.e., the execution of his wife.

The *scènes à deux* pattern of action does permit, in Whitehead's words, "full use of . . . the 'method of exclusion,'" or episodic treatment (II, xxxi). But instead of masking inherent artificialities, the pattern permits experimentation with the couple, society's basic unit. The scenes are linked to one another, furthermore, in a clear cause-effect relationship and the frame of reference, i.e., the ideal system of courtly love (*and* feudalism), imbues them with plausible psychological motivation, even the exaggerated response of the Châtelaine (her death of a broken heart).

To fail to understand why the knight does not discuss his problem with the Châtelaine (II, xviii) is to ignore the courtly value system (which, ironically, Whitehead stresses elsewhere). Between the Duchess' successful attempt to find out what she wants to know and the fateful day of Pentecost when she accosts the Châtelaine, there is an undetermined amount of time during which the Chevalier could confess his "crime." No careful reading of the text, however, would lead one to expect such a course of action. The knight is well aware of the penalty for telling the secret; he knows that it will cost him his dearest treasure, the company of the Châtelaine, if she discovers what he has done. Only when he has been twice assured by the Duke, the second time in a most solemn manner,[8] that his secret will never be repeated, does he reveal it. It would be most strange, under the circumstances, if he disclosed such a damaging fact.[9]

The second objection, that regarding the Châtelaine's hasty conclusion, fails, like the first but in a much more significant way, to take into account the circumstances influencing the character's psychological state. The lady's willingness to believe that her knight has been unfaithful is not "a very dubious piece of psychology" (II, xxxvii). This reaction and her love-death are consistent with her previous conduct during the rendezvous (the only time before her death when the reader does not see her through the eyes of her knight) and with her monologue, the sole indication of her inner disposition.[10] Far from undermining the verisimilitude of her conclusion, the rendezvous scene only reinforces it; for the memory of such exquisite tenderness enhances the bewilderment that accompanies her hurt (as certain as she is that he has betrayed her, she cannot understand why).[11] Furthermore, an examination of the monologue provides the only clues to the significance that the imposition of secrecy had in the Châtelaine's eyes. Clearly it was the symbol of the most perfect fidelity: breaking the seal of secrecy would have the specific meaning of ceasing to love. The Châtelaine obviously had never expected it to be broken, so when she discovered that it had, she imagined the worst. It is not at all surprising, therefore, that she immediately believes she has been betrayed (ll. 740–43). The evidence appears all the more damaging to her since she hears the fatal words spoken by the Duchess rather than by the Duke.

These considerations lead to the question of incongruity in the attitude of the Châtelaine. There is no contradiction that is not imposed by the artificial code to which she submits her very real love. Beyond superficial resemblances, the *ChV* is not a courtly narrative in the strict sense of the word. If the convention of secrecy was originally the *sine qua non* of love — and there is no indication whatsoever of the Châtelaine's initial motivation — it has certainly evolved very much at the moment of her death. The knight's betrayal interrupts communication between himself and his lady, but, as far as *she* is concerned, there is no moral alienation: i.e., his indiscretion may signify to her that he no longer loves her, but knowing this, she does not cease to love him. Instead, she is inspired to give the greatest proof of her fidelity and love. There is nothing in her conduct prior to the death scene which justifies calling her a haughty *dompna* (II, xxvi).[12] At the very most, the courtly convention of secrecy may be understood as a point of departure; the narrative's emphasis is on the terminus of this ill-fated love affair, and the Châtelaine's "hasty conclusion" only strengthens the impression of her as a romantic heroine enmeshed in her own extreme interpretation of her ideal. Acceptance of the romantic or broadly interpreted concept of courtly love seems to be what the poem is urging.

Thus far it has been seen to what extent the value system underlying the *ChV* is coherent, if not consonant with our own. Within that system, the poem presents "an ideal pair of lovers, each of whom more than fulfills the obligations that their love lays upon them" (II, xxx). And yet, for each the only reward is sorrow and separation: the lady dies believing the knight has betrayed her, while he dies convinced that he is responsible for her death. What can one conclude from this feeling of unnecessary waste, after repeated and reflective readings, except that the system is more to blame than its adherents? If, furthermore, as Whitehead said initially (I, xxvi), "few other works of the period allow imaginative idealism to be carried to such lengths," what other explanation seems likely than a will to magnify that idealism, the better to see its virtues *and* its limitations?

In addition, therefore, to being the tale of a great love and a greater betrayal, and the portrait of two faithful lovers, the *ChV* appears to scrutinize itself and find its value system wanting. That system, moreover, is highly complex: there is not one ideal at stake, but two, not one pledge broken, but three. The courtly ideal, already complicated by the introduction of true love into its artificial setting, is also observed in the light of the feudal ideal with which it has certain affinities. On the social level, therefore, the poem explores the question whether an asocial code of courtly love can have any enduring value. On an ontological and ethical level, it contemplates the condition of man torn between the opposing attractions of the real and the ideal, hesitating, making or refusing to make the compromises which the ideal spurns and the real demands. It is the study of the breakdown, for lack of trust or for misplaced trust, of the couple, the structure ordained by nature itself for survival.

A brief glance at the poem's prologue (ll. 1–17) and epilogue (ll. 944–58) provides several important notions regarding these various levels of meaning which a close study of the plot will subsequently substantiate and expand.

The poem's first eight lines introduce the theme of the *losengier*, a person who destroys the happiness of lovers by revealing to others their mutual affection. This theme naturally leads to that of the courtly lovers (ll. 9–17), for harm is possible only when love must be kept secret, and courtly love is by its essence in conflict with the norms of society. After the reader has familiarized himself with the poem, he may find himself wondering exactly who the "maniere de gent," alluded to in the first four lines, is meant to be, for it seems to apply equally well to the Duke, the Chevalier, and the Duchess:

> Une maniere de gent sont
> qui d'estre loial samblant font
> et de si bien conseil celer
> qu'il se covient en aus fier. . . .

Lines 5–8 leave no doubt that the Duchess is the intended referent. Since almost exactly half of the poem develops the revelation of the secret and the other half its consequences, it is clear that the *losengier* theme is vital to the story, and that the narrative will serve to illustrate the general truth just enunciated, that no good comes of a misplaced confidence. But the theme of confidence placed and subsequently betrayed is already stated in a manner which enlarges the traditional *losengier* theme to include nearly all the characters. Although the evil foreshadowed in the prologue is to be brought about directly by the recognized *losengier*, one feels, because of the purposeful lack of precision, that it will also come from the other characters as well.

The poem's conclusion confirms this suspicion. First there is the traditional lament over the misfortune of the lovers. It is not attributed to the *losengier*, however, but to the fact that the Chevalier told (ll. 947–49) what should have remained an inviolable secret. The source of the lovers' unhappiness lay, not outside themselves in a person whose *raison d'être* was to thwart the good fortune of others, but in the peculiar nature of their own relationship. Something about it was destructive of their happiness: the mistress' imposition of absolute secrecy. No explicit comment is made, but the implication is unavoidable: "If he hadn't told, they would still be happy. But if she hadn't demanded such perfect secrecy, they would have been happy even if he had told." To constrain real love with artificial restrictions could come to no good end. While it was normal for her to do this, the basic human questions posed by the poem thrust us beyond the circle of these conventions and, implicitly, call them into question.

That perfect bliss should depend on a single factor so absolutely, and that no compromise could be tolerated, however much the individuals might be constrained by circumstances, leaves the reader regretful but also uncomfortable. This you must do to be happy, the poem tells courtly lovers, all the while implying that this vital lesson in prudence cannot be applied, that even the most perfect lover will eventually be caught in the web of the real world's demands and be forced to compromise. If the other will not also bend, tragedy will ensue. In either case, the ideal situation will have been lost.

Returning to the diagram of the poem's action, one can see that the very disposition of that action is predicative as well as preparatory to the eventual failure of the ideal couple. The initial situation reveals the existence of two couples, perfectly balanced and harmonized, and apparently destined for a peaceful and happy life within the framework of this satisfying scheme. The story begins, however, at the point of its disruption, when the Duchess jeopardizes the neat pattern by trying to create a third couple from among the four persons. As the action progresses, one notices that relationships 1 through 8 fall into pairs. They involve dialogue, give-and-take, an effort at least to check the progress of evil and to maintain some sort of equilibrium. Two at a time, the characters attempt to rescue the endangered counterpoise.

The last three actions (9–11), however, are not paired. The Duchess challenges the Châtelaine who reacts against a third party, the Chevalier. After four sets of reciprocal actions, action 9, the Duchess' confrontation of the Châtelaine, is the first single action with no response from the object of the action directed back to its subject. There is no answer to it but action 10, the double death of the lovers. It is like a one-way street leading to disaster, for as evil triumphs, action 9 does not trigger a single balancing response, but instead several responses, which are destructive. As soon as dialogue is prevented, the precarious equilibrium is broken.

Just as the only answer to action 9 is 10, so action 11 (execution of the Duchess) is the only answer to 10. Actions 9 and 10 have maintained a deflected stimulus-response pattern among three people, and action 11 enlarges the frame to include the fourth person. With action 11, tragedy embraces all the members of the original scheme and the story ends. With the Châtelaine's death (action 10), three persons remain, and all hope of restoring the balance, of preserving the couples as they once were, is destroyed. This result is mirrored in the isolation of the Duke's final action: there is no direct schematic link between the death of the knight and his lord's response to it.

The diagrammatic representation of the action ends on an *impair* or odd number, whose nature eternally defies balance and harmony. Although this is only our own symbolism, it may be taken to reflect faithfully the situation and the symbolism of the poem. The ideal couple, Châtelaine-Chevalier, is defeated by the real one, Duke-Duchess, which in turn is also destroyed. As only one member of the original counterpoise of couples is left, the entire poem ends on the odd number one, indicating the complete dissolution of the initial dual "couple" relationship.

Furthermore, in keeping with the pervading tone of tragedy, even the one remaining member is, in a sense, destroyed. Unsupported by the partner of his couple, the one cannot survive. The poem illustrates in a negative fashion that we become ourselves through meaningful interpersonal relationships, and that through the selfless love of the other we discover our own identity. Without these relationships, without dialogue, there is nothing but meaningless or destructive monologue, or silence. So the Duke is never seen to laugh again; he departs from the scene of the tragedy "sanz retorner" (l. 942).

In this study of the narrative's structure, the number 2 has been stressed, and it has been seen how the harmony and balance of "twoness" is upset when the Duchess' "one-ness" introduces an element of instability.[13] But the number 3 has also been alluded to in passing. The Duchess set all in motion, for instance, by trying to create a third couple out of two existing ones. Likewise, the last three lines of action on the diagram are not paired, but occur rather in the manner of dominoes falling one on the other. And the double death of the lovers brings on a third death.

It might occur to a pragmatic reader at this point that, instead of the *scènes à deux*, which ultimately lead to grief, a few *scènes à trois* might have cleared away most of the problems in a less unhappy manner. In the first place, it is pointless to argue that something might or ought to have happened. In the second place, such speculations fail to take into account the absolutes involved in most of the narrative's relationships. Finally, the *ChV* is not a realistic novel in which external *vraisemblance* is of prime importance. Its verisimilitude lies much deeper. What does appear more pertinent is the fact that at two different times a group of three is achieved, in which the third party is *concealed*, and that on both of these occasions the result is suffering. It is another case of the odd militating against the even.

The first instance takes place when the Duke watches unseen the profuse demonstrations of affection which the Châtelaine gives to her lover. The second occurs when the little handmaid is the third and unseen party during the confrontations of the Duchess with the Châtelaine and the Chevalier with the dead body of his lady. The ideal couple is ultimately destroyed by the first spy, the real one by the second.

It might be said that, in a sense, *le petit chienet* creates a third party for the Châtelaine-Chevalier couple which is harmless because he is not human and cannot talk. This is not so; for although he cannot speak, he is nevertheless eloquent. His appearance on the night of the Duke's visit to the tower announces and ratifies the liaison existing between the Duke's niece and the knight, while his appearance in the Duchess' conversation with the Châtelaine is immediately harmful. It both announces and confirms the fact that the Châtelaine's secret has been betrayed. Like so many other elements in the poem, the little dog introduces a note of ambivalence. He is a symbol of the bond which unites the lovers (one cannot help but think of Petit Crû, the magical little dog given by Tristan to Iseut) and also of the delicate but efficacious insinuation which will snap that bond. He is the only element of the real world that dumbly witnesses and participates in the idyll lived by his mistress and her lover; in other words, he is its *only* sign or symbol. Once his symbolic value is recognized in the real world, the ideal situation is irrevocably betrayed and in a matter of time it disintegrates.

One could say, then, that the ideal couple was menaced from the very start by that which symbolized and facilitated their love: in one perspective, the dog, and in another, the very condition upon which it was established, the secret. The combination of fallible human beings obliged to live in the everyday world and exposed to its relentless demands, and an ideal situation which would tolerate no compromise with its single but absolute imperative is what will bring about the couple's downfall. "The fault . . . is not in our stars, / But in ourselves. . . ."

187

This is the underlying theme of the *ChV*. An insurmountable obstacle is inherent in the very nature of a love that strives to be perfect. Such a love cannot endure. The Châtelaine truly loves her knight, as he truly loves her. But the code by which she orders their relationship and determines its perfection obliges her to make the mistake of demanding more of him than he can humanly assure. For she expects of him perfect satisfaction of her trust (also supposedly perfect) in him. She associates a great love with a single external criterion which he may not always be able to control. This insistence on an absolute conceals an underlying egotism which casts some doubt on the altruism of her love-death. Until now the secret has spared her any burden of proof. At the one moment when she in turn must prove the faithfulness of her love for the Chevalier, she refuses (or rather it never enters her mind) to do so in the most loving way possible, that of compassionate forgiveness, or at least an effort to understand, which would be the manifestation of her perfect trust in him. It is indeed no coincidence that, in a story built upon the tribulations of two couples, the narrative's title bears her name alone.

The interpersonal problem which forms the basis of the plot arises because each member of the original couples cherishes sets of values that inevitably clash. From the Châtelaine, through the Chevalier and the Duke, to the Duchess, one can trace a definite progression from ideal to real determined by the degree to which an individual is willing to compromise absolute values. The Châtelaine brooks no compromise whatsoever. To the Duchess any compromise which furthers her end is acceptable and no absolute is sacred but her own personal satisfaction, be it lust or vengeance. Between the two women stand the men, each of them a veritable battleground of two absolute loyalties, feudalism and love. Each of them attempts to find a way out of his own impasse through compromise, the Chevalier compromising love for the sake of duty and the Duke compromising duty for the sake of love. Their compromises fail, not surprisingly, because the women, the Châtelaine especially, will not accept them. Without their inflexibility there would be no tragedy.

Of the four characters involved in the disrupted counterpoint, the Châtelaine is the most ideal: her love, in courtly terms, is most perfect. She is also the furthest removed from contact with others and the need to compromise. Both of these characteristics make her the least real character, according to the definitions of "real" and "ideal" already given. Viewed within her courtly relationship with the Chevalier, her "idealness" can be equated with total gift of self, provided it is exclusive. But beyond the narrow limits of this relationship she refuses to go. As far as the rest of men are concerned, she is, in an essential way, unreal. That aspect of her being which is the Châtelaine as perfect mistress does not exist for the world, because no one but the Chevalier knows it. As soon as it does become known, everything ideal ceases to be, and the courtly relationship is severed.

As furthest from the real world, the Châtelaine is also the most passive character. In contrast to the Duchess, she initiates no action at all, although she indirectly provokes the death of her lover by her own. The one action which does directly involve her (the Duchess' confrontation) is enough to destroy her, so great is her fragility and so powerless is she to resist or accommodate herself to the incursion of the real. She has managed to keep her knight's embraces in the realm of the ideal only by imposing on him the command of perfect secrecy. One may say that the Duchess' taunts are the very first invasion of her perfect world by the real one, even though it has been previously menaced by the Chevalier's indiscretion. It is significant that the moment reality touches her, she dies; for she represents the ideal which has nothing in common with the real. In the final analysis, the ideal can do nothing more than turn our attention beyond the here and now to an invisible world where the perfect may be attained, as in a dream, only if unshackled from the exigencies of life.

This extreme passivity is most appropriate to the character of the Châtelaine. While the ideal may suggest an attempt to escape from the real, as indeed it does in the Châtelaine's case, it may also be thought of as that which attracts a person, such as the Chevalier, to pursue it by being what it is. The Châtelaine's only act in the real world is her death, an act which reflects perfectly the duality contained in the notion of the ideal: it is both a refusal of life and a "passive action." As such, it is in perfect accord with her character.

Finally, as furthest from the real world, the Châtelaine is most faithful to her promises: she has not revealed the secret and she is dying now that she has lost her lover. But she has, in a sense, already died. The ideal mistress that she has been ceases to exist as soon as the compromise dictated by reality affects the sign of the perfection of their love, the secret. Having isolated her love and negated all else to the point where she as a person has meaning only in terms of that love, the Châtelaine must necessarily cease to exist when that love, *as she has accepted it,* ceases to exist. Physical death is thus the outward accomplishment and perfect aesthetic transposition of the spiritual death which has already taken place. The absoluteness of death, moreover, is a fitting response from one who could not tolerate life when it did not conform to her rigid demands.

Rather less passive and somewhat more involved socially than his lady, the Chevalier seems much more real. His ideal relationship with her coexists with real relationship of his allegiance to the Duke. The more involved he is with others, the more complicated becomes his life and the less secure his ideal. There are other demands on him besides that of his love. His capacity for fidelity to his word is less complete than the Châtelaine's because he lives in the real world. When the Duchess establishes another very real relationship with him, the balance is upset and there is open conflict between his two commitments. Torn between his feudal values (loyalty to the Duke) and his courtly ones (loyalty to his mistress), he seeks refuge from the Duchess' calumny in the former (i.e., confidence in his lord), in an attempt to protect his ideal love from contamination. He wants to preserve both his feudal loyalty and his love, yet it is his "real" commitment which finally takes precedence over the ideal. His loyalty to the Duke serves to destroy the other loyalty, for a man cannot serve two masters. The ideal and the real in the normal course of events cannot be completely divorced. But what becomes of the ideal in conflict with the real? Compromise cannot exist with absolutes. The dilemma of the knight is the human dilemma. His tears well out of the deepest human anguish.

The Chevalier's attempted solution is to trust his lord. Of what value are loyalty and love without trust? But more important, he has no choice except to confide in the Duke who chides him ironically for his lack of faith in his liege lord (ll. 316–17): "Bien voi que ne vous fïez pas / en moi tant com vous devriiez." Reassured by the Duke's solemn oath (ll. 332–39) that his confidence will be absolutely secure, the Chevalier breaks down and accepts a compromise. There is no other way out of this problem in human relations.[14]

Just as the Chevalier confides in his lord under pressure, so the Duke responds to the Duchess. Like the Chevalier, he is attempting a compromise based on confidence in another. It is more difficult to respect him because he ought to be more able to handle the conflict; he is probably older, and he has the authority and responsibilities of a feudal lord. But, paradoxically, his weakness is perhaps even more understandable because of the degree to which his own ideals are entangled in the reality of numerous human relationships. Even more involved in the society of others than the knight, the Duke must relate to his wife as well as to his vassal and, indirectly, to his niece, the Châtelaine. As his situation becomes more complex, solutions present themselves as far less clear-cut. Being more involved with others also causes him to be less capable of ideal fidelity than the Chevalier.

One tends to pity the Duke, and justifiably; for the pressure brought to bear by the Duchess is intense. But it must be remembered that he, too, has an active role to play until the very end. Urged by the Duchess, he sets up a relationship with his knight (actions 4–5) which makes possible the general downfall. Succumbing to his wife's subtle pressures a second time, he cooperates in another relationship (actions 7–8) which is its cause. He chooses in favor of what appears to be his own happiness, although in reality whichever alternative he adopts will thwart it. Like his vassal, he has tried to live with his feudal absolutes in a real and relative world.[15] Since social life is built on non-absolutes or compromises, the Duke is faced with the dilemma of dealing with absolutes as if they were non-absolutes, a clearly impossible undertaking. It is apparent, if one refers back to the diagram, that the direct attack of the Duchess on the Châtelaine crosses and severs the lines of the Duke-Chevalier feudal relationship. While this severance represents the Duchess' reckless disregard for both feudal and courtly values in order to attain her own selfish ends, it also concretizes the Duke's betrayal of his own values and channels it, through the Châtelaine, against the knight. The knight's complete trust in his lord now becomes the most serious incrimination of the Duke's disloyalty.

Like the Chevalier, the Duke has been caught in a conflict of two absolutes warring within him. Had the Chevalier been less faithful to his feudal obligations, he would have better defended his loyalty to his lady. Had the Duke been less distracted by his love for his wife, his feudal responsibility might have been better safeguarded. Noble, well-intentioned, confident in his set of values, the Duke is nonetheless deprived by his love of the firmness needed to make the believer in those values — himself — a sure object of trust. Indeed, one anticipates unhappy consequences from the first, for the Duke shows himself wanting when he refuses to trust his knight's word and insists on concrete evidence as well as knowledge of the secret.

The Duchess is clever enough to recognize her advantage. She knows she can attack the Chevalier through her husband. A considerable number of action lines in the diagram relate her, therefore, to the Duke. She is using his love of her and his system of feudal values to

191

attack the feudal-courtly values of the Chevalier, being herself unwilling, or more exactly, unable to respect either. The Duchess is as intransigent in her own way as the Châtelaine. Her single absolute, before which all others must give way, is personal satisfaction.[16] Her egocentricity rejects the conventional value impositions of her society. It will prevail and cause the unhappiness of all, including herself.

The "anarchistic" role of the Duchess as catalyst and destroyer of value systems as well as of couples is clear throughout the poem. The initial action undertaken by her sets in motion the destruction of the ideal couple. The final action, her execution, seals the fate of the real couple. In between, every other action is in some manner related to her.[17] It is her lust and then her desire for vengeance which destroys the ideal couple. It is her insatiable and relentless pursuit of these goals which ruins her own happiness and that of the Duke.

In the Duchess' relationship with her husband, the conflict between compromises and fidelity to absolutes is illustrated almost more dramatically than in the case of the ideal couple. In place of absolute secrecy, the destructive element in this instance (besides the wife's selfishness) is a real/ideal conflict operating on another plane. It is the misfortune of the Duke that, unlike his wife, he really loves within his own couple relationship. One sees here the reverse of the Châtelaine-Chevalier situation: within the real, the incursion of the ideal. By this is meant that the Duke, a sort of thirteenth-century Prince de Clèves, is not the husband normally conjured up in courtly situations; his wife has not ceased to be his mistress in his eyes. He has it within his power to halt the forces of evil by respecting the Chevalier's confidence, but he fails to do so despite his solemn oath. Although he has good reason to mistrust his wife in view of her previous conduct regarding the knight, he trusts her anyhow. What else could explain such an action except love, whose nature, as Marie de France said, is to oppose reason and measure?

It might be argued that love is not a sufficient motive since the Duke eventually punishes his wife for her betrayal. Is this really a contradiction? Within the context of the story, there can be only two explanations of his broken promise: love or feudalism. Obviously, feudal values are cherished by the Duke since, by virtue of his position in the social hierarchy, he represents or incarnates them. What is it, for instance, that keeps him awake all night after his wife has accused his favorite vassal? It is not that she has been dishonored, nor even he himself as her husband; rather he, as feudal lord, has been dishonored, and his feudal values have been threatened. He loves this knight, who may have betrayed his lord. There is no point in debating whether the Duke is more concerned over love or loyalty; his endangered feudal value system is what motivates him to seek out the Chevalier the very next morning.

One may assume that this same system also dominates his marital relationship at this juncture; the Duchess relates to him as a sort of feudal possession. Because his wife has been accosted, he, as liege lord, has been insulted. Naturally, then, it is in feudal terms that the Duke confronts his vassal with the situation (ll. 156–63):

> Certes, dist-il, ce est granz deus
> quant proësce avez et beauté,
> et il n'a en vous lëauté!
> Si m'en avez mout deceü,
> que j'ai mout longuement creü
> que vous fussiez de bone foi
> loiaus a tout le mains vers moi,
> que j'ai vers vous amor eüe.

Only after this lengthy introduction which establishes the tone does he broach the specific nature of the Chevalier's violation of feudal loyalty.

In view of the importance which the feudal system occupies in the Duke's mind, and the constant appeals to its values which he makes throughout his encounter with the Chevalier, in view also of the solemnity of the oath he makes before the knight, is it not then very surprising that he capitulates after a few minutes of pouting on the part of the Duchess? If she really is a feudal possession, could he not simply have asserted his rights as her husband and lord?

But this wife does not strike one, in her second dialogue with the Duke, as being accustomed to a subordinate position. She knows she is loved, for she seems to expect that by playing on her husband's affection for her she will eventually have her way (ll. 568–72):

> samblant fet que point ne li haite
> que li dus o li gesir doie,
> qu'ele set bien ce est la voie
> de son mari metre au desouz
> par fere samblant de corouz.

She does. It is important to note that, as he gives in, the Duke addresses her in courtly terms as "Bele dame," not as his wife (ll. 636–69:

> je ne sai que face, par m'ame,
> que tant m'afi en vous et croi

193

que chose celer ne vous doi
que li miens cuers sache ne ot . . .

The perfect trust referred to in these lines also conforms to the courtly code. Is it not reasonable to suppose that, feudal values being as strong as they are in the Duke, some other value (his love), which he at least momentarily places higher, prompts him to transgress against them? [18]

The threat of death which accompanies the Duke's capitulation (ll. 640–43) is more than a dramatic foreshadowing of the tragic end. It is the reassertion of those feudal values as of supreme importance after all. The Duke loves his wife enough to break his feudal promises, but he violates them lucidly. In so doing, he imposes on the Duchess a condition consonant with his feudal system. Previously she had been placed above, or rather outside that system. Now, as a result of having opposed it, she must be answerable to it. Now it is she who is solemnly bound to observe secrecy; her husband cannot violate his cherished values except in terms of those values. He betrays them for love of his wife, yet, at the same time, transposes an equal share of his responsibility to her. He sacrifices duty to love in the mistaken expectation that love (the love he believes the Duchess has for him) will conform to duty. When the Duchess proves unworthy of his trust in her, he keeps his second promise and punishes her betrayal with death. His wronged feudal values have reasserted themselves in a manner befitting their importance to him. And it may be correct to say as well that his offended love also has taken its revenge.

It has become clear, through a careful study of the narrative, that the traditional *losengier* theme does not provide the real basis of conflict in the *ChV*. The conflict develops around the feudal absolute of the Duke and the absolute of courtly love, one lived out in a social setting, the other shunning reality in order to subsist. Neither really works, even though it lies within the power of feudalism to distribute justice to the criminal. The theme of the absolute asserts itself in the narrative through the nature of every character in the poem: the Châtelaine demands absolute secrecy of her knight; the Chevalier in turn sees in absolute trust in his lord the only solution to his problem; the Duke promises to honor this absolute trust in a manner worthy of it, but weakens in the face of the absolute demands of his wife. Everything is "either/or"; there is no room for compromise — an attitude which does nothing but foster ultimately unhealthy compromises.

The poem demonstrates that a harmonious balance between ideal and real, good and evil, cannot be attained, much less maintained. On a social level, the couple has failed: the "ideal" couple, because it could not withstand the real; the "real" couple, because it could not tolerate the ideal. The ideal of courtly love, if attained, becomes real love. Yet, because this love refuses to recognize any reality but its own, it proves useless to society and to itself.

The poem goes even further. While remaining within a social framework, the *ChV* seems to be proposing reflections that would be equally true in the ontological order: man longs for the absolute; he sees in it solutions and stability; but it escapes him in this world where "what is" is forever in conflict with what he thinks ought to be, and where both failure to compromise and compromise itself are equally likely to cause unhappiness. This is the essence of tragedy.

Whatever perspective is adopted, the thread of paradox runs the entire length of the poem: to survive one must trust in another, and to trust in another is eventually to be disappointed; one must compromise to be happy although compromises jeopardize one's happiness, for the refusal to compromise entails certain unhappiness; one cannot subordinate love to duty with impunity, but neither can one subordinate duty to love without sanction.

By example as well as by precept, the story of the Châtelaine and her knight proposes prudence in the handling of absolute values. But beyond this *mise en garde*, no answers are given to the numerous questions raised by the poem, unless it be the poet's warning about the one thing that the characters forget: the weakness of men.

> Et par cest example doit l'en
> s'amor celer par si grant sen
> c'on ait toz jors en remembrance
> que li descouvrirs riens n'avance
> et li celers en toz poins vaut.
> *Qui si le fet, ne crient assaut*
> *des faus felons enquereors*
> *qui enquierent autrui amors.*[19]

NOTES

1. Gaston Paris, *La Littérature française au moyen âge* (Paris: Librairie Hachette et Cie, 1890), p. 108. Comments in the same vein can be found in the writings of Gaston Raynaud, Robert Bossuat, Lucien Foulet, and R. Weeks.

2. Paul Zumthor, "De la chanson au récit: La Chastelaine de Vergi," *VR*, 27 (1968), p. 84.

3. *La Chastelaine de Vergi*, ed. Frederick Whitehead, 1st ed. (Manchester: Manchester University Press, 1944), pp. vii–xxvi. Hereinafter referred to in parentheses in the text as I.

4. *La Chastelaine de Vergi*, ed. Frederick Whitehead, 2nd ed. (Manchester: Manchester University Press, 1951), pp. ix–xliii. Hereinafter referred to in parentheses in the text as II. References to the text of the *ChV* are taken from this edition.

5. Whitehead's first study brings to light, without developing them, these indications. For example: the idea that the irrational veto of the story's fairy-tale elements is transformed into the courtly convention of secrecy, only to be retransformed, by the extreme and unexplained interpretation given it, into something similar to the irrational veto (I, x, xiv–xv), the statement that "the lovers become the architects of their own ruin" (I, xi) (a notion later nullified or weakened on p. xxiii: the *ChV* belongs to a class of stories where "the adventures and misfortunes that happen to the lovers are produced by some agency external to themselves . . ."), the conclusion that the story illustrates "not the dangers of disclosing a secret love, but only the danger of making the disclosure to a weak and indiscreet man dominated by a vindictive wife who bears a grudge against one of the lovers" (I, xiv), the observation that the Châtelaine "regards herself as the victim of an *unavoidable*, if terrible, misfortune" (I, xvii) (italics added); the further observation that the Châtelaine dies "because being what she is, there is no other way out" (I, xx). All of these observations, even in an embryonic stage, point to another level of meaning which begs to be explored.

6. Whitehead expressed it (II, xxvi) as the use of courtly love's artificial conventions "merely as the machinery of a story of a genuinely tragic and highly emotional type."

7. In the present study, the terms "ideal" and "real" are used frequently. By "ideal" is meant a standard or model of perfection (i.e., the courtly or feudal ideal). By extension, it means that which exists only in the mind, and is beyond the perception of those not devoted to it. Being conceived in this story as an exaggerated ideal, the courtly value system entails intransigence, an inability to tolerate compromises with the real (that which is), which involvement in society requires. When describing the Châtelaine-Chevalier courtly relationship, "ideal" indicates that their love is supposedly perfect and also that, being necessarily hidden from the rest of men, it has no reality for anyone but the two lovers. On the other hand, the relationship of the Duke and Duchess is "real" or visible to men, and imperfect; because it is a marital relationship ratified by legal bonds, it automatically precludes the possibility of true love (in a courtly context). When it is suggested later that the Duke wishes it to be "ideal" as well, the word means that he desires it to be characterized by perfect love.

8. Ll. 316–22, 332–39.

9. Whitehead also remarks in this connection (II, xxxiii) that, when the knight visits the lady, he gives no sign of a sense of crisis or interior agi-

tation, as might be expected after his upsetting encounter with the Duke. Yet a period of time, at least half a day, has elapsed between their interview and nightfall. During this time the knight has been able to pull himself together and prepare for the nocturnal meeting. It is of the utmost importance that he *not* show any distress, lest he arouse in his lady any suspicion of his indiscretion. Furthermore, he has been assured by his lord, whom he has every reason to trust, that he will not be exiled and that nothing will ever jeopardize his happiness. In view of his recent dilemma, his ecstatic joy is doubly understandable.

10. See Werner Söderhjelm, *La Nouvelle française au XVe siècle* (Paris: H. Champion, 1910), p. 6: ". . . son âme ne se révèle que dans le monologue qu'elle prononce avant de mourir; mais elle y donne à sa passion et à sa douleur l'expression la plus pénétrante."

11. Whitehead himself used the words "person obsessed with one bewildering sorrow" (II, xxxix).

12. Even in his first interpretation (xvii), Whitehead anticipated the second by noting an element of surprise at her gentle and forgiving reproaches. Neither of his two supporting examples is convincing. Ll. 15–17 are a general statement and *grant dolor* can mean any number of things. Ll. 268–90 are uttered by the knight; this is *his* point of view, how *he* assesses the situation.

13. Within the context of love, of course. In another context, the one can be viewed as symbolic of unity, wholeness, and stability.

14. A further indication that courtly love must be broadly interpreted in this poem is the Chevalier's principle motivation in his choice. A perfect courtly lover would accept exile and the consequent separation from his beloved — a living death since she is the lover's life — as proof of his heroic devotion. The Chevalier is unable to rationalize to such an extent the very human longing of his heart.

15. It is relative in the sense that life in society is composed of human relationships which dictate forms of compromise, some kind of *modus vivendi*, and therefore is built less on absolutes than on the effort to adapt them to changing circumstances.

16. Of course, in one way or another, the other three characters are also seeking personal satisfaction; but they do so in a manner acceptable to society. They are not willfully destructive of the rights of others.

17. In another perspective, around the Duchess are created the exposition of the tragedy (actions 1–2), its *noeud* (3–6, which embrace 4–5), and the peripeties (7–8, 9), the second of which brings on the double catastrophe (10, 11). Whichever way one looks at it, she is at the core of the problem: the most real, by insisting that the most ideal be joined to it, entering into conflict with the ideal, which, in turn, recognizes that it cannot survive if it comes into contact with the real. The more fragile protagonist must eventually give way, for the Duchess will destroy what she herself cannot have.

18. Another indication given by the poem of the strength of the Duke's affection for his wife is the fact that, when the Duchess' accusations are proven

false, he exacts no retribution of her; he does not punish her, except by his increased affection for the Chevalier, and, what is stranger still, he does not even chide her. He merely enjoins her never again to speak of the matter (ll. 541–49). In his own way the Duke is trying, perhaps, to keep the couple immune from disintegration.

19. Ll. 951–58. Italics added.

The Illustrations of the Cædmonian Genesis

LITERARY CRITICISM THROUGH ART

Thomas H. Ohlgren

ALTHOUGH MOST STUDENTS of the Middle Ages are aware that such manuscripts as Ælfric's *Heptateuch*[1] or the *Cædmonian Poems*[2] were profusely illustrated with drawings, few realize that these pictorial representations were deliberately intercalated into the literary text for the express purpose of textual elucidation. Indeed, literary scholars have largely ignored the illustrations of medieval literary manuscripts as possible sources of information about the text. To ignore these illustrations is to ignore the manuscript as it was intended to be read.

An interdisciplinary approach in literature that employs comparisons to other art forms is still regarded with skepticism. René Wellek attacks the confusion that results when the approaches, intentions, and critical and evaluative vocabulary of one genre are forced upon another genre that has a different historical, social, and cultural development. Wellek's observation, for example, that some of these studies are "perversions on the fringes of scholarship," and hence valueless, is one of the most frequently cited dismissals of this valid critical procedure.[3] Pointing out the absurdity of interpreting poetry in terms of architecture, Wellek cites two literary studies, one by Bernard Fehr, who compares eight lines from Pope to "the string courses and cornices of a Palladian building," the other by a German scholar, who "compares the tension and bold arch of Milton's sentences with the cupola of St. Paul's cathedral." Wellek, in short, pleads for "clear

A slightly different version of this paper was presented on 30 October 1970 at the Midwest Modern Language Association, Milwaukee, Wisconsin. This article is a condensed version of sections of my 1969 University of Michigan Ph.D. dissertation, "The Illustrations of the *Cædmonian Genesis* as a Guide to the Interpretation of the Text."

distinctions in use and a scheme of relationships and emphases."[4] The enunciation of clear distinctions between artistic and literary vocabulary is of course essential to the interdisciplinary method, but instead of condemning the possibility of any valid interdisciplinary methodology, Wellek points rather to the numerous pitfalls.

Before attempting to assess the relationships between a specific literary text and its illustrations, the interdisciplinary scholar should first decide how drawings, in theory, elucidate a text. Important to this approach is the distinction between decoration and illustration. Decorations, such as foliated and zoomorphic initials, fret patterns, strapwork, rosettes, and acanthus leaves, were intended, with few exceptions, to embellish the page of a manuscript.[5] They usually had no specific reference to the meaning of a text. Manuscript illustration, by contrast, was invented in order to improve our understanding of a piece of writing — thus, diagrams were added to scientific treatises and scenic illustrations to literary texts.[6] These drawings were not intended as mere embellishments, but usually had a well-defined didactic purpose: to describe as well as to explain the text. (The Latin word *illustrare* means literally to light up; in one sense, then, to illustrate means to elucidate or to make clear by examples.) The manuscript illustrator's task was to translate aspects of the verbal content into pictures so as to explain and reinforce the text. Such illustrations, then, still function as visual aids for us, focusing our attention on specific details, situations, or dramatic elements in the text. They are not unlike the marginal glosses in manuscripts which serve to explain certain words, phrases, or concepts in the text. When these visual glosses are considered as a sequence, they may well provide a commentary on the text, revealing not only the tradition's (and to a certain extent, the artist's) interpretation of the text, but a knowledge of extrinsic but related matters, such as textual parallels and special meanings that might be useful to the reader.

It must be stressed, however, that there are certain elements of poetry, such as syntax, rhyme, and verbal connotations, that cannot be reduced to visual terms; they have no counterpart in art, just as line, shadowing, and perspective have no counterpart in literature. Herein lies the folly of describing Milton's prose style in terms of the "tension" and "bold arch" of the cupola of St. Paul's cathedral. What then does it mean to say that an illustration translates the poetic text into pictures? At best, we can say a particular picture, or part of a picture, approximates something in the text. The "language" of poetry is translated into the "language" of art, but we cannot and should not expect a literal translation.

There are two conditions, according to Kurt Weitzmann, which govern the illustration of a text. The first condition is the text's popularity; the second is a "narrative content with a considerable amount of action so that the illustrator may clearly visualize events as historical realities." [7] These two conditions are most fully realized in certain parts of the Bible, especially the Pentateuch and the Gospels. Without doubt, the Bible was the most studied and illustrated book of the Middle Ages, and religious materials, such as the Vulgate, the Apocrypha, saints' lives, homilies, and the pseudepigrapha provided the greatest single source of inspiration for literature and art for a millennium. Once the early Christian artists had established the iconography for the popular Biblical scenes, these representations crystallized into what Emile Mâle calls a "sacred script . . . of which every artist must learn the characters." [8] Mâle further states that "the artistic representation of sacred subjects was a science governed by fixed laws which could not be broken at the dictates of individual imagination." [9] Thus, as Kurt Weitzmann notes, "later generations of illustrators copied, whenever it was possible, from the established pictorial archetype, and comparatively seldom was a new cycle of miniatures invented for a text which existed already with pictures." [10] This practice accounts for the extremely conservative nature of Western art up to the Romanesque period.

Problems arose for the medieval artist when he was faced with a text requiring illustration that deviated in any way from the basic Vulgate text. The revised text could take a number of forms. It could be an excerpted version of the basic text, as in Ælfric's *Heptateuch*,[11] or it could be a metrical paraphrase which included poetic rearrangements and amplifications, as in the *MS. Junius 11*. The first poem in the *MS. Junius 11*, the *Cædmonian Genesis*, is a poetic amplification, with substantial modifications, of the Book of Genesis. The text of the 2936-line poem constitutes two parts, "Genesis A," which is of the late seventh or early eighth century, and "Genesis B," which was interpolated into "Genesis A" no earlier than the ninth century. The first part of "Genesis A," lines 1–234, begins with an account of the battle in heaven, the creation of hell, and the fall of the angels, and concludes with an account of the six days of creation. The second part of "Genesis A," lines 852–2936, commences with the meeting of God with Adam and Eve after the fall, and concludes with Abraham's sacrifice of Isaac. The poem is clearly more than a literal paraphrase of the Book of Genesis. The interpolated section, "Genesis B," for example, develops the Biblical story in Genesis II:16–III:8. These eighteen short verses have been greatly expanded to 616 lines of Old English verse. The medieval paraphrast has converted the succinct Biblical passage into an extended treatment of the war in heaven, the fall of the angels, the temptation, and the fall of man. His rendition of the Biblical text is lively and imaginative, and he apparently had no qualms about using materials from other traditions to suit his literary and narrative needs. His major deviations, for instance, from the Biblical text include the spectacular rise of the rebellious angel Lucifer, the titanic battle in heaven cast in vivid Germanic heroic diction, a detailed description of the horrors of hell with its alternating heat and frost, the defiant speeches of Satan anticipating Milton's interest in the psychology of evil, a different sequence of the temptation wherein Adam is tempted first, and an ambiguity concerning the exact form of Satan's messenger. Thus the paraphrast creates a unique dramatic narrative loosely derived from Biblical materials, and at times he seems only to pay lip service to the Vulgate account while introducing imaginative conceptions from other sources. The poem is original — original in James W. Bright's sense of "being dependent on Scripture for the most part, but independent in the selection and grouping of the material, and artistic in the interweaving of tradition with sacred history, and in observing the demands of a central theme." [12]

A study of the poetry and illustrations of the *Cædmonian Genesis* is complicated by three facts: first, the text and drawings are extant in only one manuscript, so we cannot compare the eleventh-century manuscript with its exemplar, if one existed; second, the poet and artists are anonymous, so we cannot compare this work with others from the same creative hands; third, the actual date of composition is much earlier than the date of transcription and illustration, so we cannot assume the text and drawings to be united on the basis of a common social and cultural background. As a result, we are not able to use the sources of information that would enable us to answer such important questions as: What are the sources for the text and the illustrations? Were the text and illustrations combined before the eleventh century? Were the artists simply copying from an illustrated exemplar or were they using their imaginations to adapt creatively

202

models from the Genesis pictorial tradition in order to satisfy the special requirements of the revised text?

Kurt Weitzmann suggests that the artist, when confronted with a text that had undergone changes by translation, paraphrase, or revision, instead of creating a new picture cycle, searched for the same source which the writer of the text consulted and copied from it the illustrations.[13] Weitzmann describes specifically the migration of Genesis illustrations from an exemplar, the *Cotton Genesis*, to a revised vernacular version of Genesis, the *Millstatt Genesis*, which was written in Middle High German in the late eleventh century.[14] In the *Millstatt Genesis*, however, the poet, unlike the poet of the *Cædmonian Genesis*, had not added any new elements, such as the initial temptation of Adam or the angelic tempter, that would have caused the artist to adapt models in order to accommodate the revised text. It is probable, nevertheless, that the eleventh-century artists of the *Cædmonian Genesis* did copy from an illustrated exemplar, perhaps of the tenth century, which contained stories of the fall of man and of the angels, of Enoch, Noah, and Abraham.[15] If the artists had copied from an extensive cycle of Genesis pictures, it would be reasonable to assume, as Barbara Raw points out, that the illustrations would show some resemblance to those of Ælfric's *Heptateuch*, the other early eleventh-century manuscript executed at Canterbury. But the Cædmonian pictures correspond to the Ælfric illustrations in only one point.[16] Miss Raw deduces from this fact that there was in England during the eleventh century a series of Genesis illustrations other than the early Christian cycle from which the Ælfric pictures were copied. Consequently, it is apparent that two Genesis cycles were available, both based ultimately on the *Cotton Genesis* recension but differing in details, and that the model of *MS. Junius 11* was copied from the second of these cycles.[17]

Since the uncertainties concerning the manuscript history of the *Cædmonian Genesis* cannot be resolved, I will in this study denote the artist as the one responsible for first adapting pictorial models from a Genesis cycle and other sources in order to accommodate the unusual portions of the poetic text. The artist may have considered two alternatives in his task of translating the unorthodox portions of the revised text into pictures: first, he could follow his artistic sensitivities and illustrate the text as closely as possible, but run the risk of using or inventing models unacceptable to the tradition; or second, the artist could imaginatively adapt existing pictorial models to fit the altered situations of the revised text, this alternative enabling him to express his originality within the limits of a fixed tradition. As we will see in the following representative sequence of drawings, the artist of "Genesis B" employed both alternatives, revealing in addition his nearly wholesale assimilation of the poem's content and theme.

In the illustration on the lower portion of page 20 (Fig. 1), the artist deviated from the orthodox Biblical account in order to accommodate the poem. The drawing depicts Satan fettered hand and foot over the raging hell-fires and surrounded by flagellant fiends. This scene is a visualization of lines 371–88 of the poem. The poet specifically mentions that Satan is manacled by iron rings and imprisoned by the huge gratings of the gates of hell (ll. 377–88). Although the binding of Satan episode was interpolated by the Church Fathers from the Apocalypse (Rev. XX:1–3) into their commentaries on the Book of Genesis, and transmitted to Old English poetry by means of the Christian Latin poetry of the fourth, fifth, and sixth centuries, it was not yet a part of the Genesis artistic tradition. In order to accommodate the poet's description of the binding of Satan, the artist had to adapt the scene from either an illustration of the Harrowing of Hell or an illustrated Apocalypse.[18]

The drawing, in addition, reveals Satan addressing a smaller devil, who stands before his lord and holds his chained hand. This iconographic unit corresponds to the poetic account of Satan's plea for a volunteer-devil to go to Eden in his place (ll. 409–21). Since Satan is incarcerated he cannot personally defeat God, but he can seek his revenge by having an emissary-devil cause the downfall of Adam and Eve. The poet proceeds to describe the arming of the Tempter, who places a helmet upon his head. The devil's main weapon, however, is his knowledge of craft ("feondes cræfte") and wicked deeds (ll. 447b–452). His avowed purpose is to deceive, mislead, and pervert. The success of his temptation lies in his intellectual, and, as we will see, "phantasmic" deception of Adam and Eve. The artist emphasized this element of deceit by showing the Tempter ascend through the gates of hell as a beautiful angel. The fiend's sartorial preparation later proves to be the key to his successful temptation of Eve.

The poet continues his narrative by relating the highly unorthodox initial temptation of Adam by the emissary-devil in lines 495–546. Before his rhetorical assault of Adam, the Tempter assumes the form of a serpent (ll. 491–92). He begins by telling Adam that he has just come from heaven and that God has commanded Adam to eat of the fruit of the Tree of Death. The fruit, the fiend lies, will not only increase Adam's power but will make him the most beautiful of God's creatures. The Tempter finally suggests that Adam can demonstrate his faithfulness to God by eating the fruit. Adam's initial response is cautious. He replies by reiterating God's prohibition and says he does not understand the serpent's contrary instructions. He refuses to obey the serpent because he neither looks like any of God's angels nor does he possess proof of his identity, a "tacen." Enraged, the messenger-devil turns to Eve.

This initial temptation, according to J. M. Evans, establishes two crucial points that determine the dramatic events to follow:

> First, Adam's refusal to believe him has given the Devil a weapon to use against Eve; he can appeal not only to her credulity but also to her desire to protect her husband from the consequences of his alleged disobedience. Second, Adam's request for a "tacen" has taught the Devil how to accomplish his downfall; if Eve can be persuaded to eat the forbidden fruit by offering her some concrete assurance that she is fulfilling the will of God, it should not be difficult for her to convince Adam that the emissary is all he claims to be. The prior temptation of Adam, albeit unsuccessful, suggests the means by which he can finally be brought to destruction.[19]

The Tempter, then, learns from his initial approach to Adam that Eve can be persuaded to eat the fruit by offering her a "tacen." Evans suggests that the "tacen" is the fiend's promise to Eve that she will be given a vision of the heavens to confirm the virtue of her deed. The illustrations of this portion of the poem, however, suggest a more convincing token of the Tempter's credibility: the assumption of a disguise as an angelic messenger. Adam had refused to believe the Tempter, then in the form of a serpent (ll. 491–92), because he did not look like one of God's angels (ll. 538b–539). Although the text does not specifically mention when the emissary-devil changes into his angelic disguise, we must assume he does so before he tells Eve (ll. 538–87) that he knows well the angelic court in heaven. Eve, in addition, tells Adam after her transgression that she believed the messenger because he was dressed as an angel:

> and þes boda sciene,
> godes engel god, ic on his gearwan geseo
> þæt he is ærendsecg uncres hearran,
> hefoncyninges.[20]

205

and this bright messenger
God's angel good I by his garb see
that he is the envoy of our Lord
heaven's King.

[ll. 656b–659a]

The illustrations on pages 24, 28, and the upper portion of 31 (Figs. 2, 3, 4) clearly reinforce this interpretation. The artist in all three drawings emphasized the disguise motif by showing the Tempter as a tall, graceful figure dressed in angelic robes with full wings.[21] The disguise is also enhanced by coloration. While in hell, the Tempter is drawn in brown ink — the color reserved for depictions of Satan, the other fallen angels, and the structure of hell — but when the fiend assumes his disguise as an angel he is drawn in red ink. Hitherto the artist used the color red for depictions of the Deity, the faithful angels, and the structure of heaven. After the successful temptation of Adam and Eve, the artist depicted on the lower portion of page 31 (Fig. 4) the partial transformation of the Tempter back to a naked, grizzly-haired demon with a long tail. The demon, significantly, was again drawn in brown ink. The artist created a symbolic color code also in his visualization of the story of the fall of the angels on page 3. Before the rebellion in heaven, Lucifer and his followers were drawn in red ink, but after their expulsion they were outlined in brown. The change in color visually reinforces their loss of heavenly bliss. This symbolic use of coloration has also been noted by W. O. Hassall, who, in a discussion of the coloration of the Holkham Bible, notes that the color red should have recalled to a priest the blood of Christ, and that the color red becomes the emotional keynote of the Holkham manuscript.[22] The artist's use of symbolic coloration in the *Cædmonian Genesis*, in sum, brilliantly highlights the "phantasmic" deception of Adam and Eve by the emissary-devil, and this interpretative insight can only be gained by a consideration of the drawings.

The artist, then, was capable of deviating from the Biblical account in Genesis. As a member of a religious community, he had obvious obligations to promulgate the Church's teachings through his drawings, but he also had commitments to the text he was illustrating. The deviations from the "sacred script" seen thus far may represent his conscious effort to walk the narrow line between conventionality and artistic sensitivity. The artist, however, faced a dilemma when he approached the illustration of the highly unorthodox initial temptation of Adam by the disguised emissary-devil. That he had difficulty with this section of the poem is reinforced by a consideration of the fact that the drawings on pages 20 (upper portion), 24, and 28, do not fit properly into the poetic text. The temptation-of-Eve scenes on pages 20 and 24 are prematurely placed into the manuscript — the poetic account does not occur until seven pages later than the first of these scenes. In spite of these difficulties, the artist met the dilemma by a shrewd use of conflation on page 28 (Fig. 3). There he depicted a dual temptation of Adam and Eve by the disguised demon, resolving the unusual textual account by combining both temptations into one illustration. In the center stands the emissary-devil with Adam and Eve on either side. The Tempter holds an apple in each hand, appearing to offer them to Adam and Eve at the same time. If we focus on the right half of the drawing, it seems apparent that the Tempter first offers the fruit to Adam, who rejects it. As the focus of attention shifts to the left half, we note that Eve accepts the apple with one hand and eats it with the other. The repetition of the apple indicates a sequential drawing, whereby several moments of the story are depicted as one scene without repeating any of its participants. This method violates the unity of time as several actions occur in the same scene simultaneously.[23] The clarity of the pictorial composition is impaired, yet we must conclude that the confusion or ambiguity that results from the welding of these two separate scenes was deliberately intended to resolve the unusual poetic treatment of the demon's prior approach to Adam.

Thus far we have seen how a consideration of specific drawings helps us to understand portions of the poetic text. In the drawings on pages 20 and 28, the artist could not merely borrow from the Genesis artistic tradition; he either had to adapt a model from another tradition, the Apocalypse, or he had to rearrange an existing model for the unusual dual temptation of Adam and Eve. In both situations, the resulting pictorial compositions highlight certain elements in the poem that have hitherto been slighted by critics.

In addition to elucidating specific portions of the text, the drawings may also help to clarify and dramatize the underlying thematic purpose of the poem. One of the basic principles we ought to understand when dealing with manuscript is that due to the limitations of space the artist cannot illustrate everything in the text. The artist must not only select certain passages for illustration but must decide how these episodes will be treated pictorially. Some will be amplified, others condensed, and some will be omitted altogether. If we agree that the drawings of a literary text are added for reasons of increased intelligibility of the text as well as for artistic embellishment, we will find that the artist's selection and treatment of scenes may be governed by his awareness of the theme of the poem.

The opening lines of the *Cædmonian Genesis*, according to Bernard Huppé, announce the same theme as in Cædmon's *Hymn*: man's primary duty is to sing the praises of his Creator.[24] "It is a theme that we might expect from a poem on Genesis," Huppé notes, because Genesis, "as interpreted by the commentators, not only describes man's fall, but forecasts his redemption as well; and the promotion of man's duty to praise God is the aim and logical conclusion of the traditional justification of God's ways in the story of the Creation, Fall, and Redemption."[25] Beginning with this basic theme, the poet of the *Cædmonian Genesis* develops in lines 12–77 the initial contrast between the faithful, who are rewarded, and the unfaithful, who are severely punished. The basic intention of this contrast is to help man understand his primary duty to glorify God through praise. The contrast consistently juxtaposes heavenly bliss with hellish punishment. This initial contrast is repeated throughout the poem as a central panel of the storied tapestry. The fall-of-the-angels episode, which is introduced in the first 111 lines of the poem, is twice repeated in lines 246–441 and in lines 731–60 in order to reinforce the theme of the poem. This episode functions through repetition and variation as a commentary on the action it surrounds. It directs our attention to other personages of the poem, who resemble either the fallen angels or the blessed angels. The story of Adam and Eve, for instance, is a repetition of the fall-of-the-angels story, but told in human terms; it is the catastrophic onslaught of satanic treachery against human fallibility. Man loses, but in losing he wins a way to earn heaven by praising God. The initial thematic contrast between the blessed and the damned, in addition, foreshadows later types of the faithful and faithless in other episodes in the *Cædmonian Genesis*. For instance, Abel (ll. 965–86), Seth (ll. 1104–42), Noah (ll. 1237–1601), and Abraham (ll. 1703–2936), like the faithful angels in the opening lines of *Genesis*, all retain their blessedness by praising God. By contrast, Cain (ll. 965–1054), the builders of the Tower of Babel (ll. 1661–1702), and the evil dwellers of Sodom and Gomorrah (ll. 2535–62a), like Lucifer and the rebellious angels in the opening lines of *Genesis*, all bring destruction upon themselves by not praising God. Thus, the theme that is announced in the opening lines is emphasized by repetition and variation throughout the *Cædmonian Genesis.*

By highlighting certain prominent thematic elements in his illustrations, the artist revealed his awareness of the poem's theme and structure. Like the poet, he selected and arranged his materials so that the thematic contrast between salvation and damnation is emphasized. A striking example of the way in which the artist visually reinforced the poem's theme is seen in the drawings on pages 16 and 17 (Figs. 5, 6). Here in two half-page drawings the artist encapsulated the titanic struggle between God and Lucifer. In the drawing on page 16 (Fig. 5), the angels are shown falling from heaven into hell. In hell itself, Satan, tied hand and foot to stakes, is being harassed by a demon with a flail. The most impressive aspect of this drawing is the vivid contrast between the blessed and the damned angels. Above, in heaven, the loyal angels are depicted as beautiful creatures with wavy hair, majestic robes, and full wings; below, in hell, the damned angels are small, dark, ugly creatures with unkempt hair, squat, nude bodies, exposed genitalia, and clipped wings. An even more striking visual contrast is seen in the drawing on page 17 (Fig. 6). This illustration depicts two monarchs, both enthroned and surrounded by their faithful retainers, but with pronounced differences. The Deity sits upon the cushioned throne of heaven, flanked by majestic Cherubim, while Satan sits upon hard ground, flanked by ugly fiends who hold symbols of sovereignty over his crowned head. Not only did the artist juxtapose the harmony in heaven with the chaos in hell, the beauty of the blessed angels with the grotesqueness of the damned angels, and the victorious Deity with the subdued monarch of hell, but he reinforced these thematic contrasts by means of coloration — red for the color of the blood of Christ, hence salvation; brown denoting spiritual death, hence damnation.

Just as the fall-of-the-angels episode, three times recounted in the poem and in the illustrations on pages 3, 16, and 17, focuses our attention on the theme of the poem, so too does the drama of man's life on earth after the expulsion from Eden. The battle is not between man and the superhuman, but between man and his fallen nature. If the illustrations of the entire poem were within the scope of this study, it could be shown that both the poet and the artist selected and purposefully juxtaposed significant events in the last two-thirds of the *Cædmonian Genesis* where man's attempted pilgrimage back to Paradise or his descent into an earthly hell are recorded. The illustrations of Cain and Abel, the descendants of Cain, the progeny of Seth, Noah and the Ark, Nimrod, and Abraham, like those of the fall of the angels and of the temptation and fall of Adam and Eve, are treated so as to highlight the basic thematic contrast between the "destiny of those who praise God and have joy and that of those who refuse to serve in praise and possess only a foolish boast, which leads to destruction."[26]

This study has attempted to demonstrate the importance of the illustrations of the *Cædmonian Genesis* to an understanding of the manuscript as a literary and artistic whole and, by extension, the general significance of illustrations to the study of medieval literature. Indeed, the medieval artist was able, under special conditions, to exert his originality in the selection and treatment of pictorial scenes, revealing an aesthetic assimilation of the poem's content and theme. The illustrations, in short, provide an invaluable interpretative and critical commentary on the text, eminently useful to scholars and students of literature.

NOTES

1. London: British Museum, *MS. Cotton Claudius B. IV.* It contains 418 drawings. The standard edition is S. J. Crawford, *The Old English Version of the Heptateuch* (London: Oxford University Press, 1922). A facsimile edition is being prepared by C. R. Dodwell.
2. Oxford: Bodleian Library, *MS. Junius 11.* It contains 56 outline drawings, including five recently-discovered metalpoint sketches, which are described in my article "Five New Drawings in the *MS. Junius 11*: Their Iconography and Thematic Significance," to be published in *Speculum*, 47 (1972), 227–33. I am grateful to the Bodleian Library for permission to publish the photographs of pages 16, 17, 20, 24, 28, and 31 from *MS. Junius 11.*
3. Wellek, "The Parallelism between Literature and the Arts," *English Institute Annual* (1941), p. 44.
4. *Ibid.,* p. 49.
5. One exception has been pointed out by John Leyerle, who suggests that the structure of *Beowulf* is a poetic analogue of the interlace designs common in Anglo-Saxon art of the seventh and eighth centuries. He concludes that the study of Anglo-Saxon art is "most useful as an aid to the reassessment of early English literature because it is an important reminder that the society was capable of artistic achievements of a high order which can be looked for in the poetry as well." "The Interlace Structure of Beowulf," *University of Toronto Quarterly* (1967), p. 4.
6. Kurt Weitzmann, *Ancient Book Illumination* (Cambridge, Mass.: Harvard University Press, 1959), p. 1.
7. *Ibid.,* p. 31.
8. Mâle, *The Gothic Image* (New York: Harper & Brothers, 1958), pp. 1–2.

Figure 1. Satan Sends Emissary-devil to Eden. Oxford, Bodleian Library, MS. Junius 11, page 20. Subsequent page references are to this same manuscript.

ſpa ſpa ſpige vingde · þæſ onſian blican geþeax
ſceolde þine yldo bænman· ellen dæda· opſtuniaſ
ꝼoruht ꝼaſ⁊ þim bæon oꝼad ꝼcyneꝺ· lyde hƿile
ꝼceolde he liꝼ lꝭꝭ niotan· ꝼetan þonne landa
iꝼſtantoꝛt· on ꝼyne ꝼceolde ꝼæbndum þeoþian
þiʒen iſ tulþa ꝼꝛætniu mæꝛte: læbbum to lanʒ
ne hƿile· þ ꝼiꝛteꝛe lada ʒebonne· dyſine obælſ
boda· þe ƿið oꝛuhtñ þann·

Figure 2. Temptation of Eve by Disguised Emissary-devil. Page 24.

mij gepulit. hæfde ine pacpan lige. mæcod ge
mæpcod. þ heo hine mod ongan. læcan æfter þam
lapum. forþou heo æþam laðan onfing. ofer dri
hrnet pond. þndig beamg þþpic pinne pæmn. ne
þþnd þypfe dæd. monnum gmꝼacod. þif micel
pundor þ hit ece god. æfne polde. þadm þolian.
þpnde þegn rpa monig. fon læðð beþam lygenum.
þefon þam lapum com⁘

Figure 3. Dual Temptation of Adam and Eve by Disguised Emissary-devil. Page 28.

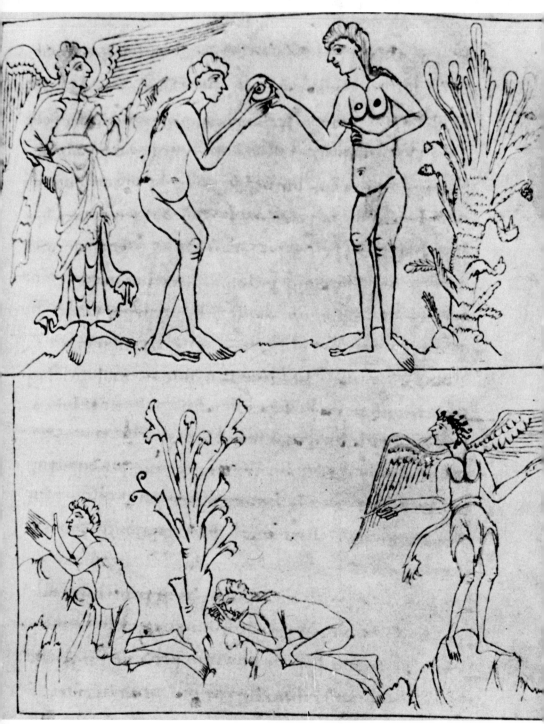

Figure 4. The Fall of Adam and Eve. Page 31.

þær þe he þann wið hæðenss waldno. ac cwæð hine
þa fram hir hyldo. ⁊hine on helle wscurp. on
þa oðwpan dala þær he to dwfle wrand. ⁊e
rwno mid hir gesihum eallum. ⁊eollox þa upon
oc hwfenum. þurh longe wra þreo niht ⁊ða
gar. þa englas oc hwfenum on helle. ⁊hwo ealle
won rewor owhten to owflum.

Figure 5. The Fall of the Angels. Page 16.

rum hæfð gefynne habban rædbodan· forhte
man he him to þice· hyra populo þær ge
hþynefð· forman rideþylde helle· mid þam
and facum· huldon ongiaf forð· heofon riht
hehde· þe ær godis hyldo geleafton· lagon
þa oðne· fynd on þam fyne· þe ær fpa fea
la hæfdon· gepinnif þið hiofna palofued· þite
þoliað· hatne hiudo þelm·helle tomioddf·

VII·

Figure 6. The Monarchs of Heaven and Hell. Page 17.

9. *Ibid.*, p. 1.

10. Weitzmann, *Illustrations in Roll and Codex: A Study of the Origin and Method of Text Illustration* (Princeton: Princeton University Press, 1947; rpt. 1970), pp. 130–31.

11. The *MS Cotton Claudius B. IV.* is chiefly composed of the narrative portions of the Heptateuch. Ælfric omitted catalogs of names, repetitions, and abstruse passages. He was interested in producing a highly readable narrative.

12. Bright, "Relation of Cædmonian Exodus to the Liturgy," *Modern Language Notes*, XXVII, 97.

13. Weitzmann, *Illustrations in Roll and Codex*, pp. 134–35.

14. *Ibid.*, pp. 139–40. The fifth- or sixth-century *Cotton Genesis* (British Museum, Cotton *Ms. Otho B. VI*) is the earliest extant illustrated Septuagint manuscript. This manuscript, or a close contemporary copy, originally contained about 330 miniatures and provided artists with models for subsequent versions of the Book of Genesis, frieze sarcophagi, silver plates, ivory plaques, and the mosaics of San Marco in Venice. See Kurt Weitzmann, "The Illustration of the Septuagint," *Studies in Classical and Byzantine Manuscript Illumination*, ed. Herbert L. Kessler (Chicago and London: The University of Chicago Press, 1971), pp. 45–49.

15. Evidence that the artists were copying has been offered by Francis Wormald and Barbara Raw. Wormald notes that the first artist's style "seems to be based on the early tenth century English work possibly of the period of King Athelstan, [and] that of the second is derived from that of the 'Psychomachia' in Corpus Christi College, Cambridge, which dates from the end of the tenth century, and from slightly earlier English portions of the Leofric Missal in the Bodleian." *English Drawings of the Tenth and Eleventh Centuries* (London: Faber and Faber, 1952), p. 40. In her M.A. thesis, "The Story of the Fall of Man and of the Angels in the *MS. Junius 11* and the Relationship of the Manuscript Illustrations to the Text" (University of London, 1953), directed by Francis Wormald, Barbara Raw seems to substantiate Wormald's assertion that the artists were copying from a tenth-century model. For instance, the coloring of the figure on page 11; the unusual tubular scroll on pages 2, 3, 41, 74, 76, 82 and the frontispiece; the dragon-like creature on pages 10 and 13; the decorated initials of the first artist; the series of cyclic illustrations depicting the stories of Adam and and Eve up to the death of Abel; the frames of the drawings depicting the descendants of Adam; and the fact that the first artist ignored the marginal instructions on pages 3, 6, and 7 all connect the first artist with tenth-century models (pp. 20–37).

16. Raw, p. 59.

17. *Ibid.*, pp. 59–60.

18. Barbara Raw notes that although there are several drawings of the bound Satan in English and Carolingian manuscripts of this period, none of them is connected with the story of the fall of the angels. As a possible model, she points to a drawing of the Harrowing of Hell, in which Satan is bound hand and foot, in the eleventh-century British Museum *MS. Cotton Tiberius C. VI.* (p. 74) The available illustrated Apocalypses may have in-

cluded Spanish Mss. of the ninth, tenth, and early eleventh centuries. Folios 17ʳ and 224ᵛ of the *Gerona Beatus Apocalypse* (Archivo de la Catedral, 975 A.D.), for instance, depict Satan enchained in hell. See plates 23 and 103 in *Sancti Beati a Liebana In Apocalypsin Codex Gerundensis*, edited by Jaime M. Casanovas, Cesar E. Dubler, Wilhelm Neuss (New York: Philip C. Duschnes, 1962). A valuable indication that the artist probably borrowed from Spanish manuscripts is that motifs other than those associated with the battle in heaven, the expulsion of the angels, and the binding of Satan also appear in the drawings of the *Cædmonian Genesis*; they include architectural details such as columns, arcades, and buildings; figure style, especially in the nudes; the circular motif for heaven; the Deity's tubular scroll; and plants and animals.

19. J. M. Evans, *Paradise Lost and the Genesis Tradition* (Oxford: Oxford University Press, 1968), p. 160.
20. All line citations from *The Junius Manuscript* (New York: Columbia University Press, 1931), ed. George P. Krapp.
21. The presence of the angelic fiend in the temptation scenes is very unusual; no pictorial precedent for these scenes is known. Barbara Raw (p. 50) suggests that if the figure of the angel is deleted from the drawing on page 24, "we find that Eve stands facing the right, her left hand raised towards the tree and holding an apple; in fact, apart from the non-appearance of the serpent in the tree, this picture corresponds very closely to that of the temptation of Eve in the mosaics and in the Grandval Bible, but it is a mirror copy."
22. W. O. Hassall, *The Holkham Picture Book* (London: Dropmore Press, 1954), pp. 11–13.
23. The "simultaneous method" is one of the three methods described by Weitzmann in *Illustrations in Roll and Codex* (pp. 12–14) for visually rendering the literary content.
24. Bernard Huppé, *Doctrine and Poetry: Augustine's Influence on Old English Poetry* (New York: State University of New York, 1959), p. 134.
25. *Ibid.*, pp. 134–135.
26. *Ibid.*, p. 137.

The Figural Style and Meaning of The Second Nun's Prologue *and* Tale

Paul M. Clogan

OF ALL THE *Canterbury Tales, The Second Nun's Tale* has received the least attention from the modern critic, despite the fact that it is generally recognized as the best-narrated example of a saint's life in Middle English poetry. For sundry reasons, the pious legend of the saintly Cecilia, her angelic coronation, the miracle of the bath of flames, and her triumphant martyrdom have never received the full, critical attention they deserve. The puritan, and especially the post-Calvinist, who insists upon a literal reading of saints' legends inevitably faces a certain difficulty in reaching an understanding and appreciation of the figural style and meaning of the Passion of St. Cecilia and its significance in the context of the *Canterbury Tales.* As a result, *The Second Nun's Tale* has been severely criticised, quickly dismissed with a degree of embarrassment, frequently ignored, and often left unedited as a mere translation and pious exercise of the young Chaucer. The present essay will first review the major criticism on the tale and will then suggest a new approach by examining the figural style and meaning of the *gloria passionis* in the legend of St. Cecilia and its social significance in the context of the marriage group of the *Canterbury Tales.*[1]

Early criticism of the tale was mainly interested in the date of composition and in possible sources and analogues, and was puzzled by the absence of a full-scale portrait of the Second Nun in the General Prologue. Scholars noted that in the Prologue to *The Legend of Good Women* Chaucer's own reference to a "Lyf of Seynt Cecyle," undoubtedly identical with *The Second Nun's Tale,* showed that the latter existed before the composition of the *Canterbury Tales,* and, therefore, was not originally written for the Second Nun or for the

213

series. Apparently, the early "Lyf of Seynt Cecyle" remained unrevised and not properly adapted when it was later inserted among the *Canterbury Tales* to mark the beginning of Fragment VIII. There is no introduction from the host or any indication of the identity of the narrator, except the manuscript rubrics which ascribe the tale to the Second Nun, a pilgrim without a portrait, who is only briefly mentioned in the General Prologue (A163–64) as "another nonne" in the company of the Prioress, perhaps serving as the latter's secretary or assistant. Because the "invocacio" in *The Second Nun's Prologue* is partly indebted to Dante's celebrated Hymn to the Virgin in *Paradiso* xxxiii, scholars conjectured that the *Tale* was probably written even as early as 1373, the date of Chaucer's return from his first so-called Italian journey.

Yet the textual evidence offered in support of the high probability of these conjectures is not convincing, nor does it stand up under reexamination. For example, Tyrwhitt was among the early scholars who cited as evidence of lack of revision and improper adaptation certain inconsistencies in the Second Nun's narration.[2] First, her reference in the Prologue, to the narrator as an "unworthy sone of Eve" 62) was taken as "striking and startling" coming from the lips of a nun. More recent critics,[3] however, have pointed out that the Nun's word pattern here is similar to that of the *Salve Regina*, which is still chanted daily by nuns, and that the word *sone* could also mean descendant of either sex, or simply human being.

Secondly, Skeat was one of the first to note the inappropriateness of "Yet preye I you that reden that I write" (G78) as clear evidence that the *Tale* was not originally intended to be narrated.[4] But the word *reden* in Chaucer can mean — in addition to *read* — *advise, interpret, counsel, describe, study* and *reckon*. Moreover, the thorough investigations into the nature and origin of saints' legends by the Bollandists demonstrate that the text of a saint's legend originated first in the official written accounts of eyewitnesses and later in the "acts" of the martyrs, "of which the principle source is a written document." These written "acts" were later adopted for liturgical purposes and *read* in the "office" of the saint's feast day. Thus arose the use of the word *legenda*, meaning "lessons to be read," for the *legenda* was based upon the saint's dossier. In this sense, "Yet preye I you that reden that I write" is not inappropriate or ill-suited to the narrator of the following legend. After the moving and elevated *Invocatio* to the Virgin, the Second Nun remembers her initial intention to translate the legend of St. Cecilia and here clarifies that intention with a word of advice and apology. The line is spoken by the Second Nun in the voice of the hagiographer and is directed to the pilgrims who are to interpret, reckon, or study the *legenda* or "lessons to be read."[5] Apologies for the unpolished style of saints' legends was a common characteristic, and it is important here to distinguish the hagiographer, narrator, and poet. The poetic of a saint's legend makes line 78 appropriate to the Second Nun.

Thirdly, the alleged close translation of the saint's life from the *Legenda Aurea* of Jacobus de Voragine has generally been accepted as clear evidence of Chaucer's early workmanship and immaturity of style, assuming, of course, that all translations are the work of only the young, and that age necessarily brings development and maturity. Yet reexamination of Chaucer's use of the *Legenda Aurea* reveals "our complete ignorance of what his copy of the *Legenda Aurea* may have contained."[6] Up to the baptism of Tiburce, where the narrative follows the source closely, Chaucer's verse is marked by a rich tonal beauty, by precise and poetic diction, compared to that of the mediocre Latin prose. From the baptism of Tiburce onwards, Chaucer's verse shows considerable abridgment of a longer version of the legend, perhaps that of Mombritius, occasional use of unexpected sources, and an artistic shaping of materials to develop theme, pattern, and imagery. No definite conclusions can be reached until there is a new study of the manuscript and textual history of the *Legenda Aurea* and the content of Chaucer's manuscript copy.

I

The structure of the *Tale* appears in the traditional form of medieval saint's legend which originally developed in response to the liturgical needs of the cult of the saint. In the period of the early Church — the time and setting of the Passion of St. Cecilia — the problem of truth, the relation of revelation and experience, was of major importance to both pagan and Christian, and the individual who would bear "witness" to the truth by suffering persecution and death for his new faith was considered to be the problem's best solution. The martyr, therefore, became the early Christians' hero, who experienced the *gloria passionis* and provided a new revelation to his fellow Christians. The martyr's confidence in his faith and the integrity of his belief inspired and edified the less heroic. The ancient world had its heroes who suffered and died in dignity for their ideals, and ancient literature had its Antigone, but the early Christian hero was, above all, the martyr who went to death not only in dignity but in triumph. His victory was the triumph of death. To preserve the memory of his faith and courage, and to console and inspire the faithful Christians, hagiographical writing developed, first as official accounts of eyewitnesses and as the "acts" of the martyrs, and later either as imaginative historical romances, sometimes with frankly fictional heroes, or as real forgeries.[7] Religious in character and edifying in purpose, hagiographical writing was inspired by pious devotion to a saint and designed to further his cult. Thus there developed a new literary genre, mixing biography, panegyric, and moral lesson.

The hagiographer's intention was to write history, but this meant everything that was said or written in books; his main concern was edification. As a result, saints' legends often presented idealized portraits, black-and-white-checkered accounts, mixing fiction and history or attempting to see history through the eyes of fiction, and flirting with potential converts by way of propaganda. In the thirteenth century, saints' legends were collected and circulated in calendars, legendaries, and martyrologies, and were finally liberated from liturgical functions by the two great Dominicans Vincent of Beauvais in his *Speculum Historiale* and Jacobus de Voragine in his masterly *Legenda Aurea*. The *Golden Legend* was one of the most popular books of the Middle Ages and one of the ten great medieval books Emile Mâle selected as presenting an adequate knowledge of medieval thought and culture.[8] There are more than 500 manuscript copies extant, and after Caxton printed an English translation in the fifteenth century it appeared in more than 156 editions and translations, outnumbering even the imprints of the Bible for the same period.[9] The *Golden Legend* was not the work of one man, nor was it in any sense an original compilation. Rather it was the work of the whole of Christendom, in which was mirrored and expressed the spirit of the age. The absence of originality should make it all the more interesting to us, for it presents the works of many writers and legends, old and new, compiled over the course of many centuries, and thereby renders the originals superfluous.

We do Chaucer and his art an injustice by dismissing *The Second Nun's Tale* as a mere translation. Clearly, it was not his intention to claim originality for his "Lyf of Seynt Cecyle," but to devote his attention to the rhyme-royal stanzas and versification. We know Chaucer was interested in hagiography and may have written other legends of

216

saints than those extant. In his Retraction at the end of the *Canterbury Tales*, he mentions among his translations several religious works:

> But of the translacion of Boece de Consolacione, and othere bookes of legendes of seintes, and omelies, and moralitee, and devocioun,/ that thanke I oure Lord Jhesu Crist and his blisful Mooder, and alle the seintes of hevene. . . .
> [(I) 1087–88]

Of the "othere bookes of legendes of seintes," only two of Chaucer's extant writings can be classified as hagiographic: *The Second Nun's Tale* and *The Prioress's Tale*. *The Legend of Good Women* is set forth as a book of martyrs, and the scattered references to saints and their cults throughout the *Canterbury Tales* are brief and passing. Even *The Prioress's Tale*, which relates the experience of the child saint Hugh the Younger of Lincoln, is strictly classified as a subdivision of hagiography known as miracles of the Virgin.[10]

Along with Agnes, Cecilia was one of the most popular Roman martyrs of the early Christian Church; her cult began in the fifth century and is still honored today in the liturgy of the Catholic Church on her feast day, 22 November, and celebrated with special ceremonies in her titular church, Santa Cecilia a Trastevere in Rome. Before the fifth century, however, little is known about the real Cecilia; her martyrdom and the origin of her cult are among the most obscured of all Roman hagiography. Her name does not appear in the early lists of feasts, nor in Jerome or Prudentius. Yet ancient pilgrim guide books to early Christian burial grounds cite the crypt of St. Cecilia adorned with frescoes near the chapel of the popes in the Catacomb of Calixtus on the Via Appia. In the fourth century, her church was built in the Trastevere section of Rome, and rebuilt by Pope Paschal I (817–24) who had her relics and supposedly those of Valerianus, Tibertius, Maximus, and Pope Urbanus removed from the Catacomb Praetextatus — where they had been transferred for fear of the invading Lombards — and reburied in the sarcophagi under the high altar of her basilica. Beyond these few facts, the rest is hagiography, romance, and legend. The "acts" of her Passion first appear in the late fifth century *Sacramentum Leonianum*[11] which contains five different masses in her honor. According to Hippolyte Delehaye, this account of her Passion owes its origin to a pious hagiographer's romantic adaptation of the virgin-marriage plot in the *Histoire de la persécution des Vandales* (486) of Victor de Vite, in which a Vandal chief encourages two of his Christian servants to marry.[12] Moreover, the legend of St. Cecilia bears many of the characteristic features of the "acts of the martyrs": numerous conversions, religious instruction to the catechumens, baptism administered by the Pope, long disquisitions with a judge, and the theme of the private house consecrated to the cult of the martyr and later transformed into a church. This theme of the private house was exploited and exaggerated especially in the "acts of the virgin martyrs," probably written by and for the edification of monks.

II

The Second Nun's legend of St. Cecilia is preceded by a so-called Prologue, actually an introduction, consisting of seventeen stanzas and composed of a dialectic of "ydelnesse" and "bisynesse" (G1–28), the eulogistic "Invocacio ad Mariam" (29–77), the narrator's stylistic apology (78–84), and the fantastic *Interpretacio nominis Cecilie* (85–119). The *Prologue* has generally been considered oblique, fragmented, and ill-suited to the legend, written later and perhaps revised when Chaucer tried to adapt the "Lyf of Seynt Cecyle" to the *Canterbury Tales*. Certain critics[13] who are impressed by the moving and elevated "Invocacio ad Mariam" consider these lines the best of the entire Tale, but fail to see how they are significantly related to the legend of St. Cecilia. Yet re-examination and a little imaginative sympathy with the medieval point of view show that the *Prologue* is artistically related to the legend in theme, pattern, and imagery. The chief function of the *Prologue* is to focus and epitomize the figural meaning of the legend.

The opening lines of the *Prologue* immediately reveal the world of the Second Nun, a world at once simple and complex, natural and supernatural, figurative and eschatological, with its strict moral vision of the virtues and vices. The *Prologue* begins with a dialectic of "ydelnesse" versus "leveful bisynesse," which at first appears simple and conventional, but as it is developed and intensified it begins to establish and express the antithetic figural style of the narrative and the basic ontological dualism of the Passion of St. Cecilia. The Nun's characterization of Idleness is conventional to the extent that the evils of Idleness were a popular topic in the Middle Ages and writers often prefaced their works with a brief invective against this subdivision of the vice Sloth. It is perhaps unnecessary to cite similar stanzas on Idleness or even to infer that the Idleness-prologue was written shortly before

Chaucer took up his active duties at the Customs office in 1373; or shortly after he petitioned for a deputy to relieve him of his duties at the Customs office in 1378 in order to write a royal-commissioned "Lyf of Seynt Cecyle" in honor of Adam Easton's nomination as cardinal priest of the church of Santa Cecilia a Trastevere.[14] Such matters are interesting from an historical or biographical point of view, but what is more important is the literary function of the Idleness invective in the context of the Second Nun's Prologue. The dialectic of "ydelnesse" versus "leveful bisynesse" uses the rhetorical figure of antithesis which is built upon the principle of contraries and consists of the rapid opposition of contrasting words in order to establish a rapprochement. According to ancient rhetoricians, antithesis could be a figure of speech, or a figure of thought, or both: for they believed that through antithesis contraries will meet.

"Ydelnesse" is not only "The ministre and the norice unto vices," it is also significantly "That porter of the gate" (1–3) which recalls Lady Idleness in the *Roman de La Rose*, the lovely portress at the gate to the garden of love. Chaucer had already translated part of the *Roman*, and he repeats the figure in the *Knight's Tale* (A1940) and again in the *Parson's Tale* (I714) where it is extended to prove that heaven is given not to idle folk but to those who will labor. Yet "That porter of the gate" may also refer to Ezechiel 44:2–3:

> And the Lord said to me: This gate shall be shut, it shall not be opened, and no man shall pass through it, because the Lord God of Israel hath entered in by it, and it shall be shut for the prince. The prince himself shall sit in it, to eat bread before the Lord. He shall enter in by the way of the porch of the gate, and shall go out by the same way.[15]

Ezechiel's gate was interpreted by Rabanus Maurus and other medieval Biblical commentators as a *figura*, or image, of the Virgin as the mother of Christ. According to Rabanus, the gate is the *uterus Virginis*.[16] In the light of this figurative interpretation, "That porter of the gate" signifies Mary's role and attitude in the mystery of the Incarnation, which will be described in the "Invocacio," and also figures the fruitful and apostolic virgin marriage of St. Cecilia, who will reveal to Valerian, Tiburce, and Maximus the mystery of suffering. In this sense, "ydelnesse" is a kind of *passio*, pathos, a passivity or affliction connoting suffering; a passive power that must be moved to action by another agent, just as vision must be stimulated by a colored object. As the

219

Prologue develops, "ydelnesse" becomes the opposite of *actio* and even *ratio*; for if unchecked, "ydelnesse" leads to the disorder of "roten slogardye" (17) and "greet confusioun" (23), implying the moral danger of uncontrolled passions.

On the other hand, its contrary, *remedium*, and antithesis is "bisynesse" which is both "leveful" and "feithful," for it checks and controls "ydelnesse" and intentions. In this sense, "bisynesse" is a kind of *actio* which perfects and realizes intentions by transforming them into "leveful" and "feithful" works. This emphasis on diligence and work echoes the monastic Rule of St. Benedict, who warned his monks against the evils of idleness and of wasteful and ineffective contemplation, and tried to establish a fruitful balance between *passio* and *actio* by stressing the value and importance of work, even manual labor, in his idea of the *opus dei*.

The danger of "roten slogardye" and "greet confusioun" brings the antithesis of the Idleness-prologue to a kind of rapprochement or resolution as the narrator reveals that she herself has been caught up in the dialectic and is moved to express her initial intention:

> I have heer doon my feithful bisynesse
> After the legende, in translacioun
> Right of thy glorious lif and passioun,
> Thou with thy gerland wroght with rose and lilie, —
> Thee meene I, mayde and martyr, Seint Cecile.
> [24–28]

In the phrase, "thy glorious lif and passioun" the two contraries, "ydelnesse" (*passio*) and "bisynesse" (*actio*), meet in a dialectical relationship. The *passio* of "ydelnesse" and the *actio* of "bisynesse" are transformed into a *tertium quid*, the mysticism of the Passion. The "passioun" or suffering of St. Cecilia will not be the result of her withdrawal from the evils of injustice, but rather her willing submission to persecution in order to transcend the world. Unlike Antigone, Cecilia will face death not in defeat but in triumph and glory. The antithesis of "ydelnesse" and "leveful bisynesse" has prepared the way for the dialectical relation of *passio* (passivity and suffering) to *actio* (perfection and fulfillment) which comes to the surface in the phrase "thy glorious lif and passioun," expressing the Christian meaning of suffering — a passionate suffering that in the end becomes a real glory and even an ecstasy.

In the early Christian centuries, the meaning of martyrdom was deeply influenced by the mysticism of the Passion of Christ which revealed a limitless love assuming the sufferings of all men. Especially in the writing of Bernard of Clairvaux, whom Chaucer mentions in the next stanza, the mysticism of Christ's Passion was expressed in terms of ecstatic love. In his famous sermon on the Passion, St. Bernard puts the mysticism of suffering in antithetical terms: "And in life he maintained a *passive action*, and in death an *active passion*, doing the work of salvation in the midst of the earth."[17] The paradox of Christ's Passion and limitless love, which can be voiced only in antithetic terms, created among mystical writers and love poets a predilection for antithetic modes of speech and thought; references to the Passion often appeared along with other secular love themes. The "glorious lif and passioun" of St. Cecilia will fulfill and perfect a rapprochement of not only passivity and activity, suffering and glory, but also desire and ecstasy. The rhetorical figure of antithesis, contrasting "ydelnesse" and "leveful bisynesse," functions therefore in the Prologue as both a figure of speech and a figure of thought, bringing into dialectical relation the basic ontological dualism of *passio* and *actio* which figure *passive action* and *active passion* in the legend of St. Cecilia. According to Bollandist Delehaye the legend of St. Cecilia develops the theme of "éclairé de lueurs mystiques." Yet Chaucer's Cecilia proves to be no speculative mystic, but rather a penitential one with a strong eschatological emphasis. Her chaste marriage and triumphant marytrdom extend and deepen the Prologue's antithesis of "ydelnesse" and "leveful bisynesse" in order to contrast and thereby reconcile the status of the *viator* now and the status of the *comprehensor* in the heavenly Jerusalem. The "leveful bisynesse" of the Prologue turns out, at the end of the *Tale*, to be the "noble wyse."

III

The Idleness-prologue is immediately followed by the beautiful and elevated "Invocacio ad Mariam" (28–84) which is generally acclaimed as the best stanzas in the Prologue and indeed the whole *Tale*. It is a mosaic of Latin church hymns, anthems, and lyrics to the Virgin that Chaucer perhaps knew by heart, artistically selected and adapted to a new harmonious pattern. The vortex of the "Invocacio," (36–56), is indebted to Dante's celebrated Prayer to the Virgin voiced by the great mystic St. Bernard in *Paradiso* xxxiii. Chaucer used Dante's Prayer again in a similar, but less successful, invocation in the *Prioress's Pro-*

logue and again for secular purposes in the lyrical love songs of Troilus and of Antigone in *Troilus and Criseyde.* Yet the Second Nun's "Invocacio" marks perhaps the first verses of Chaucer written under the influence of the great Italian poet. Despite the debt to Dante, however, the "Invocacio" remains Chaucer's own hymn to the Virgin, genuine in devotion, pious in its certitude, fresh and elevated in its lyrical form.

The style of the "Invocacio" is similar to the classical and Biblical forms of prayer that Edward Norden called "der Du-Stil der Prädikation."[18] This style employs an anaphorical *schema* or *figura* in which the same word or phrase is repeated at the beginning of consecutive tercets or clauses. Early Christian hymns and liturgical forms of prayer were influenced by classical and Biblical patterns of style structured in an anaphorical form with "thou." The style of the Christian doxology was similar to the Greek tradition of aretalogy and the Roman tradition of eulogy. Among Roman prayers of worship, Norden cites Ovid's eulogy of Bacchus (*Metamorphoses,* iv, 18–30), Virgil's praise of Hercules (*Aeneid,* viii, 293–304), and Statius' presentation of Oedipus' prayer for revenge to the cruel Tisiphone (*Thebaid,* i, 68–87) to show the classical pattern of the "tu" anaphora which involves an enumeration of the accomplishments of the god, his definite and limited sphere of earthly power and influence, and his qualities and attitudes based upon the mythical tradition. The Biblical pattern of the "tu" anaphora differs from the classical, according to Norden, in the use of "tu est" and "tua est" construction, and in the enumeration and abstract expression of the divinity's power, essence, and omnipresence. He cites for example "tu es super omnes principes, . . . tua est domine magnificentia, . . . tua est gloria" and Psalms, 88:10–15:

> Thou rulest the pride of the sea, thou restrainest the swelling of its waves. Thou hast trampled Rahab under foot as one that is pierced, with thy powerful arm thou hast scattered thy enemies. The heavens are thine, the earth is thine; the world and everything in it, thou hast founded; the north and the south, thou hast created: Thabor and Hermon rejoice in thy name. Thy arm is mighty, thy hand is firm, thy right hand is uplifted. Justice and right are the foundation of thy throne; mercy and faithfulness go before thee.

The Second Nun's "Invocacio ad Mariam" is structured and patterned in this anaphorical form with "thou" and with relative clauses that knit together seven moving stanzas into one of the most beautiful medieval English hymns to the Virgin. Chaucer draws upon the historical, dogmatic, and figurative traditions of the eulogy, but carefully organizes and condenses his material. The first stanza (29–35) begins the formal enumeration of Mary's virtues and accomplishments; the second and third stanzas (36–49) treat the Virgin's role in the history of man's salvation; the fourth and fifth stanzas (50–63) describe the Virgin's eternal role in heaven as the *viator* of all graces; and the last two stanzas (64–77) express the formal *supplicacio* of the prayer, as the eulogistic style becomes popular and emotional, less dogmatic and historical.

The first stanza of the "Invocacio" shows complete independence of Dante's Prayer to the Virgin. It begins with an invocation to Mary composed of one member in the anaphorical form with "thou" and combines figures of interpretation with figures of speech and sound.

> And thow that flour of virgines art alle,
> Of whom that Bernard list so wel to write,
> To thee at my bigynnyng first I calle;
> Thou confort of us wrecches, do me endite
> Thy maydens deeth, that wan thurgh hire merite
> The eterneel lyf, and of the feend victorie,
> As man may after reden in hire storie.
>   [29–35]

The figure of the "flour of virgines" is an abstract metaphorical expression of the history and the dogma of Mary's virgin conception of Christ. In the Old Testament, *flos, virgo,* and *virga* were often used interchangeably as figures of Mary conceiving and bringing forth her son Christ without any harm to her virginity. For instance, in Numbers 17:6–9 Moses witnesses the blooming of the rod of Aaron:

> And Moses spoke to the children of Israel. And all the princes gave him rods one for every tribe: and there were twelve rods besides the rod of Aaron. And when Moses had laid them up before the Lord in the tabernacle of the testimony, he returned on the following day, and found that the rod of Aaron for the house of Levi, was budded: and that the buds swelling it had bloomed blossoms, which spreading the leaves, were formed into almonds. Moses therefore brought out all the rods before the Lord to all the children of Israel. And they saw, and everyone received their rods.

And in Isaias 11:1 the figure is used again for the future king of peace: "And there shall come forth a rod out of the root of Jesse, and a flower shall rise up out of his root." In medieval Latin hymns, figurative and typological interpretations of Mary as the *virgo-virga* furnished not only symbolic metaphors of history and dogma but also a metrical delight in sounds and rhymes that developed to the point of becoming witty and elegant in style. In "In Purificatione Beatae Mariae," the famous tenth-century hymnologist Notker Balbulus displays the early beginnings of the witty use of the figure *flos-virgo-virga:*

> Te virga arida Aaron
> flore speciosa
> praefigurat,
> Maria,
> sine viri semine.[19]

Again in an anonymous twelfth-century Latin hymn to the Virgin based mainly on the figure of the *virgo-virga*, the poet plays with the image by referring to Mary as "virgo virga salutaris." [20] And in the mystical writings of St. Bernard, known for his devotion to the Virgin, there is a beautiful pun on the figure when he refers to Christ as "virga virgo virgine generatus." [21]

The Second Nun's "thow that flour of virgines art alle" utilizes this tradition of typological interpretation of Mary as the *virgo-virga*, combining figures of interpretation with figures of speech and sound and establishing in the "Invocacio," which expresses the mystery of the Incarnation, a playful and joyful tone and style.

The second stanza of the "Invocacio" continues the eulogistic pattern in the anaphorical form with "thou" and begins the formal praise of the Virgin. The stanza is remarkable in its rhetoric use of antithetic parallelism to set forth the basic paradox of the Virgin and the Passion of St. Cecilia.

> Thow Mayde and Mooder, doghter of thy Sone. (36)

The antithesis of "Mayde and Mooder" figures the mystery of the Incarnation and in turn the mystical marriage of Cecilia and the Church. "Doghter of thy Sone" balances the antithesis of virgin-mother with the traditional motif of *factor factus creatura.* The figure of antithesis was used in early Christian poetry, and especially by the Christian Gnostics, to represent the paradoxical dual nature of certain religious doctrines which could not otherwise be expressed or explained: the mystery of a God-man, the hypostatic union of divine and human; of the Creator and creature; logos and flesh; virgin and mother; passion and glory; death and resurrection. This antithetic mode of expression entered the poetic language of Europe through the medieval Latin hymn. Though Chaucer appears to be imitating Dante's Prayer to the Virgin in verses 36–56, re-examination shows that both Dante and Chaucer were following the popular hymn sequence formulas to the Virgin similar to, for instance, those of the "Laus Christi" of Claudian and the "Quem Terra" of Venantius Fortunatus. "Thow welle of mercy" (37), not found in Dante's Prayer, figures the Virgin's role as mediatress, "synful soules cure"; and is one of her principal virtues enumerated in medieval Latin hymn sequences to Mary. Adam of St. Victor, for example, employs a similar image to represent this virtue in his hymn sequence "In Assumptione Beatae Mariae Virginis" — "Fontis vitae tu cisterna,"[22] which refers to Psalms 35:10: "For with thee is the fountain of life." St. Bernard uses the image of an "aquaeductus"[23] to manifest the same virtue. The antithetic parallelism of the narrator's "Thow humble, and heigh over every creature" (39) imitates Dante's "umile ed alta più che creatura," but it also alludes to Mary's attitude — an important feature of the classical and Biblical eulogy — during the Annunciation. According to tradition, Mary was humble because she immediately obeyed God's will announced to her by the angel: "Behold the handmaid of the Lord; be it done to me according to thy word. And the angel departed from her" (Luke 1:38). But she is also considered "heigh over every creature" not only as being "blessed among women," but for her own attitude during the Annunciation, which St. Bernard, in his attempt to describe the incomprehensible mystery, interprets as "magnificentia tanta in secretario virginei cordis" and "videlicet nec humilitas tanta minuit magnanimitatem, nec magnanimitas tanta humilitatem."[24] Mary's humility is the antithesis of Eve's pride, and as Mary is the prototype of all virgins and brides, "humble and heigh over every creature" will also be the attitude of St. Cecilia in her legend.

> In whom that God for bountee chees to wone (38)

alludes not only to Dante's "Termine fisso d'eterno consiglio" but also recalls the rich figurative tradition of the Immaculate Conception as expressed by Adam of St. Victor's "Tu a saeclis praeelecta," as well as Proverbs 8:23–24: "I was set up from eternity, and of old before the earth was made. The depths were not as yet, and I was already conceived, neither had the fountains of water as yet sprung out." And Canticles 6:9: "Who is she that cometh forth as the morning rising,

fair as the moon, bright as the sun, terrible as an army set in array."
The issue of the Immaculate Conception of the Virgin Mary was frequently debated and attracted much of the theological interest of
the fourteenth century. Since the time of Duns Scotus' critique of
Thomas Aquinas, the battle of Maculists versus the Immaculists raged.
Aquinas rejected the doctrine of the Immaculate Conception, and
instead argued a theory of sanctification which was bestowed either at
birth in her mother's womb or occurred only at the moment of the
incarnation of Christ. The Dominicans Robert Holcot, Gregory of
Rimini, and Nicholas Trivet defended Aquinas and became known as
the Maculists. In the camp of the Franciscans, Scotus spearheaded the
attack on Aquinas' theory of sanctification and argued that God *de
facto* preserved the Virgin Mary from original sin from the very beginning of creation and that her preordained immaculate conception
exempted her at all time from the stain of original sin. Scotus' influence spread quickly at Oxford and Paris through the help of the Franciscans, who became known as the Immaculists, and in the second
half of the fourteenth century they won many influential theologians
over to their ranks. The doctrine was finally defined at the Counsel
of Basel in 1439, but the battle raged on until the doctrine became
dogma in 1864. Because both Maculists and Immaculists dedicated
chapels and altars to the Virgin, the fierce battle had its repercussions
in art: in the form of book illuminations, altarpieces, and cult images.
Chaucer's Mariology, revealed mainly here in the "Invocacio" and
in "An A B C," seems to show the influence of the Immaculists, though
not as strong as Dante's defense in Paradiso xxxiii. In fact, Chaucer
intentionally changes the meaning of Dante's

> Nobilitasti sì, che il suo Fattore
> Non disdegnò di farsi sua fattura,

which sets forth the idea "that its Maker of human nature did not
disdain to become His own creature," following the traditional theme
of *factor factus creatura*, to

> Thow nobledest so ferforth our nature,
> That no desdeyn the Makere hadde of kynde
> His Sone in blood and flessh to clothe and wynde.
> [40–42]

Perhaps Chaucer's intention was to tone down the Immaculist view
and to focus attention on the nobility of Mary and on the very human
act of nativity.

The third stanza of the "Invocacio" (43–49) is the most interesting because it digresses from Dante's eulogy and shows Chaucer's independence and skilful combination of new materials drawn from several fonts. Continuing the account of human salvation, it interweaves dogmatic and historical details in a kind of symbolic rhetoric. The opening figure of "the cloistre blisful of thy sydis" is truly Chaucer's own beautiful image of the Nativity despite its similarity to Dante's "Nel ventre tuo," the "beato chiostro" or "claustrum Mariae" of Venantius Fortunatus. The image is a symbolic expression of the union of history and dogma: the historical event of the incarnation of a God-man who figures eternal love and peace and the dogma of human salvation through redemption are put forth here in a concrete and realistic way. After the expression of eternal love in the act of the Nativity, there follows a convergent universal adoration of the three realms: earth, water, and air:

> That of the tryne compas lord and gyde is,
> Whom erthe and see and hevene, out of relees,
> Ay heryen. [45–47]

Convergent adoration was a characteristic feature of both classical and Biblical eulogies as found, for example, in Horace's ode to Augustus (*Carmina*, IV, xiv) and in the medieval hymn "Te Deum Laudamus," designed for their invocational appeal. The final lines of the stanza return to the mystery of the "Virgine wemmelees," and "The Creatour of every creature" repeats and comments upon the central paradox of the Incarnation. Though only a creature, the Virgin possessed all goodness that could be contained in a creature; or as St. Bernard so well put it: "Excellentissima quadam sublimitate prae ceteris omnibus excedit et supergreditur creaturis." [25]

The fourth stanza presents the Virgin in the community of the beatified in Heaven. The eternal appearance replaces the historical; Mary's lasting virtues take the place of her earthly deeds; and her new role in Heaven contrasts with her function on earth.

> Assembled is in thee magnificence
> With mercy, goodnesse, and swich pitee
> That thou, that art the sonne of excellence
> Nat oonly helpest hem that preyen thee,
> But often tyme, of the benygnytee,
> Ful frely, er that men thyn help biseche,
> Thou goost biforn, and art hir lyves leche.
> [50–56]

The Virgin's heavenly attributes are magnificence, mercy, goodness, and pity; and these are meant in a general sense according to the scholastic definition of "una vertù che fa compiere l'ardue e nobili cose." [26] Above all, the Virgin is "the sonne of excellence," like the force of a midday sun, an image inspired by Dante's "meridiana face di caritate" and St. Bernard's commentary on Canticles 1:6 "indica mihi quen diligit anima mea, ubi pascas, ubi cubes in meridie." [27] Yet the picture of the Virgin clothed with "the sonne of excellence" may also recall Apocalypse 12:1: "And a great sign appeared in heaven: a woman clothed with the sun, and the moon was under her feet, and upon her head a crown of twelve stars," which immediately signifies the Church of the Old and New Covenants bringing forth Christ to the World. Cecilia's chaste marriage to Valerian, symbolizing the mystical union of Christ and the Church, and the legend's theme of the private house consecrated into a church, together complete and fulfill the Prologue's figure of the Virgin clothed with "the sonne of excellence." The fourth stanza stresses the Virgin's heavenly function as mediatress of all graces, the last lines emphasizing Mary's benignity in not only helping those who pray to her, but often interceding for the needy before they seek her aid.

In the fifth stanza, Chaucer departs once more from Dante's eulogy to introduce the Biblical figure of the Canaanite woman, a Gentile and Syrophoenician by birth, who worshiped Jesus in the pagan district of Tyre and Sidon where Jesus had retired to devote himself to the instruction of the apostles. The term Canaanite underscores the importance of the miracle performed for a non-Jewish woman who belonged to the hereditary enemies of Israel:

> Now help, thow meeke and blisful faire mayde,
> Me, flemed wrecche, in this desert of galle;
> Thynk on the womman Cananee, that sayde
> That whelpes eten somme of the crommes alle
> That from hir lordes table been yfalle;
> And though that I, unworthy sone of Eve,
> Be synful, yet accepte my bileve.
> [57–62]

In the Biblical account of the incident (Matthew 15:21–28), Jesus was teaching the apostles a principle that would ultimately liberate the new Christians from the rabbinical traditions and especially the old Mosaic law regarding clean and unclean food, but they failed to understand "what goes into the mouth does not defile a man, but it is what comes out of the mouth that defiles a man" (Matthew 15:11). This principle is then dramatized in the incident of the Canaanite woman who asks Jesus to drive the devil out of her daughter. At first Jesus ignores her, but then says: "It is not fair to take the children's bread and cast it to the dogs." But she replies: "Yes, Lord, for even the dogs eat the crumbs that fall from their master's table." Then Jesus answered and said to her, "O woman, great is thy faith. Let it be done to thee as thou wilt." And her daughter was healed from that moment. The term "dogs" would be better rendered "puppies" or "pet dogs," for the passage points up the importance of priority for the children of Israel and removes the absolute idea of contempt for the unclean and uncircumcised. Chaucer's "whelpes" correctly renders the term because in the early Christian centuries up to the time of Constantine, Jews often referred to Christians as "puppies" or "pet dogs." The touching and realistic incident of the Canaanite woman, a little parable turned allegory, dramatizes therefore the breakdown of Judaic separatism and points up the importance of human solidarity of faithful believers. In the Second Nun's Prayer to the Virgin, the figure of the Canaanite woman underscores the narrator's unworthiness, heightens the image of "Flemed wrecche in this desert of galle," and prepares for and explains the "unworthy sone of Eve," which in the light of the Biblical allusion becomes more of a compliment than an inappropriate puzzle. The pure faith and witty reply of the Canaanite woman bring about the miracle she sought.

Accordingly, pure faith is tempered and made practical in stanza six (64–70) by good works. "And for that feith is deed withouten werkis" refers to James 2:17 "So faith too, unless it has work, is dead in itself." The contrast of faith and work extends and deepens the antithesis of "ydelnesse" and "leveful bisynesse," *passio* and *actio*, to signify the relation of Cecilia's chaste marriage and triumphant martyrdom. The *supplicacio* of the prayer is now intensified by figurative metaphors fused with plays on rhymes and sounds that make a direct appeal to human pity and compassion. After the events of the Incarnation, the style of the "Invocacio" becomes less dogmatic, more popular and emotional. The "thou" anaphora is voiced in the first vocative of the prayer, "O thou, that art so fair and ful of grace" (67); and a new note of joy and glory is heard in the "songe Osanne,/Thow Cristes mooder, doghter deere of Anne!" (69–70). The legend of St. Anne, the mother of Mary, is based upon the apocryphal tradition, especially the gospel of St. James which was one of the important texts of the early Christian Gnostics. According to this tradition, Anne represents the Biblical series of "long barren and lately blessed mothers." Like Sarah who gave birth to Isaac in her old age, she rejoiced: "God hath made a laughter of me. Whosoever shall hear of it will laugh with me" (Genesis 21:6). Anne first wept and later rejoiced in her nativity. In medieval Latin hymns, the joy and happiness of Anne are a familiar feature, and she is often presented as laughing.

From the angelic jubilation of the heavenly choir singing without end the song hosanna, the tone of stanza seven (71–77) falls back to the earthly melancholic prayer: "o havene of refut, o salvacioun," indicating the agony of human solicitude and anxiety in opposition to heavenly joy and security. The fear of the "derk" (66), or life without grace, now becomes a human reality as the thoughts of the narrator turn inward and begin to reflect upon the darkness of the soul:

> And of thy light my soule in prison lighte
> That troubled is by the contagioun
> Of my body, and also by the wighte
> Of erthely lust and fals affeccioun.
> [71–74]

The eulogy turns with new understanding to the difficult question of human existence. The sorrow and distress of a soul destined for heavenly existence is made a prisoner in a body's cage, subject to concupiscence and original sin. Although man knows and desires the good, he does evil; for the soul as a prisoner of the body is sold into captivity to sin, and the wages of sin is death. Yet the soul is paradoxically destined to be reunited with the body after the Resurrection. Habits of thought and will reside in the soul, and their abuses are not removed by merely removing the body. Only in the soul of martyrs, who bear witness to God's love by suffering persecution and death, is the soul by a miracle of grace instantly purified "Of erthely lust and fals affeccioun." The soul of the narrator here agonizes in its conflict with the attraction of sin, and through agony comes to a new understanding of the meaning and importance of work, not only as "leveful bisynesse" in avoiding temptations of the devil, but as the necessary means of purification and sanctification in the scheme of human salvation.

This difficult Christian doctrine, which is opposed to classical modes of thought and expression, is here set forth as if it were self-evident and credible. The rhetorical figure of antithesis and the figurative modes of interpretation employed throughout the Prologue help make the doctrine amenable. Under the stress of these ideas, the narrator is moved to clarify her general intention and apologize for the style of the legend.

> Foryeve me that I do no diligence
> This ilke storie subtilly to endite,
> For bothe have I the wordes and sentence
> Of hym that at the seintes reverence
> The storie wroot, and folwen hire legende,
> And pray yow that ye wole my werke amende.
> [79–84]

She intends to make no effort to be subtle in relating the story of St. Cecilia, but to concentrate on the versification and rhyme-royal stanzas, and, above all, to follow "the wordes and sentence" of the hagiographer who originally wrote the legend in reverence of the saint. A saint's legend is not a myth, romance, or even a tale; by its very nature it has historical and topographical connection. It presupposes the historical fact that becomes the subject or occasion of the narrative. The narrator's primary concern, however, is not to be historically precise or to seek new information on the biography of the saint, but to edify and interest others in the passion of the martyr. The style of the saint's legend is implicit in the subject matter. The Passion of St. Cecilia is both tragic and sublime depicted with the utmost realism. Like her prototype, the "humble and heigh" Virgin, Cecilia is picked out from her family and social class and asked to bear witness to a sublime event. Her dedication to the vow of virginity ultimately leads to her triumphant martyrdom. The style of the narrative, therefore, is the low, plain, unadorned style of the Bible recommended by St. Augustine in *De doctrina Christiana* (IV,12) for the purpose of instruction. Her legend is a veritable *sermo humilis* designed for all to "read" and understand, reconciling two seemingly incompatible elements, the sublime and lowly, and thereby teaching the mysticism of the triumph of suffering.

IV

The fantastic "Interpretacio nominis Cecilie" (85–119) which precedes the legend appear to contain the most perverse etymologies known or imaginable, so much so that certain translators of the *Legenda Aurea* did not include them. Modern editors of Chaucer, who should be sympathetic with the medieval point of view, consider them not only wrong, but strange and ridiculous, pointing out that the correct etymology of Cecilia is the feminine of *Caecilius*, perhaps of the noble patrician "Caecilia gens," which in turn is probably a diminutive of *caecus*, blind.[28] But this shows a misunderstanding of the nature and function of medieval etymologies. Unlike modern linguistic etymologies, the "Interpretacio nominis Cecilie" is more symbolic and figurative of the Passion of St. Cecilia, almost like reading her horoscope. Medieval philosophers generally defined a name as a *sign* of a substantive, or as a term indicating a substance, or as something represented after the manner of a substance. Etymology was the study of these *signs* and became one of the striking features of medieval thought and style. It was one of the fundamentals of all grammars from the early Roman up to Donatus and Priscian. Etymological interpretation of names had been sanctioned by Matthew 16:18 and later by St. Jerome's *Liber de nominibus hebraicis*, and is, of course, best illustrated in the monumental compilation *Etymologiarum libri* of the master Isidore of Seville. Isidore considered etymology the part of grammar that proceeds from letters and syllables to parts of speech, and argued that knowledge of the *origio* of a word leads quickly to an understanding of its *vis*, force, and that nothing can be clearly understood until its etymology is known. He recommended three etymological approaches: 1) "ex causa" (*reges a regendo et recte agendo*); 2) "ex origine" (*homo ex humo*); and 3) "ex contrariis" (*lucus a non lucendo*).[29] Isidore believed that a word is a symbol of the object. His etymological elaborations were based upon "subjective imagination," whereby he attempted to relate the concept and the name of the object the language had assigned it. He based his etymology sometimes on assonance (*homo ex humo*) and sometimes on an agglutination of syllables drawn from different words (*argumentatio est argutae mentis oratio*). According to Isidore, *reges* derives from *regere*, i.e. *recte agere*, because kings have the purpose of leading people properly (etymology from cause); *homo* comes from *humo* because by origin man is dust (etymology from origin); and *lucus*, consecrated wood, derives from *lux*, light, because it is precisely dark as opposed to light which illuminates (etymology from contrary).

In the twelfth century, etymological interpretation passed from the *ars dictaminis* to the *ars poeticae*, and in the fourteenth century the Nominalists had peculiar difficulty in defining a name because of their theory of the arbitrariness of universal concepts. Ockham called language a system of artificial signs, and by sign he meant that which, when apprehended, makes us know something else, as a barrel-hoop signifies wine in the inn. The etymological interpretations of the name Cecilia ought then to be considered as signs or figures of her substance, essence, or perfection, which will not be fully apprehended until the legend is read. In this sense, the etymologies are symbolic terms in a proposition which attempts to set forth the argument of the legend. In short, the name Cecilia is a *sign* of the person who bears it, and in its letters and syllables one can discover *signs* of what her life will be, her virtues and triumphs. Her name signifies the meaning of her Passion. As Boethius noted in *De interpretatione*, "words are signs of the impressions in the soul."

The first *interpretatacio, coeli lilia,* "hevenes lilie" (87) is an example of "ex origine" etymology and signifies "pure chaastnesse of virginitee" (88). In the legend of St. Cecilia the virtue of virginity is developed to its highest level of perfection in both the contemplative and active realms. The perfection of virginity in marriage and its sanctification through martyrdom are the chief themes of the legend and are represented in flower images of lilies and roses, traditional symbols of virginity and martyrdom. Cecilia as "hevenes lilie," the traditional flower of virginity, completes and fulfills the figure of "that flour of virgines" which is ultimately based upon Isaias 11:1 and Canticles 5:10 in which the Church mystically describes Christ to the infidels as: "My beloved is white and ruddy, chosen out of thousands." Medieval commentators on these two basic passages of Biblical figuralism interpret the flower as a figure of the Virgin and of the Church: the white lily symbolizing virginity and the red rose the flower of martyrdom. St. Bernard, for instance, commenting on the lily of virginity and the rose of passion, says:

> Virgo genitrix virga est, flos filius eius. Flos utique filius Virginis, flos candidus et rubicundus, electus ex millibus (Cant. 5:10); flos in quem prospicere desiderant angeli, flos ad cuius odorem reviviscunt mortui. . . .[30]

When Valerian returns to Cecilia's chamber after baptism by Pope Urban on the Via Appia, husband and wife are mystically united and committed to a life of chastity in marriage. At this moment, and not later at their martyrdom, appears the "Corones two" and the angel who performs the coronation.[31]

> Valerian gooth hoom and fynt Cecilie
> Withinne his chambre with an angel stonde.

> This angel hadde of roses and of lilie
> Corones two, the which he bar in honde;
> And first to Cecilie, as I understonde,
> He yaf that oon, and after gan he take
> That oother to Valerian, hir make.
>
> [218–24]

Double coronation of bride and groom was an elaborate ceremony of the early Christian Church symbolizing the mystical union of Christ and the Church. The angel in the legend explains the *origio* and *vis* of the lilies and roses:

> "With body clene and with unwemmed thought
> Kepeth ay wel thise corones," quod he;
> "Fro paradys to yow hav I hem brought,
> Ne nevere mo ne shal they roten bee,
> Ne lese hir soote savour, trusteth me;
> Ne nevere wight shal seen hem with his ye.
> But he be chaast and hate vileynye.
>
> [225–31]

The flowers are immutable and eternal because they originated in heaven, and only those committed to virginity will be able to see them. Yet the flowers have the *vis* of attracting and sanctifying others. When Tiburce, the pagan brother of Valerian, approaches Cecilia's house, he first becomes overwhelmed by the sweet odor of lilies and roses, but cannot see them:

> And seyde, "I wondre, this tyme of the yeer,
> Whennes that soote savour cometh so
> Of rose and lilies that I smelle heer.
> For though I hadde hem in myne handes two,
> The savour myghte in me no depper go.
> The sweete smel that in myn herte I fynde
> Hath chaunged me al in another kynde."
>
> [246–52]

Valerian explains to his pagan brother the miraculous power of the sweet odor by identifying the "corones two" as "the palm of martirdom" (274).

> "The mayde hath broght thise men to blisse above;
> The world hath wist what it is worth, certeyn,
> Devocioun of chastitee to Love."
>
> [281–83]

234

Virginity, or chastity in marriage, becomes then a kind of spiritual martyrdom, a means of sanctification equivalent to the heroic act of martyrdom. Cecilia, as "hevenes lilie," is twice blessed; in her "glorious lif and passioun" she achieves perfection and sanctification through both virginity and martyrdom.

The second *interpretatacio, caecis via,* "the wey to the blynde," signifies that Cecilia's Passion teaches by its good example the way of leading the blind to the light of perfection. Cecilia is the figural fulfillment of the Virgin as the *via lucis*: "The glory of her virginity shed upon the world everlasting light." Her Passion is the way of sanctifying others; it is the affirmative way of ascending from a knowledge of creatures to some understanding of God's perfections and of the nature and cause of created perfections as the possessor of all pure perfections found in creatures. In their metaphysics Augustine, Bonaventure, Alexander of Hales, and Robert Grosseteste assigned a leading role to light, the form of corporeity and the principle of action.[32] By its very essence, light is activity and is defined as "multiplicativa et diffusa sui." Light penetrates bodies and becomes the principle of all their perfection, beauty, and activity. Since God acts upon the understanding, enlightening and illuminating it, there is an analogy between light and knowledge. The life-giving properties of light enable us to liken it to the Eternal Light. Cecilia is "the wey to the blynde" because through her detailed instructions in the doctrines of faith the blind Valerian, Tiburce, and even Maximus, the Roman officer, are led to baptism and thereby enabled to see miraculous events.

Inherent in the legend of St. Cecilia are many of the ideas of Gnosticism, especially Marcionism, widespread early Christian heresies that believed salvation was achieved through knowledge. The Gnostics taught a docetic doctrine of appearances versus reality: they believed that Christ did not have a real body, merely the appearances of one. The Gnostic God was alien, unknown, and absolutely transcendent. God and creation were opposed as light to darkness, good to evil; and the world of matter was essentially evil and dark compared to the God of light. For the Gnostic, the problem of human existence was the struggle to ascend through knowledge from the world of matter to the world of the spirit. In addition, the Marcionists required baptism, celibacy, and vigorous asceticism as the condition of salvation. The legend of St. Cecilia, and especially the etymology "the wey to the blynde," suggests the presence of Gnostic themes of redemption, salvation, and liberation which are accomplished by assimilation of knowledge. Further investigation of the legend along these lines should prove fruitful.

The third etymology, a combination of *caelum* and *lya*, "by a manere conjoynynge/Of "hevene" and "lia," are figures of the contemplative and active life. "hevene" signifies "thoght of hoolynesse" and "Lia" figures "lastynge bisynesse," completing and fulfilling the basic antithesis of the Prologue. *Lia* is the Latin spelling of Leah of Genesis, who in the Old Testament symbolized the active life, just as Rachel illustrated the contemplative life. In her chaste marriage and apostolic life, Cecilia represents the perfect union of contemplation and activity.

The fourth interpretation, *quasi caecitate carens*, "Wantynge of blyndnesse" (100), is an example of "ex contrariis" etymology, similar to *lucus a non lucendo*. It is a negative way of defining Cecilia by denying to her imperfections and limitations that other creatures may have. This is definition by negative judgment, sometimes known as the way of purification or remotion, which involves the intellectual act of knowing incorporeal substances. In this sense, chastity in marriage is a negative, purifying way of the ascent of two souls to a higher, more perfect union, the fruit of which is the overflow of zeal into the apostolic life. Because Cecilia is diametrically opposed to blindness, she becomes impatient and rude with the "lewd" and "vain" Almachius during their argument over the source of human power and the nature of his idols.

The last etymology, from *coelo* and Greek *leos*, i.e., *populus*, "the hevene of peple" (104), signifies that in Cecilia the community of the faithful have a spiritual heaven; they see in her faith, wisdom, and works empyreal reflections of the sun, moon, and stars. As the heavens declare the glory of God, so also Cecilia mirrors and reflects this heavenly glory. The expression of convergent adoration of the community of Christians completes and fulfills the adoration of earth, sea, and heaven in the Prayer to the Virgin. Chaucer expands the cosmic analogy by claiming that Cecilia's heaven is composed of both the ninth *(primum mobile)*, which is swift and round, and the tenth sphere (Empyrean) which is burning. These fantastic etymologies of the name of Cecilia are, therefore, intended as artificial signs of her perfection. They express the *origo* and *vis* of Cecilia and thereby signify the figural meaning of her legend.

Since Foxe's *Book of Martyrs* and even Allan Butler's monumental *Lives of the Saints*, saints' legends have been out of style. Yet in the age which followed Constantine, esteem and gratitude toward the martyrs blossomed in legend and poetry. *The Second Nun's Tale* depicts the social world of the early days of the Church, when there were martyrs, when God's Providence was frequently revealed through the magic of miracles, when angels were ministers to the faithful, and when the Church itself was still true to its original principles. Unlike the somewhat tarnished image of the Church in the fourteenth century, the Cecilia legend embodies the victorious spirit of the first centuries of Christianity, which were distinguished by the sublimation of worldly adornments through symbolism and a vigorous asceticism which was producing monks and hermits, as well as a peculiar attitude toward saints. Indeed, the legend's theme of the chaste marriage reflects this early Christian world and its concern with ideas regarding the resurrection and apostolic asceticism.

At the vortex of the social world of Cecilia is the principle of chastity and its perfection: "what devotion to chastity is capable of effecting, not *in terms of*, but *against* love." [33] In the context of the *Canterbury Tales*, *The Second Nun's Tale* can be viewed as part of the so-called marriage group. The Cecilia legend has a significant bearing on the marriage question, for it explores the social world of a wife, virgin, and martyr; and suggests that continence and not sovereignty is the "seal of the marriage group." Like Constance and Griselda, Cecilia is one of those saintly married women who are absolutely dedicated to an ideal. Constance and Griselda are committed to the perfection of continence in marriage, a contemplative ideal. Cecilia, however, is committed to the perfection of virginity in marriage and also to an apostolic martyrdom. She is dedicated to two ideals: one *passio*, chastity in marriage, and the other *actio*, apostolic martyrdom. Because Cecilia's marriage was never consummated — and even the most rigid medieval canonist might question its validity — her relationship to Valerian ought to be viewed as a mystical marriage, similar to the mystical union of Christ and his Church. In this figurative sense, *The Second Nun's Tale* dramatizes the dignity and holiness of marriage as a sacrament and also the Biblical obligation of the believing spouse: "And if any woman has an unbelieving husband and he consents to live with her, let her not put away her husband, for the unbelieving husband is sanctified by the believing wife, and the unbelieving wife is sanctified by the believing husband" (1 *Corinthians* 7:13–14). Sanctification is an external sacredness which results from membership in the Church or from marriage with a Christian. In this regard, marriage is a real vocation, and the covenant which results is just as binding and sanctifying as any religious vow. The marriages of Constance, Cecilia, and Griselda celebrate, each in its own way, the perfection of continence in marriage, and in the wider context of the *Canterbury Tales* suggest that *gentilesse* rather than *maistrye* can be taken as the unifying theme of the whole marriage group. The figural style and meaning of the legend of St. Cecilia as narrated by the Second Nun recalls in a nostalgic way the social world of the first century of victorious Christianity, and the thematic import of the tale's *gloria passionis* depicts the high ideal of "Devocioun of chastitee to love."

NOTES

1. The text used throughout is *The Works of Geoffrey Chaucer*, ed. F. N. Robinson, 2nd ed. (Boston, 1957). In his notes, Robinson cites all the important studies of the *Second Nun's Prologue* and *Tale* up to 1956; these are also listed and brought up to date in William R. Crawford, *Bibliography of Chaucer 1954–63* (Seattle: University of Washington Press, 1967), pp. 21, 83 and in the *Goldentree Bibliography: Chaucer*, compiled by Albert C. Bauch (New York: Appleton-Century-Crofts, 1968), pp. 94–95. I am indebted to Joseph E. Grennen, who kindly sent me an offprint of his stimulating article "Saint Cecilia's 'Chemical Wedding': The Unity of the *Canterbury Tales*, Fragment VIII," *JEGP*, LXV (1966), 466–81; and to Mary Giffin, who graciously gave me a copy of her interesting study "Hir Hous the Chirche of Seinte Cecilie Highte," in her *Studies on Chaucer and His Audience* (Hull, Que.: Les Editions "Le'Éclair," 1956), pp. 29–48. For a brilliant definition and explication of "figural meaning and style," see Erich Auerbach, "Figura," *Archivum Romanicum*, XXII (1938), 436–89; reprinted in his *Neu Dantestudien: Istanbuler Schriften*, 5 (Istanbul, 1944), pp. 11–71.

2. Thomas Tyrwhitt, *The Poetical Works of Geoffrey Chaucer: With an Essay on his Language and Versification, and Introductory Discourse; together with Notes and a Glossary* (London: Edward Moxon, 1855; originally 1845), *s.v.* "The Second Nonnes Tale," note 30.

3. See especially William B. Gardner, "Chaucer's 'Unworthy Sone of Eve,'" *University of Texas: Studies in English* (1947), pp. 77–83; John P. McManus, "The Little Office of the Blessed Virgin Mary and *Invocatio ad Mariam* of the Second Nun's Prologue," unpublished Ph.D. dissertation, University of Washington Libraries (1953), reported by D. D. Griffith, *Bibliography of Chaucer 1908–1953* (Seattle: University of Washington Press, 1955), p. 240. For another interpretation of the appropriateness of lines 62 and 78 to the Second Nun, see Mary Giffin, *Studies on Chaucer and His Audience*, pp. 31–32.

4. The Rev. W. W. Skeat, ed., *The Complete Works of Geoffrey Chaucer*, 2nd ed. (Oxford, 1900), V, 405.

5. René Aigrain, *L'Hagiographie: ses sources, ses méthodes, son histoire* (Paris, 1953), pp. 126–31.
6. G. H. Gerould, "The Second Nun's Prologue and Tale," in *Sources and Analogues of Chaucer's Canterbury Tales,* ed. W. F. Bryan and Germaine Dempster (New York, 1941), p. 670.
7. Hippolyte Delehaye, *The Legends of the Saints,* trans. Donald Attwater (New York: Fordham University Press, 1962), pp. 77–78.
8. *The Gothic Image* (New York: Harper and Row, 1958), p. xiv.
9. See Robert F. Seybolt, "The '*Legenda Aurea,*' Bible, and Historia Scholastica," *Speculum,* XXI (1946), 339–42.
10. Beverly Boyd, *The Middle English Miracles of the Virgin* (San Marino, Calif., 1964), pp. 3–10.
11. On the iconography and cult of St. Cecilia, see Dom Guéranger, *Sainte Cécile et la société romaine aux deux premiers siècles* (Paris, 1877); Rohault de Fleury, *Les Saints de la messe et leurs monuments* (Paris, 1893); J. P. Kirsch, *Die heilige Cäcilia, Jungfrau und Märtyrin* (Regensburg, 1901); *idem, Die heilige Cäcilia in der römischen Kirche des Altertums* (Paderborn, 1910); Dom H. Quentin, *Dictionnaire d'archéologie chrétienne et de liturgie* (1910); E. Poirée, *Sainte Cécile* (Paris, 1920); P. A. de Santi, "Santa Cecilia e la musica," *Civiltà Cattolica* (1921); Abbé Laeger, *De l'authenticité des reliques de sainte Cécile à Rome et à Albi;* H. Delehaye, "Les caractéristiques des saints dans l'art," *Le Correspondant,* 1928; P. Benati, *Santa Cecilia nella leggenda e nell'arte* (Milan, 1928); Étienne Deville, *Sainte Cécile et les musiciens, Son culte à Lisieux* (Rouen, 1934); Hans Püttmann, "Das Tympanonrelief von St Cäcilien in Köln," *Wallraf-Richartz Jahrbuch,* XVII (1955), 48–61.
12. *Étude sur le légendier romain, les saints de novembre et de decembre* (Brussels, 1936), pp. 73–96, esp. 78–79.
13. See Carleton Brown, "The Prologue of Chaucer's Lyf of Saint Cecile," *MP,* IX (1911–12), 1–16; *idem,* "Chaucer and the Hours of the Blessed Virgin," *MLN,* XXX (1915), 231–32; Frederick Tupper, "Chaucer's Bed's Head," *MLN,* XXX (1915), 5–12; and John L. Lowes, "The Second Nun's Prologue, Alanus, and Macrobius," *MP,* XV (1917–18), 193–202.
14. See Giffin, pp. 29–48.
15. The Bible quoted here and elsewhere in the article is the Douay Version, which, it is generally recognized, is much closer to the medieval Vulgate than the King James Bible.
16. *De universo,* Book XXII, Ch. ii (*Patrologia Latina,* CXI, 385); see also *Allegoriae in Sacram Scripturam, Patrologia Latina,* CXII, 1031; *Clavis Melitonis,* in J. B. Pitra, *Spicelegium Solesmense,* 4 vols. (Paris, 1852–58), II, lxxvii.
17. *In Feria IV Hebdomadae Sanctae II* (*Patrologia Latina,* CLXXXIII, 268–69).
18. See his brilliant and stimulating study *Agnostos Theos: Untersuchungen zur Formengeschichte religiöser Rede* (Berlin and Leipzig, 1913), pp. 143–62.
19. H. A. Daniel, *Thesaurus hymnologicus,* 5 vols. (Leipzig, 1855–56), II, 10.
20. "Gaude, virgo gloriosa," in G. M. Dreves and C. Blume, *Analecta hymnica Medii Aevi,* 55 vols. (Leipzig, 1886–1922), VIII, 81.
21. *Sermones in Cantica,* XLVII, 5 (*Patrologia Latina,* CLXXXIII, 1010).

22. *The Liturgical Poetry of Adam of St. Victor,* ed. Digby S. Wrangham, 3 vols. (London, 1881), II, 164.
23. *De adventu Domini sermo,* ii, 4 (*Patrologia Latina,* CLXXXIII, 437ff.).
24. *Dominica infra Octavam Assumptionis Beatae Virginis Mariae Sermo,* 13 (*Patrologia Latina,* CLXXXIII, 437).
25. *Ibid., Sermo,* 3 (*Patrologia Latina,* CLXXXIII, 431).
26. See, for example, *L'Ottimo Commento della Divina Commedia* (Pisa, 1829), III, 726.
27. *Sermones in Cantica,* xxxiii (*Patrologia Latina,* CLXXXIII, 951).
28. See Robinson, p. 757.
29. *Etymologiarum, Lib. I de grammatica, caput xxix de etymologia* (*Patrologia Latina,* LXXXII, 105–6).
30. *De adventu Domini sermo,* ii, 4 (*Patrologia Latina,* CLXXXIII, 42).
31. For the interesting and stimulating bibliography on the "corones two," see Robinson, pp. 758–59. For the influence of St. Ambrose on the legend, see, especially, O. F. Emerson, "Saint Ambrose and Chaucer's *Life of St. Cecilia,*" *PMLA,* XLI (1926), 252–61.
32. On light metaphysics, see especially Edgar de Bruyne, *Etudes d'Esthetique Medievale* (Bruges, 1946), III, 9–29.
33. For Chaucer's modification of his source at this point, in order to make clearer the real sacrifice of St. Cecilia and to make more explicit her renunciation, by adding "to love" with the special use of "to" to mean "against," see Oliver F. Emerson, *Chaucer Essays and Studies* (Cleveland: Western Reserve University Press, 1929), pp. 416–17. For a different reading of "to" as "in terms of," see E. T. Donaldson, ed., *Chaucer's Poetry: An Anthology for the Modern Reader* (New York: Ronald Press, 1958), p. 400.

Caxton's Two Choices

"MODERN" AND "MEDIEVAL" RHETORIC IN TRAVERSAGNI'S *NOVA RHETORICA* AND THE ANONYMOUS *COURT OF SAPIENCE*

James J. Murphy

SCHOLARS HAVE examined closely the choices made by William Caxton for his press at Westminster in the 1470's and 1480's, on the assumption that his choices would provide us with an index of literary currents of that time. In some cases it has been possible to cross-check our conclusions by noting the works printed by Caxton's competitor press at Saint Alban's.

Two of Caxton's books deal with the subject of Rhetoric. One has been termed "modern" and the other "medieval." A closer examination is needed to determine whether these descriptions are justified. This in turn may enable us to assess Caxton's role in transmitting late fifteenth-century views of rhetoric.

On the 6th of July, 1478, Lorenzo Traversagni tells us, he completed at Cambridge a Latin work now usually titled *Nova Rhetorica* (though Traversagni called it *Margarita eloquentiae*). Within two years the Italian Franciscan's book had received the great distinction of being printed twice, once by Caxton at Westminster (1479?) and again (1480) by the St. Alban's printer. Howell describes the book as "thoroughly Ciceronian." It treats the five so-called canons of traditional rhetoric — invention, arrangement, style, memory, and delivery — though Biblical and not classical passages are usually used for stylistic examples. Weiss notes that it is "constructed on modern lines and was obviously inspired by classical models." [1]

At very nearly the same time somewhere in England an anonymous writer was completing, this time in English, an allegorical poem which he called *The Court of Sapience*. Written about 1475, it also received the distinction of being printed by Caxton (1481?). It has been described as thoroughly medieval. Among other things it treats the seven Liberal Arts, including of course the *trivium* of grammar, dialectic and

241

rhetoric. Atkins describes the author's conception of Lady Rhetoric as the same as that of Martianus Capella, the fifth-century encyclopedist.[2]

Does this juxtaposition of "modern" and "medieval" rhetoric in his press productions mean that Caxton was an agent of change in the late fifteenth century? Since that century requires special efforts of understanding, a brief resume of its literary background may be useful before undertaking a closer examination of these two works.

Poggio Bracciolini, the Italian humanist responsible for the rediscovery of many classical texts, had spent four unprofitable years in England (1418–22) at the solicitation of the Bishop of Winchester, Henry Beaufort.[3] He found English libraries lacking in the kind of books that interested him, and his letters to Italian colleagues disparage the state of English scholarship in the classics. He was nine years too late to meet Thomas Merke, the "courtier bishop" whose temporary political exile to Oxford (1401–5) had given him leisure to compose an eclectic work on literary composition that might have interested Poggio; Merke died in 1409 at the Council of Pisa.[4] He was too early to observe the literary patronage of the youngest son of Henry IV, Humphrey, Duke of Gloucester. It is difficult to conceive of him being fascinated by the literary output of his contemporary John Lydgate. The coming of Poggio, in short, did not at once render English letters "modern."

Roberto Weiss has carefully detailed the various other points of contact between fifteenth-century England and humanist Italy. Travelers brought books back to England, Papal Collectors sifted into and out of England, while both warfare and commerce forced Englishmen to meet continental figures. It was a Church Council at Constance, for instance, that brought Poggio and the Bishop of Winchester together in the first place. John Tiptoft, traveling in Italy in the late 1450's (at least partly for his political health) delivered a Latin oration before a pope and actually attended a lecture by the humanist teacher John Argyropoulous; he amassed a considerable library, even during the civil wars that led to his nickname as the Yorkist "butcher of England" and ultimately led to his execution by the Lancastrians in 1470. Others, like William Sellyng and John Free, had quieter careers.[5]

Other types of influence are less significant. Certainly Lydgate traveled at least to France, as well as having extensive court experience in England, and his patron the Duke of Gloucester showered him with books as well as money. But though John Capgrave did visit Italy himself he did not make a major contribution to the task of changing English cultural habits. Bibliophiles like Humphrey and William Grey, sometime Bishop of Ely, enriched English libraries but did not at once cause a significant change in English letters. And surely no one would term the *De regimine principium* of Thomas Hoccleve the work of a "modern" man.

Unfortunately the twentieth-century critic, since Descartes no longer believing in the possibility of a long-past Golden Age, tends to look back on such fifteenth-century figures with a slight sense of pity that they were not born into "modern" times. This attitude offers a temptation to distortion.

Traversagni's *Margarita eloquentiae (Nova rhetorica)*, for instance, could conceivably be valued not for its own sake but merely as a harbinger of things to come — a forerunner of Leonard Cox's *Rethoryke* (1530) or of Thomas Wilson's *The Arte of Rhetorique* (1553). Or it could on the other hand be viewed as a geographical accident, a work from a temporarily transferred Italian monk writing in the quiet of the English countryside to bring another breath of "modern" continental humanism to the backward English. Both these views depend upon a certain hierarchy of chronological values, stemming from an unstated principle that, when speaking of the fifteenth century, "the later is the better." Actually Traversagni's book must have been quite satisfactory for its immediate purpose. The Franciscan personally saw it through the press, an unusual occurrence with Caxton's productions, perhaps indicating also that Traversagni personally subsidized the book; in 1480, when he composed a short *Epitome* of his book, he sent it back to Caxton from Paris for printing.[6] In short, he was linked very closely to Caxton. His treatise was apparently intended as a textbook for his teaching in theology at Cambridge University. It must be remembered that preaching theory was taught in the faculty of theology of the medieval university; hence it is not surprising to find Traversagni adapting the doctrines of the Pseudo-Ciceronian *Rhetorica ad Herennium* to this purpose. The usual title, *Nova rhetorica*, comes from the heading on the first page of both the Caxton edition and the St. Alban's version based on it. But the colophon, more complete, indicates the real title and purpose of the book: "Pearl of Eloquence, organized for adaptation to divine eloquence."[7] The usual title, derived from the heading phrase *Prohemium in novam rhetoricam*, would merely denote a commentary on the "New Rhetoric" of Cicero (i.e. the *Rhetorica ad Herennium*). The book is in fact based on the *ad Herennium*. But the homiletic purpose is clearly explained at the outset, both by references to authorities like Gregory and Saint Augustine and by the declaration that the book aims to prevent sermonic ineptitude.[8] Howell is indeed correct when he says that the *Pearl of Eloquence* could as readily have been a product of the age of Vincent of Beauvais. It is certainly not "modern" in the sense of bringing the new humanism to bear on the preaching situation; and it is radically different from the later rhetorical works produced in England. Both Leonard Cox and Thomas Wilson were to write later about rhetoric for rhetoric's sake, not to adapt Ciceronian concepts to a specific religious purpose. Traversagni, then, provides neither a humanist intervention nor a foreshadowing of later English rhetoric.

The Court of Sapience, on the other hand, is "medieval" in a different, more parochial sense. To appreciate the centrality of its rhetorical references it might be well to sketch briefly the four major streams of medieval rhetorical theory as they appeared in the fifteenth century. The first of these is the body of ancient works transmitted directly in the treatises of Cicero and Aristotle; Cicero's *De inventione* and the Pseudo-Ciceronian *Rhetorica ad Herennium* appear in many medieval English library catalogues; in this same category may be counted commentaries like those of Victorinus, Thierry of Chartres, and a number of anonymous medieval writers, who generally transcribe the whole text of Cicero for the sake of adding their own remarks. The complete text of the *De oratore* of Cicero, his most mature rhetorical work, had been discovered at Lodi in 1422, and copies were in England by the 1440's. Aristotle's *Rhetorica*, translated twice into Latin during the middle ages, was available in numerous manuscripts and in fact in 1431 it appears for the first time as an item in an Oxford curriculum. Poggio Bracciolini had discovered the complete text of Quintilian's *Institutio oratoria* at St. Gall shortly before going to England, though it is not clear just when the first complete copy of that book became available in England.

Another medieval rhetorical tradition grew out of the *ars grammatica*. Its most directly rhetorical aspect was the *ars metrica*, or *ars poetriae*, which applied Ciceronian precepts to the writing of verse instead of the preparation of orations. The author most familiar to students of the English Middle Ages, Geoffrey of Vinsauf, composed his *Poetria nova* in hexameters about 1210.[9] Other authors were Gervase de Melkley, Matthew of Vendome, and Eberhard.

The *ars dictaminis*, or art of letter-writing, was a second major medieval rhetorical development. Basically it applied Ciceronian precepts to the writing of letters. It first appeared in 1087 at the Benedictine monastery of Monte Cassino in central Italy, then spread to major cities like Bologna and Florence by 1135 when its doctrines were stabilized. The typical *ars dictaminis* was a treatise on the theory of writing epistles, proposing a five-part format of *salutatio, captatio benevolentiae, narratio, petitio,* and *conclusio.*[10] Associated with this "Lombard art" was the *cursus,* or rhythmical prose style based on patterns of clause endings. Italian writers dominated this field throughout the Middle Ages. Except for Peter of Blois (Peter of Bath) who composed a short Latin treatise in England around 1180, there were no English contributors to the field until almost the end of the fourteenth century, when Thomas Sampson and John de Briggis produced highly derivative works associated with their dictaminal teaching in the city (not the university) of Oxford.[11]

The *are praedicandi,* or theory of thematic preaching, was the third major medieval rhetorical development. Its precise origins are not known. During the academic year 1230–31, a number of Latin sermons were preached at the University of Paris which revealed the existence of a new approach to preaching. Within a few years after that we have evidence of the production of theoretical treatises describing the new approach; more than 300 separate works of this kind have been identified. The thematic sermon — sometimes called the "university sermon" because of its frequent association with the universities — proposes that the preacher state a "theme" or Scriptural quotation, and then develop its meaning by division and amplification. One of the most influential writers was Robert of Basevorn, an Englishman whose *Forma praedicandi* was written in 1322, possibly at Oxford.[12] The English chronicler Ranulph Higden, author of *Polychronicon,* composed his own *De modo componendi sermones* (before 1349) using Basevorn's text as a guide. Thomas Waleys also wrote one. Nicholas Trevet, one of Chaucer's favorite sources, may also have written an *ars.*

In the fifteenth-century England, then, these were the various types of formal rhetorical treatises available to English writers. Beyond that, however, was the essentially French notion of "second rhetoric." If the art of writing prose was a *premiere rhétorique,* some writers felt, then the art of versification should be termed *seconde rhétorique.* So prevalent was this view, in fact, that Eustache Deschamps' *L'art de dictier* (1392) finds it necessary to urge that poetry be considered a part of music rather than rhetoric; in this view he follows John of Garland, though the tradition goes back at least as far as Boethius' *De arte metrica.* Deschamps refers to "autres" who wrote *arts de seconde rhétorique*, though neither their names nor their works are now known to us.[13] It is from this sense of *rhétorique*, no doubt, that Johan Robertet derived his title for *Les douze dames de rhétorique* (c. 1465).[14] It is of course this sense of "rhetoric" that leads fifteenth-century English writers like Lydgate to call Chaucer a "rhetorician." When Dunbar terms him "the rose of rethoris all" he means it as a generic praise, intended to mean that his poetic gifts cover a wide range.

With this background of medieval rhetorical traditions in mind, then, the picture of fifteenth-century English rhetoric might be easier to understand. Thomas Merke, writing his *De moderno dictamine* about 1404, was a well-known political figure; he used the established genre of the *ars dictaminis* as a frame for his work, introducing however some comparatively advanced ideas about composition. The popularity of his treatise may be indicated by the survival of ten manuscripts. The other Englishmen who wrote about rhetoric are for the most part minor or even shadowy figures. A Reginald Alcock appears as the author of a dictaminal tract (1456?) in Bodleian Ms. Selden Supra 65. [15] A separate writer of similar name, Simon Alcock, is the author of *De arte dictamine* which survives in an Oxford manuscript bearing the date 1427 and the scribal attribution "quod Wylton." [16] This may be the same person as the Simon Alcock (d. 1459) who wrote a preaching manual, *Tractatus de modo dividendi themata pro materia sermonis dilatanda.*[17] Several other clergy wrote preaching manuals, notably Geoffrey Schale, Thomas Penketh, and John Felton.[18]

Two short Latin pieces reveal another tendency. The better known of these short treatises, *Tractatus de modo invenienda ornata verba*, was produced at the Trinitarian priory at Ingham sometime before 1449, probably by John Blakeney, its fifth prior.[19] Ingham is of course northeast of Norwich, well within the range of King's Lynn where John Capgrave lived as an Augustinian friar, and of Bury St. Edmunds, notable for the poet John Lydgate. The town of Blakeney is near King's Lynn. Whether or not there is any truth in the tradition that Lydgate operated a school of rhetoric and poetry at Bury St. Edmunds, it is interesting to note that a man like Blakeney could easily have met both literary figures.[20] Apparently the East Anglian counties of Norfolk and Suffolk, being off the main north-south routes and away from major seaports, became a comparative oasis in those turbulent times. In 1433–34, at least, Bury St. Edmunds seemed a good place for the twelve-year-old Henry VI to spend a winter away from city plagues and other troubles. In any case Blakeney's *Tractatus de modo inveniendi ornata verba*, dealing with tropes and figures, has been linked with fifteenth-century tendencies toward highly colored or "aureate" verbal style.[21] Actually it is little more than the typical short essay on *elocutio* that one finds throughout the Middle Ages either as an offshoot of grammar training or as an adjunct to one of the major rhetorical traditions. Only its time and place are remarkable.

Another Latin piece has so far gone virtually unnoticed. This is the *Brevis tractatus de modo dilantandi et breviandi* of David Penkaer which survives in a manuscript transcribed in Oxford before 1451.[22] Penkaer was town clerk of Oxford from 1428 to 1457. His *Tractatus* discusses the standard medieval "modes" of abbreviating or prolonging material. He notes that many "colors" (figures) can be used not only to add distinction to language but to make the material either shorter or longer. Nine figures are particularly useful for brevity; while of twenty recommended for prolongation, eight are specifically recommended: "interpretatio, circumlocutio, comparatio, apostrophatio, prosopopeia, digressio, descriptio, et locus oppositorum." This doctrine is common in all the medieval rhetorical traditions, being found in metrical, dictaminal, and preaching treatises. Caplan, for instance, lists six separate preaching manuals devoted to this "eight mode" approach to amplifying material.[23] Penkaer declares that these modes of amplification and abbreviation apply "to all material equally." Among authorities quoted are Cicero, Alanus de Insulis, and Peter of Blois.

Both these works, it would seem, depend upon the existence of a generally-understood rhetorical or literary tradition that would make practical the writing of treatises dealing only with amplification or coloration. Neither writer seeks to justify his work beyond a few preliminary lines explaining its contents.[24]

Still another type of fifteenth-century treatise can only be called eclectic. The best example is an untitled work, dating from about 1435, which begins: *Preterea si dictantes ignorent materiam invenire aut tractare.*[25] A collection of model letters follows it in one manuscript, with the notation *oxon* (Oxford) in the margin. The author mixes dictaminal principles, concepts from *Rhetorica ad Herennium*, and citations from writers in every rhetorical tradition except preaching: Quintilian, John of Garland, the grammarian Alexandre de Villedieu, Boethius, Cicero, Geoffrey of Vinsauf, Master Bene (the dictaminal *Candelabrum*), Matthew of Vendome, and Horace. Then (in what might be a separate work) he includes a straightforward *ars dictaminis* in the Lombard manner, including a section on the *cursus*, and adds the model letters that usually accompany such an *ars*. Like Thomas Merke a few years earlier, he may have used the frame of an *ars dictaminis* as an opportunity to compose a broad statement about rhetoric.

Given this mixture of traditions in fifteenth-century England, what might we expect to find in an encyclopedic poem like *The Court of Sapience*?

The Court of Sapience, a clumsy poem of 2310 lines in 330 seven-line rimed stanzas, was long attributed to Lydgate.[26] The poet dreams that Sapience, after introducing him to the Four Daughters of God, takes him across a river and then to the Castle of Sapience where Theology lives with the Seven Liberal Arts. While there is much truth in Bühler's judgment that the poem is "very little more than a literary mosaic," [27] its very encyclopedic quality makes it an interesting index to some common fifteenth-century conceptions of the subjects treated. In terms of "modern" versus "medieval" attitudes toward language, the *Court's* handling of the *Trivium* is especially significant.

Lady Theology has seven other ladies with her:

> Ther was Gramor, grounde of Sciencis all,
> And Dyaletik, full of pure knowyng,
> And Rethoryk, Science imperiall,
> Dame Arsmetryke was in proporcionyng,
> Geometry that mesureth every thyng,
> The Lady Musyk and Astronomy;
> These ladyes seuen seweth Theology.
> [Stanza 221, ll. 1541–47]

Grammar has four ladies — Orthography, Etymology, Diasyntastica, and Prosody — and the authorities cited (Stanza 262) are for the most part the obvious, traditional ones: the ancient Donatus and Priscian, the medieval Peter Helias, Papias, John of Genoa (his *Catholicon* is mentioned by name), and John of Garland. Bühler has noted all of these. Two other names are unidentified: "Lambard" and "Ferryn." Given the large number of medieval treatises whose authors are still unknown to us, it is not surprising to see such unidentified authors in this list. One other name, which Bühler does not comment upon, appears in the text as "Thomas de Henneya." This may be the Thomas de Hanney who was rector of Longworth, Berkshire, from 1369 to

1391.[28] The list of authorities on grammar, however, also includes "Aristotyll. . . . Pariarmonise." This apparently puzzling entry may simply reflect the continuing interest of grammarians in the logicians' analysis of the nature of language; dialectical investigations of grammatical principles, especially strong at Paris in the 1280's and 1290's, had produced a "speculative grammar" whose practitioners (the so-called *modistae*) were neo-Aristotelian logicians rather than grammarians.[29] The Englishman William of Shirewood, writing in the fourteenth century, was one of the logicians influenced by this movement.

Logic (Dame Dialectica) has a solidly medieval function, seeking to "discerne and eke depure/ Trewthe from Falshede" (Stanza 264, ll. 1846–47). The list of authorities, however, is a curious one — Euclid, Pliny, Democritus, Demosthenes, and Alfred among them. Bühler is perhaps correct when he conjectures that the author is deliberately deriding Dialectic by positing a "preposterous" set of authorities.[30]

Dame Rethoryke takes as her province "prose and metyr of all kynde" (Stanza 276, l. 1926) as well as "speche delycious" (271, l. 1895), with a strong emphasis however on "endyting" rather than speaking orally. Not only are the authorities the traditional medieval ones, but some of them are Englishmen or have echoes of current English rhetorical practice. Cicero is of course named, "the chosen spowse vnto thys lady fre" (275, l. 1920). Geoffrey of Vinsauf, the thirteenth-century author of *Poetria nova* and *Documentum de modo et arte dicandi et versificandi*, apparently is named as "Galfryde the poete lawreate." (274, l. 1915),[31] but his two works are suggested only for their use of tropes and figures ("colours purpurate"); this is true also of the fourth book of grammarian John of Genoa's *Catholicon*, which also lists the *colores*. Vinsauf had a vogue among fifteenth-century English writers, possibly beginning with Merke's *De moderno dictamine* (1404) which includes eighteen quotations from the *Poetria nova*. The *Catholicon* of Balbus (John of Genoa: "Januense, a clerke of gret astate") does not seem to appear in other fifteenth-century English references, but his lengthy grammar was generally known throughout Europe.

A very early, almost pre-medieval view of legal rhetoric is also included, in a rather muddled stanza (275) where the author refers to "the code, also digestes thre,/ the booke of lawe." (ll. 1924–25) Apparently this stems back either to Isidore of Seville, who inserts a section on Law into his discussion of Rhetoric (*Etymologia* II.x), or to the

249

general European tradition of the Dark Ages. The stanza is the one naming Cicero, and recommends a book of "physik" as well.

The final stanza (276) in the section on rhetoric is the most medieval:

> In prose and metyr of al kynde y wys
> Thys lady blessyd had lust for to play;
> With her was Blesens, Rychard de Paphys,
> Pharas hys pisteles, clere, lusty, fresshe and gay;
> With metres was poetys in good aray,
> Oude, Omer, Virgyle, Lucan, Orace,
> Alayne, Bernard, Prudencius and Stace.
>
> [ll. 1926–32]

It is clear that "prose" is the province of *dictamen*, while "metyr" belongs to the poets. The mixture of ancient and medieval poets is interesting, but of course not unusual; a manuscript note identifies two poets more clearly as Alanus de Insulis and Bernard Silvestris respectively. "Blesens" is undoubtedly Peter of Blois (Peter of Bath) whose *De dictamine liber* (c. 1180) survives in a Cambridge manuscript. The other writer is Richard de Pophis (late thirteenth century), known for a letter collection (*dictaminum*) which survives in nine manuscripts in libraries at London, Oxford, Cambridge, and Durham.[32]

The citation of "Pharas hys pisteles" is the most conclusive evidence of the author's parochialism. Considering all the model letter collections known to be circulated widely in England — those of Peter de Vinea or Guido Faba, for instance[33] — it seems bizarre to have an English author name as a major work an arcane trifle so rare as to be almost invisible. This supposititious *Pharaonis epistolae* occurs sometimes in connection with the name of the Cistercian John of Limoges (Johannis *Lemovicensis*), who is credited among other things with an *ars dictaminis* and with a work variously titled *Somnium pharaonis* or *Somniale dilucidarium Pharaonis ad Theobaldum regum Navarine.*[34] Like the Pseudo-Aristotelian *Epistola ad Alexandrum* it purports to be a real correspondence. But compared to the extensive, realistic sets of model letters in the major collections of de Vinea and Faba, this brief overblown "correspondence" seems utterly incongruous. It certainly does not rank with the collection of Richard de Pophis, either in literary value or in usefulness.

It must be concluded, then, that the author's treatment of the *Trivium* is purely medieval. There is absolutely no awareness of the humanistic writers, the newly rediscovered classical works, or any new books on the three subjects of grammar, dialectic, and rhetoric. The

Court of Sapience could just as well have been written a hundred years earlier, in 1375.

Thus both the *Margarita eloquentiae* of Traversagni and the anonymous *Court of Sapience* prove upon closer examination to be traditional/medieval in outlook, quite out of touch with the "modern" or "humanistic" movement known as the Renaissance. Their authors should not be despised for this. From their point of view their approach was quite reasonable, with centuries of success to back them up. For instance, when the anonymous English author of the untitled *Preterea si dictantes* mixes the ancient Quintilian and the thirteenth-century John of Garland in the same sentence (f. 11) there is of course no sense of anachronism. There is also no sense of change, for when he notes (f. 13ᵛ) that in Italy the term *epetito* is used to refer to the process of matching people with their titles, he is referring to a common dictaminal doctrine going back as far as the twelfth century. For him, it is plain, Italy is merely the home of *dictatores* like Bene of Florence. Why should anything Italian be anything else for a fifteenth-century English rhetorician?

The late coming to England of the literary Renaissance, after all, may be due in part to the principle that familiarity breeds misunderstanding. When grammarians and rhetoricians had been citing Horace, Cicero, and Quintilian for centuries, side by side with Garland, Vinsauf, and locals like Peter of Blois, what is so novel, these English writers might argue, about having a more complete Quintilian text, or the full *De oratore* of Cicero? Or if Sallust or Pliny were rediscovered in Italy and copies transported to England (as William Grey did with Pliny), why then their stories could be added to the existing stock of *exempla* already collected by preachers. Even a casual reading of Roberto Weiss' marvelously detailed *Humanism in England During the Fifteenth Century* will reveal that most of the newly-discovered classical works or Italian translations had found their way into England one way or another by the 1470's. Poggio had come in hope and left in disgust early in the century, but later many English visited Italy and many Italians traveled in England. It was not opportunity that was lacking. Instead, English grammarians, rhetoricians, and literary figures maintained a kind of satisfaction with the existing forms. What we today might want to call "new," they would probably regard simply as "additional."

The two choices of William Caxton, then, should be understood in this context.[35]

NOTES

1. A description of the book may be found in Wilbur S. Howell, *Rhetoric and Logic in England, 1500–1700* (Princeton University Press, 1956), pp. 78–81. While it is usually known as *Nova rhetorica*, Traversagni also termed it *Margarita eloquentiae* ("Pearl of Eloquence"). See William Blades, *The Life and Typography of William Caxton, England's First Printer* (London, 1863; rpt. New York: Burt Franklin, n.d.), II, 74–76. For Traversagni's humanistic qualities, see Roberto Weiss, *Humanism in England in the Fifteenth Century*, 2nd ed. (Oxford: Basil Blackwell, 1957), pp. 162–63.

2. *The Court of Sapience*, ed. Robert Spindler. Beiträge zur Englischen Philologie, sechstes heft (Leipzig, 1927). See also J. W. H. Atkins, *English Literary Criticism: The Medieval Phase* (Cambridge, 1943; rpt. New York, 1952), pp. 165–66. Caxton's text also uses the title *Curia sapientiae*; cf. Blades, *Caxton*, II, 114–17. There is an excellent summary in Nellie S. Aurner, *Caxton: Mirrour of Fifteenth Century Letters: A Study of the Literature of the first English Press* (London, 1926), pp. 98–101. See also Curt F. Bühler, *The Sources of the Court of Sapience*. Beiträge zur Englischen Philologie, Heft 23 (Leipzig, 1932).

3. Weiss, *Humanism*, pp. 13–21.

4. See James J. Murphy, "Rhetoric in Fourteenth Century Oxford," *Medium Aevum* 34 (1965), 1–20. For an American manuscript of Merke's treatise, cf. Murphy, "A Fifteenth Century Treatise on Prose Style," *Newberry Library Bulletin* 6 (1966), 205–10.

5. Weiss, *Humanism*, pp. 113–22.

6. For text see Ronald H. Martin, ed., *The Epitome Margaritae Eloquentiae of Laurentius Gulielmus de Saona*; Proceedings of the Leeds Philosophical and Literary Society, Literary and Historical Section, XIV, Pt. IV (Leeds, 1971), pp. 99–187.

7. "Quibus ex causis censuit appellandum fore Margaritam eloquencie castigate ad eloquendum divina accomodatum" (St. Alban's edition [p. 364]). I have used a microfilm of the St. Alban's edition, *STC* 24190.

8. "ad tantam sermonis ineptitudionem divinam fit" (p. 2). It might be noted also that the prevalence of the usual title of this rare book (*Nova rhetorica*) may stem in part from its appearance in the Pollard and Redgrave *Short-Title Catalogue* (p. 563). The *Rhetorica ad Herennium* was of course readily available in England. Murphy, "Cicero's Rhetoric in the Middle Ages," *Quarterly Journal of Speech* 53 (1967), 334–41. Weiss (*Humanism*, pp. 62–63) notes for instance that Humphrey, Duke of Gloucester, owned several Ciceronian Texts, including one manuscript with twenty-two works in it; he gave Oxford University a number of Ciceronian manuscripts in 1439. Traversagni lectured at Cambridge on the *ad Herennium*; cf. A. B. Emden, *A Biographical Register of the University of Cambridge to 1500* (Cambridge University Press, 1963), pp. 593–94.

9. For a translation see Jane Baltzell Kopp (trans.), *The New Poetics*, in *Three Medieval Rhetorical Arts*, ed. James J. Murphy (Berkeley: University of California Press, 1971), pp. 32–108. Also translated by Margaret F.

Nims (Toronto, 1967). Vinsauf also wrote a prose version, *Documentum de modo dictandi et versificandi* which has been translated by Roger Parr as *Instruction in the Method and Art of Speaking and Versifying* (Milwaukee: Marquette University Press, 1968). Latin texts of both works are in Edmond Faral, *Les arts poétiques du XIIe et du XIIIe siècle* (Paris, 1924).

10. For a translation of a seminal treatise written at Bologna in 1135, see James J. Murphy (trans.), "The Principles of Letter-Writing," in *Three Medieval Rhetorical Arts*, ed. James J. Murphy (Berkeley: University of California Press, 1971), pp. 5–25. The most important single description of these developments is Charles H. Haskins, "The Early *artes dictandi* in Italy," in *Studies in Medieval Culture* (Oxford, 1929), pp. 170–92.

11. For these three English figures see "Rhetoric in Fourteenth Century Oxford," *Medium Aevum* 34 (1965), 1–20.

12. Basevorn's treatise has been translated by Leopold Krul, O.S.B.: *The Form of Preaching*, in Murphy (ed.), *Three Medieval Rhetorical Arts*, pp. 114–215. For manuscript listings see Harry Caplan, *Mediaeval Artes Praedicandi: A Hand-list*. Cornell Studies in Classical Philology 24 (Ithaca, 1934) and *Supplement* (Ithaca, 1936). Indispensable in this field is Th. -M. Charland, *Artes praedicandi: contribution a l'histoire de la rhétorique au moyen âge*. Publications de l'institut d'études médiévales d'Ottawa 7 (Paris and Ottawa, 1936); the Latin texts of Basevorn and Waleys are included, together with an analysis of the *genre* and biographies of authors and list of their manuscripts.

13. See Ernest Langlois, *Recueil d'arts de seconde rhétorique* (Paris, 1902). Deschamps' *L'art de dictier* is in *Oeuvres completes de Eustache Deschamps*, ed. Marquis de Quenx de Saint-Hilaire and Gaston Raynoud. Societé des anciens textes français 7 (Paris, 1891), pp. 266–92.

14. Johan Robertet, *Les douze dames de rhétorique*, ed. Louis Batissier (Paris[?] 1838). (This work is sometimes catalogued under the name of George Chastellain, one of its main characters.) The relation of Robertet and Chastellain is described in Johan Huizinga, *The Waning of the Middle Ages* (New York, 1929; rpt. 1954), pp. 329–30; though Huizinga describes the author's language as "hyperbolic effusions," it is clear that Robertet's term "rhétorique" is used to denote a wide range of poetic talents.

15. Tractatus magistri Riginaldi Alcock de arte dictandi. Oxford Bodleian Ms. Selden Supra 65, ff. 134–39. Incipit: Discantus est color rhetoricus. On folio 46 is the year, 1456, and the notation: Wilelmus Forsythe scriptor.

16. Oxford St. Johns College Ms. 184, ff. 188^v–194.

17. Edited by Mary F. Boynton as "Simon Alcock on Expanding the Sermon," *Harvard Theological Review* 34 (1941), 201–16.

18. For biographical details see Charland, *Artes praedicandi*, pp. 37, 91, 90, 84.

19. London British Museum Ms. 12 B XVII, ff. 53^v–57. Bale (p. 183) referred to it under the title *Modum rhetoricandi*, for reasons not entirely clear.

20. The tradition is discussed briefly by Atkins, *Criticism*, p. 165, and by Walter F. Schirmer, *John Lydgate: A Study in the Culture of the Fifteenth Century* (Berkeley: University of California Press, 1961), p. 23. It is also interesting to note that still another rhetorical author can be identified

with the same area: Bale (p. 352) cites a manuscript he saw at the Benedictine priory of St. Faith at Horsham, just outside Norwich, containing two works by Richard Kendale (fl. 1431). One was titled *De componendi epistolis* and the other *De dictamine prosaico*. Both are now lost.

21. For instance Weiss, *Humanism*, p. 11 and Atkins, *Criticism*, p. 164.

22. London British Museum Ms. Harley 941, ff. 80–89, transcribed in Oxford by John Edward (d. 1451). However, another version exists in Harley 670, ff. 3–10, which dates from about 1435.

23. Caplan, *Hand-list*, pp. 18–19.

24. It must be noted that each of the three major medieval rhetorical traditions developed a systematic apparatus of corollary works to support its main thrust. Collections of *exempla*, for instance, supported the *ars praedicandi* just as letter-collections (*dictamina*) supported the *ars dictaminis*.

25. There are two manuscript copies: Harley 941, ff. 91ff. and Harley 670, ff. 11–26. This second one may contain fragments of another work.

26. Stephen Hawes in *Pastime of Pleasure* (printed 1509), which is heavily indebted to *The Court of Sapience*, says of Lydgate, "He fayned also the Court of Sapyence."

27. Bühler, *Sources*, p. 17. Norman F. Blake, *Caxton and His World* (London, 1969) believes that Caxton printed the *Court* because he saw its author as one of the "courtly poets" like Lydgate, Gower, or Chaucer (p. 71).

28. Emden, *A Biographical Register of the University of Oxford to 1500*, three vols. (Oxford, 1957–59), II, 867.

29. See Robert H. Robins, *Ancient and Medieval Grammatical Theory in Europe* (London, 1951).

30. Bühler, *Sources*, pp. 72–74, notes that Alanus de Insulis, Henri d'Andeli, John of Salisbury, and Chaucer all ridicule the "sophisms" and fruitless debates engendered by dialectic.

31. This passage is somewhat confusing. It is not impossible that the author means "Geoffrey *Chaucer* poet laureate *and* (separately) the author of *Tria sunt*." The passage reads as follows:

> . . . go he to Tria Sunt
> And to Galfryde, the poete lawreate.

Vinsauf's *Documentum* begins "Tria sunt circa quae cujuslibet." (However, this is a fairly common *incipit* among medieval rhetorical works which often name three types of discourse, three types of *causae*, three levels of style, etc.) The author's verse is so clumsy, however, that precise interpretation of this and other passages is extremely difficult. Most students have accepted the passage to mean Vinsauf. Nevertheless Blake (*Caxton*, p. 164) hypothesizes that Caxton may have borrowed from this passage the term "poete laureate" to apply to Chaucer, thinking that "Galfryde" was intended to mean Geoffrey Chaucer.

32. Bühler did not know this name. For the manuscripts in England, see Noel Denholm-Young, "The *cursus* in England," in *Collected Papers on Medieval Subjects* (Oxford, 1946), p. 52.

33. See for example the fine study by Ernst Kantorowicz, "Petrus de Vinea in England," *MIOG* 51 (1937), 43–88.

34. See *Johannis Lemovicensis opera omnia*, ed. Constantine Horvath, three

vols. (Verszprem, 1932). His *ars dictaminis* occurs at I, 1–69. Fifteenth-century manuscripts of the *Somnium* are now in Oxford St. Johns College Ms. 172, ff. 99–122 and Balliol Ms. 263, ff. 114–24 (which also contains copies of Vinsauf's *Poetria nova* and of his *Documentum*, with its *tria sunt* opening line). It is of course possible that the author of *Court of Sapience* relied on a single manuscript similar to Balliol 263 containing a miscellany of rhetorical works (like, for instance, Paris Bibliothèque nationale Ms. Lat. 7695, which contains five such works).

35. Caxton's own brief words on rhetoric, of course, reveal very little about the subject. See Caxton, *Mirrour of the World*, ed. Oliver Prior. Early English Text Society, Extra Series 110. (London, 1913; rpt. New York, 1966), Cap. ix (pp. 35–36).

Cynewulf's Multiple Revelations

Jackson J. Campbell

THE INTERPRETIVE problems of Cynewulf's longest poem, *Elene*, begin with its very title. It has been recognized by a number of people for a number of years that this arbitrary yet persistent title is a grave misnomer. After absorbing the full impact of all 1300 odd lines of the poem, we are conscious that it is not a poem about Queen Elene at all, however important she may be as a part of the total structure. It is hoped that its next editor will have the courage to call it the *Invention of the Cross*, or something more appropriate.

Even if we considered Elene the principal personage in the poem, there are severe problems in interpreting her character. Some years ago a serious medievalist described her to me as a "cruel, hardbitten old harridan." This criticism obviously stemmed from her action in punishing Judas with seven days' starvation in a pit, which of course to our delicate and compassionate sensitivities seems extreme and un-Christian. Even aside from this climactic act, she often seems too business-like, curt, and efficient — purposeful and honest, perhaps, but distant and unattractive. Probably those who react negatively to her are victims of two pitfalls: that of reading too literally, and that of not reading closely enough.

A third problem involves the interpretation of the theme of the poem, particularly in the light of one or two awkward vagaries of the narrative line of the work. Several critics have been satisfied to consider the first 200 lines or so, containing the vigorous battle scenes involving Constantine, as a variety of prologue to the long, rather talky quest for the Cross in Jerusalem. The portion after the discovery of the Cross, containing the search for the nails and their discovery, has struck many people as anti-climactic, thematically repetitious, and a general artistic blemish. This objection, like the others, can easily be removed if one interprets the entire poem on a slightly broader scale than has been done before. There remains, however, a need for explaining what sort of unity these large narrative blocks add up to.

257

Finally, one annoyance, though not a major problem, faces any critic of *Elene* in that we do not know the precise source Cynewulf was using. There were current, in Old English times, two or three versions of the life of St. Cyriac and of the finding of the Cross. Aelfric uses a story in his short homily on the subject (Thorpe's Catholic Homilies II, 303) which he says is based on St. Jerome's Ecclesiastical History, and which differs almost totally from the story in *Elene*. Two other homilies, one in CCCC 303 and one in Bodleian Auct. F.iv.32, are similar to each other but very different from Aelfric and Jerome. Bede's homily on the *Inventio*, brief as it is, has elements from both versions. Cynewulf's poem is closest to a short Latin story called in most early manuscripts not *Acta Cyriaci* but simply *Inventio Sanctae Crucis*.[1] There are a number of early manuscripts of this version which differ only in some minor details; one of them is an eighth-century St. Gall manuscript which probably came from an insular exemplar. In all important respects Cynewulf's poem derives from this short version of the *Inventio*; although none of the extant Latin MSS have all the details exactly as we find them in *Elene*, yet all of the conflicting details appear in Cynewulf's form in one or another of the early MSS. Thus we can be relatively sure that Cynewulf's source was some lost or unknown MS of this *Inventio* which combined the details in a way slightly different from any of the existing Latin MSS.[2] For purposes of comparison, I shall use the edition of A. Holder, which is taken basically from a seventh-century MS. now in the Bibliothèque Nationale, with variants from the St. Gall MS. This is probably as close as we can now get to Cynewulf's source. Although the conflate and adapted texts published by Holthausen and Straubinger smooth out most of the problems of wording and certainly improve the Latin grammar, yet they are essentially an artificial construct tidied up considerably to suit modern purists.

Structurally, Cynewulf's poem falls into five main narrative blocks: Constantine's struggle and conversion (lines 1–211); Elene's search for the Cross, ending with the conversion of Judas (lines 212–1062); the finding of the nails (lines 1062–1200); a short peroration culminating in a *finit* (lines 1201–35); and an epilogue written in Cynewulf's poetic persona (lines 1236–1320). Each section has a kind of rising action, whether of story material or of gradually intensifying homiletic idea and emotion. Although it is the first section — Constantine's battle and conversion — which is most admired and most frequently anthologized, yet the core of the poem is obviously the second section — Elene's search for the Cross, which leads to the conversion of Judas. The poet spends 843 of his lines (well over sixty percent) on developing and amplifying these events. Elene's conflict with the Jews is ritualistic, formal, and stylized, but when the struggle finally narrows to one between the queen and Judas a more intimate, personalized tension appears which is eventually resolved in a burst of joy. The pattern of narrative and meaning established in this core section is one which is repeated in varied ways in the other, smaller sections, but nowhere in such a well developed state. In the opening section, Constantine's experience begins in doubt, fear, and confusion, rises to heady excitement in the battle, and reaches its Christian goal in his conversion and baptism. Judas' quest (or rather Cyriac's) for the nails begins in ignorance and humble petition, mounts to success with their discovery, and culminates in a decision about what to do with them, which I shall presently show is indeed important and meaningful enough to serve as a climax for the section. Elene's and Cyriac's final teaching (1201–35) progresses from simple instruction through various healing miracles to the promise of glory for those believing in the elemental Christian paradox of the Cross. Even Cynewulf's epilogue follows this structural movement from a low key to a high key of personalized homiletic emotion, and I think it can be shown to be far more integral to the poem than it has hitherto been thought.

These various elements, which seem rather arbitrarily and repetitiously strung together in the Latin text of the *Inventio*, are far more carefully unified by Cynewulf. At every point in the poem it is clear that his focus is on the Cross. The Cross, both as a literal object and as a symbolic idea, grows in meaning through the poem and eventually ties the poem together into satisfying thematic unity. Cynewulf could depend on his audience's knowing, of course, the fundamental idea associated with the Cross: sacrifice which proceeds from love. This of course is very nearly the essence of the Christian ethic, but the perception, and more importantly the embracing, of it can be very difficult; a teacher-poet needs to vary and shape his mode of presentation of the theme in a number of ways to make it persuasive. The notion of revelation — or the revealing of the Cross — and the conversion which follows revelation supply the thematic pattern which permeates the repeated narrative patterns just discussed. Conversion, in the sense I am using it, encompasses not merely the simple conversion of a former pagan to Christianity, as we find it in the first section

259

of the poem, but rather the deeper understanding and acceptance of the whole complex of Christian ideas concerning the meaning of Christ's sacrifice by the ordinary man — a sort of "conversion" which can come to one who, like the poet in the epilogue, has long been nominally a Christian. The effects of the revelation of the Cross in this larger sense account for the fact that throughout the poem Cynewulf constantly introduces the polarities, or better the basic Christian paradoxes, implied by the Cross. Death brings life (the Cross is *lifes treo* in line 756); sin can lead to salvation; hell and Satan give way to heaven by the spiritual action of the Cross; unbelief turns into belief; the old law is replaced by the new. In each section these mysteries or paradoxes appear, almost never as simple repetitions but as new developments, explored from some different angle of the basic idea. The movement from dark to light, from death to life, from earthly trouble to heavenly glory — or in other words the pattern of ignorance, revelation, conversion, baptism, and salvation — are not so much repeated in the poem as they are used as recurrent themes to be incrementally elaborated, explored, and developed.[3]

Working with this particular theme and with the simple narrative his source provided, Cynewulf needed, or wanted, to use only the austerest modes of characterization. The characters have a certain "minimum recognizability" which is quite sufficient for the mode of art in which he was working. Constantine is first and foremost the Emperor, a *casere* ruling people and things in this world. Few indeed are the unique human qualities which characterize him as a man. To be sure, when his army is huddled on the Danube facing a far larger hostile force, he feels fear; when his vision of the Cross reassures him, he feels relief and joy, an emotion which intensifies as he is instructed and converted to Christianity. Two emotions hardly make what old-fashioned criticism would call a well-rounded character. He seems, rather — and surely this is enough — to be the representative of civil and worldly power, seen first in confusion and peril, then in victory and strength, not only in military terms but more importantly, in spiritual ones. The vision itself, and the victory won next day by means of the newly constructed effigy of the Cross, are presented as if they were miraculous, but, as is so often true of medieval stories of this type, the outward miracle serves to adumbrate the more significant inner miracle, his changed spirit.

There is no description of Constantine at all, but the standard regal and heroic epithets occur: *hildfruma, leodhwata, beorna beaggifa, tireadig cyning, heriga helm*. He is a good (*riht*) king and God has strengthened him because he was to become (*wearð* 15) a comfort to men. A sense of resolution and vigor accompanies his first orders to prepare for battle; six and one-half lines (50–56a) are devoted to spirited imagery of the Romans' preparations, although these are made slightly ironic by the fact that we have earlier had over 20 equally vigorous lines (19b–41a) building up the feeling of menace and strength of the invading army. Constantine's fear of the superior Hunnish force is emphasized three times (56, 57, and 61), and the image of his army huddled around the *egstreame* seems to ascribe the same fear to them. During the vision of the angel and the heavenly Cross we have no indication of his emotions, but as soon as he obeys the messenger and looks up, there is the curious phrase *hreðerlocan onspeon* which has puzzled some editors.

> He wæs sona gearu
> þurh þæs halgan hæs   hreðerlocan onspeon,
> up locade,   swa him se ar abead
> [85–87]

I find the puzzlement hard to understand, for the phrase is consummately appropriate as part of an asyndetic series of clauses. "He opened his heart" to the vision, as he so patently does in the context of the entire passage; miraculous manifestations, after all, require spiritual receptiveness. The mood changes immediately to firmness and confidence. Constantine takes command: the verb *he[h]t* occurs five times in the next hundred odd lines, culminating with his instructing his mother in line 214 to seek the Cross. The vigor of the victorious battle is then followed by a tone of elation, an emotion which anticipates the joyful explanation of Christ's victory over death (187) on the Cross. Actually, Constantine throughout is a clear and impressive, though two-dimensional, sketch of a worldly king who responds positively and joyously to the revelation of the meaning of the Cross. He is changed by his new understanding of Christ's sacrifice, in a way which Elene is not, at least during this poem. At the end of this section, before focus shifts to Elene, Cynewulf uses the instruction of the *larsmiðas* to foreshadow elements in the second part:

> swa se ealda feond
> forlærde ligesearwum,   leode fortyhte,
> Iudea cyn,   þæt hie god sylfne

261

ahengon, herga fruman.   þæs hie in hynðum sculon
to widan feore   wergðu dreogan!
[207–11]

It was the old enemy Satan who influenced the Jews at the time of the Crucifixion (although they had a quite literal revelation of the Cross) to hang God himself. For that they must suffer misery forever. Rejection and acceptance of proffered revelation are important motifs in the next section.

Elene dominates the long second section of the poem in a very curious way. She also is characterized very meagerly, and her characterization develops and grows hardly at all. The movement and progress of the interest eventually shifts away from her, first to the Jews as a group, then to Judas individually. Elene's role during this crucial central portion of the poem is that of a catalyst. Perhaps she loses some human appeal because of this; she causes change in others but does not undergo any herself. Cynewulf introduces her quite abruptly, simply as *his modor* (214), fixing on her relationship to Constantine rather than her individuality. Toward the end of the poem this relationship is stressed again when church-building and bridle-making become an issue. She does have some broadly recognizable human emotions during the poem, but they are scarcely any greater in quantity or variety than those of Constantine in the first section. Epithets establish her clearly as dear (*leoflic wif* 286) and blessed (*seo eadige* 619), but we are given no physical or psychological description of her. Besides being a mother, she is preeminently a queen (*guðcwen* 331, *seo cwen* 378, *tireadig cwen* 605, *Cristenra cwen* 1068. Her participation throughout this episode is motivated by her profound and total dedication to her mission:

Wæs seo eadhreðige   Elene gemyndig,
þriste on geþance   þeodnes willan,
georn on mode
[266–68]

þeodnes could here equally well mean Constantine's will or God's will. Impressive and imperious she may be, somewhat remote perhaps as a person, but there is a feeling everywhere that this "queen of Christians" is acting not for her own benefit or from personal motives but as an agent of divine power.

Before remarking on Cynewulf's presentation of her character in her actions, it might be well to digress momentarily for a matter which

262

may explain some of the poet's technique. The Church, *Ecclesia*, that collective body of all believers in Christ, was nearly always symbolized in the literature and art of the Middle Ages as a female personage, or as W. Molsdorf would put it, a *triumphierenden weiblichen Person*.[5] Drawing his illustrations mainly from the visual arts, Molsdorf finds such feminine representations of the Church in architectural and sculptural details such as tympana as well as in illustrated MSS.

The classic symbolic representation of the *Ecclesia* is of course in the figure of the Virgin Mary, a connection made early in the history of Christian exegesis. Virtually all other good women mentioned in the Bible were also taken by St. Gregory, Bede, and other commentators as types of the Church: Sarah, Esther, Ruth, Judith, even the Magdalen in certain aspects. Another quite standard association of the *Ecclesia* was with queenhood: in the fifth century, St. Eucherius, in his *Liber Formularum Spiritalis Intelligentiae*, records the identification briefly, as if it were already traditional: *Regina, Ecclesia. In psalmo: Astitit regina adextris tuis*.[6] The Psalms provided a great number of passages where the concept of queen was taken as a figure for the Church. Cassiodorus' *Expositio in Psalterium* constantly makes use of this identification, and Bede's commentary on the Psalter is equally full of it. He is often unequivocally definite about it: *regina, id est, Ecclesia*.[7]

Motherhood has also always been an attribute of the Church from early times down to the recent decretal *Mater et Magistra*. It was another of those figural meanings which was so common that St. Eucherius again felt the need only of a brief, shorthand explanation: *Mater, Ecclesia, vel Hierusalem coelestis*.[8]

All these associations make me wonder if Cynewulf was not using the character of Elene in his story as a figure of the Church in its action *vis à vis* the Jews as well as in its interactions with Christians. I must admit that I have so far failed to find any clear and definite identification in early medieval sources, though there may be scholia or glosses doing so in the continental manuscripts of the *Inventio* which I have not been able to see. There is, however, one very interesting spot in the Latin *Inventio* which served Cynewulf as a source. The text in most manuscripts reads, "Gratia autem spiritus sancti requievit in beata Helena matre Constantini imperatoris. Haec autem in omnibus scripturis se exercebat, et nimiam in domino nostro Iesu Chr possedit delectionem.[9] These remarks could, of course, be made equally appropriately of a figure symbolizing the Church or of an individual human person who later became a saint. In the Paris MS, however, the oldest exemplar we have of this text, the last sentence reads: "Haec autem in omnibus domibus dominicis scribturis se exercibatur et nimiam in domino nostri Ihu Xro possedit dilectionem." Quite aside from its doubtful grammar, that *domibus dominicis* seems very odd if the story is purely and solely literal. The passage may mean something like: "She occupied herself with scriptures in every house of God," which would be difficult for one mere woman to do.

In short, the associations were available in the traditional *figurae* of the time, and although the case is built on circumstantial evidence, I suspect that Cynewulf viewed Elene at least partly as a type of the Church. His stress on her queenhood and her motherhood, plus the manner in which he presents her character in action, make such an interpretation extremely plausible.

Elene's first action in the poem is to embrace her mission joyfully and set out on her sea voyage for Jerusalem. It has often been pointed out that this voyage is not in any of the possible sources for the poem, so Cynewulf's addition to the poem must have been motivated by some artistic or structural or doctrinal consideration. It has also been pointed out that sea voyages of this sort in OE poetry do not necessarily indicate, as some nineteenth-century critics assumed, that the English were great sailors, and that their poets therefore wrote sea poetry with intimate realistic knowledge of the sea. This passage is mainly constructed out of the standard formulas which often describe sea voyages in the most general way. Cynewulf combines them, however, in such a way as to produce a feeling of elated adventure, creating a tone of vigorous anticipation as Elene leads her men and women across the sea to discover the Cross.

The traditional metaphor of the sea as the tribulations of this earthly life over which man must sail may well be at work in this passage. It has long ago been shown that this metaphor was virtually omnipresent in the early Middle Ages [10] and that it was quite clearly being used by a number of OE poets.[11] The expedition to recapture the cross could very easily be couched in terms of the Church leading Christian people joyfully toward rediscovery of the basic concept in their religion. Though the passage may have this figural significance, it is naturally presented in the best of standard OE poetic diction, and has a rich and stirring flavor of native feeling and action. I find it hard to believe that Cynewulf added this to the source merely to show off the vigorous sea poetry he could write; but the excitement of the voyage coupled with the suggestions of mystical meaning make an ideal introduction to the issues at stake in the central section of the poem. The joy at the inception of this block of the poem is balanced by the joyful poetry Cynewulf writes at the end of the successful completion of the mission, forming a kind of envelope emotional response.

Taking the poem as a whole, joy and praise are the emotions most frequently mentioned in connection with Elene. Her actions quite often, however, appear schematic and monumental rather than intimately naturalistic. Most of her speeches are introduced by simple phrases specifying the speaker: e.g., "Elene maðelade him on andsware" (642). A stern anger appears a few times (573, 685), but it is invariably of the type which Chaucer's Parson shows when he reproves the blaspheming of the Host. Her three calls to the Jews — first to an assembly of 3000, then 1000, then 500 — are serious and firm, but by no means vindictive. The first speech (288–319) dwells rather sadly on the fact that they once were dear to God but have brought misery on themselves by their rejection of Christ. At the end of it she sends them away quite simply and dispassionately to choose those who know the Jewish law best. Her second speech also is calm and reasonable (345–76), and she herself quotes passages from the Old Testament which were universally taken in the Middle Ages to refer to Christ in typological fashion. Again she requests men with wide knowledge and deep wisdom about Jewish writings. To the 500 she points out the frequency of the foolish acts of the Jews (and of course none of them could deny the many lapses into idolatry in their history) and is quite explicit about their sinfulness in refusing to recognize the son of God born in Bethlehem. When the Jews reply somewhat pitifully that they do not know how they have offended her (þec 403) and aroused her anger, we realize that it is true that no transgression (*aebylgð* 401) has been committed against her personally, but that against the community of Christian believers and against the Christian God evil was done. At least one member of the 500 does know about the events of the Crucifixion, as we discover immediately after they leave Elene, and one wonders if the others are completely candid when they say they have never heard of it. Judas gives a remarkable account of the knowledge that has been passed down from his fathers, and the Jews hand him over to Elene for questioning. They may well have been *geomormode* (555), but they were also harder than stone (565) in wishing to deny knowledge of their secret. Only after this duplicity is made clear to the reader does Cynewulf write a truly stern speech for Elene (574–84).

The alternative Elene puts to Judas during his questioning may possibly be taken in both a literal sense and the sense of his ultimate spiritual destiny:

> þe synt tu gearu,
> swa lif swa deað   swa þe leofre bið
> to geceosanne
>
> [605–7]

Life or death can be his, but in the context of this poem the anagogical polarity is also between eternal life or eternal death. Judas' response also contains a polarity with overtones of wider meaning. His analogy of the weary traveller in a wasteland who is offered bread or a stone can hardly avoid recalling the recently mentioned stoniness of the Jews on the one hand and the bread of the Eucharist, the bread of life, on the other. Elene picks up the positive side of this analogy and, speaking in spiritual terms as well as literal ones, tries to persuade him with the promise of heavenly existence as well as earthly life (621–22). Judas does not respond to this fair promise, however, and in his subsequent two speeches he not only becomes wily and evasive, but eventually utters a blatant and intentional lie. At line 660 he says that until now he has never heard any man speak of the matters Elene refers to, when of course the audience has just heard Judas himself speaking very movingly about them. This direct lie does not appear in the Latin at this point, and Cynewulf undoubtedly added it for the effect he wanted in his narrative. Elene's response also has a small element that is not in the Latin: she apparently knows, in some strange way, that he only shortly before was speaking to his people about the tree of life and victory (665). Cynewulf does not pursue the supernatural suggestions here, but he certainly had not told us earlier, or later for that matter, that Elene had some avenue of knowledge about what went on in the Jewish community.

Judas' next direct speech contains a further lie, and it is then that Elene ordains his punishment. Now some modern interpretations of Christian principles seem to deny that punishment exists in Christian terms, and that it is evil when it appears. This lovely sentimental view certainly does not hold up when one views the life of man on this earth, where punishment is an existential reality and evil acts often contain within themselves their own punishment. The Middle Ages looked unflinchingly at this matter. Though the individual must not indulge in vengeance, yet the collective Church had to "snibben" evil whenever it found it. What the thought of the Middle Ages most often did, moreover, was to see spiritual significance in literal events. The hunger Elene threatens Judas with may also mean the lack of psychic food which in Judas' case already exists, and will continue to exist as long as he denies Christ. The chains and the seven days in the dry pit may also be not only factual but representative of his state of sin. It is the very function of the Church to help sinners repent for their own ultimate health, and quite possibly Elene's action here should be viewed not so much as stemming from a human being's sadistic vengeance as from the duty of an institution charged with responsibility for not only one individual's soul but those of the mass of its own limbs or members. The results of the punishment are in any event salubrious not only for Judas, with his conversion, but for the whole Christian community, with the finding of the Cross. There is more joy in heaven, according to St. Luke (15, 7), over the repentance of one sinner than over ninety-nine who do not need repentance. Judas is taken out of the pit *mid arum* (714), and Elene's reactions to virtually everything that happens in the rest of the poem are those of joy and gratitude. To choose but one illustration from the many in the latter part of the poem:

> Gode þancode,
> wuldorcyninge þæs hire se willa gelamp
> þurh bearn Godes bega gehwæðres,
> ge æt þære gesyhðe þæs sigebeames,
> ge ðæs geleafan þe hio swa leohte oncneow,
> wuldorfæste gife in þæs weres breostum.
> [961–66]

Though her mission had been but to recover the Cross, her final rejoicing is for two things: the sight of the Cross and the belief received into the breast of the man Judas. Belief, after all, is the special province of the Church. Through this latter part of the poem, where the Latin *Inventio* is very laconic about Elene's rejoicing, Cynewulf is fulsome, expanding and amplifying at every turn. The action, such as it is, in the latter part of the poem is performed mostly by the believing Judas while Elene becomes an appreciative bystander.

From the modern point of view, the most interesting character in the poem is Judas. It is he who seems to experience some internal conflict, and who is not only changed by conversion but becomes a saint literally before our eyes. Although central and extended, Judas' finding the Cross is only one of a number of such inventions, as Cynewulf varies and develops the theme in several different forms. The growth and progression of Judas' character, however, is almost impossible to understand if we apply the standards of naturalistic or psychological criticism. Judas is introduced in line 418 as *gidda gearosnotor* and *wordes craeftig*. He tells the assembled Jews immediately that he knows that Elene wants the *sigebeame* on which *Godes agen bearn* suffered his passion. This distinctly Christian vocabulary is curious from an unconverted Jew and needs some sort of explanation. It is possible that the poetic formulas were so ingrained into a Christian poet like Cynewulf that he would use them automatically whenever he mentioned Christian matters, regardless of whether he was violating verisimilitude — in this case putting them in the mouth of a character whose real attitudes would not permit such vocabulary. The matter is more complex than that, though, for during Judas' long speech which follows, both the Latin and Cynewulf's elaboration of it show that this ambiguity was intentional. As Judas reveals what had been passed down from Sachius to Simon and from Simon to Judas, he shows not only knowledge of the Crucifixion but apparently a belief in its deeper truths. He speaks quite movingly of Christ, Stephen, Paul, and the Christian God. A dilemma arises in this situation, for if he believes in Christ why should he deny both the knowledge and the belief? The only reason we are told is that the matters must be hidden

> þylæs toworpen sien
> frod fyrngewritu   ond þa fæderlican
> lare forleten
> [430–32]

Fear that Jewish lore would be lost and overthrown seems to be Judas' motive; he has a type of dogged loyalty to the old faith. In reporting Simon's speech, this idea is repeated (448–50). Judas then reports his earlier puzzlement about this very thing: if the Jews knew that Christ was the true son of God, why did they crucify him? Simon's answer is rather unsatisfactorily mystical, but he adds that he had tried to dissuade his fellow councillors from the foolish deed. He reports the Resurrection accurately and with apparent belief, and in relating Stephen's conversion and martyrdom he reveals an understanding of the sort of self-sacrifice which is at the heart of the crucifixion story:

> ne geald he yfel yfele,   ac his ealdfeondum
> þingode þrohtherd,   bæd þrymcyning
> þæt he him þa weadæd   to wræce ne sette
> [493–95]

Judas proceeds to expatiate on the spiritual effects of St. Stephen's martyrdom on Saul, and ascribes Saul's conversion to his reaction to Stephen's act. These two classic Christian stories are extremely important to the theme of revelation and conversion with which Cynewulf is working; Stephen was the model of the *imitatio Christi* in paralleling the Crucifixion itself, and Saul's transformation to St. Paul represents the perfect paradigm of revelation and belief caused by the vision of the principles of the Crucifixion. Again it might be said that Cynewulf found these references in the Latin and wanted them in his poem for providing doctrinal and narrative parallels to the materials in the foreground of his poem, and therefore he violated all realism by putting them in the mouth of a Jew who apparently never received baptism. Such awkward and odd handling of this speech is possible, I suppose, but it hardly solves the problem of this passage. Simon goes on (ll. 518ff.) to state clearly that he and his father sincerely believed in Christ, although they apparently never did much about it.

In recommending Judas to Queen Elene, the Jews again use epithets for him which stress his wisdom in dealing with words (*wordcraeftes* 592, *meðle* 593, *gencwidas* 594). Cynewulf's emphasis here must be intentional, for it is not in the Latin at this point, yet among Anglo-Saxon poetic formulas, word-wisdom was not the only kind he had formulaic terms for. Juliana, for instance, is often characterized with epithets indicating a very different kind of wisdom. This partial and superficial wisdom is endemic to Judas' nature at this point, and probably explains his whole action in this passage. Although he knows the truths of Christianity in a superficial way, and, judging by his speech to the Jews, more than half believes them, yet his conviction is weak. A lesser good — loyalty to his people — can overpower the greater good in him — truth. When pressed with words, he replies skillfully with words, though he is apparently not conscious that the pathos he intends to elicit in his speech about the bread and the stone is capable of irony and ambiguity for the Old English audience. Because of the Eucharistic associations, it loses most of its power to inspire pity. His words eventually go so far as to utter direct lies about never having heard of Christ's crucifixion (660). Another lie, which also appears in the Latin source, occurs at line 683; that he knows the place is well demonstrated by his stepping out directly to it at line 716. Elene must put more tangible pressure on the guilty one (*scyldigne* 692). His imprisonment is parallel to the *haeftnung* in which his mind is living, and at the end of it he is enlightened by the truth which he himself had known before (708).

When Cynewulf's poem is considered closely, there is almost no indication of internal struggle in Judas' psychology. The situation could easily have allowed it, but those fascinating psychological ambivalences which intrigue us moderns apparently did not interest Cynewulf very much. Judas is knowledgeable, devious, and erring up to a certain point, and thereafter he is strong, direct, and devout. His long prayer on Calvary (725–801) is humbly and sincerely Christian. His mention of the fall of the angels and the fate of Lucifer emphasizes again the great polarities around which Cynewulf is building his poem, as does his later fliting with Satan. With Elene's help, his internal Lucifer has already been put down. The final petition in the prayer is that he may believe:

> ic gelyfe þe sel
> ond þy fæstlicor ferhð staðelige
> [795–96]

His soul did need firmer underpinning, and firmer belief will produce it. Ironically, Judas has to make a revelation in order to receive one, somewhat in the pattern of confession before absolution. Cynewulf makes it very clear that the revelation of the Cross is directly responsible for the conversion of Judas from a partially wise Jew to a man filled with the *sapientia* of Christ.

The miracle of the steam and smoke arising from the burial place of the three cosses is obviously closely tied to the miracle of the changed Judas. His transformation is total and complete. He immediately settles the mater of which of the three crosses was Christ's by bringing about a miracle himself. The dead boy appears on the scene at exactly the ninth hour; Cynewulf repeats the time (873) to emphasize the parallel with the time of Christ's death. The Cross, instrument of death, becomes the instrument of life, and the dead youth demonstrates in a new way the paradox of the Crucifixion. The father of the resurrected boy (missing in the Latin *Inventio*) voices the praise and rejoicing which always accompanies this major theme.

As Judas' fliting with the devil begins, the fiend laments the loss of one he had held securely in death, thus recalling the Lazarus story and the Harrowing of Hell which followed Christ's own death. Again we are offered a Christological parallel to the immediate human events of the poem. It is in this speech also that we have attention called to the irony of the name of Judas — one Judas gave hope to the devil and this Judas takes it away. The verbal combat (*geflitu* 953) between the incipient saint and the devil crystalizes the polarities on which the poem is built; his words now are imbued with true wisdom. By this time there is no question that Judas has become the soldier of God. Incidentally, the use of the word *wigan* in line 937 would have caused no trouble to the many editors and commentators if they had simply recognized the metaphor of spiritual warfare which so often occurs in OE poetry. Judas is not a literal warrior, any more than his brother Stephan was (*He hafað wigges lean* 824), but he is a warrior nonetheless. His baptism and ordination as bishop complete his transformation in an overt way. The new positive power which he acquires had already been acquired, however, at the moment his revelation led to his conversion. Like the action of decorating the newly discovered Cross with gloriously bright jewels, these honors may be merely the outward manifestation of a spiritual reality.

There is much talk in the early stages of Elene's mission of Jews who know the law. During her calls to the various groups, they chose their wisest, that is, those who know best the *Ebreisce ae* (397), and *aeriht* (590). In setting up this opposition between Elene and the Jews, Cynewulf may well have taken the Jews to represent the Synagogue. Elene twice refers to their blindness (*modblinde* 306, *blindnesse* 389) and the darkness of their beliefs (*þeostrum geþancum* 312), although they had earlier received great benefits from God. They had all the revelation they needed for belief, but they had closed their minds to the final step of simple acceptance. These are the qualities most often brought out in connection with the Synagogue during the Middle Ages in such works as the Pseudo-Augustinian *Altercatio Ecclesiae et Synagogue*.[12] The Jews as a whole, of course, are essentially untouched by their experience with Elene, yet Judas, who formed part of the group up to the time of his incarceration, became marvellously enlightened. Cynewulf points out the irony of the conflict between the Church and the Synagogue when he explains the etymology of the new name Cyriacus, a thing not done in *Inventio*. The old law of the treacherous *littera* has given way to the *ae haelendes* (1062), the bright new law of the spirit.

After Cyriac takes on priestly functions, Elene usually defers to him, asks his advice, and, certainly in the case of the nails of the Cross, takes it. Cyriac's status as a *halga* (1093) and as a bishop caring for his people is amply demonstrated from the narrative point of view.

271

After this passage, however, his relationship to Elene and Constantine is even clearer if one takes the whole episode on a metaphorical level.

It is only at first glance that the revelation of the nails — this time with a miraculous light — seems merely to repeat the more elaborate revelation of the Cross which has preceded it. When the traditional meanings of the bridle are understood, the whole episode becomes significant, and indeed fits into the poem at this precise point as a climax rather than an anticlimax. I will pause briefly to establish the traditional symbolism Cynewulf was probably dealing with.

The nails, of course, were the things which actually pierced Christ's flesh, causing the physical suffering which necessarily accompanied the life-giving sacrifice. Once Cyriac's prayer reveals them, it seems at best trivial and at worst sacrilegious to put them into a horse's mouth as *salivares* of a bridle. Yet the bridle of a horse had long been used figuratively in several senses. Prudentius had made suggestive use of both the horse and the bridle in the portion of the *Psychomachia* dealing with *Superbia*:

> forte per effusas inflata Superbia turmas
> effreni volitabat equo
> [178–79]

The fierce unbridled horse thus associated with Pride, Prudentius develops the restraints on that quality:

> nec minus instabili sonipes feritate superbit,
> inpatiens madidis frenarier ora lupatis.
> huc illuc frendeus obvertit terga, negata
> libertate fugae, pressisque tumescit havenis.
> [190–93]

Humility eventually conquers Pride in Prudentius' allegory, of course, but in the imagery of the poem, the *frenum* in the mouth is the restraint which most enrages the proud horse of Superbia.

Taking a different line, St. Jerome develops the horse and bridle imagery in his commentary on Zacharias.[13] It is precisely this passage in Zacharius which the *Inventio* quotes in the nail episode, and which Cynewulf expands and elaborates (1191–95). Interestingly enough, Jerome mentions the very events of the Constantine legend with which we are here dealing. Though Jerome at the end casts some doubt on the literal truth of the legend, he had already supplied an excellent metaphorical interpretation immediately above:

272

Sin auten voluerimus, ut LXX transtulerunt, *frenum*, accipere sermonem Dei, intelligamus in freno, eum qui equos insanientes libidine, et mulos steriles atque lascivos refrenat a vitiis, et coercet, et non patitur ire per praeceps, de quibus dicitur: *Nolite fieri sicut equus et mulus, quibus non est intellectus. In freno et chamo maxillas eorum constringe, qui non approximant ad te* (Ps. XXXI 9, 10). De hoc freno et Jacobus loquitur: In equorum ora mittimus frenos, et omne corpus eorum circumagimus (Jacob. III, 3) ut scilicet recto gradiantur itinere, et mollia ad sedendum Domino possint terga praebere. Tale frenum et talis sermo auri et argenti varietate compositus, feros equos Salvatori praeparat ad sedendum; et sanctos facit, ac proprie illius cultui consecratos. Audivi a quodam rem, sensu quidem pio dictam, sed ridiculam. Clavos Dominicae crucis, e quibus Constantinus Augustus frenos equo suo fecerat, sanctum Domini appellari. Hoc utrum ita accipiendum sit, lectoris prudentiae relinquo.

Here the horse represents the unhealthy lasciviousness of the flesh which must be controlled and restrained by reins or bridle. The Word of God supplies such a restraining force. There is nothing wrong with the horses, of course, since they were made by God, but restraint and direction are needed to produce a sound Christian life for the individual. Haymo of Auxerre had obviously read these remarks of Jerome when he commented on the same passage. It seems that the allegory was still viable in his time, and that he took the connection with Constantine slightly more seriously than did Jerome:

Hebraei more suo juxta litteram dicunt, quod postquam cum aequitate rex eorum venerit, et regnaverit in aurea Hierusalem, pace cuncta obtinente, non erit opus equis aut equitatu, sed frena et ornatus phalerarum ad cultum Domini transferentur; et in eo quod dicitur: "super frenum equi" omnem bellicum ornatum intelligamus. Secundum sensum mysticum, frenum disciplina coelestis est magisterii, qua insaniens libido et petulans lascivia refrenatur; de qua Psalmista: "In chamo et freno maxillas eorum constringe." Hoc frenum in ore equi ponitur, ut, relictis errori anfractibus, recta gradiatur via, et mollia ad sedendum terga praebeat Salvatori. Talia ornamenta et tale frenum, auro et argento, id est sensu et eloquio decorata, sancta sunt Domino, et ejus cultui proprie consecrata. Sane quod in libello inventionis sanctae crucis legitur, hoc tunc impletum fuisse, quando Helena Augusta, mater Constantini imperatoris, clavos Dominicae crucis fieri salivares in freno equi regis jussit; beatus Hieronymus pio quidem sensu, sed ridiculo dicit esse confictum.[14]

273

Ridiculous as the story of Constantine's horse may seem if taken literally, in the context of Cynewulf's poem it assumes figurative significance which is richly meaningful. Constantine early in the poem was established as the supreme worldly ruler. Once converted, he more than other people needed reminders that secular power is not ultimate. As a Christian ruler, his physical power must be limited by the knowledge that even secular affairs must be governed by divine principles. Whether the horse is taken as his own pride, or perhaps as the self-centered physical desires of secular humanity, the bodily suffering of Christ on the Cross, recalled by the nails, can conduce to both humility and a healthy, controlled treatment of desire. The Church may be the secular world's mother and loves it as Elene did Constantine, but the individual must pull the reins on himself, must supply his own discipline, whether he be an emperor or a cottar. Memory of Christ's sacrifice, supplied by the *sermo Dei*, can help him to do so.

It is interesting to me that Cyriacus the bishop gives this advice, not Elene. The Church as a community is concerned with belief, yet it is the priests who must deal with the application of moral principles, not only among ordinary Christians but the powers and potentates of this world. Elene continues her way at the end of the poem doing God's work in her fashion:

> Huru weroda god
> gefullæste,　　fæder on roderum,
> cining ælmihtig,　　þæt seo cwen begeat
> willan in worulde.
> 　　　　[1149–52]

Cyriacus continues his way also, healing the lame and the blind, until his hour of suffering and martyrdom come. The memory of these events, and their meaning, must be kept fresh by celebration every year of the finding the Cross on May 3. The purpose of this, and indeed the purpose of the whole poem, is again stated in terms of polarity:

> Sie þara manna gehwam
> behliden helle duru,　　heofones ontyned,
> ece geopenad　　engla rice,
> dream unhwilen,　　ond hira dæl scired
> mid Marian.
> 　　　　[1228–32]

Union with Mary as the Church triumphant is the goal Cynewulf wishes for all men.

As an epilogue, Cynewulf adds one more parallel to the series of life-giving revelations on which his poem has been constructed. Many critics have taken this signature passage as a separate excrescence on the poem, written solely to supply the runic enigma by which we can identify the author.[15] The fictive autobiography of this conclusion, however, is far too close in pattern to the patterns of the rest of the poem for this to have been merely a mechanical device for the signature. It is integral to the themes of the entire poem, and treats them in a fresh way. Using his own persona, his meaning can be more immediate and arresting to the ordinary Christians of his day. He is here speaking to his audience directly as one man to another. This is a real experience. Even if the poem were being read aloud to a group a hundred years after his death, the same effect would be produced on the auditors. Though he (the poet, reader, speaker) had read and thought, well into old age, he had never had a true revelation of the Cross. When it came, it finally revealed wisdom (*wisdom onwreah* 1242). Like other men, particularly Judas, he had been stained with sin, full of sorrow, bitterly enchained, until the brilliant gift of understanding released him, body and soul, and unlocked the poetry we have just heard. Possibly he had been a man "indifferent honest," accepted by his fellows as a good Christian, but his poetic fiction here claims that his early days had been filled with the "pride of life." He had indeed received honors in the meadhall, had enjoyed horsemanship, had indulged in fact in all the *gomen* which the standard OE poetic vocabulary associated with youth. Indeed, in one of the very rune sentences, Cynewulf may be using some of the symbolic imagery I have spoken about earlier:

>   þær him M fore   [*eh* or *eoh*]
> milpaðas mæt,   modig þrægde
> wirum gewlenced.
>   [1261–63]

Youth, like the horse, tends to be *modig* and *gewlenced*, spirited, headstrong, proud, handsomely accoutred, and carnally unrestrained.[16] But in spite of such natural worldly pleasures, he also had been sad and oppressed with care. All these worldly things pass rapidly and turbulently like the wind. This *ubi sunt* message as well as the Judgement Day theme which follows are part of the revelation of the meaning

275

of the Cross that has come to the poet. The true earthly Church may be composed of the *soðfaeste* who suffer Judgement easily; the ordinary sinners who become enlightened, like Cynewulf and Judas-Cyriacus, may be purged of their guilt; but the unrepentant members of the Synagoga (and this concept of course applies to all, Jews or gentiles who reject Christ) are likely to suffer pain forever. Most emphasis is placed on the *synfulle*, as it had been placed on Judas in the poem at large. Ordinary sinners, however benighted, can possibly emerge from their darkness and sorrow into bright, golden glory:

> Hie asodene beoð,
> asundrod fram synnum,　　swa smæte gold
> þæt in wylme bið　　womma gehwylces
> þurh ofnes fyr,　　eall geclænsod,
> amered ond gemylted.　　Swa bið þara manna ælc
> ascyred ond asceaden　　scylda gehwylcre,
> deopra firena,　　þuhr þæs domes fyr.
> [1308–14]

The unwelcome restraints which produce freedom, the sufferings which precede bliss, the death which begets life, and the darkness which yields to light — these are the paradoxes which Cynewulf has tried to induce his audience to absorb. Multiple revelations and revelation in multiple senses have provided him a persuasive poetic structure. As always in the four poems he signed, he ends on a note of the glorious promise of salvation.

NOTES

1. The title *Acta Cyriaci* appears in some later MSS. The text of this work has been published several times; two editions can be considered good in varying degrees: Alfred Holder, *Inventio Sanctae Crucis* (Leipzig, 1889); J. Straubinger, *Die Kreuzauffindungslegende* (Paderborn, 1912). Holthausen's edition of *Elene* (1905) prints a text of the Latin at the bottom of the pages of the Old English poem, but it is taken from the late text printed in the *Acta Sanctorum*, with numerous unannounced "*Verbesserungen*" from other texts.

2. Miss Pamela Gradon traces fairly clearly the problems of this source in the introduction to her edition of *Elene* (London, 1958), pp. 15–22. Her treatment, however, leaves untouched the artistic questions of Cynewulf's handling of the material.

3. In this essay I deal very little with the light-dark imagery, since that has been well handled in the superb recent article of Robert Stepsis and Richard Rand, "Contrast and Conversion in Cynewulf's *Elene*," *NM* 70 (1969), 273–82.

4. We certainly do not need parenthetical punctuation for 86b, nor do we need to look further afield than *He* in 1. 85 for a subject for *onspeon*, as does Miss Gradon in *Elene* (London, 1958), p. 29.

5. *Christlichen Symbolik im Mittelalterlichen Kunst* (Leipzig, 1926), p. 175.

6. Migne, *Patrologia Latina*, 50, col. 755.

7. *In Psalorum Librum Exegesis, PL* 93, 721. In fact, all of Psalm 44, on which Bede is commenting here, is taken as an address of Christ to his bride the Church.

8. Migne, *PL*, 50, col. 755.

9. Reconstructed by J. Straubinger, *Die Kreuzauffindungslegende* (Forschungen zur Christliches Literatur-und Dogmengeschichte 11 [Paderborn, 1912]), pp. 15–16.

10. G. V. Smithers, "The Meaning of *The Seafarer* and *The Wanderer*," *MÆ* 26 (1957), 137–53, and *MÆ* 28 (1959), 1–22, 99–104.

11. J. E. Cross and S. I. Tucker, "Allegorical Tradition and the Old English *Exodus*," *Neophilologus* 44 (1960), 122–27.

12. Migne, *PL* 42, col. 1131. A great deal of other evidence along this line is adduced in W. Molsdorf, *Christliche Symbolik der mittelalterlichen Kunst* (Leipzig, 1926), pp. 177ff.

13. Jerome's commentary on Zacharias 14:20 occurs in Migne, *PL* 25, cols. 1539–40.

14. Migne, *PL*, 117, col. 277. This book has long been ascribed to Haymo of Halberstadt, but recent scholars grant it to Haymo of Auxerre. See F. Stegmüller, *Repertorium Biblicum Medii Aevi*, III, 7.

15. The most recent is C. L. Wrenn, who speaks of the "quite separate meditative Epilogue" containing Cynewulf's signature. *A Study of Old English Literature* (London, 1967), p. 124.

16. In a slightly different metaphor, the *sundhengestas* at the end of the Ascension are firmly tied to the ancor of Christ.

The Fair Field of Anglo-Norman: Recent Cultivation[1]

Ruth J. Dean

ANGLO-NORMAN may appear at first glance to be merely one of several dialects in which medieval French literature was composed. A considerable body of distinctive literature is, however, preserved in this dialect, and it forms part of the culture of two countries. During the twelfth century Anglo-Norman writers were pioneers in two domains. They used French instead of Latin for historical and religious material in England before this vernacular was used in France. And they composed romance and drama in their vernacular before English writers did so in theirs. For more than two centuries Anglo-Norman flourished as a literary medium, and it was only during the fourteenth century that English became a serious rival. A number of works in English were in fact translated or adapted from Anglo-Norman, while authors in several other countries also borrowed from Anglo-Norman writers. In short, the varied body of material in this dialect is to be reckoned with in the study not only of French and English, but also of comparative European literature.

The study of Anglo-Norman dates back well into the nineteenth century, but for some time it was carried on irregularly and with varying degrees of evaluation. A juster appraisal and more systematic work began to be developed in the 1920's, greatly helped by Vising's manual, which set forth the features of the language, classified known works with their bibliography, and listed manuscripts containing Anglo-Norman writing.[2] Anglo-Norman studies have been growing steadily since the Second World War. For reasons which will shortly appear, the present review will comment chiefly on work which has been published since 1965.

The outstanding landmark in recent years is of course Professor Legge's book surveying Anglo-Norman literature and its historical setting.[3] As is by now generally known, she presented a study, both

279

chronological and generic, of all the known works that fall into the general category of "literature," while she excluded treatises of a pragmatic character, such as those dealing with the law, husbandry, falconry, medicine, and the teaching of the French language; nevertheless she called attention to the importance of documents and Year Books for the study of language and society. Among the many valuable features of this book are the studies of patrons and of the sociopolitical setting of literature. Analysis of many of the more important works and felicitous translation of illustrative passages add to the value of the book, which contains a further original contribution to literary history in the long chapter devoted to Anglo-Norman lyric poetry. Not least valuable, especially for students in the field, are the many suggestions, thrown out along the way, of texts that need editing and studies that need investigation or further development.[4] Needless to say, Professor Legge has continued in lectures and articles to develop topics touched on in her book.[5]

The next most important general work is the bibliographical review of Anglo-Norman studies published by Dr. Sinclair, which covers approximately 1945 to 1965.[6] After rapidly surveying earlier bibliographical work, Sinclair proceeded systematically through the genres and titles, and brought together an enormous amount of information clearly set out and briefly commented on, including a number of additions and some corrections to Miss Legge's book. Such a comprehensive survey could hardly escape having, itself, an occasional slip or misinterpretation, for we are all human, but they are relatively minor ones. A detailed index and a concordance of Vising's serial numbers with Sinclair's page references make this review an essential tool.

The advance of Anglo-Norman studies is systematically maintained by the series of "Anglo-Norman Texts." Begun in 1939, unavoidably delayed by the war and austerity, the series now numbers twenty-three volumes.[7] Four of these have appeared since Sinclair's study and will be discussed below. In accordance with the general plan, the introductions to these editions stress the linguistic interest of the texts. There are brief comments on the manuscripts (usually with a frontispiece plate) and on the literary setting. These introductions often leave scope for further development elsewhere of the literary interest of the work edited. Notes on the interpretation of the text, followed by a glossary and a table of proper names, complete the book in each case.

Although both volumes of Professor Pope's edition of the *Romance of Horn* were recorded by Sinclair, a few comments about this, one of the most important editions in the A.N.T. series, will not be out of place here.[8] This *Horn*, by a Master Thomas not to be identified with any of the other Thomases known in AN literature, is one of the more interesting of the AN romances because its adventures are told with some of the vigor of the chansons de geste and its form is the twelve-syllable laisse rather than the octosyllabic couplet usual in romances. *Horn* is the central portion of a trilogy. There seems to be some evidence that the first part had been written, though it is now lost. But the third part was still to be composed and no trace of it has yet been found. The two-volume edition prepared by Miss Pope was brought to completion after her death by the care of Professor T. B. W. Reid, Miss E. A. Francis, and other colleagues devoted to Miss Pope and to Anglo-Norman studies. It stands as a memorial to the scholar who did so much to advance the subject. The two double volumes are more ambitiously developed than most of those in the A.N.T. series. Besides a literary study of the poem there is a long analysis of the language which supports or develops Miss Pope's major linguistic work *From Latin to Modern French*.[9] Advantage was taken of the section "Explicative Notes," prepared for volume II by Miss Pope, to include corrections of a number of errors in volume I. Among reviews of the second volume, pointing up its many values, useful additions or corrections are given by Sinclair, Trethewey, and Miss Legge.[10]

Another AN romance which has been the subject of recent work is the *Roman de toute chevalerie* by Thomas of Kent,[11] which is perhaps the first cyclic romance of Alexander in French, earlier ones being episodic. It is also a moral treatise about chivalry and a source of the Middle English *Kyng Alisaunder*. Discussion of the problems it raises has been hampered by the lack of an edition, but this should soon be rectified, for Dr. Brian Foster's edition was submitted to the A.N.T. Society in 1970. Meanwhile opinions on two points which have been conflicting at intervals for over eighty years have now been treated again. The position taken by Miss Legge in *ANL*, pp. 105–7, was that Thomas' work probably had no connection with continental vernacular forms and that the date of its composition could not be guessed. The succession of opinions on these points has been reviewed by Professor Foulet.[12] He has offered textual evidence to support the subjective views of Schneegans and Hilka that Thomas did know some continental Alexander material. Comparing three versions of a brief episode, Foulet has proposed that Thomas knew the episodic *Alexandre en Orient* by Lambert le Tour of Châteaudun but not the

281

cyclic romance by Alexandre de Paris. His argument has merit, but is not without its own subjective elements. We must await Foster's edition to see whether these problems and others can be resolved. The provenance of the Robartes fragment may indicate that the *Roman de toute chevalerie* was known also on the continent, for it is not safe, with so small a specimen of the writing, to assert that this fragment was copied by an English rather than a continental scribe.[13]

The *Roman de Fergus* is one of the borderline works which enter into consideration for AN literature only if one shares Miss Legge's view that what was written in French for insular society should be taken as culturally Anglo-Norman, even if it was composed by an author who was born on the continent and whose language does not betray Anglo-Normanisms.[14] See, for example, her treatment of *Guillaume d'Angleterre*, of Guernes's life of Becket, and of the work of Guillaume le Clerc de Normandie and Marie de France.[15] Such works do not appear in Vising or Sinclair, nor does *Fergus*. In an article on the origin of *Fergus* Miss Legge set out details about the remarkable knowledge of Scottish geography possessed by the non-Norman Guillaume le Clerc who wrote *Fergus*.[16] This Guillaume was possibly Picard or Walloon. A somewhat similar situation exists with regard to the *Secret des Secrets* by Jofroi of Waterford and Servais Copale. Jofroi, a Dominican, was apparently a member of the Anglo-Norman colony in Ireland.[17] He was more than once posted abroad by his Order and he collaborated on several translations with Servais, a native of Huy. Their translation — one of numerous versions in French[18] — of the *Secretum Secretorum*, a treatise on government represented as written for Alexander by Aristotle, has no AN character but it found its way to Waterford and was later adapted into English for the lord of Ormonde. Jofroi and Servais collaborated also on translations of Dares and Eutropius. M. Monfrin, whose Ecole des Chartes thesis treated French translations of the *Secretum Secretorum*, published a few years ago a study of the sources of the Jofroi-Servais version, in which he showed that these translators were less original than Gaston Paris had thought, but that the material they drew from many sources besides their basic text was put together with some variety and freedom.[19] Monfrin's edition of this version was ready for publication in 1964 but does not seem to have come out yet. An edition of the joint translation of Dares was announced some time ago as in preparation by F. W. A. George of University College, London.

Another edition in the A.N.T. series makes available a short text for some brave soul working on the tangled problems of the compilations known as "Bruts." This text is an AN translation into verse of a portion of Geoffrey of Monmouth's *Historia Regum Britanniae.* In an AN copy of Wace's *Roman de Brut,*[20] Wace's text is interrupted after line 52 by an AN translation, running to about 6236 lines, after which the copyist resumes Wace's text at the episode of the begetting of Arthur (line 8729). This extraneous text has been known for some time and has been thought by some critics to be part of Gaimar's lost "History of the Britons." The editor of Gaimar, Dr. Bell,[21] showed several years ago that this AN passage, "the Royal *Brut* interpolation," is neither composed by Gaimar nor abridged from Wace, but is an independent version.[22] Bell has now followed that study by editing the "interpolation," which he dates early in the thirteenth century on the basis of linguistic evidence and some internal details.[23] He gives an interesting frontispiece, showing the column where the interpolation ends and Wace's text resumes, in order to draw attention to a slight change in alignment. It is as though the scribe had paused in his work, having perhaps come to the end of the exemplar before him, and lacking any more of this version had turned to the appropriate part of Wace to continue the history. Bell suggests that this text is not so much an interpolation into Wace as an unfinished work which the copyist completed from Wace. If this was the case, the copyist evidently felt that the AN version was incomplete or too abrupt at its beginning also, for he copied, as has been said, fifty-two lines of Wace before starting the AN text, which resulted in the overlapping of some material. The Anglo-Norman translator, whose style is briefer than Wace's, followed Geoffrey's *Historia,* though not without making both additions and omissions. He may have used a redaction of *HRB* related to the source of the Welsh version translated in Griscom's edition.[24]

Some comments on AN prose "Bruts" may be appropriate here. These "Brut" chronicles were composed in several forms and in different reigns. They eventuated in the ME *Brut* and in the "Common Chronicles" of England or *Caxton's Chronicle,* on which histories of England were chiefly based until the seventeenth century. Dr. Taylor discussed AN prose "Bruts" in an article cited by Sinclair with approval but with a few reservations.[25] Subsequently, Taylor published a study of Higden's chronicle.[26] In the second chapter of this book, "The Chronicle Background," he devoted a few paragraphs to the fourteenth-century prose "Brut," calling it an Anglo-French compilation.

He gave a succinct account of the various forms in which the AN prose "Brut" has survived, but he made several statements that are confusing or ambiguous. He referred (p. 15) without date to Brie's "introduction which was published separately." As Brie's work turned out, it is misleading to call his first book the "introduction" to his edition of the ME *Brut*, although he may have originally intended it so. In 1905 he published in German, as a first part, an account of the history and sources of the ME prose *Brut*, and a classification of manuscripts in both AN and English. In 1906 and 1908, in the Early English Text Society series, he published the text of the ME *Brut* in two parts. The introduction (properly so called), the notes, and the glossary, which were all mentioned on the title-page of both parts, were, however, put off for a third volume in this series; but this volume, alas, never appeared. The classification of manuscripts in the preface to part I of this edition is a revision of the 1905 German study.[27] To return to Taylor: farther along on p. 15, after some discussion of the "French" (i.e., AN) versions, he described continuations which go to 1377 and to 1419, without making clear that he was there referring to the English version. In the following sentence he mentioned other continuations but failed to specify that these belong to the AN version. To them can be added a continuation in AN to 1398 in an Oxford manuscript of the turn of the century, Corpus Christi College 78. Other forms of the history of England from the arrival of Brutus to that of William of Normandy, confusingly presented in nineteenth-century editions, were edited in detail by Dr. Foltys.[28] In the area of local history, the AN chronicle of Wigmore Abbey has recently been edited with a translation by Messrs. Dickinson and Ricketts.[29]

A recent volume in the A.N.T. series belongs to the area of moral and didactic literature: *Le Petit Plet*, edited by Professor Merrilees.[30] The editor agrees with the generally accepted attribution of this work to Chardri (proposing, further, that the name may be an anagram for Richard), but the author's name does not appear on the title-page. Chardri's "little debate or discussion" is built up of commonplaces on death, fortune, women, friends, and so on, but it is composed with a light touch. This is noticeable from the beginning, for the poet reverses the conventional roles so that here it is the old man who complains and mourns, while the young one undertakes to comfort him — with many reasons, often cynical, and not much sympathy. The young man joins a few others in medieval literature by his attitude toward the path of virtue: he would rather die young laughing than have a long life full of ascetic sorrow in the hope of eventual beatitude. There are occasional passages of poetic description, others facetious in tone, with homonymic puns, and a general air of mirth when the young man is talking. Although these qualities are commented on in the introduction, they are obscured by philological literalness in the glossary.

One of the sources of *Le Petit Plet* was Cato's *Distichs*. A recent study of this popular medieval text-book was published by Herr Ruhe.[31] Examining the Latin, AN, and continental French texts, he considered the sources of the several versions, the nature of the translation, and the influence of one version on others and on proverb literature. While he discussed the order of writing of the AN versions, he did not take into account the linguistic evidence. Miss Legge, pointing this out in a review, slightly modified the conclusions about dating the versions that she gave in *ANL*.[32]

Young people of the present day should find Chardri sympathetic, for he makes his old man say that in a young person one can often see great wisdom. But they might not understand the young man's motivation: he seeks joy in order to escape the sadness which upsets the body and which God curses. Few people of any age nowadays recall that there is virtue in avoiding *tristitia*, which was sometimes included among the capital sins. Another sin not in the usual list of seven is *vana gloria*. The history of this idea has been treated by Mme. Joukovsky-Micha, beginning with the work of an Anglo-Norman, Simund de Freine, who adapted Boethius' *de Consolatione Philosophiae* in AN verse toward the end of the twelfth century.[33]

Sin and vices are treated in three further AN works in the moral-didactic category. The most elaborate is St. Edmund's *Merure de Seinte Eglise*.[34] Although an edition of this work by someone skilled in Latin, AN, and ME, urged by Miss Legge, has not yet appeared, there is now hope that it may be in hand. An important preliminary study was submitted as a thesis by Miss Forshaw.[35] It has unfortunately not been published, but permission to consult it can be obtained. The author takes issue with some of the conclusions of the earlier editor, H. W. Robbins, and of Miss Legge; describes the contents of twenty-two manuscripts in French; re-edits the Latin text printed by LaBigne which was based on the British Museum MS. Royal 7 A. I (ca. 1400); and edits on facing pages that in the Bodleian MS. Hatton 26 (mid-14th century). Since Miss Forshaw has projected an edition of the two vernacular versions, we may yet have the complete work that is so much needed.[36]

285

A passage on vices and virtues is included in Robert Grosseteste's allegorical *Chasteau d'amour*. Mr. Sajavaara recently edited the ME versions of this work and is preparing a new edition of the AN text.[37] The third work concerned with sin and vices is a hitherto unknown little poem on the lay "orders" (celibacy, widowhood, marriage) and on the virtues with which to combat vices. It was found and published by Monfrin.[38] Like so many of the pious works that followed the Interdict and the decrees of the Fourth Lateran Council,[39] this piece has no poetic value, but it does possess a slight literary interest. Its homiletic tone is relieved by occasional dialogue. The treatment of marriage is not as commonplace as that of the other "orders": marriage is advised by Holy Church (lines 43–44); it was consecrated by Jesus Christ when He created Adam and Eve (lines 61–65); and it was exalted because Joseph married Mary of whom Christ was born (lines 115–20). Another unusual treatment is that of the vices, which are presented as the "sergents" of the devil. If the poem is surely of the early thirteenth century, as seems possible, this is perhaps the earliest example in the vernacular of the confronting of each vice by a corresponding virtue. Similarly, this is apparently the first known vernacular example of presenting the vices in the order which, in Latin, gives the mnemonic S A L I G I A.

A more ambitious homiletic work of this same period is the series of verse sermons on the Sunday Gospels by Robert of Greatham. A fairly extensive study which appeared several decades ago included long extracts from this text, but, in spite of a recent publication, a complete scholarly edition is still lacking.[40] The sermons, composed to divert a lady from her fondness for romances and chansons de geste, contain counterbalancing exempla, besides the appropriate evangelical commentary and interpretation.[41]

Legends of the Virgin may be associated with exempla or with hagiography, and ultimately with drama. The first French translation of Mary legends was made by the Anglo-Norman Adgar, who lived in the second half of the twelfth century and wrote earlier than the more famous Gautier de Coincy. There seems to have been no publication dealing primarily with Adgar later than those reported by Miss Legge, but his work figures briefly in a recent study of miracles in medieval Romance literatures.[42]

Hagiography in AN has had a share of attention. Two lives of saints appeared in the A.N.T. series and a fragment of a third in *PMLA*, each having an individual interest: the life of St. Catherine is one of the first pieces in AN by a woman, the life of St. Alban treats of the first English martyr, and the acts of Andrew bring a new figure into AN literature.

Shortly before Marie de France, there were English women composing French verse. They were nuns of Barking Abbey, the most important nunnery in England, of which the abbess was appointed by the king. One of these nuns, who wrote of Edward the Confessor, remained anonymous, but it has been argued that she is the same person as the one who recorded her name, Clemence, at the end of another work from Barking so that those who should hear her book read might pray for her. Clemence took for her subject St. Catherine of Alexandria, a fourth-century martyr whose legend and cult were immensely popular all over Europe from at least the ninth century, and whose relics had reached Rouen by the eleventh. The poem by Clemence has been difficult of access, because the only edition, from two Paris manuscripts, was published in Czech. The new edition by Professor MacBain is the more welcome that it takes account also of a third manuscript unknown to the Czech editor, and provides us with further material for twelfth-century studies.[43]

Besides picturesque details, the legend of St. Catherine has the less usual element of being built around a disputation in which the saint defeats and converts fifty of the most subtle masters — philosophers, grammarians, rhetoricians, dialecticians — summoned by the emperor to uphold pagan doctrines. He himself had failed in argument with this beautiful young lady, whose royal father had taken care that this his only child should be highly educated. In the vocabulary, consequently, abstract words are more numerous than concrete ones. Miss Legge underlined the courtly language of the poem and thought that the text was intended to be mimed. MacBain was more impressed by the presence of terms of chivalry.[44] The work foreshadows the multiplying of exhortations and preaching which followed the Fourth Lateran Council two and three generations later.

Another welcome edition in the A.N.T. series is that of the life of St. Alban prepared by Professor Harden.[45] The edition published by Robert Atkinson in 1876, which caused such a stir among Romance philologists, has long been out of print. No other manuscript of the poem has come to light in the intervening decades, but work by M. R. James and Richard Vaughan[46] has vindicated Atkinson's contention that the manuscript was composed, written, and illustrated by Matthew Paris, the versatile monk of St. Albans. It is now generally accepted that Matthew translated his verse Life from a prose one in Latin by another St. Albans monk, named William. It would have been useful to have the new book include the text of William's work, of which there is no readily accessible edition, in order to study Matthew's methods as translator and versifier. Harden confirms, from his study of the language, earlier estimates that Matthew probably composed his poem not long after 1230, possibly even in the preceding decade (pp. xv–xvii). Although he refers to Vaughan's work on Matthew Paris' script, he does not use it to support his own dating, as he could have done since the St. Alban manuscript is one of Matthew's earliest works. Harden does not solve any problems about the irregularities in meter, but he does point out some passages where variations in line-length have affective value and may therefore be considered intentional (p. xviii). He misreads the word *rumantz* in a rubric (f. 49^C) and a colophon (f. 50^B).[47] There is room for comparison of this text with other lives of saints as well as for re-editing the others associated with Matthew Paris.[48]

In view of other recent work on Matthew Paris, Professor Ross' conjectures about the possible existence of a lay workshop perhaps under Matthew's influence are timely.[49] As Ross has had so much experience with illustrated manuscripts, and particularly those of the Alexander romances, we should like to see him pursue his own suggestion that someone write a monograph on manuscripts illustrated in the style of Matthew Paris, a style that persisted in England for more than a century.

Miracles performed by St. Andrew appear for the first time in Old French verse in an AN fragment, found in an American library, that was identified, described, and published by Professors Bertin and Foulet.[50] Previously known French material about St. Andrew is all continental and, with one exception, in prose. This poem was composed perhaps about 1200, and the fragment preserves 206 lines of it (187 are decipherable) copied in the thirteenth century.

One of the best known pieces of religious literature in AN is the *Jeu d'Adam*, often described as the first known drama written entirely in French. In an article describing and analyzing this play afresh, Professor Noomen upholds the originality and skill of the playwright, but suggests that undue emphasis has always been put upon the proportion of French to Latin in the composition.[51] He studies the relation between the complete liturgical texts (not always printed in full by editors) and the vernacular development that follows each. This "bilinguisme" is the keystone in the structure of the play, in his view, and the drama is developed by a process that he calls "la technique de la farciture." He takes issue with Professor Calin[52] in his thematic analysis and contends that the play has two parts (not three), one which is dramatic based on Genesis, the other which is homiletic based on the Pseudo-Augustinian sermon. The interest of each episode is concentrated within itself and there is little relation of one to another, coherence being achieved by the relation of each episode to the general subject, sin and redemption. This construction "by addition" Noomen finds characteristic of literature in the Romanesque period. In an appendix he suggests, as a very tentative hypothesis, a new concept of the staging of the play. This discussion will no doubt be drawn on by those who want to produce the drama. Some of these students of stagecraft will welcome two new translations of the *Jeu d'Adam* into English, both of which are published with production in mind.[53]

The miscellaneous studies that have been appearing in the AN field indicate the variety of interest that it offers. We have become accustomed to hearing about the cultural influence of the courts of Henry II and Eleanor of Aquitaine. Miss Legge has pointed out the number and variety of works that emanated earlier from the court and the aristocracy in the reign of Henry I, although Beauclerc exercised little personal influence in the literary domain.[54] She discussed in more detail the role of some of these people in disseminating the matter of Britain.[55] Adeliza of Louvain, second queen of Henry I, and one of the important patronesses of the twelfth century (as Miss Legge pointed out in both *ANL* and *Mélanges Lejeune*[56]) attracted also the attention of Professor Holmes who would like to attribute to her the launching of the rhymed chronicle in AN.[57]

Two recent studies have been made of translations into AN. The first, and apparently unique, version in French verse of the book of the Tiburtine Sybil was examined by Mr. Shields, who was planning to edit it. On the basis of the language, the versification, certain traits of style, and the dedication to the Empress Matilda, he attributed it to Philippe de Thaon.[58] Miss Legge referred to this attribution, without committing herself to accepting it, in the course of discussing AN versification in a recent article.[59] We await the edition with interest. Another translation, this one into AN prose from the Proverbs of Solomon, has already been edited. Called "commentary" by Vising (§ 72), it is entitled "paraphrase" by its editor.[60] Such variant titles have arisen more than once from medieval practices in translation.

Translators often used commentaries to add a homiletic quality to their work as well as to interpret words or expressions for which custom and glossaries did not provide adequate equivalents in the developing language. Consequently, vernacular forms of Latin works may be called by modern editors translation, paraphrase, adaptation, or commentary. In fact, this version of *Proverbs* supplies a fairly close translation of the Biblical text interspersed with commentary translated from Latin writers, both sacred and profane: Juvenal, Cato, Bede, Peter Comestor, and so on.

A different form of Biblical material in AN is found in the *Holkham Bible Picture Book*. This fourteenth-century manuscript (now British Museum, Add. 47682) has been available in a facsimile edition with introduction, commentary, and glossary prepared by Dr. Hassall, but without a printing of the text.[61] Professor Pickering has now brought out an edition of the text, with a more extensive glossary and some discussion of the language.[62] His particular interest lies in examining the relation between texts and pictures, and he shows us the importance of this apparently unique manuscript as an example of Anglo-Norman culture. This "Bible picture book" is quite different from such "pictured Bible books" as the *Biblia Pauperum* and the *Speculum Humanae Salvationis*. "For the Holkham undertaking," Pickering tells us, "some two hundred subjects were selected, for treatment by the practitioners of two distinct crafts," an artist and an author. Each treated the chosen themes according to his own competence. The artist was not illustrating a continuous text, nor was the author describing the pictures. The artist was of course familiar with standard iconography and the author fitted into the space available around the pictures material in AN adapted from Genesis, the Gospels, Pseudo-Matthew and — again — Peter Comestor. In order fully to appreciate all the points of the editor's commentary one would like to have Hassall's facsimile alongside this latest A.N.T. volume, but copies of the facsimile, as Pickering says, "now cost nominally rather more than Coke of Norfolk" paid for the manuscript (£30) some 155 years ago. Still, the edition has two plates, which is twice the usual provision of the A.N.T. series.

A number of works in AN, as in English (and no doubt in other languages), have a social and philological, rather than a literary, interest. In this category have recently appeared a collection of beauty recipes and a treatise on heraldry. Many recipes, medical, culinary, and cosmetic, are found scattered in manuscripts of miscellanea or scribbled on margins and blank pages. Vising gives references to some of them (§ 319). A collection edited by M. Ruelle was put together in the second half of the thirteenth century and equipped with a versi-fied prologue in twenty-three couplets chiefly of seven- and eight-syllable lines, a common AN rhythm. The collection contains refer-ences to several Latin works and echoes of others, especially those attributed to Trotula of Salerno, but it is not a translation of any of them.[63] An early treatise on heraldry, composed in AN and found in a miscellany compiled at St. Albans in the 1380's, was published by the present writer.[64]

Besides the material that successive editions of texts have been making available for further refining our knowledge of AN language, there have been several discussions of one or another aspect of this dialect. Messrs. Richardson and Sayles have presented evidence of the existence of an important class of literate laymen, as early as the twelfth century, some knowing Latin, others French, or a little of each.[65] Dr. Bullock-Davies has stressed the role of bilingual people living along the borders of England in disseminating the matter of Britain in French (i.e., AN).[66] Professor Rothwell has pointed out that the bilingual problem is more complex than such discussions suggest, showing how a close linguistic study can contribute to the picture.[67] Miss Legge has on various occasions called attention to the psychologi-cal and linguistic interest of the AN Year Books (e.g., *ANL*, p. 310). Professor Baugh has now had recourse to them to explain a long-puz-zling couplet of Chaucer's.[68]

Lyric poetry in AN is not extensive nor of international moment, but it has varied form and content, as well as occasional charm or feeling. It raises, of course, as do all metrical works in AN, the ever-vexing problem of versification. Miss Legge proposed a re-examina-tion of the question by periods, and as a beginning she discussed the twelfth century.[69] She pointed out with justice that when AN verse began, early in the twelfth century, there was little French verse on which to base it (or with which we can compare it), and that it has nothing in common with Anglo-Saxon verse. The AN poets composed much as the continental French poets did — they adapted to the ver-nacular the Latin rhythms to which they were accustomed — but their results were different. AN lyric poetry received its first extended treat-ment in Chapter XIII of *ANL*. We can now look forward to a study of the AN secular lyric, with more than sixty texts newly edited and all assembled in one place, when Professor Legge's pupil, Dr. Carol Harvey, publishes her Edinburgh dissertation.

The migrants to England from the latter half of the eleventh century on were more forward in trying out their vernacular in literary forms than their contemporaries who remained at home. Were they perhaps inspired by the discovery that the land they were occupying had long been accustomed to vernacular writing? As generations passed, they developed forms and themes which influenced literature not only in the English language and in continental French but also elsewhere in western Europe. It is good to see that a subject which occupies such a significant position has passed out of its former stepchild status and is evoking widespread and continuing interest. A number of editions and studies in AN by both older and younger scholars are in hand. There remain, none the less, other plots to till. It has been remarked above that an edition which concentrates on linguistic problems may leave scope for further study of literary interest. The growing series of editions is making material available for comparative work in versification, in linguistic problems, and in literary history and criticism. Further study is needed of individual writers, such as Matthew Paris and John Gower, of the French and AN sources of ME romances, and in the area of AN-English linguistics.[70] Careful perusal of *ANL* and Sinclair will yield a considerable choice of areas in which to toil. The fair field, though now better cultivated than in 1954, still welcomes folk.

NOTES

1. This title recalls that of an article, now superseded, "A Fair Field needing Folk: Anglo-Norman" by the present writer, in *PMLA*, LXIX (1954), 965–78.
2. Johan Vising, *Anglo-Norman Language and Literature* (London, 1923); hereafter referred to as Vising, with the serial numbers of his list of titles.
3. M[ary] Dominica Legge, *Anglo-Norman Literature and Its Background* (Oxford: Clarendon Press, 1963; reprinted 1972); hereafter referred to as *ANL*.
4. Some of these were drawn together and discussed by the present writer under the title "What is Anglo-Norman?" in *Annuale Mediaevale*, VI (1965), 29–46.
5. These include the originality of Anglo-Norman authors in producing various genres before their like appeared in continental French, the geographical origins of literary Anglo-Norman, AN works from Wales, Ireland, and Scotland, and the legacy of AN literature to that of Europe: *Cahiers de Civilisation Médiévale*, VIII (1965), 327–49; *Revue de Linguistique Romane*,

XXXI (1967), 44–54; University of Edinburgh, Inaugural Lecture, No. 38, 26 Nov. 1968. Other studies by Miss Legge are noted below.

6. Keith V. Sinclair, "Anglo-Norman Studies: The Last Twenty Years" in *Australian Journal of French Studies*, II (1965), 113–55, 225–78; hereafter referred to as Sinclair. Although this periodical was not easy to consult in this country in 1965, the *Union List of Serials* recorded its presence in nearly 40 American libraries by 1968; but some libraries had subscribed late and missed one or more of the early issues.

7. Anglo-Norman Texts, published at Oxford by Basil Blackwell for the Anglo-Norman Text Society; hereafter referred to as A.N.T.

8. Mildred K. Pope, *The Romance of Horn*, I, A.N.T., IX–X (Oxford, 1955); II, with T. B. W. Reid, A.N.T., XII–XIII (Oxford, 1964).

9. *Ibid.*, II, 21–124. Pope, *From Latin to Modern French with Especial Consideration of Anglo-Norman* (Manchester, 1934; reprinted 1952). It is curious that of the five manuscripts used for the edition of Horn (all incomplete, two very fragmentary), only the two from which the text is printed are described (Cambridge, Univ. Libr. Ff.6.17, and Oxford, Bodl. Douce 132). The reader is referred by implication (I, ix) to studies by Braunholtz and Brede for descriptions of the Brit. Mus. fragment Harley 527 (ff. 59ᴬ–73ᴰ, incomplete at beginning and end) and two small fragments in Cambridge (Univ. Libr., Add. 4407, 4470). It may be useful to add a few details to those at I, ix–xii. The size of Ff.6.17 is 6¼ x 4½ inches and the period of its script is the first half of the thirteenth century. Harley 527 measures 9 x 6⅜ inches; the *Horn* section is in a tiny hand of the mid-thirteenth century. The Cambridge fragments may be of the second half of the thirteenth century.

10. Sinclair, pp. 229–30; William H. Trethewey in *French Studies*, XX (1966), 169–70; Legge in *MLR*, LXI (1966), 309–13. A note by James Cable in *Romania*, XC (1969), 515–27, supports Godefroy's definition of *muntarsin*, applied to a falcon in line 731 of the AN *Horn*. The editors had rejected this in favor of an origin in a proper name (II, 134). Dr. Cable, who investigated the vocabulary of the hunt for his 1967 thesis at Nancy, explains the adjective as referring to a falcon captured young in its mountain eyrie.

11. Vising § 37; *ANL*, pp. 105–7; Sinclair, p. 230.

12. Alfred Foulet, "La Date du *Roman de toute chevalerie*," in *Mélanges offerts à Rita Lejeune*, II (Gembloux: Duculot, 1969), 1205–10.

13. Oxford, Bodl., Lat. misc. b. 17, f. 140; first half of the fourteenth century.

14. *ANL*, pp. 161–62.

15. *ANL*, pp. 141–42; 249–50; 207; 72–73.

16. Legge, "Sur la Genèse du *Roman de Fergus*," in *Mélanges de linguistique romane et de philologie médiévale offerts à M. Maurice Delbouille*, II (Gembloux, 1964), 399–408.

17. *ANL*, p. 304; J. Quétif and J. Echard, *Scriptores ordinis praedicatorum . . .* , I (Paris, 1719), 467–69; Victor Le Clerc, in *Histoire Littéraire de la France*, XXI (1895), 216–29.

18. An AN version, *Le Secré de Secrez* by Pierre d'Abernun of Fetcham, was edited by Oliver A. Beckerlegge in A.N.T., V (Oxford, 1944); see also *ANL*, pp. 214, 216.

19. Jacques Monfrin, "Sur les Sources du *Secret des Secrets* de Jofroi de Waterford et Servais Copale," in *Mélanges . . . Delbouille (supra cit.,* in n. 16), II, 509–30.

20. London, Brit., Mus., Royal 13 A.XXI; ca. 1300.

21. Alexander Bell, ed., *L'Estoire des Engleis by Geffrei Gaimar,* A.N.T., XIV–XVI (Oxford, 1960).

22. Bell, "The Royal *Brut* Interpolation," in *Medium Aevum,* XXXII (1963), 190–202.

23. Bell, ed., *An Anglo-Norman Brut (Royal 13.A.xxi),* A.N.T., XXI–XXII (Oxford, 1969); for discussion of the date see p. xxxiv.

24. Acton Griscom, *The Historia Regum Britanniae of Geoffrey of Monmouth* (London, 1929).

25. John Taylor, "The French 'Brut' and the Reign of Edward II," in *EHR,* LXXII (1957), 423–37; Sinclair, p. 238.

26. Taylor, *The Universal Chronicle of Ranulf Higden* (Oxford: Clarendon Press, 1966).

27. Friedrich W. D. Brie, *Geschichte und Quellen der mittelenglischen Prosachronik The Brute of England oder The Chronicles of England.* I. Teil (Marburg, 1905). This work was published twice in the same year, one form ending at p. 51 after the study of the French "Brut," the other continuing to p. 130 with a study of the English "Brute." Evidently it was intended as part of the introduction to the edition; but II. Teil did not follow and the edition came out under other auspices, as will presently appear. The review by J[ames] T[ait] in *EHR,* XXI (1906), 616–17, conveniently summarizes Brie's conclusions regarding the composition of the whole chronicle in its various forms. Two volumes of Brie's edition were published two years apart, and the organization and title of the edition were changed in the meanwhile: *The Brut or The Chronicle of England,* edited from MS. Rawl. B.171 . . . with introduction, notes and glossary, Part I, E.E.T.S., Orig. Ser., 131 (London, 1906); Part II, E.E.T.S., Orig. Ser., 136 (London, 1908).

28. Christian Foltys, *Kritische Ausgabe der anglonormannischen Chroniken Brutus, Li Rei de Engleterre, Le Livere de Reis de Engleterre* (Inaugural-Dissertation, Berlin: Free Univ., 1962).

29. J. C. Dickinson and P. T. Ricketts, "The Anglo-Norman Chronicle of Wigmore Abbey," in *Transactions of the Woolhope Naturalists' Field Club,* XXXIX (1969), Part III, 413–46.

30. Brian S. Merrilees, *Le Petit Plet,* A.N.T., XX (Oxford, 1970).

31. Ernstpeter Ruhe, *Untersuchungen zu den altfranzösischen Übersetzungen der Disticha Catonis,* Beiträge zur romanischen Philologie des Mittelalters. Editionen und Abhandlungen. Hgg. v. Hans-Wilhelm Klein. Bd. II (Munich, 1968).

32. Legge in *Erasmus,* XX (1968), cols. 486–88; cf. *ANL,* p. 182.

33. Françoise Joukovsky-Micha, "La Notion de 'Vaine Gloire' de Simund de Freine à Martin le Franc," in *Romania,* LXXXIX (1968), 1–30, 210–39.

34. Vising § 156; *ANL,* pp. 211–12; Sinclair, p. 143; edited by H. W. Robbins (Lewisburg, Pa., 1925).

35. Helen P. Forshaw (Mother Mary Philomena, S. H. C. J.), "The Speculum Ecclesie of St. Edmund of Abingdon (a critical study of the text, with edition)" (History Faculty, University of London, 1964).
36. Project listed by Rossell H. Robbins in "Middle English Work in Progress, 1963–64," in *Neuphilologische Mitteilungen*, LXV (1964), 367.
37. Kari Sajavaara, *The Middle English Translations of Robert Grosseteste's "Château d'Amour*," Mémoires de la Société Néophilologique de Helsinki, XXXII (Helsinki, 1967).
38. Jacques Monfrin, "Poème anglo-normand sur le mariage, les vices et les vertus, par Henri (XIIIᵉ siècle)," in *Mélanges de langue et de littérature du moyen âge et de la renaissance offerts à Jean Frappier, Professeur à la Sorbonne*, Publications Romanes et Françaises, CXII (Geneva, 1970), pp. 845–66.
39. See *ANL*, Ch. IX.
40. Marion Y. H. Aitken, *Etude sur le Miroir ou les Evangiles des Domnées de Robert de Gretham* (Paris, 1922). Eight of the sermons were published in an unsatisfactory manner by Saverio Panunzio: *Robert de Gretham, Miroir ou les Evangiles des Domnées: edizione di otto domeniche*, Studi e Testi di Letteratura Francese diretti da Gianni Nicoletti (Bari: Adriatica, 1967); see the review article "The *Miroir* of Robert of Gretham" by Linda Marshall and W. Rothwell in *Medium Aevum*, XXXIX (1970), 313–21.
41. *ANL*, pp. 212–13.
42. *ANL*, pp. 187–91. Uda Ebel, *Das altromanische Mirakel*, Studia Romanica, 8. Heft (Heidelberg, 1965), 62–68.
43. William MacBain, ed., *The Life of St. Catherine by Clemence of Barking*, A.N.T., XVIII (Oxford, 1964).
44. *ANL*, pp. 67–69; MacBain, p. xxiv.
45. Arthur Robert Harden, ed., *La Vie de Seint Auban: An Anglo-Norman Poem of the Thirteenth Century*, A.N.T., XIX (Oxford, 1968).
46. Cited by Harden, p. xii, notes 2, 4.
47. The misinterpretation of *rumantz* as "a romance" was made also by Miss Legge in *Anglo-Norman in the Cloisters* (Edinburgh, 1950), p. 23, but silently abandoned in *ANL*, p. 268. The rubric (f. 49ᶜ) precedes and summarizes an epilogue about the authorship in which the work is attributed to a Saracen converted to Christianity "ki estoit presenz a tutes cestes aventures e tut mist en escrit, ke puis fu translaté en latin e aprés ço fu translaté de latin en rumantz." The colophon (f. 50ᴮ) has: "Ci finist le [corrected from li] rumantz de l'estoire de Seint Auban. . . ." *En rumantz* in the rubric indicates the language into which the adventures were translated from Latin; the colophon then means: "Here ends the Romance [i.e., vernacular] version of the story . . ." The sense of "vernacular" or "French" for *rumantz* is borne out by the text written in tiny letters along the bottom margin of f. 49ᵛ to guide the rubricator, where *franceis* is the final word, instead of *rumantz* which the rubricator preferred; and the word *franceis* appears in the epilogue itself (the Saracen is speaking):

> La geste ai, cum la vi, escrit en parchemin.
> Uncore vendra le jur, ben le di e devin,

La estoire ert translatee en franceis e latin.
Ne sai autre language fors le mien barbarin . . .
                                            [1821–24]

48. Suggested in the review by Alexander Bell in *Medium Aevum*, XXXVIII (1969), 313–16.
49. David J. A. Ross, "A Thirteenth Century Anglo-Norman Workshop Illustrating Secular Literary Manuscripts?" in *Mélanges . . . Lejeune* (*supra cit.*, in n. 12), I (1968), 689–94, with two plates.
50. Gerald A. Bertin and Alfred Foulet, "The Acts of Andrew in Old French Verse: The Gardner A. Sage Library Fragment," in *PMLA*, LXXXI (1966), 451–54.
51. Willem Noomen, "Le *Jeu d'Adam*. Etude descriptive et analytique," in *Romania*, LXXXIX (1968), 145–93.
52. W. C. Calin, "Structural and Doctrinal Unity in the Jeu d'Adam," in *Neophilologus*, XLVI (1962), 249–54.
53. Lynette R. Muir, *Adam, A Twelfth-Century Play translated from the Norman-French with an Introduction and Notes,* Proceedings of the Leeds Philosophical and Literary Society. Lit. and Hist. Section, vol. XIII, Part V (Leeds, Jan. 1970), 149–204. John Stevens and Richard Axton, "Le Jeu d'Adam," in *Medieval French Plays* (Oxford: Blackwell, 1971).
54. Legge, "L'Influence littéraire de la cour d'Henri Beauclerc, in *Mélanges . . . Lejeune* (*supra cit.* in n. 12), I, 679–87.
55. Legge, "Gautier Espec, Ailred de Rievaulx et la matière de Bretagne," in *Mélanges . . . Frappier* (*supra cit.* in n. 38), 619–23.
56. *ANL*, Ch. II; *Mélanges . . . Lejeune, supra,* n. 54.
57. Urban T. Holmes, "The Anglo-Norman Rhymed Chronicle," in *Linguistic and Literary Studies in Honor of Helmut A. Hatzfeld* (Washington: Catholic Univ., 1964), pp. 231–36.
58. Hugh Shields, "Philippe de Thaon, auteur du *Livre de Sibylle?*" in *Romania*, LXXXV (1964), 455–77.
59. Legge, "La Versification anglo-normande au XII⁰ siècle," in *Mélanges offerts à René Crozet*, I (1966), 641 (Supplément aux Cahiers de Civilisation Médiévale, Poitiers).
60. Heiner van Bömmel, *Eine altfranzösische Paraphrase der Proverbia Salomonis: Edition des MS. Bibl. Nat. fonds fr. 24862,* Inaugural-Dissertation zur Erlangung des Doktorgrades der Philosophischen Fakultät der Justus Liebig-Universität (Giessen, 1968).
61. W[illiam] O. Hassall, *The Holkham Bible Picture Book, Introduction and Commentary* (London: Dropmore Press, 1954).
62. F[rederick] P. Pickering, ed., *The Anglo-Norman Text of the* Holkham Bible Picture Book, A.N.T., XXIII (Oxford, 1971). The study on which this edition is based is related to the thesis of Professor Pickering's important book *Literature and Art in the Middle Ages* (London: Macmillan, 1970).
63. Pierre Ruelle, ed., *Ornement des dames (Ornatus mulierum): Texte anglo-normand du XIIIᵉ siècle*, Université Libre de Bruxelles, Travaux de la Faculté de Philosophie et Lettres, Tome XXXVI (Brussels: Presses Universitaires, 1967).

64. Cambridge, Univ. Libr., MS. Ee.4.20; Dean, "An Early Treatise on Heraldry in Anglo-Norman," in *Romance Studies in Memory of Edward Billings Ham*, ed. by Urban Tigner Holmes (Hayward, Calif., 1967), pp. 21–29. References to date and provenance on pp. 21 and 22 of this article require correction. Since the miscellany was compiled at St. Albans over a period of several years beginning in 1382, this copy of the treatise (of which no other is known) is perhaps three or four decades later than was previously thought. The manuscript was excluded from the St. Albans group by Ker p. viii) as a business book (see n. 3 of the article), but probably should have been included because it is a formulary. Besides the Cambridge catalogue (cited in n. 2 of the article), see W. A. Pantin, "English Monastic Letter-Books," in *Historical Essays in Honour of James Tait* (Manchester, 1933), p. 220; H. G. Richardson, "Business Training in Medieval Oxford," in *AHR*, XLVI (1941), 277–79; *idem*, "Letters of the Oxford *Dictatores* in H. E. Salter, W. A. Pantin, H. G. Richardson, *Formularies which Bear on the History of Oxford, c. 1204–1420*, II, Oxford Historical Society, n.s., V (Oxford, 1942), 370, 406.

65. H. G. Richardson and G. O. Sayles, *The Governance of Mediaeval England*, Edinburgh Univ. Publications: History, Philosophy and Economics, No. 16 (1963), Ch. XV: "Statecraft and Learning."

66. Constance Bullock-Davies, *Professional Interpreters and the Matter of Britain* (Cardiff, 1966); reviewed by Rachel Bromwich in *Medium Aevum*, XXV (1966), 282–84.

67. William Rothwell, "A Study of the Prefix De/Des in Anglo-Norman and Some Considerations Arising Therefrom," in *Transactions of the Philological Society*, 1966, pp. 24–41.

68. Albert C. Baugh, "Chaucer's Serjeant of the Law and the Year Books," in *Mélanges . . . Frappier* (*supra cit.* in n. 38), pp. 65–76.

69. Legge in *Mélanges . . . Crozet* (*supra cit.* in n. 59), pp. 639–43.

70. See Herbert H. Petit, "A Wood Needing — Clearing," in *Annuale Mediaevale*, I (1960), 102–7.

Must We Abandon the Concept of Courtly Love?

Francis L. Utley

E. Talbot Donaldson, "The Myth of Courtly Love," *Speaking of Chaucer* (London: The Athlone Press, 1970).

F. X. Newman, ed., *The Meaning of Courtly Love* (Albany: State University of New York Press, 1968).

John V. Fleming, *The Roman de la Rose: A Study in Allegory and Iconography* (Princeton: Princeton University Press, 1969).

The Comedy of Eros: Medieval French Guides to the Art of Love, trans. Norman R. Shapiro with Notes and Commentary by James B. Wadsworth (Urbana: University of Illinois, 1971).

IN AMERICA today one must be valiant to use the term *courtly love* without radical surgery. Nothing is more fashionable than a decision to abandon any view held by a century of scholars as orthodox, for the demolition of an academic house of cards brings excruciating joy to youthful Weathermen. How much greater this is when one can rest beside such talented but strange bedfellows (or is it weathervanes?) as Peter Dronke, E. Talbot Donaldson, John Fleming, and D. W. Robertson, Jr.? Yet there is an ethics of belief, and there may be some decency in refusing to abandon a belief simply because a few winds blow in a contrary direction.

The case can be conveniently re-examined with the above four recent books, each a strikingly different contribution to the question.[1] Donaldson's essay is a *tour de force*, only half serious; Newman's book records a symposium, in which the polite antagonists, with two exceptions, talk more around than about the subject at issue; Shapiro provides a modest popular translation of a few Ovidian tracts which may, when they receive the study they merit, put the whole problem of medieval love on a sounder basis; Fleming's book is a brilliant contribution to the controversy, and ones response to it must combine intense gratitude with extensive disagreement. These books but scratch the surface of medieval love, for what is needed is a vigorous and

299

well-planned survey of all the countless works from the eleventh to the sixteenth century which have talked about women and love, perhaps an organized group effort like Roger Loomis' *Arthurian Literature in the Middle Ages,* which despite its own biases put historical order into opinionated confusion. Some years ago John Hurt Fisher attempted to organize such a survey, but his arduous duties as Secretary of the Modern Language Association and a certain disillusion with collaborative projects have combined to dampen his ardor. Are there no more valiant younger soul brothers among us?

For the moment one can only address oneself briefly to the four books I have mentioned, and to draw some very tentative conclusions which will not, I prophesy, be too enthusiastic for the nihilistic challenge, a model of modern *desmesure,* laid down by Robertson (Newman, p. 17):

> Do my colleagues really believe that Chaucer had no moral or social responsibility? I think it is time we stopped teaching medieval texts to the tune of "Hearts and Flowers." The sophistication of the tune with things like pseudo-Albigensian heresies, pseudo-Platonic philosophies, or pseudo-Arabic doctrines does not conceal its true nature, nor do these wailing ghosts on the sidelines make it any more respectable intellectually. The study of courtly love, if it belongs anywhere, should be conducted only as the subject is an aspect of nineteenth and twentieth century cultural history. The subject has nothing to do with the Middle Ages, and its use as a governing concept can only be an impediment to our understanding of medieval texts.

In fear and trembling, faced by the Either/Or of the nineteenth century, which forgot God, and the twelfth Century, which had no Eros — by flat and uninviting polarities, we proceed to our four books.

Donaldson's essay (1965), the earliest of the four, represents a fairly late stage in the controversy, since the lists were opened years before by early Robertson articles, most notably his devastating "The Subject of the *De Amore* of Andreas Capellanus," *Modern Philology,* L (1952–53), 145–61, in which he argued that the subject is *"fornicatio* used with its full connotations as the opposite of *caritas,* and Andreas does nothing except condemn it" (p. 161). With a certain dreary consistency he continues, "Theories to the effect that Andreas and the great poets who took up his themes were swayed by scurrilous

Albigensian doctrines, by Arabic or Andalusian cults of sensuality [*pace* Parry and Denomy], if such indeed existed, or by obscure neo-Platonic heresies are little short of ridiculous." Everything we have construed as a support for "courtly love" is irony; we are sobersides who have missed the joke. Of this gambit, calculated to win hearers to the side of the preacher as the Pardoner's *gaude* did with his audience, Donaldson remarks:

> My impression is, after a rereading of the Chaplain that could not help being more exhausting than exhaustive, that Andreas hoped he was being funny, and that Robertson is quite right to point out that one Drouart la Vache records that in 1290, when someone gave him a copy of Andreas, "after he had read a little of it, he found the book so pleasing and he laughed so much at it," that he ended up by translating it into French. . . . I say I think Andreas meant to be funny: my sense of humor is insufficiently robust for me to agree with Robertson and Drouart that he succeeded.[2]

Donaldson is not exactly known as a Simon Zelotes who has made Robertson his "goodly fere," and indeed (p. 159) he asserts flatly that he does not agree with "Robertson's oft-stated premise that any serious work written in the Middle Ages that does not overtly promote St. Augustine' doctrine of charity will be found, on close examination, to be doing so allegorically or ironically," nor does he agree "that Andreas can be made to read as a good disciple of St Augustine." So we must not repeat the irreverence of certain smoke-filled rooms, and say that Donaldson is Yale's Robertson. The irony in his essay remains vastly more controlled and lucid than that ascribed to Andreas. He begins (p. 154) with a tribute to "the eighty-second anniversary of *amour courtois*," invented, except for an embarrassing single example in the troublador Pierre d'Auvergne, by Gaston Paris. "I had no idea, when I undertook this paper, of how much writing on the topic I was not going to be able to read." The idea belongs to modernistic desires "to find in the past something strikingly and excitingly different from the drab present, and to talk about love, especially a love that is suspected of being naughty but whose naughtiness has attained archaeological respectability." Though the Middle Ages were much preoccupied with love, his confreres' definitions for *amour courtois* are "so widely divergent from one another as to be mutually exclusive." The major culprit is C. S. Lewis, with his compact tetrad "Humility, Courtesy, Adultery, and the Religion of Love." Donaldson observes that there is very little adultery in the succeeding pages of Lewis' *The Allegory of Love.* (Many of us have shared his disappointment, but most have not shown the enterprise shown in the English Department Library of Ohio State some years ago, when Lewis' book was made the common hiding place for notes leading to clandestine assignation). In England, says Donaldson, the prudery of the race made romance heroes and heroines "dwindle into marriage." The troubadours, or rather the scholars who write about them, manifest two contradictory views: "first, that the troubadours normally loved married ladies with whom they wished, above all, to consummate their love; second, that the troubadours' chief desire was to achieve a state of idealized frustration — one scholar, indeed, seems to suggest that they loved married ladies so that they would not have to spoil their love by consummating it" (p. 157).

We have no right to complete a vicious circle, and to say that the poems teach us that a Bernard of Ventadour loved Eleanor of Aquitaine and then explicate the poem with this "historical fact." Donaldson thus shows his obligation, which we all share, to J. F. Benton, who has shown us in his sensible articles that Gaston Paris' magnificent network of cause and effect, woven around the names of Eleanor and Marie de Champagne and Andreas, has very little historical foundation. Andreas is more likely to have been a chaplain of the royal French court than of Marie's, Marie probably had no contact with her mother Eleanor after Eleanor went to England, and "from what little is known of Marie it is not probable that she had either the desire or the temperament to preside over a court of immoral love, or, if she did, that the Count her husband, while he lived, would have let her get away with it" (p. 159). Robertson and Lewis agree on one thing, says Donaldson, that the third book of Andreas is to be taken seriously: "For his retraction is just as outrageous in its own way as what it retracts." It begins with a proper orthodox statement, that "God hates and will condemn the lustful," but it ends with "an extended antifeminist tirade in which Andreas strives to out-Hieronymo St Jerome." [3] Andreas' *De Amore* is a debate, like *The Owl and the Nightingale*, and it "has about as much to do with erotic practices in Champagne at the end of the twelfth century as the debate of *The Owl and the Nightingale* has to do with ornithology" (p. 161). [4]

Aware of the paradox that certain scholars who assign a cult of adultery to the Middle Ages are actually severe moralists, like Lewis, Donaldson sees in medieval secular writers more of a process of spiritualization than of moral didacticism. The "morality" is often modern, the product of a nineteenth- or twentieth-century bias which identified "immorality" with sexual lapses and went on to bleed the poor, flaunt the white man's burden, and refuse gruel to Oliver Twist. "I conclude that at least a part of what is called courtly love was no more real in the Middle Ages than it had been before and has been since," and that "what was really new and significant in medieval love has become part of our inherited response to existence" (p. 163). Though one is unwilling to grant Donaldson the last word on the subject, his charming humor and good sense make him perhaps the most able spokesman for the opposition to "courtly love."

Much more elusive are the lectures which Newman edits as *The Meaning of Courtly Love*, the product of a conference held at Binghamton in 1967. Cheerful perhaps because of his unexpected ally at Yale, Robertson begins the debate with great jocularity. In England there was little "courtly love," since there an adulterer was shorn of his locks, paraded, and sent to prison, and "pure" courtly love could have been no fun.

> We are told . . . that the lady involved should be of much higher station than the lover, that she should be located at a distance, that the lover should tremble in her presence, and that he should obey her slightest wish. . . . All this seems to me a terrible nuisance, and hardly the kind of thing that Henry II or Edward III would get involved in.

(No mention is made of Richard II, who seems to have loved Anne of Bohemia, and whom John Fisher believes to be the inspiration of the courtly poems of Chaucer and Gower.) Responding to those who have challenged him to explain the "ironic and humorous" butt of the satire he finds in Andreas, Chrétien, and the *Roman de la Rose* in default of a real code of courtly love, he answers that the object of satire is "idolatrous passion," as in the Old Testament, Lucretius, and Ovid's *Remedia amoris* (it is not quite clear why Roman writers in their invincible ignorance are attacking idolatry). Since Christianity was a religion of love, the aberrations of love or passion were "a useful vehicle for the expression of literary and poetic themes. But it was not regarded in terms of sentiment, romantic rebelliousness, sentimentality, or, that great criterion for aesthetic appeal in modern novels, plays, and television programs, stark psychological realism" (p. 4). He admits (as well he might) that "medieval poetry shows

303

what might be called frank physical optimism," but denies that courtly love is a useful concept for interpreting such poetry. There follows an attack on Kittredge's "romantic" interpretation of *The Book of the Duchess*; in Robertson's eyes John of Gaunt is an exemplum of sloth whose excessive tears for his lost wife wet her winding sheet. (One more authority thus bites the dust, and the sage of Harvard will be restless in his Unquiet Grave.)

Now Robertson returns, as usual, to his Boethian reduction of *Troilus and Criseyde*, but he combines it with his newest interest, Troynovant or medieval London.[5] "The fall of Troy loomed as a warning to all Englishmen," and *Troilus* was a particular case of that fall. With Bishop Bradwardine Chaucer admonishes the English not to succumb to the religion of Venus, since that is what brought down the French at Crécy. Apparently heeding modernist warnings that his monolithic concupiscence and charity allegories were somewhat reductive, Robertson succumbs to the topical allegory we had thought he had come to save us from. He would have been wiser had he read widely enough to know Kittredge's famous spoof which shows that *Romeo and Juliet* is an allegory of the Overbury murders, which by a lapse of history took place about twenty years after the event. In general we may say that Robertson has succeeded in his demonstration that courtly love is a concept of no value in reading medieval texts — no value to him, that is. For others he is of course no authority.

With relief we turn to John Benton, hailed as Robertson's ally, because he has ably criticized some of Gaston Paris' conjectures about Marie de Champagne and Andreas. He reminds us of what we have always known, that the Middle Ages strengthened St. Paul's counsels about marriage by a sturdy institutionalization of the social conventions: despite the prevalence of celibate ideals (only one part of St. Paul), marriage was a normal and desirable course for most people, and the clerical ideal if not the secular practise encouraged love between the spouses. We are somewhat impeded by the nature of the documents, since most of them reflect marriages which failed and therefore came into court. There is plenty of premarital passion and some evidence that marriage followed it, as in Philippe de Beaumanoir's account of the custom of legitimizing bastard children by placing them between the sheets in a marriage after the fact of birth. With his usual scholarly homework and courtesy he commends Jackson for his association of this custom with Tristan's infancy. "For the highly placed, the noble and the wealthy, arranged marriages remained the common pattern," but poorer folk could often really marry for love (p. 23). Extra-marital love or adultery were severely chastised, but the penalties for the wife were usually greater than for the husband, and they were greater in southern France than in northern France or England. The private vengeance of the early Middle Ages was later replaced by repudiation. "Adultery with the lord's wife was treason," and the seducer came off badly when the lord had anything to do with the punishment. "Instances like these should have been enough to destroy the idea that medieval troubadours roamed about the countryside advocating adultery and addressing suggestive songs, more or less thinly disguised, to the wives of the local lords, for a poor troubadour was certainly a vulnerable rival" (p. 27). The easy morality of the fabliaux was "more acceptable in the camp of William IX than in the sewing circle of his wife." Ulrich von Zatzikhoven's Lancelot loves four women, but the *Charrette* of Chrétien is a sign of the poet's irony as well as of Guenevere's displeasure.

In his treatment of Andreas, Benton recognizes the kinship of Aquinas, thus renouncing pure Augustinianism. "The hypocrisy of seduction provides much of the humor of the treatise on love by Andreas," and the book owes nothing to the Cathars. "Admiring sexual purity was not peculiar to Cathars, and to assume that a poet advocating chastity was a heretic would be equivalent today to assuming that anyone advocating racial justice is a Communist" (p. 30). The notion that courtly love reflected a new liberation of woman is a fallacy: "Courtesy was created by men for their own satisfaction, and it emphasized a woman's role as an object, sexual or otherwise. . . . The second feudal age, like the first, remained a man's world" (p. 36). With wry humor Benton "would therefore like to propose that 'courtly love' be banned from all future conferences." A delightful essay, which combines the needed wit with the critical spirit we expect from historians. One may, perhaps, suggest that skill in the interpretation of historical documents is not always the same as skill in literary interpretation, and there are some problems still unsettled.

Charles Singleton, the next lecturer, moves on relatively safe ground for him, "Dante — Within Courtly Love and Beyond." Dante lies within the tradition of the troubadours, above all in the *Vita Nuova*, where he gives the prize in *amoris accensio* to Cino da Pistoia. Singleton reminds Benton that "the *social* reality of this cult of courtly love in Florence, in Dante's time, is firmly attested by documentary evidence: courtly love, as practised by poets, *did* exist, then and there"

(p. 47). But this love, like all poetry, was play, and the carnival spirit is an essential part of Christianity. In the *Commedia*, on the other hand, we have *directio voluntatis*, in which Beatrice becomes Lady Philosophy and ultimately the means by which the will of the poet is directed to God. Thus Dante, like Aquinas, reconciled Aristotelian nature with Christian grace.

W. T. H. Jackson confines himself to Germanic reactions to the French models. Germans read Chrétien without perceiving his irony, and emerged with an ideal for the secular knight of love-service, courtly love, love-in-court. Though *Erec* ends with loving companionship between husband and wife, at no time does the hero indulge in love-service, and Chrétien ridicules these extremes in his Joie de la Cort episode, with the knight who is a silly thrall of his lady. Hartmann von Aue, reworking the poem, intensifies the mutual bond between husband and wife. In *Yvain* the haughty Laudine is an unsympathetic portrait of the dominant lady, but Hartmann in his revision makes her fall at Ywein's feet and destroys the irony. Though Wolfram von Eschenbach denies that he owes anything to Chrétien's *Perceval*, it is certain that he has transformed that poem — in Parzifal's night with Blanscheflur the atmosphere is not that of *Minnedienst* but rather that of rank sensuality, and there is a streak of anti-feminism running all through the poem. Wolfram, closer to the Church than to romance tradition, "rejects the two basic constituents of courtly love, the right of a woman to demand unquestioning service in whichever triviality she fancies, and the need for a knight to gain honor for his lady by embarking on a series of otherwise pointless adventures." Chrétien's criticism of the code is ironic, but Wolfram's is for real, and openly didactic.

To French irony Gottfried reacts in a different way. Though he finds no certainty in love, he admits its immense power. Love is sensual and not unattainable, and Gottfried's major concern is with "the reasons why people fall in love." Thus he creates an infancy story for Tristan, and Riwalin, more for honor than for continued love, marries Blanscheflur to give her child a father. Tristan first attracts Isolde through his music, and "the most enduring love affair in all medieval literature begins with no sign of affection on either side" (p. 69). The slaying of the dragon is almost a parody of love-service, since Tristan won the princess not for himself but for another. Only on the ship does love begin, and the love-potion means simply "that a wave of conscious physical attraction sweeps over them both." Though this love is indeed intense, there is no sign of *Minnedienst*, for Isolde is as racked by passion as Tristan is. The allegory of the grotto of love is not courtly, but antisocial; "courtly society is inimical to true love." An artist with a sense of mission, Gottfried's "characters are exemplary, they are martyrs of love, but they belong to the literary and artistic world." And the lyric writers, climaxed by Walter von der Vogelweide, drop the courtly conventions and move to naturalism in love.

With much grace Theodore Silverstein ends the argument, but his point is plain; he calls his essay "Guenevere, or the Uses of Courtly Love." Andreas' *De Amore* is a kind of *summa* on "How to Practice Love and Be a Gentleman," while Chrétien's *Charrette* is love's earliest *Commedia*. Whatever its ultimate intention, there is much seriousness in Andreas, and Chrétien is in truth the poet of love, whatever kind you call it: *Erec* the testing of man and wife together and *Yvain* the testing of the man alone, the *Charrette* the constraints on a lover both from Love and his lady, and *Perceval* the progress of a knight through mother love to less domestic varieties. "To purists like the late Father Denomy only the *Charrette* among the works of Chrétien might be said strictly to deal with courtly love, call the other loves romantic, chivalresque, noble, ideal, or what you will." But Chrétien was no purist. Ovid is plainly a carnal source for the troubadours, and Bernart Marti accepts the carnality, but Marcabru keeps it as *fin'amors*. Neo-Platonism and Christian varieties of the same, as well as Bernardine mysticism, all contribute to the medieval picture of love, and Silverstein, who once criticized Father Denomy for his orientalist theories, now pays him a good deal of credit, perhaps as a result of Dronke's recent demonstrations of the importance of eastern parallels to *amour courtois*. De Rougemont's myth of degradation can be dismissed as a kind of poetry rather than being accorded the name literary criticism. Thus courtly love has many uses — grammatical or descriptive (Dronke); dialectical and tensioned (de Rougemont and Broadbent); rhetorical or moral (Coomaraswamy and Robertson); poetic or aesthetic (as yet too little practised). Silverstein, and the whole conference, wind up this appeal to the categories with some waggish Latin.

> Amor curialis est infernus non coelestis
> Qui affliget homines semper tam quam pestis.

Amidst all these jests and unjoined battles, the book closes with its solidest contribution, a valuable selected bibliography of the theory of courtly love. From this, in the future, we must proceed to do the solid work the subject needs.

John Fleming's book on the *Roman de la Rose* is thoroughly Robertsonian; the author unashamedly confirms himself as a convert. At first Robertson's reading "excited not merely incredulity but outrage," but it led him to further dialectic and an allegiance more papist than the Pope. He has even caught the polemic tone: "My own opinion is that the vast bulk of recent scholarship dealing with Jean de Meun's poem, much of it from the pens of learned and distinguished scholars, is fundamentally wrong-headed" and absurd (p. vi). It is strange that these anti-modernists arouse almost as much iconoclastic passion in themselves as the New Left, which I am sure they ascribe to Hegel. Indeed, I have never been threatened with fists in a scholarly argument before, but within the past year I met one young Robertsonian prepared, after a few drinks, to do battle. Augustinian, or better, Pauline charity seems to be forgotten.

Most of Robertson's disciples are rather dreary, but Fleming is anything but that. His own humor almost disposes one for a moment to take seriously his descriptions of irony in Andreas and the *Roman*. While reading this witty book I several times almost concluded that if Robertson has caught such a Leviathan with a hook, there might someday be a chance for me, either as fisherman or as fish.

The answer to such a book must be one twice as long and twice as painstaking, and there is a danger of losing one's sense of humor into the bargain. Fleming's uncompromising reading, which equates Guillaume de Lorris and Jean de Meun despite the usual belief that their tone and commitment are miles apart, awes one with its promise to subject their literary puzzle wholly to the critic's control. We come to the *Roman* with less "modern" prejudice than we do to *Troilus and Criseyde*, which we have long accepted as a magnificent and ambivalent poem about the ennobling effect of human love and its final impermanence.[6] Except perhaps by its obscenity, which Fleming thoroughly appreciates, the *Roman* has not captured the allegiance of modern readers, and a new and consistent reading therefore seems appealing enough. Fleming provides one, based less on the text of the poem than upon various glosses like *Les Eschecs Amoureux* and the *querelleurs* Pierre Col and Jean de Montreil (all three of the fourteenth century) and the many illustrated MSS of the poem. If Fleming had plainly called the study one confined to the illustrations we might

308

go farther along with him in his skilful analyses. Our hesitation comes when one is asked to accept such visual and lettered glosses, composed a considerable time after the text, as true to its spirit, and as better evidence of the intention of the poem than can be provided by scholars of Old French or historians of literature.

Fleming believes that the allegory adds up to something of this kind: Oiseuse, Pygmalion, and Narcissus are all exempla of the absurdity of all human love; the Garden of Deduit combines an infernal Eden with a mystic *hortus inclusus* from *Canticles*; of Love's Preceptors — Lady Reason, Amis, Faussemblant, and La Vieille — only the first is divine and the rest are false counsellors; Genius is natural concupiscence, and the final allegorical approach of the Lover to the Rose, a clear sexual assault, is not natural but unnatural. Pornography has no terrors for Fleming, and his Puritanism is more like that of Stubbes and Jeremy Collier than like that of a nineteenth-century Bowdler or a twentieth-century John Bircher. As with Daniel Defoe or even Fanny Hill, one is allowed both to have a *frisson* and the pleasure of moral condemnation. Far from the spiritualization of love which a Bernard or a Bonaventura or a Dante sought, we lie in doleful dumps. If one can reconcile Jean and Guillaume one can reconcile anything; there is no contradiction in the poem; it is a psychomachia with a sordid ending, and Fleming compares it again and again to a morality play like *Everyman*, but he does not explain why, unlike that play and its kindred, this play ends with a simple orgasm and no actual word of disapproval for the forces of evil. This is irony with a vengeance; where Robertson had made simplicities out of artistic complexities, Fleming makes complexities out of the plain truth.

Though one does not always disagree with the meaning of the artwork, Fleming has many interesting things to say about it. The Robertsonian vogue has helped many a captive of literary departments to discover the brilliant iconographic studies of Erwin Panofsky, Edgar Wind, Jean Seznec, the Princeton Index of Christian Art, and the Warburg School in all its manifestations. The illustrations of the *Rose* may, as Fleming says, provide one aspect of a contemporary reading of the poem, some evidence of audience reaction, and even some glimpse of auctorial intent. Yet illustrators then as now are notoriously capable of misreading an author; in the times we can document there has often been a battle between the two. Not only do the illustrators of the *Rose* themselves disagree, but, as Fleming admits, their respective period styles lead to widely different interpretations.

The piety of the glossators, both verbal and visual, does cover disturbing truths which the text seems to display; since visual art is usually more explicit than literary art, it may destroy the ambivalences an author consciously or unconsciously wrote into his poem.

At the center of this school's attempt to extend the single rhetorical device of irony to the whole of medieval secular literature there lies a basic paradox, in that the medieval authors themselves seem again and again to have been disappointed at the results of their supposed irony. Andreas tries to be funny, and yet he was condemned for Averroism by Bishop Simon Tempier of Paris in 1277, about a century after he wrote. Whether Tempier entered a similar objection to Jean de Meun (see Fleming, p. 215) is not quite clear, but it is certain that the brilliant Chancellor Gerson so "misread" it in the late fourteenth century (pp. 47–48). Despite Book III, sensual and ironic in a different sense than that implied by Robertson and Fleming, Chaucer's *Troilus* is supposed to be wholly a moral Boethian tragedy, and yet Chaucer at the end of the *Canterbury Tales* rejects it by including it with his "translacions and enditynges of worldly vanitees, the which I revoke in my retracciouns: / as is the book of Troilus; the book also of Fame," and, we assume, the translation of the *Rose*. My spies in the Robertsonian camp suggest that this is because Chaucer saw his contemporaries misread him. Or it may be that he did have second thoughts about *Troilus* and *Fame* as worldly vanity, as Boccaccio is reputed to have done with the *Decameron*, though the Italian poet copied out the Hamilton holograph himself in the early 1370's, ten years after he was supposed to have rejected it from monkish fears and Petrarchan distrust of the vernacular. None of these rejections tell us anything certain about the Augustinian significance of the poems themselves, none of the *Wahrheit* about the *Dichtungen*, but there seems to be ample evidence that contemporaries could misread the "irony."

Despite the firm rigor of his reading and the unprecedented interpretation of the obscene ending of the *Rose*, which does not even have a contrastive word or phrase to point out the supposed irony, Fleming keeps his sense of humor. Indeed, he denies his own rigor: "In spite of recent attempts to find in Jean's poem a taut, not to say a remorseless, unity, I remain unconvinced that he has achieved, or indeed attempted, anything more than a loose poetic structure" (p. 53). He admits that his iconographic method "is merely one of the many tools at the scholar's disposal, and an imperfect one at that" (p. ix).

The allegory is "hardly *recherché*; its few tricky aspects are carefully glossed within the text of the poem itself" (p. 5). Glosses are not cryptic, and the fourfold method has been overextended (p. 6). Fleming is obviously sensitive to the charges of puzzle-solving. What we call Chaucer's realism is only "stunning verisimilitude" (pp. 29–31); perhaps nobody since Carlyle has used the rare coinage "verisimilar" more often than Fleming (see the *NED*). (Do we have the right to use so nineteenth-century a term for a technique of the Middle Ages?) At least we may laugh instead of holding up our hands in horror at the vices; Viellesse of the *Rose* becomes Chaucer's January (p. 32).

Many illustrations reflect cliché rather than profound meaning (p. 38). The use of Kuhn's study of the illustrations of the *Rose* is usually acknowledged with respect and without polemics, yet Fleming occasionally tends to bluster with an *ad hominem* argument: "The temptation to explain unusual iconographic features . . . as the artist's misunderstanding of the text seems to be almost irresistible to many students of . . . art and literature, although, on the face of it, it is likely that a medieval painter knew as much about how to read medieval poetry as a modern philologist" (p. 44). Possible, of course, or even likely, but was not that what was to be proved? Styles change; may not the shift of Bel Accueil from man to woman in the illustrations reflect period style (p. 46), just as the great Gerson's misreadings of the poem do? Fleming has listened to the critics of Robertson's views about medieval gardens, who question whether vernacular authors really understood "specialized" scriptural exegesis, and who ask whether the techniques of scriptural interpretation developed by Augustine and others for the reading of the Bible really can be used by modern students to explain secular literature (p. 62). The answer, that there is no distinction between secular and religious literature in the Middle Ages, is still monolithic; it appears that all our efforts to trace a gradation of subject matter from the human to the divine in, say, *Troilus and Criseyde, The Parliament of Foules, Piers Plowman, Pearl, Patience,* and the *Parson's Tale,* in order to discover creative variety and to avoid the usual charges of stereotyping, are wistful and vain. Yet Fleming, though he recognizes the *hortus inclusus* from *Canticles* as a theme in the Garden of Deduit to balance off the Edenic fall, resists Glunz' error of reading the Garden merely as an allegory of Divine Love, of Christ, Mary, and the Church (p. 66). And though he believes that Guillaume and Jean share the same moral goal and meaning, he does admit that there is a striking difference in their tones

311

and styles (p. 70). One cannot go further and hope from a historicist of this school, so conscious of liberation from the "modernism" of the New Criticism, for any reconsideration of the axiom that it is impossible finally to divorce form and content. Fleming even, in growing sophistication, uses the term "reduction," though he reserves it for an illustrator he doesn't approve of (p. 71). Though he admits that C. S. Lewis' reading of Guillaume is "more sensitive and ambiguous" (p. 79) than his own, he still believes his own to be more accurate.

Yet he has sensitivity, at least to the charges directed at the Princetonian school, and the power of that school is shown by his refusal to do more than combat them. Even his favorite glossators, Deguilleville, Laurent de Premierfait, and Pierre Col, who in his view translate the text as a moral poem, may be guilty of practicing "reductionism, as is all medieval literary criticism with which I am familiar, with the exception perhaps of some technical rhetorical analyses of very limited interest" (p. 80). But he asserts that C. S. Lewis and Alan Gunn are likewise reductionists, and this is likely enough, since it was a canon once more of the New Criticism that any paraphrase reduces. The mention of rhetoric is interesting, for the scriptural exegetes have notoriously ignored this useful tool, the equivalent of modern formalistic criticism, probably because it seems to imply that medieval poets, despite their moral preoccupation, might be artists after all.

Only irony, from the rhetoricians' armory, remains a favorite. The code of love which Amours gives to Amant is merely "a parody of the Ten Commandments" (p. 97); its resemblance to the unexceptionable commandments in *The Court of Love* or the more carnal ones in some of the early Ovidian tracts is ignored. Fleming's own jocular ribaldry must not lead us to fully accept him as one of the boys in the back room; he is a moralist like many a modern preacher, who is more anxious to win his hearers than to keep his language pure: "The injunctions of Amours seem no more sinister than the Boy Scouts' pledge — be reverent, be clean, be cheerful; but what of the fruits of these commandments, the toothache and the masturbation, the sordid lies and the hypocritical clean speech?" The preacher has been listening to Tom Lehrer, perhaps.

Countering Gorce and Paré (p. 116), who attempted to define Thomistic and scholastic elements in Jean de Meun, Fleming at least recognizes the existence of Aquinas, as the Augustinians rarely do, but he brushes the two modern authorities aside too easily. The "historicists" are plainly uninterested in any kind of historical evidence other than their own. When Reason describes her right, after Amant's rebuke, to use the word *coilles*, she is obviously anticipating blind modern readers, including Lewis and Gerson (pp. 135–36). There were prudes among the earlier conners of the illustrations, who did not respect their noble aim; some of the pictures have been expurgated (p. 136). Genius, whom most of us might consider an advisor who countered the excesses of La Vieille and Faussemblant, Fleming admits to be something of a puzzle; he tries to unlock the secret by making him, in William of Conches' phrase, "naturalis concupiscentia," an instinct made ambiguous and inglorious by the Fall (pp. 193–96). Nature is always ambiguous, which is why we cannot use it (as the Fathers or modern bishops did in discussing procreation) as a guide. Apparently, if the historicist critic wishes, he can depart from authority, for Jean's Nature is not Alain de Lille's Nature: "Nature does not use Venus; Venus uses Nature," and Reason is at the helm of all (p. 197). In the *Roman* the religion of love (p. 206) does not parody religion: "it ridicules the idolatry of the lover."

Fleming is willing to admit that modern readers have some grounds for their erroneous readings:

> It may be that Jean's method is here too bold; certainly the most serious misunderstandings of his poem, from the time of Gerson up to our own, spring from the intricacies of his handling of Nature and Genius. But if Jean is at fault, he is generously at fault, for he has assumed that his audience will have the learning and the literary sensitivity, not to mention the sense of humor, to follow his text with both laughter and logic. His poem makes the reader do some hard thinking about difficult Christian concepts such as love, nature, and grace" [p. 225].

This much, though we may be wary like the Pardoner's temporary flock and jealous of our learning and literary sensitivity and humor and logic, we must accept. Indeed, we too must be generous and admit that the reading has shaken us to the point where we seek the therapy of further careful reading, which will fill up the interstices in Fleming's argument, such as why Danger is consistently drawn as a rather stupid ogre or devil-figure (figs. 13, 31; pp. 99, 188), when he is supposed ironically to be on the side of the angels. Fleming's argument, from which we have had to select a few points in need of demurrer, we have tried to give with page numbers; Fleming's view of the argument of the *Rose*, which I would charge has many lacunae which do not deal with the text properly, is rarely documented with line-numbers. One would forgive his argument more, and his supposed discovery of the argument of the *Rose*, were it not for the complete failure to deal with the flatly obscene climax of the poem, surely the strangest ending to a didactic poem opposed to love that was ever written. All that he can offer to take off the heat from the plain phallicism and orgasm of the last lines is one single formal line, at the very end, "Atant fu jours, et je m'esveille." Petrarch clearly saw the ending was not one for a moralist (p. 248).[7] To end his book, as Fleming does, with an exhortation from St. Paul is wholly to beg the question, as Jean did not. Jean de Meun added no moral, no retraction, no epilogue, no awakened understanding; only John Fleming has done so.

Thus the great heirs of twelfth-century Ovidianism have written a mere tract for the times, an apologia for a degenerated Nature. The cure for such readings as Fleming's lies in a more painstaking reading of the poems these exegetes undercut, and also in making the countless readings they have refused to make, since there would be no profit in them — they are too patently on the other side of the question. Among such poems are both plainly religious pieces like *The Quest of the Grail* or *Quia Amore Langueo* and such plainly secular pieces as the Ovidian tractates of the thirteenth, fourteenth, and fifteenth centuries.[8]

Shapiro and Wadsworth, in their modest selection of some of the thirteenth-century works, merely whet our appetite. They sample three Ovidians, Maître Elie, *La Clef d'Amors*, and Guiart's *L'Art d'Amors*; an advice to young men, the Anglo-Norman *De Courtoisie* in rimed couplets from Bodleian Selden *supra* 74, and an advice for ladies, Robert de Blois's *Le Chastoiement des Dames*. In addition we have the rules of love from Drouart la Vache's paraphrase of Andreas Capellanus, *Li Livres d'Amours*, and Richard de Fournival's *Consaus d'Amours*. The translations are Shapiro's, and James Wadsworth provides a brief but pleasant introduction.

Maître Elie medievalizes his translation of Ovid by shifting the Roman scene to Paris, but his own cynicism matches Ovid's, and we can scarcely find in him a pious Augustinian indulging in irony. *La Clef d'Amors* works with considerable freedom, but the author retains Ovid's cynicism about love and marriage and speaks for *carpe diem*, in a vein which Shapiro and Wadsworth call a Renaissance motif, but a vein scarcely absent from an age where repentance is always

314

an available opiate in the pharmacy of sin. The author of *La Clef* is no moralist, but he is opposed to the "crude Don Juans" and to the embraces of old women, which Ovid found a practical solution to lust. One assumes his audience consists of the "yonge fresshe floures" of Chaucer's *Troilus*. Those who argue all such codes are ironic fail to mention the good advice most of them contain, and the author of *La Clef* takes a position ignored by the Augustinians, that these codes are necessary idealistic counsels for restraint (p. 17) for feudal aristocrats who are despots on their fiefs, and who need both secular and religious sanctions in a kingdom which has no Supreme Court and no FBI. But Guiart brings us to the conventional moral realm, for his version of Ovid contains more *Remedia* than *Ars*. He begins, without irony or guile, with a firm commitment to set forth both good and ill, and discusses with no great enthusiasm the works of love; then he spends the rest of the poem, about three-fifths of it, counselling a man how to get rid of his mistress and offering Christ and the Virgin as proper remedy. The point is plain, yet even in Guiart the Middle Ages refuses to wear blinkers in the presence of the libidinal drive. Though it is in general gnomic and banal, *De Courtoisie* has a few idealistic touches; Robert de Blois is ostensibly a counsel to married women (of the upper middle class?), but the tone is that of the fabliaux and the parodies on courtly love, not ironic or moralistic but boisterous and funny. Drouart, perhaps more human in his language than Andreas with his dry Latin, is on the whole faithful to his master. Richard de Fournival's prose piece is a letter addressed to a young lady, called "sister," and though it reproduces Andreas' popular account of the hell reserved for sinners against the codes of love, Richard seems to be urging a romantic love without adultery.

So unassuming a book needs no heavy-handed criticism; we must await from another time or author the thorough study of such treatises and their allegorical progeny which may halt the casual dismissal of "courtly love." Yet, in view of the present controversies, Shapiro might have done better to avoid the term in his translation. One passage reads:

> Icest livre que j'ai sommé
> la clef d'amours sera nommé;
> quer par lui porra l'en ouvrir
> les arz d'amours et descouvrir.[9]

Shapiro translates:

315

> This book of mine will bear the name
> The Key to Love; for I proclaim
> That with this key, one will uncover
> Canons to guide the courtly lover.

Later (lines 1001–2) the original says:

> Quant a ta dame parleras
> en lieu ou cen fere oseras,

which is rendered as:

> A courtly lover must, as well,
> Be glib of tongue.

The treason is plain, yet on the whole the selections read pleasantly, without either excessive colloquialism or archaism, and the introductory matter is sound and informative, though we yearn for a much fuller treatment of the subject. So far as I know, none of these tracts have been translated before into English; some of them are modernized in La Grand d'Aussy's *Fabliaux et Contes*, third edition (Paris, 1829), volume II.

Interesting as all four of these books are, none of them settles the vexed question of the term or the concept *courtly love*. Nor can we do so, but this is a propitious time to comment on six key-words invoked again and again in the controversy:

(1) Beyond question the term *amour courtois* is a nineteenth-century coinage, and the unique Provençal example of *amor* combined with *cortezia* is as good as no evidence at all. Yet the point may be a petty one after all. A philological roll call is not always necessary to demonstrate a phenomenon; the Middle Ages itself had no name for itself, and the term seems to have been common in English only since the eighteenth century. Moreover, the modern Augustinians use the terms *romantic* and *Hegelian* without assuming that every culprit accepts the designations.[10] After his first contemptuous denial of the term, Robertson has been playing with such substitutes as "courteous love" and "passionate love." This would seem to betray not a nominalist but rather a Platonic-realist or even Hegelian concern with the word and not the idea. If there was *amour* and there was *courtoisie* in related circles of context there can be no scholarly sin in combining them, perhaps with a warning. Better, one might use consistently the more common medieval term, *fin'amors*, which despite its early application

to an perfectionist unconsummated love, becomes common enough for aristocratic love in general.[11] There is no doubt that there were such sensitized words in the period, and they may be useful despite their ambiguity. We may be courteous enough to accept Robertson's denial of its use for him without turning his blind spots into our own.[12]

(2) The charge is common that the experts (i.e. the opposition) do not agree on their *definition,* or on the origins of "courtly love" or its special appropriateness to the Middle Ages. Since the period of time and the body of literature is so great, it is not surprising that inductive definitions should vary. Peter Dronke has shown that the origins or analogous situations lie in both North and East;[13] yet he believes that the strong infusion medieval love has from Christian mysticism gives it uniqueness. Clearly we find contradictions galore when we range beside each other all of the following writers: the troubadours (who themselves differ despite attempts to codify them as pioneers), the trouvères, and the popular poets; the *dolce stil nuova* and Dante's transcendence of it (or his own several stages); the German *Minnesinger* and the Ovidian treatise writers; the twelfth, thirteenth, fourteenth, and fifteenth centuries and the Renaissance derivatives including Petrarchism (the last so often glibly separated from its courtly forebears); the romances and those anti-romances the fabliaux and the *Roman de Renard,* the massive body of late medieval allegories. But to avoid disputes over origins, I would accept the condition that we speak of medieval rather than of "courtly" love, since the feudal elements are in part those of an age and time, the bourgeois imitators and parodists are many, and the noteworthy ambiguities of Eros and Agape and Caritas are in part the reason for the extraordinary preoccupation of that time with the subject of love, ranging from *amor dei* to *amor dominae* to *amicitia* to *amour propre,* or Narcissism as the Freudian Augustinians would have it. Whatever its moral tensions, no age saw better the universal correspondences between human love and divine love: no age could write more moving stories about passionate lovers, in which the tragedy triumphs over the exemplary: Héloise and Abelard, Tristan and Isolde, Lancelot and Guenevere, Paolo and Francesca. Even the abused definition of C. S. Lewis, Humility, Courtesy, Adultery, and the Religion of Love, works well in three of its components. Humility is both an appropriate Christian and feudal virtue; Courtesy cannot be denied to a system of precepts which perpetually asserts its aristocratic bias and its association with one court after another; the Religion of Love is reinforced both by the use of the

pagan gods both audaciously and with reservations and by the constant reciprocity between the literature of divine and human love. For the last phenomenon, one need only recall that romantic passage in which the wise psychologist of the thirteenth-century *Ancrene Wisse* appeals to his well-born and romantic anchoresses with the story of the King Christ who wooed the Lady Religious,[14] and contrast it with the ecclesiastical imagery of Book III of the *Troilus.*

(3) But most of us will concede that the term *adultery* in Lewis' definition and in most commentators since Paris has been overplayed.[15] Lewis' own examples, as opposed to his precept, minimize it; and whether Andreas' famous paradox which denies the possibility of love in marriage is irony or sober social history in an age of marriages of convenience, the bulk of the romances generally, as Donaldson put it aptly, "dwindle into marriage." Paris unfortunately chose the *Charrette* and the love of Lancelot and Guenevere as his prime example; Chrétien may well have believed that Lancelot did love inordinately, though in his treatment and even more in that of Malory Lancelot generally has the reader's sympthy. Surely, even in the Middle Ages, there are degrees of the "inordinate." A Lancelot who in Malory is taken to heaven by angels (after repentance, of course) is a different case than old January in the *Merchant's Tale*, whose inordinateness is *in* marriage and whose impotence is not forgotten by the virile reader; and the three incestuous brothers in the *Quest of the Holy Grail* are different again.[16] Nothing is surely gained by lumping all these together. Lancelot may be in some sense an anti-Tristan; de Rougemont has even said that the love and death theme makes Tristan an anti-Tristan. As Jackson shows, *Parzifal* is notoriously unsympathetic with adultery. Benton is right in reminding us of some of the penalties for this crime, notably for the wife and for the lover rather than for the nobleman himself at play. But of course literature has normally involved an element of wishful thinking, from the twelfth century to *Pamela, Anna Karenina*, and *Women in Love.* We really don't need to be scolded for forgetting that Christian orthodoxy had sharp views on the matter; for the romances themselves are notoriously equivocal, as in the case of Isolde's oath about the beggar (Tristan) who carried her over the ford and in that of Lancelot and Sir Urry, where the sinful knight is allowed by God to cure a wound which none but Lancelot can cure. Tedious as it might be, we need a census of the cases of extra-marital love and those sanctioned by marriage in medieval romance.

(4) The issues have been particularly clouded by the injection of the term *realism* into the controversy. As Benton shows,[17] the surface statements of the codes or the narrative motifs of the romances are not historical facts; we need only remind ourselves that the old debate about literature and life was fought many years ago by E. E. Stoll and a host of other critics. Political history uses different documents than social history, and the fictions of a time are as important as charters or court documents. In the beginning too much was made of the legal status of "courts of love," and Gaston Paris himself was one of those to deny that the decisions ascribed by Andreas to Marie de Champagne were anything but fiction.[18] Knowledge of this point was common among the Hegelians and philologists among whom I studied some time before Robertson appeared on the scene. Amy Kelly was somewhat too enthusiastic a popularizer in her revival of the courts,[19] which even in later imitative manifestations could have been little more than examples of *homo ludens*. In reality there may have been nothing in the Middle Ages called "courtly love" or meriting that title, any more than there was a philosopher's stone. But the phenomena and the apparatus which go under that name are real enough, and to ignore an entity because it cannot be physically demonstrated is a strange action for a historian of ideas. Some people still say that there is no such thing as democracy; what will our Robertsons and Bentons say about that five hundred years from now?

(5) *Apparatus* seems an appropriate word to introduce, in view of the multiplicity of *codes* and precepts. No doubt these owe something to the Ten Commandments, but they cannot be dismissed wholly as ironic or parodic, as Fleming tries to do for the precepts of *Amours* in the *Roman de la Rose*. Indeed, if we wanted a really useful term for the phenomena we are considering, it might well be "the formalized codification of love." Such formalization is certainly common in the Middle Ages, and common nowhere else, though we might find parallels in feudal counterparts of the age in Persia, Japan, China, or India. Whatever may be the case with Andreas, I will vouch my reputation for literacy and sensitivity on the assertion that the twenty precepts in the fifteenth-century *Court of Love* are soberly and seriously offered: worship of the God of Love, secrecy, fidelity, praise, denunciation of Danger, meditation on the lady's beauty, patience, service, humility, sovereignty of the lady even with a nobler lover, skilled and secret communication, malady, gift-giving, hope and trust, chivalric combat, avoidance of sloth, loving in September as in May, decorous

dress, fasting, and pain in the lady's absence. None would deny that certain clerics might not accept this particular kind of sobriety, since there was a frame of mind which considered anything at all associated with the world suspicious. One of the restraints on love urged by the period was Paulinian and Augustinian, another was the codes of love. That neither was totally effective needs no urging; were they so we as descendants would never have been born. The codes are one more of the period's many formalizations, like the seven sins and the seven virtues, the five joys of Mary and the fifteen joys (or sorrows) of marriage, the fifteen signs of doomsday and the commentaries on the Ten Commandments. As Sidney Painter has shown us,[20] these restraints on noble practice which we call the Codes of Love were probably honored more in the breach than in the observance. The irony is that of life, not that of intent but of haphazard performance, the inevitable human deterioration of the ideal.

(6) And this brings us to our final point, the nature of medieval *irony*. Benton cites a Latin definition of irony *per antifrasim* (Newman, p. 37) from the *Rhetorica antiqua* (c. 1215) of Boncompagnus de Signa. He uses it in support of his humorous reading of Andreas, and further urges (p. 31) that "medieval authors and audiences enjoyed ambiguity in literature, not because it reflected a basic ambiguity in the universe or the heart of man, but because their natural tendency was to think in very rigid categories," as when *Roland* says "Pagans are wrong and Christians are right." Admittedly we cannot attribute to Andreas the elaborate double vision which poets since Eliot have been cultivating, and which the sixties has tended to reject under the influence of the new either/or philosophies of Maoism and Krishnaism and Robertsonianism. Kierkegaard is as modern a fashion as his opponent Hegel, and much of the Robertsonian appeal is to a generation which does want its decisions cleared of double vision, its Hobbits unambiguous, its wars plain and without disturbing questions. Unfortunately the subtle Augustine, who urged ambiguity in scriptural exegesis, never gave us himself a literary exercise to show how the technique of obscurity was to be used. We have to wait until someone like Boccaccio, whose glosses to *Il Filostrato* show us the technique. Yet even attempts to save the *Decameron* for modern morality present their problems.

Most of us might accept irony *per antifrasim* in the "stream of consciousness" passage which some ascribe to January in the *Merchant's Tale*, since it has a clear dramatic purpose in demonstrating the old fool's rationalizations about marriage.[21] The irony is here cued by such unconventional statements as bachelors singing "alas," the buxomness of a wife, the twisting of antifeministic statements by Theophrastus, and such obvious reversals with a "destroying burden" as:

> A wyf wol laste, and in thyn hous endure,
> *Wel lenger than thee list, paraventure,*

or

> The hye God, when he hadde Adam naked,
> And saugh hym all allone, *bely-naked*,
> God of his grete goodnesse sayde than,
> "Lat us now make an helpe unto this man
> Lyk to hymself"; *and thanne he made him Eve.*

This is simply the technique of "cuius contrarium verum est,"[22] somewhat more subtly used. Chaucer was also capable of the irony of double vision, as in the Wife of Bath's "Allas! allas! that evere love was synne!" or in the epilogue and indeed the whole of *Troilus and Criseyde*. It is not surprising that some young people today, half-taught by the Audens and Eliots and half-taught by Abbie Hoffman and Jerry Rubin, find the Robertsonian approach imminently satisfactory: it reverses the plain text and makes all simple. Moreover, it has a striking similarity to the technique of Freudian inversion, in which overt respectability, say, is undermined by covert homosexuality or the like; the football players and Huck and Jim are all really homoerotic, a great consolation to intellectuals such as we who have no pass to the locker room or the raft. Only a skeptic will suggest that there is considerable difference whether you accept the sin or hide it, and that goes as much for Freud as it does for Boccaccio or Andreas.

Great literature in any age has double vision, and the meta-medieval Boccaccio and Chaucer and Dante share the richness of the meta-romantic Keats and the meta-classical Corneille or Swift, without denying that they are in some measure also medieval, romantic, and classical. Andreas is simply not in this class, as Donaldson sees, and we may have missed some of the irony and humor in his first part,[23] just as we have missed some of that of Jean de Meun in the last part of the *Roman of the Rose*, and owe gratitude to Fleming for showing it to us. But serious and mature critics surely will be chary of the continued use of irony *per antifrasim* to get one's argument out of a tangle.

321

Fin'amors, then, was a medieval term, and can be a useful one to-day, though we cannot apply it to one definition of *courtly love* in the Middle Ages. Rather we must do what we have been trying for generations to do for medieval art and philosophy and letters, not to "modernize" it — though we should like to explain why we generally choose to write about some medieval works (Chaucer, Dante, Boccaccio) rather than others (the *Cursor Mundi*, the *Orrmulum*, the *Ovide Moralisé*) — but to demonstrate its great variety, its changes and its permanency. What Robertson and Fleming do so ably for shifts in "style" in art and letters from the twelfth century to the fifteenth they refuse to do for the philosophy and the ideas, and thus fly in the face of Gilson and McKeon, who assert that there is real progress from the pseudo-Dionysius to Albertus Magnus to Aquinas to Ockham and Duns Scotus and Nicolas of Cusa. Love may, as that ubiquitous genre of poetry called "The Twelve Abuses" says, be lechery, yet Dante gave it the easiest place in hell and Chaucer described it with enthusiasm, as most secular authors do. Surely we therefore are not too far wrong in finding some emotional and artistic residue in love, even when faced by a strict "fruit and chaff" critical doctrine.

There is not one courtly love but twenty or thirty of them, warring with theories of divine love and with popular reductions, such as those few which seem at times to condone adultery. The realm of most of them is not the real but the ideal, and the ideal is usually plain and open and well-cued, like medieval irony and medieval allegory, and needs no mystic interpreters. Though love, which of all passions best fits the proverb "Plus ça change, plus la même chose," is by no means unique to the Middle Ages, that time is especially prolific in elaborate codifications, a few of which may perhaps be ironic. Irony is a useful device for both author and critic, but it must not be run to the ground by either, lest we are led to over-simplify or to over-complicate the nature of human passion. Rejection of the term *courtly love* will not sweep the social phenomena and the literary expression under the rug, and it is time for serious housecleaning, where we roll up our sleeves and go to work bringing together the multiple and variable evidence with all the skill we have for careful reading, including philology and linguistics, patristic exegesis, glosses literary and artistic, rhetoric, historical externals, the variety of medieval philosophies, a sense of the value the past has for the present, and plain common sense.

NOTES

1. Donaldson's essay originally appeared in *Ventures: Magazine of the Yale Graduate School*, V (Fall, 1965), 16–23, and was reprinted in his *Speaking of Chaucer*. I use the more available book.
2. *Speaking of Chaucer*, pp. 159–60.
3. I can share what must be Andreas' posthumous sadness at the many misreadings of his book, including the condemnation of the Sorbonne, since I have just been informed that my own early essay on the themes of satire and defense of women, *The Crooked Rib* (Columbus, Ohio, 1944; reprinted New York, 1970) labels me among the penetrating and liberating youth as a "sexist." I had thought it was a deeply sympathetic demonstration of male chauvinism's conspiracy to condemn the women they did not understand with projection and stereotypes.
4. On such debates see *The Crooked Rib, passim*, and a forthcoming fascicule by the reviewer in the Severs-Hartung revision of Wells' *Manual of the Writings in Middle English*, which appeared in February 1972.
5. See his *Chaucer's London* (New York, 1968).
6. See a recent reading of the epilogue by F. L. Utley, "Stylistic Ambivalence in Chaucer, Yeats, and Lucretius — The Cresting Wave and the Undertow," *The University Review*, XXXVII (1971), 174–98.
7. One fourteenth-century reader, not cited by Fleming and perhaps very much to his purpose, is the author of *Purity*, who speaks of the divine love expounded by "Clopyngel in the compas of his clene Rose." See *Purity*, ed. Robert J. Menner (New Haven, 1920), line 1057. Menner believes that the author has misunderstood Jean de Meun (pp. xliii, 101–2); one wonders if the poet had read to the end of the *Roman*.
8. See the forty or so treatises and other works cited by Robert Bossuat, *Manuel bibliographique de la littérature française du Moyen Age* (Melun, 1951), pp. 252–66.
9. *La Clef d'Amors*, ed. Hermann Suchier, Bibliotheca Normannica V (Halle, 1890), p. 9.
10. The revered term "humanities" is another example: a recent coinage despite the aura of antiquity it carries today; see J. C. Laidlaw, ed., *The Future of the Modern Humanities* (Leeds, 1969), pp. 18–19, 107.
11. For the phrase see Tobler-Lommatzsch, *Altfranzösischer Wörterbuch* I (Berlin, 1925), 363.25, 365.36; III (Wiesbaden, 1953), 1868.39–42; 1870.22–36.
12. One wonders why nobody has brought into the discussion the English word, "to court" for "to make love to" or "to woo." It would certainly explain, much better than Hegel, why English commentators have so commonly accepted Paris' coinage. See NED *court* sb.[1] V. 17 and *court* v. II. 3–4 (for the noun the earliest cited use is Spenser 1590 and for the verb Lyly 1580; the provenience is of course French).
13. *Medieval Latin and the Rise of European Love-Lyric*, 2 vols. (Oxford, 1965), I, 9–46.
14. J. R. R. Tolkien, *The English Text of the Ancrene Riwle: Ancrene Wisse*, edited from MS. CCCC 402 (London, EETS 249, 1962), pp. 198–200.

15. I cry *mea culpa* for calling the *Troilus* "adulterous" in *The Crooked Rib*, p. 87.
16. See the translation of P. M. Materasso (Harmondsworth, 1969), pp. 241–42.
17. "The Evidence for Andreas Capellanus Re-examined Again," *Studies in Philology*, LIX (1962), 471–77; "The Court of Champagne as a Literary Center," 36 (1961), 551–91, see especially 587–88.
18. See his important but neglected review of Trojel in the *Journal des Savants*, 1888, pp. 664–75, 727–36.
19. "Eleanor of Aquitaine and Her Courts of Love," *Speculum*, XII (1937), 3–19.
20. *French Chivalry: Chivalric Ideas and Practices in Mediaeval France* (Baltimore, 1940).
21. For the controversy based on this passage see Fred N. Robinson, *The Complete Works of Geoffrey Chaucer*, second edition (Boston, 1957), p. 713.
22. *The Crooked Rib*, pp. 165–66, 256.
23. So far as I can see Moshé Lazar has not yet been incorporated into the ranks of the scapegoats, Paris, Parry, Lewis, and Kelly, though his book *Amour courtois et fin'amors dans la littérature du XIIe siècle* (Paris, 1964) appears in the Newman bibliography. After a lengthy study he concludes that "L'oeuvre d'André le Chapelain, en fin de compte, possède plus qu'une valeur littéraire. C'est un document important sur la crise morale et philosophique que traversait la société de son temps. Il reflète le divorce qui existait entre la vie sociale-laïque des classes aristocratiques et les exigences de la tradition chrétienne." In general I have found foreign and American romance scholars to be less impressed by the Robertsonian school than American students of Middle English.

BOOKS RECEIVED

This list was compiled from the books received between 16 May 1971 and 14 January 1972. The publishers and the editorial board would appreciate your mentioning *Medievalia et Humanistica* when ordering.

Adams, Jeremy D. *The Populus of Augustine: A Study in the Patristic Sense of Community.* New Haven and London: Yale University Press, 1971. Pp. viii, 278. $12.50.

Allen, Judson B. *The Friar as Critic: Literary Attitudes in the Later Middle Ages.* Nashville, Tenn.: Vanderbilt University Press, 1971. Pp. xi, 176. $11.50.

Bailey, Terence. *The Proceedings of Sarum and the Western Church* (*Studies and Texts*, No. 21). Toronto: Pontifical Institute of Mediaeval Studies, 1971. Pp. xv, 208, 15 illustrations.

Baxendall, Michael. *Giotto and the Orators: Humanist Observers of Painting in Italy and the Discovery of Pictorial Composition 1350–1450.* London: Oxford University Press, 1971. $12.00.

Benson, Larry D. and Theodore M. Andersson, eds. *The Literary Content of Chaucer's Fabliaux.* Indianapolis, Ind.: The Bobbs-Merrill Co., 1971. Pp. xv, 395. $4.95 paper.

Blackley, F. D. and G. Hermansen, eds. *The Household Book of Queen Isabella of England for the Fifth Year of Edward II, 8th July 1311 to 7th July 1312* (The University of Alberta Classical and Historical Studies I) Edmonton, Alberta: The University of Alberta Press, 1971. Pp. xxvii, 255. $15.00.

Bolgar, R. R., ed. *Classical Influences on European Culture,* A.D. *500–*

1500 (Proceedings of an International Conference Held at King's College, Cambridge, April 1969). Cambridge: Cambridge University Press, 1971. Pp. xvi, 320. $15.00 in the U.S.A.

Borchardt, Frank L. *German Antiquity in Renaissance Myth.* Baltimore and London: The Johns Hopkins Press, 1971. Pp. xi, 356. $12.50.

Brucker, Gene, ed. *The Society of Renaissance Florence: A Documentary Study.* New York: Harper and Row, 1971. $3.95 paper.

Bulletin de Philosophie Médiévale, édité par la Société Internationale pour l'Etude de la Philosophie Médiévale, 10–12. Louvain: Secretariat de la S.I.E.P.M., 1968–70. Pp. 439.

Burrow, J. A. *Ricardian Poetry: Chaucer, Gower, Langland, and the Gawain Poet.* New Haven: Yale University Press, 1971. $5.75.

Cabanis, Allen. *Liturgy and Literature.* Tuscaloosa, Ala.: University of Alabama Press, 1971. $6.00.

Davis, Norman, ed. *Paston Letters and Papers of the Fifteenth Century*: Part I. London: Oxford University Press, 1971. Frontispiece, 12 plates, map. $38.50.

Five Comedies of Medieval France, trans. and introd. by Oscar Mandel. New York: E. P. Dutton & Co., Inc., 1970. Pp. 158. $1.95 paper, in Canada $2.35.

Forster, Robert. *The House of Saulx-Tavanes: Versailles and Burgundy 1700–1830.* Baltimore and London: The Johns Hopkins Press, 1971. Pp. xii, 277. $15.00.

Greco, Aulo, ed. *Vespasiano da Bisticci, Le Vite,* Volume I. Edizione critica con introduzione e commento. Florence: Instituto Nazionale di Studi sul Rinascimento, 1970. Pp. lxvi, 601.

Haesaerts, Paul and Roger H. Marijnissen. *L'Art Flamand D'Ensor à Permeke.* Antwerp: Editions Fonds Mercator, 1970. Pp. 304, 97 color reproductions, 25 drawings. $50.

Heers, Jacques. *Fêtes, jeux et joutes dans les sociétés d'occident à la fin du moyen-âge* (Conférence Albert-le-Grand 1971). Montreal and Paris: L'Institut d'études médiévales, 1971. Pp. 146.

Hill, W. Speed. *Richard Hooker: A Descriptive Bibliography of the*

Early Editions, 1593–1724. Cleveland and London: The Press of Case Western Reserve University, 1970. Pp. xiii, 140, $5.00 paper.

Jackson, W. T. H. *The Anatomy of Love: The Tristan of Gottfried Von Strassburg.* New York: Columbia University Press, 1971. $12.50.

McKisack, May. *Medieval History in the Tudor Age.* London: Oxford University Press, 1971. $7.25.

Morrison, K. F., ed. *Rome and Medieval Culture: Selections from History of the City of Rome in the Middle Ages,* trans. Mrs. Gustavus W. Hamilton. Chicago: The University of Chicago Press, 1971. Pp. xxviii, 465. $18.50.

Murphy, James J., ed. *Three Medieval Rhetorical Arts.* Berkeley: University of California Press, 1971. $8.00.

Okasha, Elizabeth. *Hand-List of Anglo-Saxon Non-Runic Inscriptions.* Cambridge: Cambridge University Press, 1971. Pp. xv, 159, 2 maps, 158 plates. $35.00 in U.S.

Powell, James M., ed. *The Liber Augustalis or Constitutions of Melfi Promulgated by the Emperor Frederick II for the Kingdom of Sicily in 1231.* Syracuse, N.Y.: Syracuse University Press, 1971. Pp. 208. $8.00.

de Rachewiltz, I. *Papal Envoys to the Great Khans.* Stanford, Cal.: Stanford University Press, 1971. Pp. 230. $7.95.

Radcliff-Umstead, Douglas, ed. *Innovations in Medieval Literature: Essays to The Memory of Alan Markman.* Pittsburgh: Medieval Studies Committee, University of Pittsburgh, 1971. Pp. v, 75. Paper.

Riggs, David. *Shakespeare's Heroical Histories: Henry VI and Its Literary Tradition.* Cambridge, Mass.: Harvard University Press, 1971. $6.50.

Robertson, D. W., Jr., ed. *The Literature of Medieval England.* New York and London: McGraw-Hill Book Co., 1970. Pp. xxiii, 612, illustrated.

Smart, Alastair. *The Assisi Problem and the Art of Giotto: A Study of the Legend of St. Francis, Assisi.* London: Oxford University Press, 1971. 110 plates. $25.75.

Strayer, Joseph R. *Medieval Statecraft and the Perspectives of History: Essays by Joseph R. Strayer, with a Foreword by Gaines Post.* Princeton: Princeton University Press, 1971. Pp. xix, 425. $13.75.

Tierney, Brian and Sidney Painter. *Western Europe in the Middle Ages, 300–1475.* New York: Alfred A. Knopf, 1970. Pp. 576. $10.50

Wade, Ira O. *The Intellectual Origins of the French Enlightenment.* Princeton: Princeton University Press, 1971. Pp. xxi, 678. $20.00.

Wimsatt, James I. *Allegory and Mirror: Tradition and Structure in Middle English Literature* (Pegasus Backgrounds in English Literature Series). New York: Pegasus, 1970. Pp. xiii, 224. $1.95 paper.